This book is to be returned on or before
the last date stamped below. MALVERN

MALVERN COLLEGE
LIBRARY

13 DEC 1995

8 JAN 1996

-8 FEB 1996

13 SEP 1996

14 FEB 2000

31 OCT 2000
5 FEB 2003

7 NOV 2003

-9 JAN 2004

12 DEC 2007

7 FEB 2012

820.8

EVESHAM COLLEGE OF FURTHER EDUCATION
LIBRARY

020094

LIBREX

D0239491

Longman Literature in English Series

General Editors: David Carroll and Michael Wheeler
Lancaster University

For a complete list of titles see pages x–xi

EVESHAM COLLEGE OF FURTHER
EDUCATION

LIBRARY

CLASS NUMBER	820.8
ACCESSION NUMBER	020094 x

The Victorian Period

THE INTELLECTUAL AND CULTURAL CONTEXT OF ENGLISH LITERATURE, 1830–1890

Robin Gilmour

Longman

London and New York

Longman Group Limited
Longman House, Burnt Mill,
Harlow, Essex CM20 2JE, England
and Associated Companies throughout the world.

Published in the United States of America
by Longman Publishing, New York

© Longman Group UK Limited 1993

All rights reserved; no part of this publication
may be reproduced, stored in a retrieval system,
or transmitted in any form or by any means, electronic,
mechanical, photocopying, recording, or otherwise
without either the prior written permission of the Publishers
or a licence permitting restricted copying in the United Kingdom
issued by the Copyright Licensing Agency Ltd,
90 Tottenham Court Road, London W1P 9HE.

First published 1993
Second impression 1994

ISBN 0 582 49346 3 CSD
ISBN 0 582 49347 1 PPR

British Library Cataloguing-in-Publication Data

A catalogue record for this book is available from the British Library

Library of Congress Cataloging-in-Publication Data

Gilmour, Robin, 1943–
    The Victorian period : the intellectual and cultural context,
1830–1890 / Robin Gilmour.
        p. cm. – (Longman literature in English series)
    Includes bibliographical references and index.
    ISBN 0-582-49346-3 (CSD). – ISBN 0-582-49347-1 (PPR)
    1. English literature – 19th century – History and criticism.
2. Literature and society – Great Britain – History – 19th century.
3. Great Britain – Intellectual life – 19th century. 4. Great
Britain – History – Victoria, 1837–1901. 5. Great Britain–
Civilization – 19th century. I. Title. II. Series.
PR461.G55   1993
820.9′008–dc20   92–44545
                                                                                        CIP

Set by 5L in 9½/11pt Bembo
Produced by Longman Singapore Publishers (Pte) Ltd.
Printed in Singapore

Contents

List of Plates

Acknowledgements

My greatest debt in the writing of this book has been to the University of Aberdeen, which granted me a year's research fellowship to work on it. I am grateful to my colleagues for their insistence on the inviolability of this year, especially Ian Alexander, who took on administrative tasks that might have turned into major distractions. Of others, I would like to thank David Hewitt for his encouragement, Ronald Draper for wise advice given at a crucial time, and Paul Schlicke for many fruitful discussions on things Victorian. Michael Wheeler has proved an open-minded, encouraging, and patient general editor – especially patient, for which I am grateful. I owe more than I can say to my wife Liz for putting up so cheerfully and helpfully with the strains attendant on authorship. And I owe something to my Jack Russell Terrier, Tiffin, for pestering me into taking walks during which much necessary thinking was done. All have helped to bring this book to birth; I alone am responsible for whatever faults the offspring has.

R.G.

We are grateful to the following for permission to reproduce illustrations:

(Photograph from) Bodleian Library Oxford (Plate 18); British Museum (Plate 8); Leicester University Press (from Pugin, *Contrasts*, 1836, reprinted LUP 1969, Plates 5 and 6; from Eastlake, *A History of the Gothic Revival*, 1872, reprinted LUP 1970, Plates 15 and 16); The Board of Trustees of the National Museums and Galleries of Merseyside (Walker Art Gallery, Plates 2 and 4); The National Museum of Photography, Film and Television, Bradford (Plate 13); *Punch* Publications (Plate 19); Royal Pavilion, Art Gallery and Museums, Brighton (Plate 17); The Royal Photographic Society, Bath (Plate 7); Scottish National Portrait Gallery (Plate 12); Tate Gallery, London (Plates 3, 9 and 10); The Board of Trustees of the Victoria and Albert Museum (Plates 1 and 11).

Editors' Preface

The multi-volume Longman Literature in English Series provides students of literature with a critical introduction to the major genres in their historical and cultural context. Each volume gives a coherent account of a clearly defined area, and the series, when complete, will offer a practical and comprehensive guide to literature written in English from Anglo-Saxon times to the present. The aim of the series as a whole is to show that the most valuable and stimulating approach to the study of literature is that based upon an awareness of the relations between literary forms and their historical contexts. Thus the areas covered by most of the separate volumes are defined by period and genre. Each volume offers new and informed ways of reading literary works, and provides guidance for further reading in an extensive reference section.

In recent years, the nature of English studies has been questioned in a number of increasingly radical ways. The very terms employed to define a series of this kind – period, genre, history, context, canon – have become the focus of extensive critical debate, which has necessarily influenced in varying degrees the successive volumes published since 1985. But however fierce the debate, it rages around the traditional terms and concepts.

As well as studies on all periods of English and American literature, the series includes books on criticism and literary theory, and on the intellectual and cultural context. A comprehensive series of this kind must of course include other literatures written in English, and therefore a group of volumes deals with Irish and Scottish literature, and the literatures of India, Africa, the Caribbean, Australia and Canada. The forty-seven volumes of the series cover the following areas: Pre-Renaissance English Literature, English Poetry, English Drama, English Fiction, English Prose, Criticism and Literary Theory, Intellectual and Cultural Context, American Literature, Other Literatures in English.

David Carroll
Michael Wheeler

Longman Literature in English Series

General Editors: David Carroll and Michael Wheeler
Lancaster University

Pre-Renaissance English Literature

* ★ English Literature before Chaucer *Michael Swanton*
  English Literature in the Age of Chaucer
* ★ English Medieval Romance *W. R. J. Barron*

English Poetry

* ★ English Poetry of the Sixteenth Century *Gary Waller*
* ★ English Poetry of the Seventeenth Century *George Parfitt (Second Edition)*
  English Poetry of the Eighteenth Century, 1700–1789
* ★ English Poetry of the Romantic Period, 1789–1830 *J. R. Watson (Second Edition)*
* ★ English Poetry of the Victorian Period, 1830–1890 *Bernard Richards*
  English Poetry of the Early Modern Period, 1890–1940
* ★ English Poetry since 1940 *Neil Corcoran*

English Drama

  English Drama before Shakespeare
* ★ English Drama: Shakespeare to the Restoration, 1590–1660 *Alexander Leggatt*
* ★ English Drama: Restoration and Eighteenth Century, 1660–1789 *Richard W. Bevis*
  English Drama: Romantic and Victorian, 1789–1890
  English Drama of the Early Modern Period, 1890–1940
  English Drama since 1940

English Fiction

* ★ English Fiction of the Eighteenth Century, 1700–1789 *Clive T. Probyn*
* ★ English Fiction of the Romantic Period, 1789–1830 *Gary Kelly*
* ★ English Fiction of the Victorian Period, 1830–1890 *Michael Wheeler (Second Edition)*
* ★ English Fiction of the Early Modern Period, 1890–1940 *Douglas Hewitt*
  English Fiction since 1940

English Prose

* English Prose of the Seventeenth Century, 1590–1700 *Roger Pooley*
  English Prose of the Eighteenth Century
  English Prose of the Nineteenth Century

Criticism and Literary Theory

Criticism and Literary Theory from Sidney to Johnson
Criticism and Literary Theory from Wordsworth to Arnold
Criticism and Literary Theory from 1890 to the Present

The Intellectual and Cultural Context

The Sixteenth Century
* The Seventeenth Century, 1603–1700 *Graham Parry*
* The Eighteenth Century, 1700–1789 *James Sambrook (Second Edition)*
  The Romantic Period, 1789–1830
* The Victorian Period, 1830–1890 *Robin Gilmour*
  The Twentieth Century: 1890 to the Present

American Literature

American Literature before 1880
* American Poetry of the Twentieth Century *Richard Gray*
* American Drama of the Twentieth Century *Gerald M. Berkowitz*
* American Fiction 1865–1940 *Brian Lee*
* American Fiction since 1940 *Tony Hilfer*
* Twentieth-Century America *Douglas Tallack*

Other Literatures

Irish Literature since 1800
Scottish Literature since 1700
Australian Literature
* Indian Literature in English *William Walsh*
  African Literature in English: East and West
  Southern African Literature in English
  Caribbean Literature in English
* Canadian Literature in English *W. J. Keith*

* *Already published*

Author's Preface

It is necessary, Matthew Arnold wrote in 1849 to his friend and fellow-poet Clough, 'to begin with an Idea of the world in order not to be prevailed over by the world's multitudinousness'. The period covered by this book is the first in which the multitudinousness of the world begins to be felt as an intellectual burden. The sheer accumulation of information produced by the development of modern communications and technology, combined with the growing intellectual pluralism of the period, made it a much more difficult business for Arnold's contemporaries to bring their mental universe into focus than it had been for any of their predecessors. There was simply so much to know, and the impossibility of mastering that knowledge was a frequent complaint of intellectuals from 1830 onwards. The same is true for anyone working in the field today. A book of this kind also needs an 'Idea of the world' if it is not to be overwhelmed by the multitudinousness of the period's intellectual and cultural life, and it may be as well to state that idea at the start, if only to declare prejudices and justify omissions.

There can, of course, be no single key to a period so vast and complex as this; it depends on where one is looking, and for what. That reservation made, however, I believe that the Victorian period and its products were profoundly conditioned by two forces, one intellectual and the other socio-historical. The first is the nineteenth-century discovery of what has been called 'deep time', not the comfortable, imaginable time of recorded history and biblical record, but the aeonic time of geology and evolution. The shock waves from that discovery were felt in every area of intellectual life, and out of it comes the pervasive time-hauntedness of the period, seen also in history and its cognate forms of autobiography and anthropology (the subject of Chapter 1). The second force is the energy released in the emergence of new groups of people from the obscurity in which the old Anglican, aristocratic state had cast them, groups who had a direct interest in the development of a modern, religiously plural society – provincial industrialists, secular intellectuals, doctors and other men of science seeking professional status, radicals and reformers brought into local politics by the 1835 Municipal Reform Act and into national politics by the campaign against the Corn Laws, and Nonconformists of all denominations who scented the abolition of historic grievances. The expectation of reform vitalised their campaigns against aristocratic and religious protectionism, and inspired a middle-class involvement in the development of intellectual and cultural life which is of the greatest importance in understanding the ideological basis of Victorian science, religion, politics, and art. This social context of intellectual life is discussed in the Introduction and in the Prefatory sections of Chapters 2, 3, 4, and 5.

Ideas do not exist in a vacuum, as the older kind of intellectual history tended to assume, nor in watertight compartments. Science cannot be excluded from the study of religion or political ideas, religion and politics from the history of science; and in time all these categories may collapse into the growing field of cultural history. At present, however, and for the purposes of a book of this kind, there seems more to be gained than lost by organising the narrative in the traditional categories. This means that, for example, the principal discussion of 'Evolution' is in Chapter 3 (Science), although its ramifications can be traced by using the index to the development of anthropology in Chapter 1 (History) and its influence on political ideas in Chapter 4 (Politics). For the same reason I have chosen to consider the cultural and artistic life of the period in a separate chapter (5) although throughout the others regular linkages have been made with painting, photography, architecture, and – of course – literature.

If ideas do not exist in a vacuum, nor do they exist in detachment from the lived experience of individuals. The autobiographical writing of any period may be an unreliable witness but it is the only one we have of what people thought was happening to them. This is sometimes interestingly different from what later historians have concluded they should have thought was happening to them. Also, it helps to 'earth' abstractions and gives access to minority voices, especially those of women, which tended not to be heard in the predominantly masculine intellectual discourse of the time. I have made as much use of Victorian autobiography as the constraints of space allowed, considering it both as a general phenomenon (Chapter 1) and in relation to specific individuals and topics.

The word 'Victorian' occurs frequently in this book, unfortunately. No one is more conscious than I of the important differences of class, gender, generation, locality, and ideology which are obliterated when that historical adjective is used. Besides, it does not quite fit 1830–90, since Victoria reigned from 1837 to 1901. But to have attempted a more precise historical definition at every point would have made for a much lumpier and longer book, so for the sake of convenience I have settled for the looser 'Victorian', knowing how unsatisfactory it is.

Finally, it is only fair to the reader to point out that I write this book as a Scot and as a non-Anglican. These facts may have made me more aware of the frustrations felt by the growing body of religious and secular dissenters about the powers enjoyed by the Anglican Establishment in 1830, and therefore more sympathetic to the liberal ideology which emerged from their struggles. For too long now students of literature have been encouraged to see Victorian liberal culture through the eyes of its great accusers – Arnold, Newman, Carlyle, Marx. I have tried to redress the balance a little, whether successfully or not is for others to decide.

Robin Gilmour
University of Aberdeen

Note: In the notes at the end of each chapter and in the General Bibliographies and Individual Authors sections at the back of the book, place of publication is London unless otherwise stated.

For Peter and Karin Wood
In gratitude and affection

Introduction

A parvenu civilisation

We generalise confidently about the people we call the Victorians, although a moment's thought should make us realise how partial and unsatisfactory such generalisations are likely to be. The period is, in the first place, a very long one: Queen Victoria reigned from 1837 to 1901 and even within the narrower limits of the present study a statement about the early Victorian period (1830–c. 1850) is likely to need modification for the mid-Victorians (c. 1850–c. 1870), and may not be true at all for the later Victorians (c. 1870–c. 1890). Then generalisations about the Victorians (including my own) tend to be unduly derived from the society's public discourse about itself, which, since this was the great age of the middle classes and they had most at stake in that discourse, was predominantly middle-class, masculine, and metropolitan. Then again the surviving record is, relatively speaking, so very full. Time has winnowed the products of earlier periods to a quintessence of style, but the artefacts of Victorian Britain are still all around us in their baffling stylistic variety. The painting, architecture, and design of the period pose problems not only of evaluation but of definition: in an age of such fertile revivalism, is it possible to speak of a Victorian *style* at all?

And yet the impulse to generalise about the Victorians is a natural one, for at least two reasons. The first is that we still live, even at the end of the twentieth century, in the aftermath of that powerful and seemingly assured civilisation, a further complicating force in undermining our ability to generalise about something so close. The modern urban-industrial world was born, and passed from confidence to anxiety and crisis, in the hundred years separating two famous European battles, Waterloo in 1815 and the Somme in 1916. We are still the spiritual great-grandchildren of that century and look back to our Victorian ancestors with conflicting feelings of envy, resentment, reproach, and nostalgia; like the speaker in the Larkin poem locating the source of inherited unhappiness in those

fools in old-style hats and coats,
Who half the time were soppy-stern,
And half at one another's throats.

('This Be the Verse')

The other reason why generalisations about the period come so easily
is that we have picked up the habit from the Victorians themselves. No
previous generation of people had been so conscious of the uniqueness
of the times they were living through as the early Victorians, so drawn
to compare themselves with their ancestors, or so aware of their time
as an 'age' requiring definition. Dickens mocked this tendency at the
start of *A Tale of Two Cities* (1859): 'It was the best of times, it was
the worst of times, it was the epoch of belief, it was the epoch of
incredulity . . .'. Single labels are too static and, as Dickens implies,
too open to contradiction, but there is perhaps a clue to the special
character of the period in the very fact of the contemporary eagerness
to characterise it. The frequency of Victorian retrospect and cultural
evaluation – their debates about the 'spirit of the age' or the 'condition
of England', their anxious scrutiny of the reality or otherwise of their
'progress' – testifies to their historical exposure. 'They themselves knew
that they were peculiar,' Humphry House wrote in a seminal essay,
'they were conscious of belonging to a *parvenu* civilisation. At one
moment they are busy congratulating themselves on their brilliant
achievements, at the next they are moaning about their sterility, their
lack of spontaneity. In either mood they are all agog at being modern,
more modern than anyone has ever been before. And in this they were
right.'[1]

A *parvenu* civilisation: at first glance this may seem a rather surprising
definition. The idea of Victorian society as a kind of historical upstart is
at odds with the imposing solidity of the monuments it has left behind
and the high seriousness with which it conducted its moral, religious,
scientific, political, and domestic life. The solidity and the seriousness
are not illusory, but they exist against – and almost in defiance of
– a background of uncertainty, the uncertainty of people who knew
they were moving in uncharted waters. Their exposed modernity is
evident in the material and technological developments of the period: the
doubling of population (in England and Wales) to 18 million between
1801 and 1851, and near doubling again, to 32.5 million, by 1901; the
growth of large industrial cities; the coming of steam navigation, the
railways, and the electric telegraph in the 1830s and 1840s, transforming
the speed of communications and the rhythm of everyday life. All this is
a dynamo hum in the background of Victorian literature. Modernity is
evident in intellectual life, in the accumulation of knowledge beyond the
power of the individual mind to digest it, and in the rise of science and

the steady expansion of the scientific methodology into other areas of human enquiry, with the difficulties this posed for revealed religion and institutional Christianity. It is also evident in the successive extensions of the franchise through the Reform Acts of 1832, 1867, and 1884–85, whereby not only the middle-class male householder but also, by 1885, his working-class equivalent had the right to vote. In the sixty years covered by this book Britain as a whole, and England more specifically, passed from being a predominantly rural and mercantile society, ruled by an aristocratic élite and a powerful Established Church, with a largely unofficial and only incipiently specialised intellectual life, to being a predominantly mercantile and industrial society, increasingly democratic and (within Christian bounds) religiously plural, whose intellectual life was fragmenting into the various specialisations we are familiar with today. The middle classes were the chief agents and beneficiaries of these unprecedented developments, the parvenus who transformed a 'feudal' society into a 'modern' state.

It is possible to be more socially and historically precise about this. The transformations of the period were to a significant extent brought about by groups and individuals who, in terms of the existing polity in 1830, were outsiders. That polity was Anglican; it ensured the civil and ecclesiastical dominance of a state church, the Church of England. Those outside the Anglican communion, the small minorities of Jews and Roman Catholics, the larger numbers in the various Protestant Dissenting churches, had justified grievances against the Establishment – something which should always be borne in mind when considering Matthew Arnold's patronising treatment of 'Dissent' in *Culture and Anarchy* (1869). They had to conform to Anglican rites if they wished the state to register their marriages or the births of their children, and in the burial of their dead, since often the only local cemetery was in the Anglican churchyard. In parts of the country they had to pay rates for the upkeep of a church in which they did not worship. They were prevented from taking degrees at Oxford and Cambridge (until 1826 the only universities in England), and nominally excluded from Parliament by Test Acts dating from the seventeenth century. The repeal of the Test and Corporation Acts in 1828 was largely symbolic, since an annual act of indemnity enabled Protestant Dissenters to participate in public life. But Catholic Emancipation the following year was a different matter: an Act designed to appease the large Roman Catholic population in Ireland, its passing seemed to call into question the Protestant character of the constitution and initiated a decade and more of anxious debate about the relations of Church and State. Out of that debate was to come the Oxford Movement and a spate of articles and books, including Coleridge's *On the Constitution of Church and State* (1830), Thomas Arnold's *Principles of Church Reform* (1833), and the young William Gladstone's *The State in Its Relations with the Church* (1838).

It is difficult now to appreciate the intensity with which this issue was worried over by the Anglican establishment in the 1830s, but the reasons were largely political. The privileged position of an unreformed Established Church focused a burgeoning conflict at the heart of English society between two nations – not the rich and poor of Disraeli's *Sybil* (1845) but what has been described as 'an old nation based upon the old nobility, upon the squires and upon the Established Church, and a new nation based upon commerce and industry, and in religion largely Dissenting'.[2] Wealth, power, and prestige in the old nation went with the ownership of land and was mirrored in the structure of the Church: squire and parson at local level, nobleman and bishop at national, the monarch at the apex – on this pyramidal hierarchy was based the 'Anglican hegemony' of England's *ancien régime*.[3] It is the hierarchy underlying the novels of Jane Austen, Trollope, and scores of lesser nineteenth-century writers. The new nation found its identity by sidestepping the State Church (hence the zeal with which Nonconformism guarded its religious practices and resented the privileges of Establishment), and then increasingly came to challenge it, as the Church seemed less and less in touch with the new social order brought about by industrialisation. The old nation was strongest in the south of England and in the rural areas; the new nation became stronger as one moved from the centre to the periphery, particularly to those areas – in Wales, the midlands, and the north of England – where industrialisation had brought about rapid urban growth.

At this point it is necessary to pause and qualify what may seem to be emerging as a rather simplified (and traditional) opposition between Church and dissent, industry and land. The picture is, of course, much more complex than this. It has long been established, for example, that landowners were involved from the beginning in industrial development; and recent work in economic history suggests that industrialisation, far from being the major factor in Victorian wealth-creation, may always have been secondary to land, banking, and finance.[4] Many in the new nation belonged to the Established Church, and many in the old sympathised with the grievances of dissent: it was, after all, a predominantly landed House of Commons which enacted the great political reforms of the pre-1850 period, the 1832 Reform Act and the Repeal of the Corn Laws in 1846, acting in what a majority of its members believed to be the best interests of the country. In other words, the new nation could not have succeeded without the support of the 'progressive' elements in the old, and the corollary is its willingness after 1850 to accept aristocratic political leadership. It is salutary to be reminded by Norman Gash that Lord Palmerston's cabinet of 1859 'was composed of seven peers, three baronets and only three untitled commoners. This was a slightly more aristocratic body than Liverpool's cabinet of 1825 which had five commoners in a membership of thirteen.'[5]

The willingness of influential members of the new nation to accept aristocratic social and political leadership can be seen as a triumph for compromise and the Westminster way, or as a great historic opportunity missed. The radical Richard Cobden (1804–65) was in no doubt:

> We have the spirit of feudalism rife and rampant in the midst of the antagonistic development of the age of Watt, Arkwright and Stephenson! Nay, feudalism is every day more and more in the ascendant in political and social life. So great is its power and prestige that it draws to it the support and homage of even those who are the natural leaders of the newer and better civilisation. Manufacturers and merchants as a rule seem only to desire riches that they may be enabled to prostrate themselves at the feet of feudalism.[6]

Cobden was writing in 1863, seventeen years after the repeal of the Corn Laws, an event which he and other leaders of the Anti-Corn Law League had seen as an historic victory for trade over land, liberalism over feudalism. The struggle for leadership of the new society, for cultural dominance, was to be much more prolonged and inconclusive than he anticipated; the triumph of the bourgeoisie was much slower to come than Marx predicted – if indeed it can be said to have come at all in a society so insidiously and multifariously 'feudal' as Britain.

Something of the interaction between the old nation and the new can be seen in the family background and political career of William Gladstone (1809–98). His father began life outside the Anglican hegemony and ended securely within it: a Scots Presbyterian who came from Leith to Liverpool to make his fortune, he changed his religion to Anglicanism at the time of his second marriage (to an Anglican evangelical), and his politics from Whig to Tory, and became a substantial landowner in the process. Two of his four sons were sent to Eton and Oxford. William Gladstone began his political life as a Tory, making his maiden speech in defence of compensation for the slaveowners in the emancipation debate of 1833, and all his life was a High Churchman. But when he became Prime Minister in 1868 at the head of the first Liberal government it was on the strength of Nonconformist support and on the understanding that he would carry forward legislation on Church reform. One thus has the seeming paradox of a prime minister who was a High Anglican and believer in aristocratic government, enacting legislation which his younger self would have deplored, such as the disestablishment of the Irish Church (1869) and the abolition of compulsory Church rates (1868). Gladstone's eventual leadership of the party from which his father defected represents not so much the triumph of the new nation as the compromise with the old, which enabled it to achieve political power in the first place.

Victorian intellectual and cultural life was profoundly shaped by this struggle of new groups to reform or reconstruct the old aristocratic Anglican state. The new men and women of 1830 formed a wide spectrum: Nonconformist manufacturers and their spokesmen; old-fashioned radicals who looked back to Tom Paine (1737–1809) and the ideals of the French Revolution; the newer 'philosophic radicals' who took their cue from Jeremy Bentham (1748–1832) and wanted to reform British institutions along utilitarian lines; influential Scottish intellectuals such as Francis Jeffrey (1773–1850), first editor of the *Edinburgh Review*, Thomas Carlyle (1795–1881), and James Mill (1773–1836), father of John Stuart, friend and disciple of Bentham, and founder (in 1824) of the *Westminster Review*, the organ of the philosophic radicals; provincial freethinkers (often Unitarians) who provided a rallying point in their communities for new ideas and the spirit of reform, as the Bray family did for George Eliot in Coventry; a new generation of would-be professional people, of whom Darwin is perhaps the most famous example, whose imaginations had been caught by science and for whom clerical Oxbridge provided neither intellectual challenge nor institutional support. These groups were all in various ways middle class; a different challenge to the existing order came from the industrial working class in the rise of Chartism in the later 1830s.

The intellectual failure of Oxbridge in the first half of the nineteenth century is a consideration of some importance in any attempt to understand the direction intellectual life was to take between 1830 and 1890. Until 1826, when the philosophic radicals founded the University of London to provide a more broadly secular education along the lines of the Scottish universities, Oxford and Cambridge were the only two universities in England. (One might have obtained a better education at several of the Dissenting Academies, but not the social cachet.) They were indolent, Anglican institutions, offering a 'liberal education' in classics and mathematics but little support for the study of science and other modern subjects – despite the fact that distinguished scientists were to be found among the dons, and that in Cambridge at least there were professorships of geology and mineralogy, and an active network of intellectuals promoting extra-curricular interest among undergraduates in the cause of science.[7] The campaign for university reform yielded a slow trickle of concessions: optional Honours courses in science, law, and history at Oxford in 1850 (but only after a qualifying examination in classics), University Acts in 1854 (Oxford) and 1856 (Cambridge) abolishing religious tests for undergraduate degrees and making provision for a broadened curriculum. But these developments came too late for the first generation of Victorian scientists, with the consequence that much of the most innovative intellectual activity was unofficial, conducted in the pages of the periodicals and in the meetings of such societies as the Royal Institution and the British Association for the Advancement of Science (BAAS), founded in 1831. Science was the pursuit of enthusiastic amateurs and to some extent cut across social boundaries: it could bring to national eminence such men as Hugh Miller (1802–56), a Cromarty stonemason and self-taught geologist who wrote a number of best-selling books on the subject, won the respect of the leading scientists and writers of the day, and became a hero of Victorian self-help through his autobiography, *My Schools and Schoolmasters* (1854). Literary and philosophical societies developed in the major provincial cities as an expression of new nation commitment to modern knowledge, often with the support of local industrialists; and these could sometimes employ full-time scientists of distinction, such as John Dalton (1766–1844) at Manchester.

This state of affairs had advantages as well as disadvantages for the wider cultural life of society. If clerical Oxbridge hindered the professionalisation of science in the universities, and both the code of gentlemanly amateurism and new nation individualism were hostile to the formation of an intelligentsia on the continental model, this meant that until the 1860s or so intellectual debate was not the preserve of the specialist and the expert, but part of a wider discourse which thoughtful men and women could share by reading the magazines and periodicals in which the latest developments in science, philosophy, religion, and politics were reviewed. As these reviews were usually long and contained lengthy excerpts from the work in question, it was possible to derive an informed awareness of contemporary intellectual and cultural life from the reviews alone. Moreover, the prestige and comprehensiveness of the great periodicals (a nineteenth-century phenomenon in itself) helped to sustain a common discourse. A subscriber to the *Edinburgh Review* or the *Quarterly* was accustomed to move from, say, a review of Tennyson's poems to a discussion of the latest work in geology, from an article on contemporary astronomy to one on the Oxford Movement, without feeling that science, literature, and theology belonged in separate intellectual compartments. The discoveries of science fertilised the imagination of such writers as Tennyson, Dickens, Ruskin, Kingsley, and George Eliot; and could do so because science itself was so literate. There were energetic literary middlemen – like George Henry Lewes (1817–78), George

Eliot's companion – who communicated science and philosophy to the educated reader; more importantly there was a tradition of popular lecturing and writing by the great scientists themselves. It was through hearing Sir Humphry Davy lecture at the Royal Institution that Michael Faraday (1791–1867), then a stationer's apprentice, was inspired to become an experimental scientist, and his lectures at the Institution were in turn a popular draw because of his talent for explaining the complex through the familiar – like his *Course of Six Lectures on the Chemical History of a Candle* (1861). That tradition survives at the Royal Institution to the present day, but science's availability to the layperson was not a situation that could last; the expansion of knowledge made specialisation inevitable, and with specialisation came the fracturing of the common cultural context which, until *On the Origin of Species by Means of Natural Selection* (1859) at least, kept the discoveries of science in touch with the moral, religious, and aesthetic concerns of the informed general reader.

The climate of reform

What the different groupings in the new nation had in common, and what brought them into sympathetic relation with the more progressive elements in the old, was commitment to the cause of reform. The parliamentary and institutional reforms of the 1830s – the Reform Act of 1832, the Factory Act of 1833, the New Poor Law Act of 1834, the Municipal Reform Act of 1835, and so on – are important indications of a changed climate (although not all of this legislation was equally welcome to opponents of the old regime). These changes need to be seen against a wider background of awakened conscience and imagination, a widespread contemporary revulsion from the brutality and lawlessness of much everyday life in the early nineteenth century. It needs to be remembered, although often forgotten, that the world in which the first Victorians grew up was in many ways a violent, anarchic place. The old criminal code, aptly named the 'Bloody Code', was both ferocious and inefficient – 'the curse and disgrace of the country', as Macaulay wrote in 1818, 'at once too sanguinary and too lenient, half written in blood like Draco's, and half undefined and loose as the common law of a tribe of savages'.[8] One famous Victorian barrister described the county assizes at this time as being 'like a tiger let loose upon the district', and recalled, as a formative childhood experience, seeing the body of a seventeen-year-old youth, executed for rick-burning, being carried past his schoolroom window on a cart followed by the youth's parents.[9] That was in 1830, and it is worth recalling that only in this decade was the pillory abolished (1837), the baiting of animals made illegal, and a police force extended from London to the rest of the country by the Rural Police Act (1839). As late as 1850 a band of thieves terrorised the country districts in the south of England, murdering a clergyman in his garden at Frimley and compelling Charles Kingsley to put extra bolts on his doors and to sleep with a loaded gun and two pistols beside his bed; even so, there were several attempts to break into his house, and on one occasion Kingsley had to escort his wife home from Reading with a loaded pistol.[10]

The very fact that the adjective 'Victorian' is now associated – however erroneously – with restraint, repression, inhibition, and an oppressive decorum, is a sign of the magnitude of the change that took place between 1830 and 1890. The civilisation of everyday life was a Victorian achievement as remarkable and far-reaching as the democratic and industrial developments of the period, although, like the sewers they laid beneath the streets of their towns and cities, it is one that we now take for granted. In most accounts of the period, credit for this achievement is usually given to the evangelical revival of the eighteenth and early nineteenth centuries (see Chapter 2). A movement dating from John Wesley's conversion experience in 1738, it was by 1800 operating in upper-case form within the Church of England (Evangelicals) and in lower-case form among the newly formed Methodists, through whose influence it passed to other Nonconformist groups (evangelicals). Evangelicals of both sorts constituted the first modern pressure group: assiduous in forming societies and organising public meetings, relentless in distributing free pamphlets or 'tracts', they were credited by Macaulay's biographer with being 'nothing short of the pioneers and fuglemen of that system of popular agitation which forms such a leading feature in our internal history during the past half-century'.[11] Their activities were conspicuous and extensive. Evangelicals helped to restore spirituality and a sense of parish responsibility to the Church of England when indifference and absenteeism were rife. They were instrumental in abolishing slavery in the British colonies and, through Lord Shaftesbury, in the passing of Acts limiting child labour in factories. For good and ill they were active in the movement for the reformation of manners, setting up scores of societies to combat licentiousness and indifference, such as the Vice Society (1802) and the Lord's Day Observance Society (1831), and to convert the heathen. If they were largely responsible for the gloom of the Victorian Sunday, they were also leaders in the campaign against cruelty to animals, helping to set up the Society for the Prevention of Cruelty to Animals in 1824. Through their aristocratic converts they helped purify the domestic life of the upper classes, making marital fidelity no longer unfashionable and setting standards of family piety and domestic decorum for others to follow.

The record is impressive and historically important, yet it does not in itself explain the Victorian moral revolution. The Evangelicals were always a minority: even in the 1850s, when it was reckoned that they were at their most numerous, they accounted, according to one witness, for just over one-sixth of the clergymen in the Church of England.[12] Their success in converting an influential section of the aristocracy, and the undoubted influence this had on the manners of the aspiring middle classes, has to be set against the resentment that many of their activities caused, in particular their attempts to impose their own strict sabbath observances on the population at large, which led to riots in Hyde Park in 1855. They could claim a part in the shaping of some famous Victorians, including Macaulay, Gladstone, Newman, Ruskin, and George Eliot, but it is striking how many of these slipped the yoke in adult life, and how many more remained resistant or hostile to Anglican and non-Anglican evangelicalism. Dickens, for example, to take an important and representative figure, loathed evangelicalism, as the portraits of Mr Stiggins in *Pickwick Papers* (1836–37) and Mr Chadband in *Bleak House* (1852–53) abundantly attest. The spirit of humanitarian reform and love of hearth and home in his work seem to owe little to the movement, and his immense contemporary popularity suggests that these sentiments were much more widely diffused in his audience, and much less tied to specific religious doctrines, than is sometimes allowed. Indeed, the prominence given to children in his work, the sense of childhood as a special and precious state, run counter to evangelical ideology and have their roots in Romanticism. The Victorian moral sense was shaped as much by Wordsworth as by Wilberforce. In fact evangelicalism, like its secular equivalent utilitarianism, may only be tributaries to a much wider historical stream, the one described by Professor Harold Perkin as 'the tide of middle-class moral superiority to the aristocracy which . . . was flowing so strongly in the early nineteenth century'.[13] The Victorian moral revolution can be seen, in part, as another aspect of the middle-class challenge to aristocratic social leadership in the period, in which the challenge was legitimised by laying claim to the high ground – to a more inward religion, a tenderer domestic life, a more scrupulous and efficient conduct of public business, than the civilised classes traditionally practised. Here again the parvenu label is apt. With its roots in the eighteenth century, however, this tide was part of a broader movement still in response to the pressures of a rapidly changing society, cutting across the boundaries of the propertied classes, though it was the new nation which gave the movement its greatest momentum and urgency.

The ideology of the early Victorian reformers was strongly individualistic. It had been forged in the historical experience of social groups who had either been excluded from the Anglican hegemony because of their beliefs, such as the Nonconformists, or who were bent on transforming the rambling gothic structure of the old society into an efficient, secularised modern state, as the followers of Jeremy Bentham wanted to do. Whatever their differences about religious belief, these shared the psychological inheritance of embattled social groups in what they saw as an unregenerable society; committed to religious freedom and (usually) economic individualism, they were to find a common home in the Liberal Party which rose to power in the third quarter of the nineteenth century. By then the Nonconformists could hardly be described as a religious minority. The 1851 census revealed that they comprised just under half of those attending worship on a given Sunday in March (see Chapter 2). They were proportionately stronger away from the Anglican south, in Wales and the industrial north, where religious affiliation formed a strong cultural bond between industrialist and employee. In a recent study of ten nineteenth-century industrialists who were also noted philanthropists, there are three Quakers, three Congregationalists, one Baptist, one Presbyterian, and one Anglican, and only one figure who was not a member of any denomination – Andrew Carnegie.[14] For men of this background the idea of the state had been shaped by their memory of a privileged state church which was legally intrusive and culturally remote. Macaulay sounded their note in his review of Southey's *Sir Thomas More: or, Colloquies on the Progress and Prospects of Society* (1829), where he took Southey to task for proposing a revived paternalist state built around the Established Church as an antidote to the supposed evils of the industrial system:

> It is not by the intermeddling of Mr Southey's idol, the omniscient and omnipotent State, but by the prudence and energy of the people, that England has hitherto been carried forward in civilisation. . . . Our rulers will best promote the improvement of the nation by strictly confining themselves to their own legitimate duties, by leaving capital to find its most lucrative course, commodities their fair price, industry and intelligence their natural reward, idleness and folly their natural punishment, by maintaining peace, by defending property, by diminishing the price of law, and by observing strict economy in every department of the state. Let the Government do this: the People will assuredly do the rest.[15]

Here, in characteristically ringing and simplified tones, is the notion of a nightwatchman state: a fair field and no favours in matters of trade and industry, and the officers of the state to come out only after dark and in an emergency. Of course things were not as straightforward as Macaulay tried to make out (they rarely were) or as his readers would have liked to believe. The doctrine of *laissez-faire* was something of a necessary myth in Victorian society – a bogeyman for the old nation to use in its attacks on the new, a rallying cry for the new in its assault on protectionism (the Corn Laws, for example) and privilege. Liberal reformers might be inspired by the idea of cheap, efficient, and minimal government, but the effect of reform was always to increase the element of control at local and national level. This was inevitable in a society undergoing rapid growth in population and rapid urbanisation. The public health of cities, put on the political agenda by the 1848 Health of Towns Act, was not a job for nightwatchmen. Nonconformist manufacturers might resent the State Church and the interference of Parliament, but they could be as generously paternalistic towards their employees as any Tory squire: men like Sir Titus Salt (1803–76), the Bradford textile manufacturer who built a model industrial village, Saltaire, to house his employees in clean and civilised surroundings.

Liberalism set the agenda for much of the social, political, and religious debate of the period. The work of the so-called 'Victorian sages' – Carlyle, Newman, Mill, Arnold – is to a significant degree concerned with the nature of authority in an age of individualism: in Mill's case with the extent of the authority which the state had a right to exercise over the individual, in Arnold's and Carlyle's with reconstituting authority in what they saw as the anarchy of their times. The climate of reform also stimulated the Church of England into redefining the role it might come to play in modern society. Liberalism (in the sense of intellectual relativism and independence from dogma) is a dirty word in the writings of Newman and his fellow-Tractarians: their response to the challenge of the times was reactionary, in the strict sense of the word, meaning a return to the traditions and beliefs of the historical Church. But there was also an influential group of liberal Anglicans who wanted to reform the Church and widen its appeal in the 1830s. Thomas Arnold (1795–1842) and Lord John Russell, the Whig Home Secretary and later Prime Minister, were among its leaders and their thinking was influenced by the writings of Coleridge, in particular by his work *On the Constitution of Church and State* (1830). Coleridge saw the way the world was going – the trigger for the book was Catholic Emancipation in 1829 – and he wanted to save the cultural baby from being thrown out with the ecclesiastical bathwater. The baby was the national network of parish churches and clergymen which could become, in his view, the basis for a 'National

Church', manned by a body he called the 'clerisy' whose task would be 'to preserve the stores, to guard the treasures, of past civilization, and thus to bind the present with the past; to perfect and add to the same, and thus to connect the present with the future'.[16] The extent to which the clerisy would overlap with the existing clergy is never made entirely clear, and a cynic might say that Coleridge's National Church was simply a means of rescuing the *de facto* Established Church by other means. Still, to those who studied him – and this included such progressive thinkers as John Stuart Mill – Coleridge suggested two ideas of far-reaching consequence: that a special class of intellectuals and men of letters might exert an influence in society out of all proportion to their numerical size, and that a national church might find its modern justification not only as a repository of doctrine and dogma (which was Newman's view) but as a rallying point for the values and traditions implicit in Coleridge's notion of 'cultivation'. As the nineteenth century progressed and orthodox religion became more problematic, the idea of cultivation widened into Matthew Arnold's 'Culture' and came to be seen as a cohesive force distinct from Christianity and even as a replacement for it.

Coleridge saw a struggle going on between the forces of what he called 'Permanence' and those of 'Progression', and he hoped that the National Church might provide a third, reconciling force. The years between 1830 and 1850 saw that struggle at its sharpest. In politics there was the conflict between the old nation and the new over parliamentary reform and Corn Law repeal; in religion the institutional conflict between the Established Church and Dissent, and later between the supernatural claims of belief and the increasingly confident naturalistic premises of science; in philosophy and ethics the conflict between the spirit of rationalism, utilitarianism, and the inductive method, and the romantic–conservative defence of imagination, tradition, and intuition. By the mid-1850s these conflicts had worked themselves through to a recognisably 'Victorian' state of equilibrium. The success of the 1851 Great Exhibition, a witness to the international dominance of British manufactures, seemed to have set the seal on the wisdom of the 1832 Reform Act and Corn Law repeal in 1846: the new society was working. The proposals for Church reform emanating from the Ecclesiastical Commission set up by Sir Robert Peel in 1835, the collapse of the Oxford Movement in the 1840s, and the vindication of the non-doctrinal believing temper in the writings of Carlyle and Tennyson, all made for a certain religious reconstruction before the upheavals that followed the publication of *The Origin of Species* in 1859. The threat of revolution at home and abroad had passed in 1848. Domestically, the arrogance and licentiousness of old nation style was banished from the middle-class home (if not always from the country-house or the castle), while deference was maintained through the example of domestic piety set by Queen Victoria, and by the widespread acceptance of such multivalent social doctrines as respectability and gentlemanliness. In these and other ways the parvenus of 1830 both reflected and shaped the changes at work on the old aristocratic society, stamping Victorian culture with the values that had inspired their emergence: hard work, energy, self-help, individualism, earnestness, domesticity.

The parvenu accepted

What has been said so far applies largely to the earlier part of our period. By the 1860s important changes were taking place in Victorian society, changes that were to bring social acceptance for many in the new nation but were also to create a new agenda of reform. In one respect, this is the decade when the parvenus finally came into their inheritance, as Gladstone's government of 1868–74 abolished their great historic grievances: church rates, religious tests for teaching posts in Oxbridge, the Established status of the Church of Ireland, aristocratic patronage in the civil service and the army. The effect of these reforms was to signal traditional society's acceptance of new nation priorities, and, in doing so, to draw the sting of rebellion. What depressed Cobden, in the passage quoted above, was the willingness of the new to accommodate the 'feudalism' of the old; it was as if the Nonconformist manufacturer and artisan, the dissenting shopkeeper, the ambitious doctor or civil servant, had aspired merely to respectability within the traditional social order, not to changing the order itself. As many of the parvenus became more respectable – the wealthier sending their children to public schools and almost all acknowledging a transcendent social value in 'gentlemanliness' – they drifted away from the cutting edge of social reform. A combination of new-found respectability with historic individualism blinded them to the fact that the problems created by the new urban-industrial society required state action to a degree not allowed for in their ideology.

For in the 1860s the reform agenda was changing. This decade also saw the start of organised campaigns for women's rights and the resurgence, twenty years after the collapse of Chartism, of trade unionism. The first meeting of the Trades Union Council (TUC) took place in Manchester in 1868. The Reform League was set up in 1865 to increase working-class representation in Parliament. As some radicals split off from the liberals to pursue these causes, there was a leakage on the right wing of the Liberal Party towards conservatism, especially in the London suburbs. In 1868 Westminster and Middlesex went Tory against the tide, to be followed in 1874 by Surrey, Kent, and Essex.[17] An increasingly conservative middle class, having won its own share of social and political rights by 1870, found itself out of sympathy with the next stage of reform. Women's rights, the extension of democracy beyond the propertied classes, the necessity for state action in areas like education and public health, the rise of socialism towards the end of the century: these were the issues on the reform agenda of a modernising society, and the individualistic ethic of the new nation had great difficulty in adjusting to them. (See the section on 'Democracy, the state, and socialism' on page 169.)

An archetypal social and political trajectory of the century can be seen in the case of Beatrice Webb (1858–1943), the pioneering sociologist and founding mother of Fabian socialism. Both her grandfathers were radical Nonconformists who became successful businessmen from lowly origins; one, 'Radical Dick' Potter, was a founder of the *Manchester Guardian* and a prominent opponent of the Corn Laws. He sent his son to Clifton and University College London, the dissenters' university, with a view to a genteel career in the law, but the loss of Richard's fortune in the financial crisis of 1847–48 forced him to begin a new career as a timber merchant and railway director. Beatrice's father proved to have all 'Radical Dick's' entrepreneurial skill, but he dropped both the radicalism and the family unitarianism, becoming a political conservative and regular attender at the local Anglican church, where, despite not having been confirmed, he would read the lesson.[18] By the time Beatrice came to full political awareness, in the 1870s and 1880s, she decided that old radicalism had become new conservatism, based on a now-complacent economic individualism which she saw as irrelevant to the needs of the contemporary urban–industrial world: the future for her and many like her lay in socialism.

Cobden was an increasingly isolated figure in protesting that those he called the 'newer and better civilisation' should carry on their quarrel with aristocracy. The parvenus were mostly happy to settle for their own social and political acceptance, content to preach to others the doctrine of gradualism which had once been applied to them. For England was

> A land of settled government,
> A land of just and old renown,
> Where Freedom slowly broadens down
> From precedent to precedent.[19]

There is an important historical truth in Tennyson's famous lines, but also an almost infinite blandness that is both comical and deeply characteristic of the later Victorian mood. Only those who have 'Freedom' are content that it should '*slowly* broaden down'.

Exclusion had given the different elements in the new nation, and their sympathisers in the old, a cohesion that was starting to disperse in the 1860s, if not earlier. The parvenu accepted was too often the parvenu absorbed, and the cause of reform was fragmented in the process. No other single issue could unite the Liberal Party as the old civic disabilities had done, but one could fatally divide it: imperialism, the poisoned chalice of Disraelian conservatism (see Chapter 4).

Art and society

The social and technological developments of the period also made their impact on the visual arts. Industrialisation gave a powerful stimulus to contemporary interest in art and design, and to its dissemination, through inexpensive prints and illustrated newspapers, to all classes in society. The link between 'art' and 'manufactures' was early perceived as essential to the promotion of good industrial design, especially in those products where ornamental drawing was important, such as silk, ceramics, and wallpaper. A Government School of Design was set up in 1837 as a result of a recommendation by a Commons select committee on design, and in 1841 Sir Robert Peel appointed a Royal Commission chaired by Prince Albert to see how the fine arts could be promoted in relation to the rebuilding of the House of Commons at the time. It concluded that not enough was being done: more education was needed and the provision of free galleries, museums, and parks for the working classes, which could be justified even on strictly utilitarian grounds, 'since it is admitted that the cultivation of the more exalted branches of design tends to advance the humblest pursuits of industry, while the connexion of art with manufactures has often developed the genius of the greatest masters of design'.[20] Out of this awareness of the interdependence of art and design was to come the Great Exhibition of 1851.

The six million visitors to the Exhibition were visually literate to a degree that no previous generation had been. Technological change meant that quality engravings were no longer the preserve of the well-to-do. The perfecting of the steel-plate process in 1822 and the introduction of electrotyping in 1845 multiplied by several hundred times the number of impressions that could be taken from the old copper-plate, bringing the possession of prints within reach of all but the poor. The lowest entry charge to the Exhibition, one shilling (5p), was the cost of one of the monthly parts in which many of Dickens's novels were published, each of them containing two illustrations requiring to be 'read' as carefully as the text. The Exhibition was enthusiastically promoted by the *Illustrated London News*, that invaluable pictorial record of Victorian life and manners. Founded in 1842, it was the first paper to subordinate letterpress to illustration; according to one recent historian, the paper was responsible for stimulating 'a much greater visual sophistication' in its readers, making them aware of what the wider world looked like and of changing fashions in dress, painting, architecture, and interior design: 'A great step had been taken towards the imposition of a uniform taste. Never before had so many people been aware of how others outside their own locality, or outside their social class lived.'[21] The developments in technology also made possible the spread of photography in the 1840s and 1850s as a medium of public and domestic record.

Changes in the nature of patronage had important consequences for the development of painting in the nineteenth century. Traditionally, art collecting had been the preserve of the aristocracy and their dependents, whose tastes, formed by the European Grand Tour, tended to be for the Old Masters. New wealth had less time for leisured travel, less certainty about its judgement, and gravitated to the work of living artists instead. 'The increase of the private patronage of Art in this country is surprising', the painter C.R. Leslie wrote in 1851. 'Almost every day I hear of some man of fortune, whose name is unknown to me, who is forming a collection of the works of living painters; and they are all either men in business, or who have made fortunes in business and retired.'[22] One of the first of these men was John Sheepshanks (1787–1863), a Leeds manufacturer who retired to a suburban villa in Blackheath and left his collection to the nation in 1857 (it is now in the Victoria and Albert Museum). His tastes were typical of the first generation of new collectors in being predominantly for narrative genre painting of the kind produced by Sir David Wilkie (1785–1841) and William Mulready (1786–1863). The characteristics of their work are well summarised in the official catalogue to the collection:

> The present collection . . . consists of pictures of cabinet proportions, illustrative of every-day life and manners amongst us, appealing to every man's observation of nature and to our best feelings and affections, without rising to what is known as historic art; and as such, they are works that *all* can understand and all more or less appreciate. And this is especially to be insisted on, since a wrong impression is all too widely entertained that art does *not* appeal to the

multitude but only to those specially educated to appreciate it.[23]

Of 'cabinet' size (to fit the walls of a suburban villa rather than a castle), taking its subject from everyday life and appealing to nature and the heart, and readily comprehensible – these are the incipiently democratic artistic criteria which, by their patronage of living artists and by their public-spirited bequests, men like Sheepshanks helped to encourage.[24] There is evidence, too, of a regional shift in Victorian patronage, to the midlands and the north, where businessmen and industrialists were willing to support such groups as the Pre-Raphaelites before it became entirely respectable to do so – for example, Thomas Fairbairn of Manchester purchased *The Awakening Conscience* (1854) and commissioned a family portrait from Holman Hunt and a sculpture of his two children from the Pre-Raphaelite sculptor Thomas Woolner. 'The principal support of British Art proceeds from wealthy Lancashire', the *Art Journal* declared on the retirement of the influential Manchester-based dealer Thomas Agnew in 1861, claiming that he had been influential in encouraging the taste for contemporary painting: 'he may justly claim the gratitude of many who have prospered by the transfer of Art-patronage from the dead to the living'.[25]

Like the Victorian novel, to which it is often and rightly compared, and like the Dutch genre painting of the seventeenth and eighteenth centuries which provided inspiration to painters and writers alike – a comparison famously made by George Eliot in chapter 17 of *Adam Bede* (1859) – Victorian painting was predominantly narrative and domestic in character. Whether it dealt with contemporary life or dramatised a character or incident from the national past, the emphasis was on character and situation, sometimes catching the dramatic moment when these are revealed – the sudden access of remorse which brings Holman Hunt's fallen woman to her feet in *The Awakening Conscience* (1854), or the husband's stunned reaction to the letter which reveals his wife's unfaithfulness in Augustus Egg's *Past and Present – I* (1858). These famous and frequently reproduced paintings suggest comparisons not just with the Victorian novel but with the dramatic monologue as well, which in the hands of Browning is similarly concerned with crucial turning-points in the lives of his men and women. The iconography of genre painting derives from and reinforces the pieties of hearth and home, and the same is true of paintings dealing with military and historical subjects. Battle scenes are eschewed in favour of the tender and pathetic treatment of the victims of battle – wounded, maimed, or elderly soldiers, suffering widows and sweethearts. Mulready's *The Convalescent from Waterloo* (1822; see Plate 1) may be compared with Thackeray's *Vanity Fair* (1847–48) for its sober, unillusioned, and above all domesticated treatment of the subject: the wounded father sits beside his wife, who is in mourning, and both look at the re-enactment of the old stereotypes in their children – the wife apprehensively at the little girl sheltering beside her father, the husband at the two scrapping boys. History is typically seen in terms of public figures caught in poignant moments of private life, like Cromwell on his farm in Ford Madox Brown's painting *St Ives, AD 1630* (1874; see Plate 2 and Chapter 1), or in revealing and pathetic moments of high drama, or in terms of children. It is notable that the two most famous historical paintings of the period involve children: Millais's *The Boyhood of Raleigh* (1870) and W.F. Yeames's *And When Did You Last See Your Father?* (1878).

Approaching the age

This introductory chapter has been concerned particularly with the forces at work in the first half of our period which made the Britain of 1850 a different place – socially, culturally, intellectually – from the Britain of 1800, and set an agenda for the rest of the period which only gradually emerged into focus. To that extent it has minimised important continuities and discontinuites. Many in the new nation or in sympathy with it were Anglicans, as has already been noted above, and many Anglican clergymen, perhaps a majority by 1850, needed no lessons in spirituality or pastoral duty from reformers of the day. Equally, there were virtues in the old liberal education if one were fortunate enough to be taught by someone like Newman, who took his teaching duties seriously, and in the unofficial science education that Darwin received from J.S. Henslow (1795–1861), the Professor of Botany at Cambridge. The difference by 1850 was that no one, not even the conservatives, believed that the old attitudes and institutional structures could be sustained without exposure to the spirit of the age: they might be reaffirmed or they might be overthrown, but they had to come to terms with the most significant intellectual development of the previous fifty years, which was the growth of the *expectation* of change.

The Victorians confronted their unique historical exposure without the security of a confident world-view (Christianity being in crisis) until science began to provide one in the 1860s and 1870s (see 'The Spread of Science' in Chapter 3). The acceleration of everyday life, and the accumulation of knowledge about a new society which left individuals conscious of crisis but impotent to act, bred a new kind of *angst* – pervasive but unfocused. There were no precedents that industrialisation and urbanisation could fall back on, and no canons of taste dominant enough to forge their painting and architecture into a self-sufficient contemporary style. More than any previous generation the people we call Victorians were driven to find models of social harmony and personal conduct by means of which they could understand, control, and develop their rapidly changing world.

Some of these 'models' were historical. Just as the archaeologists of the time plundered the Ancient World for its artefacts, so educators, historians, writers, and politicians plundered the classical past for symbols of authority or desire. Greece, in particular, proved a fascinating model, attracting reformist historians at the start of our period, conservative Hellenists in the middle, and Platonists and pagans at the end (see Chapter 1). The Middle Ages were plundered even more selectively, to provide the period's most distinctive style of architecture (Gothic) and its richest stock of alternative images to the prevailing modern, urban–industrial world. The medieval model could inspire the Catholic polemic of Pugin's *Contrasts* (1841), the secular satire of Carlyle's *Past and Present* (1843), the Christian gentlemanliness of Tennyson's King Arthur; and through Ruskin's profoundly influential 'On the Nature of Gothic' (1853) it could take on new life in the writings and designs of William Morris, influencing both socialism and the Arts and Crafts Movement towards the end of the century (see Chapters 1 and 5).

The Victorians also had more modern, or modernised, models. One of the most important of these was the idea of the gentleman (and lady). The gentleman was a respected rank in traditional society – a 'grand old name' as Tennyson called it (*In Memoriam*, cxi) – and carried the prestige of its historic landed origins. However, partly because it could never be defined satisfactorily, it was not the possession of a caste, like the French *gentilhomme*. This meant, Alexis de Tocqueville shrewdly observed in *The Ancien Regime and the French Revolution* (1856), that 'we find its connotation being steadily widened in England as the classes draw nearer to each other and intermingle'. Its history, he thought, was 'the history of democracy itself'.[26] The gentleman model played a central part in the political and cultural assimilation of new social groups (see Chapter 4), and it also provided a focus for the moralisation of traditional society. Reformers could develop both the potential for 'gentleness' and 'manliness' in the concept: the first in the civilisation of domestic life, the second in promoting an ideal of conduct for young men which was decent, generous, open, of the world but not worldly, and brave without the recklessness and licentiousness of aristocracy.

Here again it is possible to see changing patterns and emphases between 1830 and 1890. In the 1830s and 40s, as the new middle classes sought to define their identity in relation to aristocracy, there is a defensiveness about re-definitions of gentility which is reflected in the earlier fiction of Dickens and Thackeray. By the 1850s a new model – middle-class, manly, and modern – had established itself, partly through the influence of Prince Albert (who was all these things) and partly in the fusion of Christianity with gentlemanliness in the doctrine of Christian manliness – what is sometimes rather misleadingly called 'muscular Christianity'. Just as the hero of Thomas Hughes's *Tom Brown's Schooldays* (1857) stands up to the upper-class bully at school and succours the weak, so the manly Christians like Hughes and his friend Charles Kingsley repudiated the economic selfishness of their class and espoused a form of socialism as a response to the sufferings and injustice of industrial society.[27] Gentlemanliness was the badge of acceptance sought by the new professional groups, but even as they won it there were voices in the 1870s and 1880s saying that it was too bland and diluted to have much value: e.g. Mrs Swancourt in Hardy's *A Pair of Blue Eyes* (1873), who tells Elfride that '"you mustn't say 'gentlemen' nowadays. . . . We have handed over 'gentlemen' to the lower middle class"'; and when Elfride asks what she should say, she is told '"'Ladies and *men*', always."' (ch. 14) By the 1890s the model of the gentleman had done its work and was beginning to look rather old fashioned and irrelevant to most of the concerns of the time (feminism, socialism, political and social reform) except for imperialism.

Industrial society had its own legitimating myths and models, and two of these were celebrated in the writings of Samuel Smiles (1812–1904): self-help, in his book of that title (1859), and the heroic myth of the Victorian engineer portrayed in his biography of George Stephenson and *The Lives of the Engineers* (1867; 1874). The independent, night-school-attending, self-helping artisan was one of the models which middle-class writers held up to the working class, in novels like George Eliot's *Adam Bede* (1859) and Mrs Craik's *John Halifax, Gentleman* (1856). Smiles did not so much develop a new model as codify an old one, which seems more appropriate to the pre-factory stage of industrial development and to the minority which has usually been seen as the 'labour aristocracy'; yet recent work in Victorian history has argued that the aspiration to an independent 'respectability' was much more widely spread in the mid- and late-Victorian working class.[28] The ideology of self-help appealed to this and to the individualism which was the religious inheritance of the new industrial proletariat, and may explain something of their resistance to trade unionism in the nineteenth century. Self-help, like the gentleman – and Smiles's final chapter is called 'Character: the True Gentleman' – may have played an important part in reconciling new groups to the respectability-seeking thrust of the new society. Equally, the engineer was a reconciling model. He might have, and often had, risen from the ranks; everyone could see how essential his work was to this heroic age of British engineering; and the mythology was that of an officer leading from the front rather than the back, not asking his workmen to take any risks he was not prepared to take himself. He made people feel the pride and exhilaration of participating in a uniquely modern social experiment.

These and other models were various means of assimilating, comprehending and directing change; their success can be judged from the fact that they enabled Victorian Britain to undergo a revolutionary change without revolution. The price paid, culturally, was a deep ambivalence about past and future, an ambivalence which Tennyson captured and which Whitman recognised as the source of his appeal:

> His very doubts, swervings, doublings upon himself, have
> been typical of our age. We are like the voyagers of a ship,
> casting off for new seas, distant shores. We would still
> dwell in the old suffocating and dead haunts, remembering
> and magnifying their pleasant experiences only, and more
> than once impell'd to jump ashore before it is too late, and
> stay where our fathers stay'd, and live as they lived.[29]

That sense of life as a voyage on uncharted seas is now a cliché but had then something of the force of an intellectual discovery: it is there in Tennyson's 'Ulysses', pervasively in the poetry of Matthew Arnold, and comes in at the climax of Newman's *Apologia Pro Vita Sua* (1864), when he transcribes a letter written to a friend in 1846 recording the loneliness he felt at his departure from Oxford after his conversion to the Church of Rome: 'I realize more that we are leaving Littlemore, and it is like going on the open sea.' Newman describes saying goodbye to his old tutor at Trinity:

> There used to be much snap-dragon growing on the walls
> opposite my freshman's rooms there, and I had for years
> taken it as the emblem of my own perpetual residence even
> unto death in my University.
>   On the morning of the 23rd I left the Observatory. I
> have never seen Oxford since, excepting its spires, as they
> are seen from the railway.[30]

Here, as reasonantly juxtaposed as in a poem by Tennyson, is the private symbol of the life surrendered, the snap-dragon, and the public symbol of the forces of modernity, the railway. In the abruptness of the second paragraph one can hear the iron gates of the present and the future shutting on the lost garden of the past. This sense of emotional exile in a changing world is at the heart of the Victorian *angst*, and comes over most powerfully in their obsession with time – the private time of autobiography, the public time of history – to which we must now turn.

Notes

1. 'Are the Victorians Coming Back?', *All in Due Time* (1955), p. 93.

2. G. Kitson Clark, *An Expanding Society: Britain 1830–1900* (Cambridge, 1967), p. 11.

3. The phrase 'Anglican hegemony' is used by J.C.D. Clark in his *English Society 1688–1832* (Cambridge, 1985).

4. See J.T. Ward and R.G. Wilson (eds), *Land and Industry: The Landed Estate in the Industrial Revolution* (Newton Abbot, 1971), and W.D. Rubinstein, 'The Victorian Middle Classes: Wealth, Occupation, and Geography', *Economic History Review*, 30 (1977), 602–23. C.H. Lee, *The British Economy since 1700: A Macroeconomic Perspective* (Cambridge, 1986) is a recent history arguing against the view that manufacturing industry was predominant in Victorian wealth creation.

5. *Aristocracy and People: Britain 1815–1865* (1979), p. 347.

6. John Morley, *Life of Cobden* (2 vols, 1881), II, pp. 481–2.

7. See T.W. Heyck, *The Transformation of Intellectual Life in Victorian England* (1982), and for the Oxbridge professoriate's involvement in the early years of the BAAS, J. Morrell and A. Thackray, *Gentlemen of Science* (Oxford, 1981).

8. G.O. Trevelyan, *The Life and Letters of Lord Macaulay* (2 vols, 1876), I, p. 83.

9. Sir Henry Hawkins, *The Reminiscences of Sir Henry Hawkins*, edited by Richard Harris (1904), pp. 87, 15–16.

10. See Robert Bernard Martin, *The Dust of Combat* (1959), pp. 124–5.

11. Trevelyan, *op. cit.*, I, pp. 64–5.

12. See W.J. Conybeare, 'Church Parties', *Edinburgh Review*, 98 (1853), 273–342.

13. *The Origins of Modern English Society 1780–1880* (1969), pp. 283–4.

14. Ian Campbell Bradley, *Enlightened Entrepreneurs* (1987).

15. *Critical and Historical Essays* (1872), p. 122.

16. *On the Constitution of Church and State*, edited by J. Barrell (1972), pp. 33–4.

17. See E.J. Feuchtwanger, *Democracy and Empire: Britain 1865–1914* (1985), p. 53.

18. See Carole Seymour-Jones, *Beatrice Webb: Woman of Conflict* (1992), pp. 3–4, 45.

19. '"You ask me why, though ill at ease?"', *Poems of Tennyson*, edited by C. Ricks (1969), p. 490.

20. Quoted in B. Denvir (ed.), *The Early Nineteenth Century: Art, Design and Society* (1984), p. 203.

21. *Ibid.*, p. 23.

22. Quoted in Dianne S. Macleod, 'Art Collecting and Victorian Middle-Class Taste', *Art History*, 10 (1987), 328–40 (see esp. p. 329).

23. Quoted in E.D.H. Johnson, *Paintings of the British Social Scene: From Hogarth to Sickert* (1986), pp. 139–40. I am generally indebted to Johnson's book here, and to the article by Macleod cited above.

24. When he made a gift of his collection to the nation, Sheepshanks stipulated that access should be given to the public, 'and especially the working class', on Sunday afternoons (Macleod, p. 330).

25. Johnson, *op. cit.*, pp. 186–67.

26. *The Ancien Regime and the French Revolution*, translated by S. Gilbert (1966), p. 109.

27. See Norman Vance, *The Sinews of the Spirit: The ideal of Christian manliness in Victorian literature and religious thought* (Cambridge, 1985).

28. See F.M.L. Thompson, *The Rise of Respectable Society* (1988).

29. 'A Word about Tennyson' (1887), in *Tennyson: The Critical Heritage*, edited by J.D. Jump (1967), p. 350.

30. *Apologia Pro Vita Sua*, edited by D.J. DeLaura (New York, 1968), ch. IV, p. 183. At the start of the next chapter Newman described his conversion to Rome as 'like coming into port after a rough sea' (p. 184).

Chapter 1
The Sense of Time and the Uses of History

Time and autobiography

People of the nineteenth century were fascinated by time because they were conscious of being its victims. This was the age of Lewis Carroll's White Rabbit, anxiously consulting his watch ('Oh dear! Oh dear! I shall be too late!'), but it was also the age of the memento, the keepsake, the curl of hair cherished in the brooch, the photograph in the locket – all those sentimental stays against the quickening pace of time's erosion. An awareness of time as history inspired the intellectual discoveries of the period, in geology, evolution, biblical criticism, archaeology, anthropology; and the search for origins and continuities was common to an agnostic scientist like Darwin and an Anglo-Catholic theologian like Newman. Wherever one looks, in almost every area of Victorian intellectual life, one encounters a preoccupation with ancestry and descent, with tracing the genealogy of the present in the past, and with discovering or creating links to a formative history. And what is true of the culture's public discourse about itself was also true of individuals, driven in an age of rapid change to find coherence and meaning in the shape of their own lives, in autobiography.

Geology was the leading science in the first half of the nineteenth century and its message was of the immeasurability of time. The early Victorians were the first people to receive the chilling impact of 'deep time', as John McPhee called it: an expanse of time so vast that we can only grasp its scale metaphorically. Mark Twain's metaphor in his '"Was the World made for Man?"' of 1903 is more suggestive than most:

> Man has been here 32,000 years. That it took a hundred
> million years to prepare the world for him is proof that
> that is what it was done for. I suppose it is, I dunno. If
> the Eiffel Tower were now representing the world's age,
> the skin of paint on the pinnacle-nob at its summit would

represent man's share of that age; and anybody would
perceive that that skin was what the tower was built for. I
reckon they would, I dunno.[1]

Today we live in a universe that is four and a half billion years old.
Only custom muffles for us the thrill which the 'terrible muses' of
geology and astronomy inspired in Tennyson and Edward FitzGerald:
'it is not the poetical imagination, but bare Science that every day
more and more unrolls a greater Epic than the Iliad; the history of
the World, the infinitudes of Space and Time! I never take up a book
of Geology or Astronomy but this strikes me.'[2] The two sciences
were often linked. Throughout his *Principles of Geology* (1830–33) Sir
Charles Lyell compares the 'immensity of past time' opened up by
contemporary geology to the 'sublimity' of the astronomer's view:
'Worlds are seen beyond worlds immeasurably distant from each other,
and, beyond them all, innumerable other systems are faintly traced on
the confines of the visible universe'.[3] Time and space, geology and
astronomy, combined to open up dizzying perspectives which seemed
to dwarf mankind and its history, calling in question the consolations
of religion and the optimism inherited from the Romantics.

There is one remarkable painting which seems to capture the existential
emptiness of this moment in history – somewhat surprisingly, since
the painter was a devout High Churchman who might have been
supposed immune to such intimations of cosmic despair. This is
William Dyce's *Pegwell Bay: A Recollection of October 5th, 1858* (1860;
see Plate 3). Dyce (1806–64) was a man of developed scientific as
well as religious and artistic interests; he knew that Pegwell Bay was
particularly rich in fossils and the cliff's geological strata are painted with
knowledge and precision. Here they dominate the human figures in the
foreground. It is a family scene, but worlds away from the cheerful
bustle of W.P. Frith's seaside paintings. The figures stand separate,
the woman and the child looking beyond the spectator, perhaps out
to sea, the other two gathering shells in the centre, and the tiny
figure of the artist in the middle distance. Apart from the donkeys
and their drivers beneath the cliffs, no other figures can be seen,
and no houses, but in the centre of the sky is the faint streak of a
comet. As Marcia Pointon has shown, this is Donati's comet, which
was 62 million miles away but at its brightest on 5 October 1858:
hence the painting's subtitle.[4] Here Tennyson's two 'terrible muses'
are brought together and seen in contrast to the human figures on the
shore, who look vulnerable and lost: isolated, straying figures rather
than a cheerful family group. *Pegwell Bay* is a unique capturing of the
great gulf which was opening up in the nineteenth-century's experience
of time, between the family album 'recollection' of a visit to the

seaside and the terrifying vastness of geological time and astronomical distance.

To the modern mind there is something a little strange, even ironic, in the precision with which Dyce here attempts to fix his moment of recollection. When the very rocks on that desolate foreshore are likely to be older than the human species, why bother to record the day, month, and year? Because they belong to the private universe of memory, which has its own logic and importance. There is a saying of Goethe's which Matthew Arnold copied many times into his *Notebooks:* 'The highest happiness, says Goethe, is to find what it is that holds the world together within.'[5] Holding the world together within, finding a coherence in the self which would at the same time impose some meaning and coherence on a rapidly changing world outside: this involved searching for the logic in one's own memories, which is the task of autobiography. The autobiographical pressure which is felt so strongly in Victorian writing of all kinds – fiction, poetry, literary criticism, theology – is an expression of the desire to make sense of an evolutionary universe by discovering evolution in one's own universe of memory. Or if not evolution, since the idea belongs to the second half of the century, then what Arnold called in his poem of that name the 'buried life' (1852), in discovering which 'A man becomes aware of his life's flow' – 'And then he thinks he knows / The hills where his life rose, / And the sea where it goes.'

No sooner does one recognise this phenomenon, however, than one encounters a major paradox of Victorian culture. The very forces which made the autobiographical task urgent also made it problematic. The prophets of progress saw the backward glance of autobiography as regressive, its surrender to introspection as a failure to measure up to the active, public virtues of a new civilisation. The consequence was the kind of strain which can be felt in *In Memoriam* (1850). Wordsworth's self-exploration in *The Prelude* (1805; 1850) is epic and unabashed, whereas Tennyson always seems aware of the accusations of morbidity that might be directed at his song of private grief:

> A third is wroth: 'Is this an hour
>   For private sorrow's barren song,
>   When more and more the people throng
> The chairs and thrones of civil power? (XXI)

Introspection is not quite 'manly', this voice implies, and it is out of step with the spirit of the age. The fact that the age created profound dislocations in everyday life, and was throwing up problems in science and belief which made introspection almost inevitable for a thinking person, did not make autobiography of the frank Romantic kind respectable. It was still too closely associated with the turbulence of the French Revolution.

The early Victorian ambivalence about exploring the self is both revealed and transcended in one of the most influential books of the century. Carlyle's *Sartor Resartus* (1833–34) seems a strange and uncouth work today, but for readers of George Eliot's generation it marked, as she said in 1855, 'an epoch in the history of their minds'.[6] They wrote about it in terms almost of personal gratitude, and it now seems clear that the book's power for them lay in its addressing of the spiritual crisis of the time. However, *Sartor* differs markedly in form and tone from other spiritual autobiographies. The narrator is a student of German literature engaged in interpreting for British readers a work by a German philosopher, Diogenes Teufelsdröckh ('God-born Devil's-dung'), called *Die Kleider*, a dissertation on the philosophy of clothes. It is not clear for much of *Sartor Resartus* – which means 'the Tailor Re-Tailored' – whether Teufelsdröckh is a seer or a madman, and in the course of answering this question, and interpreting his friend's writings, the narrator is compelled to write his biography – or rather to assemble, from notes stuffed into six bags, the philosopher's autobiography. This reconstructed autobiography forms the second of the work's three books.

Sartor is a kind of narrative onion – a review article on *Die Kleider*, leading into an editorial essay on the problems of interpreting the notes stuffed in the bags, which then becomes a biography of Teufelsröckh, which then leads to a confessional core, which in turns explains and authenticates the clothes-philosophy in Book 3. Parodic and self-reflexive, *Sartor* plays fictively with the realities of Carlyle's own situation and past. Like the Editor he was a reviewer who had made his reputation by introducing the German Romantics to British readers through a series of articles and reviews in the 1820s, by translating Goethe's *bildungsroman* (novel of self-development) *Wilhelm Meister's Apprenticeship* (1824), and by writing a *Life of Schiller* (1825). He had also begun, but not completed, his own version of a *bildungsroman, Wotton Reinfred* (1827), and some of the formative experiences that would have been dealt with romantically there emerge here, distanced by irony and editorial commentary: his disillusionment with the dry rationalism he had encountered as a student at Edinburgh ('Pedagogy'), disappointment in love (the Blumine episode), and the religious crisis of his early manhood, which is treated in the central chapters of Book 2 – 'The Everlasting No', 'Centre of Indifference', and 'The Everlasting Yea'. It was these chapters above all which seem to have inspired and consoled the first generation of Victorian agnostics. They describe a process of religious loss and negation leading through a period of philosophical suspension to the rediscovery of faith – not in the

Christian God, for that 'vesture' of the Divine has passed, but in an Eternal God behind all those particular manifestations. Belief-systems are only clothes, not the thing itself, and what is needed now is a spiritual retailoring: hence the book's title and clothes symbolism.

This may sound banal enough in summary, but what gave it emotional punch was Carlyle's topical awareness of the new immensity of time coupled with his religious feeling for the eternal behind it, for 'only in the transitory Time-Symbol is the ever-motionless Eternity we stand on made manifest'.[7] The one met the conditions of the scientific universe while the other satisfied religious longings which Christianity could no longer meet: modern men, such as the scientist T.H. Huxley, learned from *Sartor* that 'a deep sense of religion was compatible with the entire absence of theology'.[8] But not the absence of morality: the book's power owed much to the austere solution Carlyle/Teufelsdröckh offered to the modern search for fulfilment.

> Foolish soul! What Act of Legislature was there that *thou*
> shouldst be happy? A little while ago thou hadst no right
> to *be* at all. What if thou wert born and predestined not to
> be Happy, but to be Unhappy! Art thou nothing other than
> a Vulture, then, that fliest through the Universe seeking
> after somewhat to *eat*; and shrieking dolefully because
> carrion enough is not given thee? Close thy *Byron*; open thy
> *Goethe*. (p. 146)

This is an important moment in nineteenth-century autobiography. Carlyle may have solved for a while the religious problem but in doing so he seemed to close the other great route to existential self-understanding which the romantic autobiographers had opened up (Byron here stands for self-indulgent introspection). Instead, the contemporary reader was left with the hard doctrine of work:

> Produce! Produce! Were it but the pitifullest infinitesimal
> fraction of a Product, produce in God's name! 'Tis the
> utmost thou hast in thee; out with it then. Up, up!
> Whatsoever thy hand findeth to do, do it with thy whole
> might. Work while it is called To-day, for the Night
> cometh wherein no man can work. (p. 149)

As is the case with Carlyle's work generally, the scriptural references here – Ecclesiastes 9: 10 and John 9: 4, to be precise – reinforce his moral exhortations with the emotional associations of the faith whose time, *Sartor* tells us, has passed. This rhetorical device looks suspect today, but it was almost subliminal for Carlyle and his readers, imbuing his severe doctrines with an emotion and authority they would not otherwise have had.

The liberation which *Sartor* brought to the first generation of Victorians was not achieved without a cost. Its influence was directly related to its power as spiritual autobiography, but the way in which the religious doubts were resolved, in a therapeutic turning-away from introspection (Byron) to renunciation (*entsagen*), work, and duty (Carlyle's reading of Goethe), had the effect of slamming the door on introspection and autobiography. The book's form and tone mock the self-indulgence of 'these autobiographical times of ours' (p. 73). The well-meaning but ironic narrator is never far away; we are made aware of him assembling Teufelsdröckh's autobiography and consequently are never allowed the entirely unironic view of the making of the self one has in a great Romantic autobiography like Wordsworth's *Prelude*. The persistent dualism in his presentation of Teufelsdröckh – is he 'spirit' or 'dung', seer or charlatan? – is calculated to fend the reader off. The fact that many contemporary readers nonetheless identified with him meant that they imbibed a scepticism about autobiography in the process of being consoled by it. *Sartor Resartus* fulfilled the functions of a contemporary version of Rousseau's *Confessions* while simultaneously questioning the validity of confessional writing. Carlyle had his cake and ate it, but his readers were to be denied that luxury; their medicine was to be Aristotle's dictum that '*The end of Man is an Action, and not a Thought*' (p. 120).

In this way Carlyle's most influential work did much to reinforce pressures coming from the outer life of society telling individuals to abandon their fruitless and self-indulgent search for the buried life, and sublimate their existential anxieties in work and duty. Such cultural prohibitions did not prevent the writing of many remarkable autobiographies in the period, but they also had the effect of forcing the confessional impulse underground, where it surfaced indirectly in various symbolic forms like the *bildungsroman* (*Jane Eyre*, published in 1847, is subtitled 'An Autobiography'), the personal elegies of Tennyson and Arnold, the dramatic monologue, even the critical essay in the hands of Arnold and Pater – these give us often a more vivid and intimate sense of the inner life than formal autobiography, which tended to be reticent in crucial areas.

There were no such cultural inhibitions about the writing and reading of biography and history. To close one's Byron and open one's Gibbon or Herodotus or Macaulay was to move from the dangerously subjective to the fruitfully objective. History was a record of people and events, of action rather than introspection, and in the hands of a Whig historian like Macaulay, a record of progressive national development. Yet the antithesis is neither as sharp nor as simple as Carlyle liked to make it seem. History-writing is also an act of memory, a form of cultural autobiography. The various pasts which a period chooses to investigate, and the contemporary uses to which these pasts are put, tell us much about the anxieties of the present and the identity – or identities – which a society chooses to affirm. Serious historians like Macaulay and Froude were drawn to the 1688 Revolution or Elizabethan England out of a sense of ancestry, of a formative past that had set in motion forces still at work in their own society which they wished to clarify and defend. Others, like the artists and writers of Victorian medievalism, were less concerned with recovering the actuality of the past than with using it as a model to be set against the present, a mirror in which the ills of the present could be seen by force of contrast. The variety of historical models evoked in the competing styles of art and architecture – classical, Gothic, Italian Renaissance, Elizabethan and Queen Anne vernacular – is evidence of how thoroughly the consciousness of the period was steeped in time and history, and of the restless relativism which drove the Victorians in the search for an authenticating ancestor who would redeem their parvenu age. In fact, the writing of history in the nineteenth century was a much more subjective enterprise than its respectably 'objective' status admitted.

Two versions of Victorian historiography: Carlyle and Macaulay

The collapse of the Soviet Union in the late twentieth century is a final collapse not only of a political system but also of an assumption which almost no secular thinker now holds, but which almost everyone held in the nineteenth century: that history has a design and a purpose. So strongly did people believe this that it led them to read into Darwin's essentially directionless theory of evolution a moral progressionism which defused its darker implications (see Chapter 3). There were several different theories of history but they were nearly all theories of inevitable, progressive development: in this sense most nineteenth-century theorists of history – including Karl Marx – were whigs. In his *Lectures on the Philosophy of History* (1831) Marx's mentor Hegel traced the development of human freedom as an inevitable process working through the rise and fall of ancient civilisations, the growth of Christianity, its corruption in medieval Catholicism and re-emergence after the Reformation, and its culmination in modern Germany; he also contributed the idea of history as a dialectic, the incompleteness of one period (thesis) breeding a reaction against its particular conditions in the next (antithesis), leading either to a synthesis of the two or to a further antithesis – but always with a forward movement to the desired goal of human freedom. Hegel's thesis–antithesis–synthesis is one philosophical triad; Saint-Simon's notion of 'organic' and 'critical' phases leading to a 'Golden Age' is another, and out of Saint-Simon's three phases the French philosopher Comte built his own more influential system of the Theological, Metaphysical, and Positive (Scientific) stages of human history (see Chapter 4).

Hegel's and Saint-Simon's theories of history were not blandly progressive. They allowed for alternating movements within the historical process and thus for the sufferings of individuals and societies before the goal of the good society was reached. Many Victorian intellectuals, for example, saw themselves as living in a Saint-Simonian 'critical' phase after the break-up of the 'organic' phase of Christianity, believing in a redemptive future that they would not live to see: like the speaker in Arnold's 'Stanzas from the Grand Chartreuse' (1855) – 'Wandering between two worlds, one dead, / The other powerless to be born'. Indeed, as Peter Bowler has argued, Victorian thinking about both past and future was conditioned by a tension between a linear model of development and a cyclical.[9] On the linear model civilisations followed an arrow's path of development, onward and upward in the vulgar rhetoric of progress; but – and here the evidence of archaeology began to darken the picture – they also declined and passed away. On the cyclical model each successive civilisation could be seen as contributing something to the growing revelation of a divine purpose in history, and so the natural pattern of birth, growth, and death in the story of civilisations could be redeemed and, in the case of Christianity, stayed and reversed. The two greatest histories of the period – both histories of revolutions – correspond approximately to these two models. Macaulay's *History of England from the Accession of James II* (1849–61) is linear and progressive, and has always been taken as the great exemplar of 'whig' history. Carlyle's *The History of the French Revolution* (1837) has a vision of history that is apocalyptic and cyclical (though hardly Christian), where men and women dance to the increasingly frenzied music of the Time-Spirit, whose more or less helpless victims they are.

There are interesting continuities between *Sartor* and *The French Revolution*: the spiritual crisis Teufelsdröckh experiences in his contact with Enlightenment rationalism becomes the crisis of a whole society, and the 'Time-Spirit' presides over both works. Carlyle's attitude to history cannot be separated from his sense of time, which differs in important respects from that of his contemporaries brought up in the English romantic tradition of Wordsworth and Coleridge. Influenced by the more rigorous Idealism of the German romantics, he saw time not as linear progression but as a garment that reveals God, or as a loom weaving that garment. One of his favourite quotations was the speech of the Spirit of the Earth in Goethe's *Faust Part One*, which he quotes in *Sartor*:

> 'Tis thus at the roaring Loom of Time I ply,
> And weave for God the Garment thou seest Him by. (p. 44)

Not for Carlyle the long perspectives of geological time which oppressed the early Victorians with a sense of unceasing process; his vision is apocalyptic: the garment of Time can at any moment be rolled away to reveal an unchanging Eternity (one naturally slips into capitals when discussing Carlyle's concepts). Time the loom is a machine over which we have no control: 'Fearful: how we stand enveloped, deep-sunk, in that Mystery of TIME; and are Sons of Time; fashioned and woven out of Time; and on us, and on all that we have, or see, or do, is written: Rest not, Continue not, Forward to thy doom!'[10] Revolutionary time accelerates the loom to the point at which the 'Sons of Time' pass from sight with bewildering speed.

Carlyle captures the speed and terror of revolutionary events by the simple but brilliant device of writing in a dramatic present tense, bombarding the reader with a multitude of simultaneous events. 'Narrative is *linear*, Action is *solid*', he had written in his earlier essay 'On History' (1830), and it is the solidity of acted history which his book aims to convey; for

> It is not in acted, as it is in written History: actual events
> are nowise so simply related to each other as parents and
> offspring are; every single event is the offspring not of one,
> but of all other events . . . and will in its turn combine
> with all others to give birth to new: it is an ever-living,
> ever-working Chaos of Being, wherein shape after shape
> bodies itself forth from innumerable elements.[11]

This view of history and the writing of history is rather more complex than the cult of the heroic leader which Carlyle was later to propound, and it differs also from the Whig or progressive view associated with Macaulay, where linear narrative, cause and effect, and the steady descent from 'parent' to 'offspring' in political development are all emphasised. *The French Revolution* is unique among Victorian histories in portraying a society in the grip of large, impersonal forces over which the single individual can exert only a limited and temporary influence. It is also unique among Carlyle's works, for he was later to turn to a more individualistic view of history, not only in his *On Heroes, Hero-Worship and the Heroic in History* (1841) but also in his portrait of Abbot Samson in *Past and Present* (1843), and his edition of Cromwell's letters and speeches (1845) (see 'Usable pasts' below, p. 41 ff). But the nearest we get to a Carlylean hero in *The French Revolution* is Mirabeau, who 'if not Epic for us, is Tragic'[12]; but he dies before he can affect the later course of the Revolution. Otherwise most of the characters in the drama are not so very different from Louis XVI's courtiers, 'Light mortals', walking their 'light life-minuet, over bottomless abysses, divided from [them] by a film'.[13]

The French Revolution was an unprecedented event and Carlyle recounts it in an unprecedented way. A reader looking for an intro-duction to the historical event in Carlyle's book is likely to feel bewildered: a chronological account of the Revolution is there, but Carlyle chooses to treat it as the Greek tragedians had treated their myths, on the implicit assumption that the audience knew the story beforehand – as indeed his first readers would have done, being less than fifty years away from the Fall of the Bastille. His book is epic in scope and tragic in shape, taking the story from the death of Louis XV to the death of Robespierre – 'Our fifth-act of the natural Greek Drama'[14] – and the end of the Terror. It can be read as a tragedy in two parts: the first the tragedy of the *ancien régime*, represented by Louis XVI and his family, who are the unlucky scapegoats for a corrupt and dying social system; the second, represented perhaps by Robespierre, a tragedy brought on by what Carlyle saw as the hubris of the Enlightenment mind, when the militant rationalism of the heirs of the French *philosophes* ends with tragic irony in the whirlwind of the Terror.

Carlyle's narrator participates in these events, gesturing towards the historical figures, addressing them directly, appealing to the executioner not to delay his work with the wounded Robespierre. He ventriloquises historical destiny even as he runs along beside the actors like a modern television reporter caught in a crisis; he can do this because the dramatic present tense always has access to the future, and knowledge of the future floods the present with a tragic light. So, as the deputies of the Three Estates process with the court from Versailles to Notre Dame on 4 May 1789, 'the baptism day of Democracy. . . . The extreme-unction day of Feudalism', the reader is button-holed and has the principal characters pointed out to him, as by a knowing onlooker, but the scene concludes –

> And so, in stately Procession, have passed the Elected of France. Some towards honour and quick fire-consummation; most towards dishonour; not a few towards massacre, confusion, emigration, desperation: all towards Eternity![15]

The sudden widening of perspective creates an effect of grave irony: between the 'stateliness' with which these notabilities process and the violent death or shame that awaits most of them, and between the absorption of historical life and the awesome inevitability of Eternity which waits all (including the reader). It is this ability to command both the immediate and the eternal that gives *The French Revolution* its tragic power.

Carlyle had little interest in or talent for historical analysis of the dispassionate, sequential kind we expect from the professional historian today. His feeling for historical reality is most effective in particular episodes and events – the flight of the royal family to Varennes and their return to Paris, the trial and execution of Louis, Charlotte Corday's murder of Marat and her own execution, the failed suicide of Robespierre and his execution. No writer has ever captured the mob better, perhaps because there was a daemonic element in Carlyle's nature which made his response to events like the Fall of the Bastille and the Siege of the Tuileries ambivalent: the violence unleashed was terrible but it was also inevitable, retribution exacted by the Old Testament god of history for the frivolities of the *ancien régime*. The contrast between the violence of the mob and the processions and pageants celebrating reason brought out the savage ironist in Carlyle. On the one hand there was the march of the women on Versailles, when the 'Boundless Chaos of Insurrection' presses round the Palace 'like Ocean around a Diving-bell'[16]; on the other the enthronment, at the very height of the Terror, of a 'Goddess of Reason' in the shape of an actress from the Opera:

> Demoiselle Candeille, of the Opera; a woman fair to look upon, when well rouged; she, borne on palanquin shoulder high; with red woollen nightcap; in azure mantle; garlanded with oak; holding in her hand the pike of the the Jupiter-*Peuple*, sails in: heralded by white young women girt in tricolour. Let the world consider it! This, O National Convention wonder of the universe, is our New Divinity; *Goddess of Reason*, worthy, and alone worthy of revering. Her henceforth we adore.[17]

Such comically grotesque pageants of rationalism were for Carlyle the natural counterparts of the unreason of the Terror, for he saw the scepticism of the Enlightenment as a symptom of the last stages in the decay of religious vision. In this respect *The French Revolution* is a historical embodiment of the religious crisis in *Sartor Resartus*. Teufelsdröckh passes from the simple faith of his parents to a rationalism-induced religious crisis, and then experiences the

'Baphometic Fire-baptism' (II, 7) which is the prelude to his spiritual re-tailoring. French society passes from feudalism to scepticism to the fires of revolution, but to no new vision beyond a recognition that in the destructiveness of revolution the old shams have been burned up: 'The new Realities are not yet come' ('Finis').

For Carlyle's vision of history is ultimately a religious one. In *Sartor* he wrote: 'As in longdrawn Systole and longdrawn Diastole, must the period of Faith alternate with the period of Denial; must the vernal growth, the summer luxuriance of all opinions, Spiritual Representations and Creations, be followed by, and again follow, the winter dissolution' (II, 3). Faith and Denial correspond to 'organic' and 'critical' periods in the philosophical historiography of Goethe, Saint-Simon, and Novalis which influenced Carlyle.[18] These periods are cyclical: in *The French Revolution* the gradual departure of the Divine spirit from social institutions is seen as inevitable, their decay leads with equal inevitability to violent change, and this violence is both an eruption of titanic forces and something terrible, awesome, cleansing. And if this is a religious vision it is also, curiously, in touch with current scientific thinking about the formation of the earth's crust. What if, the narrator asks at one point, 'the *sub*marine Titanic Fire-powers came into play, the Ocean-bed from beneath being *burst*? If they hurled Poseidon Lafayette and his Constitution out of Space; and, in the Titanic melly, sea were mixed with sky?'[19] The reference is to the work of the Scottish geologist James Hutton (1726–97), whose *Theory of the Earth* (1795) advanced the theory which is the basis of modern geology: that the processes of geological erosion, consolidated under great pressure on the ocean floor, create the heat necessary for the eruption of the earth's core into new land masses, which are eroded in their turn to similar effect. The universe becomes an endlessly self-renewing machine. This cyclical view of time is at odds, as Stephen Jay Gould has recently argued, with the linear 'arrow' of history.[20]

Another scientific analogy might be drawn, with Darwin. It may seem strange to compare Carlyle's rhapsodic *French Revolution* with Darwin's cautious *Origin of Species* but there is one point of significant similarity: both offer a vision of the universe in which individuals and groups are passive rather than active participants in their destinies. The 'Time-Spirit', like Natural Selection, works through them, largely indifferent to influence by individual decision. Most Victorians liked to believe otherwise, and events after 1832 seemed to confirm their belief: a people who could beat Napoleon, reform their political institutions without incurring the revolutions abroad, and become the world's leading industrial power, did indeed seem to have found the key to progress. Macaulay's *History of England* was so popular because it gave a kind of historical certificate to the contemporary faith in progress.

History was not an indifferent and chaotic process but a kind of railway engine which, once properly set up and freed from over-manning, would naturally draw societies along the line to peace and prosperity. There are other comparisons and contrasts that could be made between Carlyle and Macaulay. Both are historians of revolutions, for although Macaulay originally planned to cover the period from 1688 to 1789, the bulk of the completed work deals with the 'Glorious Revolution' of 1688–89 and its immediate consequences. Carlyle's dramatic present tense participates in the violence of revolution and invites the reader to do so also; Macaulay uses the past tense, writing from a present that is always seen as the legitimate offspring of the past, but also uses 'dramatic' effects of characterisation and dialogue to bring the past alive. Carlyle was deeply influenced by German idealism, believing that mind or spirit was the fundamental reality of the universe; Macaulay was a materialist and empiricist, heir of the Scottish commonsense tradition (see Chapter 4).

Thomas Babington Macaulay (1800–59) was a brilliantly precocious child of whom any parent might have been proud, who never quite succeeded in pleasing – or pleasing enough – his gloomy evangelical father Zachary. Instead, he found the admiring intellectual stepfathers he seems to have needed in the circle of mildly reforming Whigs who edited and wrote for the *Edinburgh Review*, men of an older generation like Francis Jeffrey (1773–1850) and Sydney Smith (1771–1845). With the success of his essay on 'Milton' (1825), a dazzling defence of Milton from Dr Johnson's charge of 'surly republicanism', he established himself as Whiggism's brightest young hope, and confirmed that reputation by his demolition of James Mill's *Essay on Government* (1820) in 1829 (see Chapter 4), which destroyed, for a while, the confidence of the philosophic radicals of Macaulay's own generation. But one pays a price for pleasing one's elders, and Macaulay paid it by allowing their sense of history and political possibility to limit his own. He never developed beyond the 1832 Reform Bill, which he saw as the political settlement of his generation. It was not; it was the political settlement of his father's generation. Macaulay is presented as the spokesman for Victorian 'progress' in its vulgar, materialist sense, which in part he was; what tends to be forgotten is how out of step with progressive liberal opinion he was becoming by the time he started to write his famous history in the 1840s. On the great issues of industrialisation and democracy he had almost nothing to say, beyond a general welcome for the one and a distrust of the other when it was proposed to extend the franchise much beyond his own class. This may explain why the *History of England* (1849–61), although technically highly innovatory, gives off a slightly old-fashioned air: if it is the past seen through the present, like all history, the present is not

1848 but 1832, a time when national destinies were decided on a heroic platform, where powerful orators (such as Macaulay himself) debated great matters of principle before an audience of their peers. It is such a grand, not to say grandiose, vision of history which informs Macaulay's great work.

Like his political beliefs, Macaulay's prose did not really develop after 1830, and even then it must have seemed closer to the eighteenth century than to that of his contemporaries. Carlyle, whose own prose is a bizarre medley of styles, justified the seeming eccentricities of *The French Revolution* on the grounds that 'purism of style' was no longer possible when 'the structure of our Johnsonian English [was] breaking up from its foundations'.[21] Macaulay writes with that structure still in place. His sentence structure is heavily reliant on the resounding antithesis: it is as if he had gargled with Gibbon every morning before getting down to work. Consider the following sentence describing the differences between the two 'races' in Ireland:

> There could not be equality between men who lived in houses and men who lived in sties, between men who were fed on bread and men who were fed on potatoes, between men who spoke the noble tongue of great philosophers and poets, and men who, with a perverted pride, boasted that they could not writhe their mouths into chattering such a jargon as that in which the Advancement of Learning and the Paradise Lost were written.[22]

One can see here how a habitual idiom and rhythm betray Macaulay into saying both more and less than he probably intended. The opposite of 'houses' would of course have to be 'sties', not the less emotional and possibly more accurate 'cabin' or 'cottage', and the little spark of contempt which the word carries has flamed out into a roaring insult by the time we get to the third 'between', when the 'noble tongue' of Bacon and Milton is being contrasted with the 'perverted pride' of those who prefer to speak their own language – 'writhe', 'chattering', and 'jargon' boomeranging to its discredit. But it is doubtful if Macaulay really wanted to insult the Irish peasantry; on the contrary, he was a supporter of Catholic Emancipation and of government grants to the Catholic seminary at Maynooth (for which he landed in trouble with his Edinburgh constituents), and one of the great strengths of his *History of England* is the detailed consideration he gave to Ireland. But his style did not make it easy for him to resist the pointed, dramatic contrast. It is a style, as Matthew Arnold said, 'brilliant, metallic, exterior; making strong points, alternating invective with eulogy, wrapping in a robe of rhetoric the thing it represents; not, with the soft play of life, following and rendering the thing's very form and pressure'.[23]

Macaulay's rhetoric of antithesis expresses a vision of history and politics. As W.A. Madden has shown, the antithetical structure of Macaulay's style and thought enacts a conviction that truth tends to lie between two untenable extremes.[24] In contemporary terms these were the extremes of toryism and radicalism, with whiggism as the path of moderate reform and therefore of true progress; translated back into the seventeenth century they become Stuart absolutism and its acolytes on one hand, and the various forms of religious extremism on the other. The unlikely friendship between the Catholic James II and the Quaker William Penn does not surprise Macaulay: 'For they deviated in opposite directions so far from what the great body of the nation regarded as right that even liberal men generally considered them both as lying beyond the pale of the largest toleration. Thus the two extreme sects, precisely because they were extreme sects, had a common interest distinct from the interest of the intermediate sects' (ch. 4). Conversely, when traditional opposites meet in a moment of reconciliation, something of historic importance has taken place. This happens when the Seven Bishops rebel against James's Declaration of Indulgence, are prosecuted, and acquitted:

> The prosecution of the Bishops is an event which stands
> by itself in our history. It was the first and the last occasion
> on which two feelings which have generally been opposed
> to each other, and either of which, when strongly excited,
> has sufficed to convulse the state, were united in perfect
> harmony. Those feelings were love of the Church and
> love of freedom. During many generations every violent
> outbreak of High Church feeling, with one exception, has
> been unfavourable to civil liberty; every violent outbreak of
> zeal for liberty, with one exception, has been unfavourable
> to the authority and influence of the prelacy and the
> priesthood. In 1688 the cause of the hierarchy was for a
> moment that of the popular party. (ch. 8)

The opposition is characteristically just a little too neat, set up by the syntactical parallelism of 'every . . . with one exception'. The 'one exception', the moment when rebellion against the temporal head of the State Church at last becomes justifiable, is the turning-point in Macaulay's historical argument, rendering William's invasion justifiable and revealing the true current of historical destiny.

Antithesis and opposition make for drama, and Macaulay wanted to give his history of England something of the narrative excitement of the novels he read so enthusiastically. His original plan was to take the story from 1685 to 1832, from 'the revolution, which brought the crown into harmony with the parliament, and the revolution which brought the parliament into harmony with the nation' (the idea that Parliament might have some way to go before achieving 'harmony with the nation' did not excite him).[25] Ill-health, shortage of time, and possibly a subconscious reluctance to complete a task which had become an emotional refuge,[26] meant that he only got as far as the death of William in 1702, but what he completed has its own narrative and thematic coherence. The story tells of Charles II's death, the accession of his brother James, the violent and successful defeats of rebellions, James's apparently consolidated power in 1685, and then his downfall as a result of suicidal attempts to impose a Roman Catholic Establishment on an increasingly hostile country. It has a rich cast of villains (Judge Jeffreys, Tyrconnel), cowards (Monmouth), sneaks (Penn), noble heroines (Alice Lisle), fawning courtiers, and one hero, the improbable figure of William. The controlling theme is the transition from Stuart absolutism to constitutional monarchy which Macaulay saw as having laid the foundations for the future progress of the British people. The famous third chapter, 'The State of England in 1685', is often read out of context as a vainglorious celebration of material progress, whereas it is really a reminder of the success of the revolution he is about to narrate: the energies released by this historic change have made possible the contrast between then and now which is there for all to see. It is Macaulay's 'progressive' retort to the more familiar doctrine of decline advocated by Pugin, Carlyle, Ruskin, and others (see below).

Talk of 'cast', 'characters', 'story', 'drama' point to the literary and imaginative dimension of Macaulay's *History of England*. His innovation was to combine that ambition with a much greater use of archival material than any previous historian of Britain had had access to. His idea of the 'perfect historian', he wrote in 1828, was someone 'in whose work the character and spirit of an age is exhibited in miniature. He relates no fact, he attributes no expression to his characters, which is not authenticated by sufficient testimony. But by judicious selection, rejection, and arrangement, he gives to truth those attractions which have been usurped by fiction.'[27] In selecting, Macaulay often slanted the evidence (his treatment of William Penn and of Quakers generally is an egregious libel), and we have seen how the very structure of his prose was likely to distort his argument, but there is such a weight of authenticating contemporary detail there that the 'spirit of the age' does not elude him. He is the first modern social historian. If the notion of history as an untidy flux was alien to his habit of mind (Carlyle is better at that) he captured more of its thickness of texture than his predecessors. He travelled to Ireland before writing about it, surveying the main sites of conflict carefully, exploring their history and examining the archives in Dublin. Because he had so much detail at his hand he could afford to use it economically and artistically, with an eye to the effectiveness of his narrative: nothing brings home the starvation at the height of the siege of Londonderry more tellingly than learning, for example, that the price of a dog's paw was five shillings and sixpence (27p).

Macaulay's presentation of historical character is less impressive than his command of detail and narrative momentum. They tend to be seen externally, at a stroke, and thereafter to bring their fixed identities to the various set-pieces and *tableaux* which portray the drama of historical development. For a man who loved reading novels he learned little of the novelist's inwardness. It is here most of all that Anold's 'soft play of life' is missing. Macaulay's style was too Augustan and oratorical for the exploration of human complexity: a man who could use words like 'clowns' (for 'peasants') and 'the vulgar' in the 1840s had a mind operating with pre-Romantic, patrician categories. But intense Romantic emotion was operating within these pre-Romantic categories, and operating, in a sense, on behalf of them. Macaulay's deepest feeling was for the aristocratic political tradition which ran from 1688 to 1832 and had admitted him, the thwarted son of an evangelical father, to its ranks. The *History of England* is the act of a grateful son, its style weighted with a sense of the solemnity of that inheritance, its narrative shaped to bring out the enduring significance of King William's triumph, its contempt reserved, flared-nostrils style, for any who presumed to be above or beyond the demands of parliamentary accountability, whether they were Stuart absolutists or unworldly Quakers. This was the meaning of the book as offered to his Whig stepfathers; to his contemporaries it was both a reassurance and a warning – progress had happened and would happen, but only if a nation learned to avoid the dangerous extremes of reaction and radicalism. With such awesome but also slightly comic caution, Macaulay addressed himself to a future already slipping behind him to the past.

Usable pasts

'There must always be a connection between the way in which men contemplate the past, and the way in which they contemplate the present', wrote H.T. Buckle.[28] Carlyle saw his revolution through the flaming torches of Reform Act rioters and the first stirrings of working-class movements; Macaulay saw his in the aftermath of Chartism and the successful parliamentary adjustment of Corn Law repeal. But much of the period's historicism was more directly ideological, and Buckle's sentence needs to be rephrased to describe it accurately: men choose the pasts that will serve their needs in the present. There was a plethora of available pasts in the nineteenth century. In examining three of them – Greece and Rome, the Middle Ages, and the English Civil War – I want to indicate some of the cultural and ideological uses to which history was put. Comprehensiveness is impossible here; whole books have been and could be written about each of these areas. The aim is rather to suggest something of the variety of Victorian historicism and, more importantly, of the contemporary needs that these pasts satisfied.

Greece and Rome

Augustanism, the admiration and emulation of the civic virtues of Augustus's Rome, was a legacy of the eighteenth century; Hellenism, the love of things Greek, was mainly a nineteenth-century development with roots in the Romantic re-discovery of Greece. The Victorian equivalent of Gibbon's great history of Rome was George Grote's twelve-volume *History of Greece* (1846–56), which portrayed the course of Greek history as a progressive development towards Athenian democracy and freedom of thought. Gibbon's theme was decline; Grote, a political radical and friend of John Stuart Mill, saw in Greek history a rise towards a modern state in its liberal, democratic, British form. It is worth underlining the fact that Victorian Britain's most impressive Hellenic historian was a member of the new nation and shared its values, for Hellenism, and classicism generally, was often a force for cultural conservatism, and was used as such by writers like Matthew Arnold. In England a classical education was the sign of a gentleman: a handy quote, a reference to the Roman Senate, a command of the classical historians, a deferential nod to Homer or Cicero – these were the small change of Establishment discourse in Parliament or gentlemen's club. So powerful was the mystique that Trollope, a dunce at Harrow, taught himself Latin again in middle life and redeemed his early failure with a *Life of Cicero* (1880), the deadliest Roman of them all. The classics were responsible for more humbug than almost anything else in the Victorian age. Poor Cobden was not allowed to live down his remark in 1850 that there might be more use in a single issue of *The Times* than in all of Thucydides, and yet, as his biographer noted, the journalists who made it a standing joke against him probably knew as little about Thucydides as he did.[29] The remark is philistine, of course, but there were some fictional victims of the cult of the classics who would have raised a rousing cheer for such moments of honesty – like the pupils at Dr Blimber's Academy in *Dombey and Son* (1846–48), so browbeaten by his classical drilling that they look on the Romans as a 'terrible people, their implacable enemies' (ch. 12), or Tom Tulliver in *The Mill on the Floss* (1860), forced against the grain of his practical nature to study classics because his father has fallen victim to the snobbish prestige associated with studying them.

Classicism was not a static ideology but passed through different phases in the course of the century as separate groups adapted the Ancient World to their needs. To Romantic poets like Byron and Shelley, Greece was the cradle of liberty and rebellion. Byron died in the struggle to liberate modern Greece, Shelley celebrated the God-defying Prometheus in *Prometheus Unbound* (1820). Twenty years later Macaulay, too, celebrated the heroic exploits of Horatius guarding the bridge in the buoyant rhythms of his *Lays of Ancient Rome* (1842). Grote's *History of Greece* was immensely more detailed, but still progressive and democratic in movement. It is with Matthew Arnold in the 1850s and 1860s that the classical past starts to be put to culturally conservative purposes. Arnold saw Greece through the eyes of Goethe and Heine as a culture of health and sanity, but he was less interested in historical scholarship, which by then was starting to alter the romantic image, than in the uses to which this image could be put. His ancient Greece is a metaphor for what he saw as missing from Victorian Britain – the spirit of intellectual enquiry, 'spontaneity of consciousness', 'sweetness and light' (*Culture and Anarchy*). Following Heine, he ranged these attributes against 'Hebraism', the instinct for conduct, in the famous and influential fourth chapter of *Culture and Anarchy*. It seems a balanced opposition but, as Frank Turner says, both it and the supposed historical analysis are 'profoundly deceptive': 'Hellenism for Arnold was not the experience or thought of ancient Greece but a set of more or less traditional humanist values long employed to oppose commercialism, excessive religious zeal, dissent from Anglicanism, philosophical mechanism, political radicalism, subjective morality, and social individualism.'[30] In this respect, Arnold's Hellenism was a prosecution of old nation politics by other means – as indeed is much in *Culture and Anarchy*.

But the conservative, implicitly Christian classicism of Matthew Arnold was soon being challenged by different interpretations in the 1860s and 1870s – interpretations variously rebellious, idealistic, erotic, and with the rise of Empire in the last quarter of the century (see Chapter 4), grandly imperial. There was a turn towards decadence which can be dated to Swinburne's *Poems and Ballads* (1866). His 'Hymn to Prosperine (After the Proclamation in Rome of the Christian Faith)' laments in lines of rhythmical vigour the victory of Jesus and his 'grey' religion: 'Thou hast conquered, O pale Galilean; the world has grown grey from thy breath.' Swinburne's elders were shocked: he had broken the uncomfortable, unstated pact which prevented Christian classicists from exploring the differences between paganism and Christianity, and had gloried – albeit through a dramatic monologue – in the pagan vision. Once cut loose from its Anglican shackles, Hellenism became available as an outlet for the expression of ambiguous sexual feelings. Plato had written approvingly of the love between men and boys and Benjamin Jowett (1817–93), master of Balliol, talked admiringly of Plato (though not of homosexuality) to two generations of Oxford undergraduates. The idea of the youth beautiful fitted naturally into the image of Greece derived from German Hellenism and Matthew Arnold: a land young, sunlit, unsullied by the intellectual strife of later times, where a public-school atheleticism was married to a delightful 'spontaneity of consciousness'. The public schools are very much to the point here: the massive expansion of the system in the second half of the century, with the attendant separation of boys from sisters and mothers, and the prominence schoolmasters gave to study of the classics in them, made Hellenism an ethos which intensified and prolonged the normal homo-erotic phase of adolescence. For the post-adolescent, classical literature and mythology, with its delight in the beauty of the male form and acceptance of androgynous sexuality, constituted a sort of code in which homosexuals could express their feelings. References to the friendship of Achilles and Patroclus or to Plato's *Phaedrus* were clear signals, but kept within the bounds of respectability: after all, Gladstone was devoted to Homer and Jowett to Plato.

A few dates may indicate the wider cultural change Hellenism brought about: Swinburne's *Poems and Ballads* in 1866, Walter Pater's sophisticated treatment of paganism and Christianity in his 1867 essay on 'Winckelmann', and in the same year the exhibition of Frederick (later Lord) Leighton's *Venus disrobing for the Bath* – the first nude to be exhibited at the Royal Academy for many years. Venus is shown against a background of Doric columns, right arm balanced on a ledge, left thrown somewhat coyly across the pubic area to her right knee, while she attempts to kick off a remaining sandal. It is a provocative if not especially erotic picture because it puts the viewer in the position of a Peeping Tom who has just surprised the woman in her privacy. But it provoked only approval in the reviews of the day: 'eminently chaste' was the verdict of the *Art Journal*.[31] Even a bared breast would have caused an outrage in a painting of contemporary life, but almost complete nudity could be considered chaste when a model with a well-trimmed head was put in a setting of marble and Grecian columns. It says much for the power of classicism to hoodwink the Victorian moral censor.

But hoodwinking is not quite the right word to describe the use of nudity in the revived classicism that dominated British art in the 1870s and 1880s. Lord Leighton (1830–96) was nothing if not a respectable man, the friend of the leading writers and politicians of the day, President of the Royal Academy at the age of forty-eight, an academician to the core (his last words are said to have been: 'Give my love to the Royal Academy'). He was the leading figure of a group of painters known as the 'Olympians' from their predilection for subjects from Greek mythology, among whom were the scarcely less respectable figures of Sir Edward Poynter (1836–1919), also President of the Royal Academy, and G.F. Watts (1817–1904). Sir Lawrence Alma-Tadema (1836–1912) shared their enthusiasm for classical subjects but tended to choose his from Egypt and then increasingly from Rome; his 'Victorians in togas', as they have been described, inhabit a world as wealthy and leisured as that of his patrons – young women lounging on marble terraces lit up by the intense blue of sea and sky, or swimming untoga-ed in baths meticulously recreated from the latest archaeological research. But always marble, marble – that passport to respectability which allowed even a teasingly erotic picture like *In the Tepidarium* (1881; Plate 4) to pass the censor. An impressionist who painted a nude in a modern setting would have been hunted from town, a pack of clergymen at his heels; but put her on a marble slab, with a feather coyly covering her most private parts and a phallic symbol in her other hand, and the painting becomes acceptable, if not exactly 'eminently chaste'. But hypocrisy is not the main charge posterity has levelled against the Olympians. Their sin against art was their acquiescence in their wealthy clients' desire for respectable escapism. They are the Andrea Del Sartos of nineteenth-century art, settling like Browning's character for finish rather than struggle, and this makes so many of their paintings empty of life and movement today.

The Middle Ages

No period was used so promiscuously and unhistorically in the nineteenth century as the Middle Ages. Historical understanding lagged far behind symbolism until professional historians turned to the task in the later part of the century. In the minds of most people the Middle Ages was a largely undifferentiated stretch of time between the Norman Conquest and the Reformation, and their ideas of what daily life was like in medieval society was derived from the work of antiquarians, poets, and novelists. All three were combined in the immensely influential figure of Sir Walter Scott (1771–1832). Scott in turn had been influenced by the eighteenth-century reaction against its own sceptical materialism in the form of the gothic novel and the rediscovery of ballad. Inspired by his youthful reading of Percy's ballad collection, *Reliques of Ancient English Poetry* (1765), and drawing on his knowledge of border history, he became famous with narrative poems like *The Lay of the Last Minstrel* (1805), *Marmion* (1808) and *The Lady of the Lake* (1810), poems which may not all have been strictly medieval in chronological terms but were entirely so in action and sentiment; they told of knights and ladies, of pages and wizards, of trysts and disguises and imprisonment in monasteries, of family feuds and conflicts settled by heroic single combat. Keats's 'Eve of St Agnes' (1820), a story of passion and conflict in a medieval setting, belongs to the same moment of feeling and was a favourite with Victorian painters. But perhaps Scott's most influential contribution to Victorian medievalism was his novel *Ivanhoe* (1819), set at the time of Richard I and the Crusades, which contained two features which captured the imaginations of future readers: the fictional (and therefore highly suggestive) embodiment of the old myth of England as a 'Saxon' land usurped by 'Norman' invaders, and a famous jousting tournament at Ashby de la Zouch, where Ivanhoe and King Richard in disguise defeat the Norman knights. Trollope gives these aspects of *Ivanhoe* a comic treatment in the Ullathorne Sports in *Barchester Towers* (1857), which the 'Saxon' Thornes win, metaphorically, when the arrogant 'Norman' Countess De Courcy is defeated in the social lists by Madeline Neroni.

The idea of the jousting tournament was to the early Victorian imagination what the Western shoot-out is to the twentieth century, and just as societies exist today to stage mock-gunfights so there was one famous attempt then to stage a joust. This was the Eglinton Tournament of 1839. A carefully selected gathering of wealthy Tory aristocrats, kitted out at great expense from Samuel Pratt's armour showroom in Lower Grosvenor Street, met together with their retainers at Lord Eglinton's Ayrshire castle to tilt at the lists he had built and contest for the honour of the Queen of Beauty. Thousands came to watch. The August day began brightly, and if the thirteen knights had been out of their beds earlier and quicker to arm and mount, it might have been a different story. But the procession did not start until three in the afternoon, at which point torrential rain descended and lasted for the rest of the day. Knights with umbrellas and ladies in long dresses slithered around in the mud to get to shelter, the grandstand started to leak, and the pavilion put up for the evening's ball collapsed. Although the tournament was completed more or less successfully later in the week, the damage to the image of the knight in armour had been done; hereafter the ghost of ridicule haunted any attempt to enact medievalism too literally.[32]

Nevertheless, the potency of chivalry as an ideal of conduct and medievalism as a cluster of ideologies remained. It is paradoxical that

Scott should have been so influential in encouraging idealisation of the Middle Ages, because the great theme of the novels that are valued today – like *Waverley* (1814) and *Redgauntlet* (1824) – is precisely the inevitable and (on the whole) desirable supersession of feudal by modern codes of conduct, their outcome being the education of a sensitive young man in achieving the right balance of prudence and chivalry. And when Victorian medievalism lost its polemical edge, this was the compromise between past and present that most people accepted. In 1830, however, past and present were in opposition and the Middle Ages were used, as they had been by the Romantics, as a weapon against the mechanism, calculation, selfishness, and ugliness of the emerging industrial civilisation.

It was in architecture, particularly church architecture, that research into the Middle Ages was most advanced. Thomas Rickman's *Attempt to Discriminate the Styles of Architecture in England from the Conquest to the Reformation* was published in 1817 and much reprinted; he defined the phases that were used by subsequent writers, permitting more precise description – Norman, Early English, Decorated, Perpendicular. The fourth edition of Rickman's work appeared the year before the publication of a major work of polemical medievalism by the architect Augustus Welby Pugin (1812–52), *Contrasts, or a Parallel between the Architecture of the Fourteenth and Fifteenth Centuries and Similar Buildings of the Present Day* (1836). Pugin was an Anglican convert to Catholicism who disliked the Roman element in Catholicism almost as much as he did Dissent; 'strange as it may appear,' he wrote in the Preface to the second edition, 'there is a great deal of connexion between the gardens of the Medici, filled with Pagan luxury, and the Independent preaching-houses that now deface the land; for *both are utterly opposed to true Catholic principles, and neither could have existed had not those principles decayed.*'[33] Strange indeed, but here is an early shot from one of the loose cannons in the Victorian 'battle of the styles': Gothic is devout, Catholic, English; classicism – whether Roman Catholic or not – is pagan, worldly, foreign and (therefore) decadent.

Gothic was also caring, and caring because Catholic. Pugin set pictures of idealised pre-Reformation buildings against their bleak modern or eighteenth-century counterparts in ways that accentuate what he thought had been lost. The two poor-houses are pregnant with topical symbolism (see Plates 5 and 6). The Poor Law Act of 1834 had been designed to reorganise an inefficient old system on the basis of discouraging the able-bodied poor from depending on the rates: the harshness of the resulting poor-houses was deeply resented at the time for bearing heaviest on the weak and defenceless. Their architect was Edwin Chadwick, a disciple of the utilitarian philosopher and jurist Jeremy Bentham (see Chapter 4), and Pugin's modern poor-house is based on Bentham's infamous plan for a model prison, the Panopticon. This 'all-seeing' institution (the meaning of the Greek word) features a central hub from which an inspector could, quite literally, inspect the behaviour of inmates housed in cells along the walls of the octagon. The drawings at the side illustrate the dehumanising features of the system. The 'Antient Poor Hoyse', on the other hand, looks like a Victorian public school, with a dominant chapel but plenty of open ground where the inmates could wander; and the side drawings emphasise the obvious contrasts – gowned bedesman in place of modern prisoner, a Master carrying instruments of punishment against one distributing alms, meagre as against plentiful diet, a corpse being carried off for dissection by medical students and one being lowered gently into the ground with the full rites of Christian burial. Secular rationalism plans for order and achieves destruction, while the age of faith cherishes the individual.

In the 1830s and 1840s medievalism was a consciously reactionary movement, High Church and often Catholic in religion, Tory-radical in politics. On the scholarly side, the Cambridge Camden Society began as an undergraduate antiquarian society around 1836, and was formally founded in 1839; its original aim was to re-issue works of antiquarian interest, and one of these was the Chronicle of Jocelin of Brakelond, which Carlyle drew on for his portrait of the medieval monastic community at St Edmund's Abbey in *Past and Present* (1843). The Society also encouraged research into church architecture with a view to making restoration more historically accurate: the papers published in its journal *The Ecclesiologist* became an important source for later architects to draw upon. Politically, there was a tradition of looking to pre-Reformation England for the socially responsible hierarchial community which modernisation had corrupted and dispersed. William Cobbett's *History of the Protestant Reformation in England and Ireland* (1824–26) linked the decline of community and the coming of the Reformation. His ideas and others equally anti-modern were taken up and made into a political programme by the 'Young England' movement, a small group of wealthy young aristocrats within the Tory Party led by the improbable figure of Benjamin Disraeli (1804–81). Their vision of society is encapsulated in the lines from Lord John Manners's poem, *England's Trust* (1841):

Each knew his place – king, peasant, peer, or priest –
The greatest owned connexion with the least;
From rank to rank the generous feeling ran,
And linked society as man to man.[34]

The best epitaph for the Young Englanders is that they tried to live up to their imaginings of what feudal responsibility should be; they supported campaigns to limit the working hours of children and women, opposed oppressive sabbath legislation, spoke out against the new Poor Law, and generally left behind, after their group split on the rocks of Corn Law repeal, the idea that aristocratic government might have something still to offer a democratising society. If they used the Middle Ages for their purposes, then the suspicion lingers that Disraeli used them for his, not only in his 'Young England' novels *Coningsby* (1844) and *Sybil* (1845), but to legitimise his own rise in a party which otherwise distrusted his exotic appearance and undisguised ambition.

With Carlyle's *Past and Present* (1843) medievalism took a turn away from Anglo-Catholicism and Tory myth-making. He was inspired to write it by visiting the St Ives workhouse and the ruins of St Edmund's Abbey, and then reading Monk Jocelin's account of the career of the Abbot Samson in the Camden Society reprint. In the first two books he employs Pugin's technique of contrast, setting the society which creates and tolerates the workhouse against the medieval world of the monastery. But it is a more complex contrast than Pugin's: there is crisis in the present – hunger and unemployment – but there is also crisis in the past, for the monastery is run down and in debt, and the choice of their new abbot is a crucial one. Carlyle does not simply posit an idealised medieval world against the desolate industrial present; he moves between them, using irony and invective, to suggest parallels as well as contrasts, and possibilities in the present as well as lessons from the past. The chief lesson is the need for leadership: just as the abbey's fortunes are turned around by the wise and strong leadership of Abbot Samson, so contemporary *laissez-faire* England (as Carlyle saw it) needs leadership too; but Carlyle breaks with the tradition in locating the potential for this leadership among contemporary groups like the 'Captains of Industry', who need awakening to their responsibilities. Previous medievalists had yearned for a restoration of the Catholic hegemony or a revived chivalry, but Carlyle's irony concedes that the past was not to be revived. It can provide images of faith and leadership, the two going together for Carlyle, but these have to be applied in the present.

By loosening medievalism from the doctrinal bias of Pugin, Carlyle made it more accessible for Victorian Protestants; and by engaging images of authority and community from the Middle Ages with the *laissez-faire* individualism and democratic reforms of his times, he established a line of authoritarian social criticism which was taken up and developed in the medievalism of Ruskin and William Morris (see Chapter 5). Within this tradition, the Middle Ages pass from being the property of Tory radicalism to being the property of socialism, without going through the stage of being historically examined. That came only in the work of such major professional historians as Edward

Freeman in his *History of the Norman Conquest* (1867–76) and William Stubbs in *The Constitutional History of England* (1874–78), who laid the foundations for studying the period on which the medieval dream had been superimposed. As for the dream, it gradually lost its edge of theological controversy and faded, if not into the light of common day, then at least into the everyday furniture of the Victorian imagination. Architects continued to fight the battle of the styles between Goths and Romans, but in painting and literature after 1850 medievalism became domesticated, and in the rediscovery of the Arthurian legends Saxon and Norman, Catholic and Protestant, past and present were reconciled. Although the historical Arthur was a pre-medieval figure, this hardly matters in Tennyson's *Idylls of the King* (1859, 1869, 1885), where the noble king is the apotheosis of chivalry. He is also a troubled Victorian gentleman at the heart of a middle-class national epic. The success of the poem is a sign of how completely medievalism had been digested by the liberal, democratic culture it set out to challenge at the start of the century.

The Civil War

'The seventeenth century, and particularly the Civil War period,' J.W. Burrow has written, 'held the imaginations of nineteenth-century English people to a degree only second to the Middle Ages.'[35] The reason for this, put very crudely, is that the Cavalier/Roundhead opposition of popular mythology corresponded to the old nation/new nation division in Victorian society. 'We are Cavaliers or Roundheads before we are Conservatives or Liberals', as the historian W.E.H. Lecky put it in 1892.[36] The Cavaliers had had the best of the argument before 1800: Clarendon's *History of the Rebellion* (1702–04) had seen it from the Stuart side and David Hume's influential *History of Great Britain* (1754–62) portrayed the Parliamentarians as wild 'enthusiasts'. But the issues of the present inspired a re-examination of the past – or perhaps it would be more precise to say that the past provided rhetorical and ideological tools with which to fight the battles of the present. Parliamentary reformers encountering conservative obstructions turned back to an earlier period when Parliament had asserted the will of the people against Stuart tyranny. High Churchmen who saw with fear a Parliament which had agreed to abolish Irish bishoprics and set up an Ecclesiastical Commission to reform their Church, found inspiration in the seventeenth-century churchmen who had suffered at the hands of an interfering Parliament – men like Archbishop William Laud (1573–1645), whose execution by Parliament sealed off the memory of his spirituality and loyalty to King Charles I from the abundant evidence of his political incompetence.

The important development in the nineteenth century was the re-habilitation of Oliver Cromwell. There are signs of it in Macaulay's 1825 essay on Milton, which refuses to approve the execution of Charles but otherwise presents Cromwell as an upholder of liberty in an age of tyranny, the key actor in a drama of historical destiny: 'That great battle was fought for no single generation, for no single land. The destinies of the human race were staked on the same cast with the freedom of the English people.'[37] But the turning-point was undoubtedly Carlyle's two-volume edition of *Oliver Cromwell's Letters and Speeches* (1845). Two centuries of denigration were reversed almost overnight; Cromwell the ruthless and ambitious regicide became Cromwell the visionary leader and man of destiny. Stuart hagiography now had a rival. 'Evangelical in religion,' Roy Strong observes, 'a self-made man, anti-aristocratic and anti-establishment by inclination, a reformer of passionate moral conviction, Cromwell had all the ingredients to make him the hero of the reformers, liberals and new men of nineteenth-century Britain.'[38] A hero for radicals and Chartists, too, who encountered his writings in the 1840s when their hopes for parliamentary reform were running high. Strong demonstrates how paintings of Cromwell were invested with religious inconography. In Augustus Egg's *Cromwell before Naseby* (1859) he is shown praying fervently in the moonlight, like Christ in the Garden. In David Wilkie Wynfield's *Death of Oliver Cromwell* (1867) he lies like a saint, hands clasped, in a bed brightly lit in a darkened room, with two women praying on their knees at the foot. Ford Madox Brown's painting of Cromwell on his farm, *St Ives, AD 1630* (1874), see Plate 2), captures the man of destiny in a moment of personal crisis, as he looks down abstractedly at the burning stubble at the bottom left while his wife tries to engage his attention on the right. This is a puritan alternative to the Royalist iconography of Charles the Martyr: Cromwell is shown coming to terms with his destiny, and with the realisation that it will not allow him to remain a private citizen; and in the burning stubble there is perhaps a symbol of the dead growths in national life which he will have to burn away.

Carlyle's *Cromwell* appeared in the year of Newman's conversion to Rome, 1845, an event which effectively spelt the end of the Oxford Movement. Newman and his fellow-Tractarians had made a very deliberate and self-conscious identification of their movement with Oxford and the Caroline divines of the seventeenth century. Charles I had been devoted to the Church of England, and Laud had been devoted to Charles, to Oxford, and to the liturgy and church-discipline of a purified Anglo-Catholicism. The Oxford Movement saw in Laud a martyr to state interference with the roots of true Catholicity, which for them lay in sacramental worship, episcopal church-government, and the spiritual authority of King rather than Parliament. The 'National Apostasy' – the title of Keble's Assize sermon in July 1833 which marks the start of the movement – of the seventeenth century was being repeated in the nineteenth. It was never a very plausible reading of Laud's role in seventeenth-century politics, and the rediscovery of Cromwell knocked it on the head.

The English Civil War was therefore an area of contesting ideologies, providing a code in which contemporary loyalties could be declared and contemporary issues debated. In Elizabeth Gaskell's *North and South* (1855) the heroine, Margaret Hale, moves from a Hampshire vicarage to a northern industrial town called *Milton*-Northern, where she meets an industrialist, John Thornton, who declares a Carlyle-like admiration for Cromwell. But he also seeks classical culture at the hands of Margaret's lapsed-vicar father. Mr Hale is a product of Oxford, yet he admires and seeks to understand Thornton and his world, something his best friend, an Oxford don, is not prepared to do. The relationship of Margaret and Thornton develops in proportion as they learn to negotiate the Civil War stereotypes and come to understand and adapt to each other, Thornton learning from Margaret's 'royalist' paternalism, and she delighting in his 'parliamentary' energy.

Cromwell was a Protestant hero, and his ascendancy in Victorian historical iconography reflects a reassertion of Protestant nationalism after the small epidemic of Roman conversions which ended the Oxford Movement. This took other historical forms: Carlyle's biographer, J. A. Froude (1818–94) published a famous and widely influential review-essay in 1853 called 'England's Forgotten Worthies', in which the Elizabethan seadogs (Drake, Raleigh, Frobisher, Grenville) are presented as heroes of the Reformation and pioneers of imperial expansion. The first half of the essay is an account of Spanish atrocities in South America, providing a black historical context against which the sailors shine out as 'the armed soldiers of the Reformation, and . . . avengers of humanity'. They are the leading edge of a specifically Protestant renaissance in English history:

> The England of the Catholic Hierarchy and the Norman Baron, was to cast its shell and to become the England of free thought and commerce and manufacture, which was to plough the ocean with its navies, and sow its colonies over the globe; and the first appearance of these enormous forces and the light of the earliest achievements of the new era shines through the forty years of the reign of Elizabeth with a grandeur which, when once its history is written, will be seen to be among the most sublime which the earth as yet has witnessed.[39]

This is not only a past in which a particular allegiance in the present is affirmed ('the England of free thought and commerce and manufacture'), it is a past which prophesies the future. Froude's essay inspired Kingsley's *Westward Ho!* (1855) and Tennyson's 'The Revenge: A Ballad of the Fleet' (1878), and may also have played a part in the genesis of perhaps the most famous of all Victorian historical paintings, Millais's *The Boyhood of Raleigh* (1870). At one point in his essay Froude imagines the young Raleigh and his friends exploring the ships in Dartmouth harbour and perhaps 'climbing on board, and listening, with hearts beating, to the mariners' tales of the new earth beyond the sunset' (p. 318). In Millais's painting Raleigh and his friend are sitting by the sea-wall, having deserted their model galleon to listen to the tales of a sailor who is pointing with outstretched right arm to the horizon. We are so familiar with the picture now that we may well miss the intensity of the sailor's gesture and its significance: he is pointing to the Empire.

Biblical history

These pasts, however mythologised, existed as matters of historical record; there might be, and was, debate about the interpretation to be put upon the records, but there was no feeling that uncovering and exploring them was in any sense taboo. Nor were there many inhibitions about pursuing the archaeology of other civilisations. Lord Elgin's plunder of the Parthenon statuary (admittedly to save it from worse than plunder at the hands of the Turkish soldiers in Athens) set the tone for the century. Sir Austen Layard's bestseller *Nineveh and its Remains* (1849) is well titled: not content with excavating the sites of the old Assyrian Empire he brought its remains home with him – bas-reliefs from the palaces and two huge winged bulls. The European rape and destruction of Ancient Egyptian monuments, which begins with Napoleon Bonaparte, is a shameful story, but in an ironic way these ancient civilisations had their revenge on the 'advanced' Judaeo-Christian societies which plundered their remains. As more and more were brought to Europe, the hieroglyphics of Ancient Egypt were first decoded, and then the cuneiform writings of Babylon; a new library of near-Eastern antiquity was opened up, in which scholars discovered that there were many and uncomfortable similarities between the mythologies of these pagan religions and the sacred texts of Judaeo-Christianity – like the fact that the Babylonian myth of creation seemed to be related to the first book of Genesis, or that deluge-stories figured in both. Furthermore, a visit to museums in which these 'remains' were displayed opened new areas of disquiet: there was a strange otherness about ancient Egypt or Babylon absent from Greece and Rome. The Greeks and Romans were honorary middle-class Britons; their civilisations might have declined, but they lived again in classical education, and imperial Britain would complete the unfinished business they had left behind. But the funerary culture of the pyramids, or the heavy, brutal statuary of Nineveh, came from another world and spoke of darker things. They were a reminder of how little, relatively, was known about the world of the Old Testament.

Hitherto, scholarship had put a ring-fence around Christianity and its origins. Men like Dr Arnold of Rugby School went at ancient history like an express-train and then pulled up short when it came to the Old and New Testaments: these belonged in the realm of Revelation rather than history. The German biblical scholars of the late eighteenth and nineteenth centuries thought differently. They were influenced by the Enlightenment discovery of history and by an important distinction made by the founding-father of biblical criticism, Johann Semler (1725–91), between 'theology', the dogmas of the Church derived from the Bible, and 'religion', the historical experience of the individuals which had inspired the writing of Scripture. It was this second, empirical reality which was the origin of religious inspiration, and the way to reach it was by approaching the Bible in a spirit of historical enquiry and examining the surviving records in a spirit of scientific criticism (i.e. analysis). There was a 'lower criticism' concerned with establishing the original form of the text, as far as this was possible, and a 'Higher Criticism' concerned with questions of date, authorship, source, influence, literary form, and interpretation. The aim of both was to recover the living reality of religious experience behind the surface of the canon. As has been said of Heinrich Ewald (1803–75), author of a massive history of the Jews, 'the historian can perform a theological task by enabling us to get closer to the very basis of the divine revealing activity'.[40]

The historicising activities of the German critics and those influenced by them took various forms. Wilhelm Gesenius (1786–1842) put the study of the Hebrew language on a proper historical footing, thereby making it available as a tool of interpretation. One of his pupils, the American Edward Robinson (1794–1863), was inspired by his teaching to visit Palestine where he identified many of the ancient sites and compiled an ecclesiastical geography of the Holy Land; he also discovered, as many after him were to do, how relatively unchanged everyday life was there. Palestine became a favourite route of pilgrimage as well as the inspiration for some of the nineteenth century's more painful acts of literalism, such as Holman Hunt's

The Scapegoat (1858). J.G. Eichhorn (1752–1827) drew attention to similarities between the Creation and Deluge stories in classical and biblical narrative, using the word 'myth' for the first time to describe them – stories which were records not so much of actual happenings as of the religious consciousness of pre-scientific people, symbolic narratives which expressed their spiritual conceptions of the universe. 'Myth' was the most contentious of Higher Critical terms: that an episode in the Bible could be both fictional (i.e. unsupported by history and science) and true to the existential needs of primitive people, and that this false belief could also be a true embodiment of genuine religious insights, was too much to ask of people who feared that any further surrender of Christianity to history must end in atheism. So when David Friedrich Strauss (1808–74) used the term extensively in his life of Christ, *Das Leben Jesu* (1835) – an English translation by George Eliot was published in 1846 – there was a predictable outcry. Strauss's life of Jesus was the first to draw upon the work of German scholars; accepting their view of miracles and of the unreliability of the gospel narratives, he pressed on to uncover the historical Jesus. This Jesus was entirely human, a great prophet and teacher around whose life and death Messianic hopes had gathered. The fact that these hopes were illusory did not, to Strauss, invalidate Christianity, for the ethical teachings remained as well as the profound symbolic truth about human destiny expressed in Christ's life and death.

It should be noted in passing that the historicisation of Christianity was not confined to Germany. Henry Hart Millman (1791–1868), the liberal Anglican clergyman and historian, wrote an important *History of the Jews* (1829) which for the first time treated the Hebrews historically, as an ancient people to be approached with the same dispassionateness that classical scholars expected from their histories. Milman had some acquaintance with German scholarship; George Eliot's friend Charles Hennell (1809–50) seems to have had none, which makes his *An Inquiry Concerning the Origin of Christianity* (1838) all the more remarkable, since he arrived at Strauss's naturalistic interpretation of the life of Jesus independently. As George Eliot liked to say, there was nothing in Strauss that she had not already learned in the Hennells' free-thinking, Unitarian circle in Coventry. Hennell's book made little impact in Britain but was translated into German and published there with a preface by Strauss.

More than enough has by now been said to establish the power of the intellectual forces which were sucking Christianity into history in the nineteenth century. But the historicisation of belief was a much more untidy matter than intellectual history makes it seem. Most Victorians did not read Strauss and begin to doubt Revelation: for a start, few of them knew enough German to read his work before George Eliot's translation, and even then it took some stamina to get through those three volumes. They knew of the Higher Criticism as an avalanche that was gathering in distant mountains, as something discussed in reviews and debated by clergymen, but brought home as an idea in its relation to developments in geology. The vastness of the geological time-scale was the setting for their reading of the Old and New Testaments, and one did not need to study at Tubingen to reflect that this new time-scale had disturbing implications for the security of the traditional explanations. History, science, and religion interpenetrate. 'It was not science itself', as Noel Annan observes, 'but science interpreted *as history*, which upset the traditional cosmology.'[41] The significance of this work lay, rather, in its reflection of a new scientific consciousness which, in various forms, was eroding the traditional bases of belief.

The German biblical critics were Protestant. They held the Enlightenment view of the historical Church as a corrupt steward of its spiritual assets and looked for truth behind its encumbering dogmas and metaphysical speculations. They did not perhaps stop sufficiently to consider that 1800 years of continued growth was itself a phenomenon to be accounted for in any search for the 'truth' of religion. Historical myths tend not to last so long or spread so widely. Those who were tied to the Church by loyalty or conviction, the Catholics and Anglo-Catholics, faced a different problem when confronted by the evidences of history. Should they retreat behind Church authority, or should they try to come to terms with the historical consciousness of the age? The second course was taken by John Henry Newman in *An Essay on the Development of Christian Doctrine* (1845). Newman was aware of the work of the German scholars although not particularly exercised by it: deriving religious authority from the fact of the historical Church rather than from Scripture, he was untroubled by the thought that the Bible was a collection of historical documents rather than a sealed book of revelation. Nor did he share the German view that a religion was most itself at the time of origin. 'It is indeed sometimes said that the stream is clearest near the spring. Whatever use may fairly be made of this image, it does not apply to the history of a philosophy or sect, which, on the contrary, is more equable, and purer, and stronger, when its bed has become deep, and broad, and full.'[42] A great religion worked on and was worked by the forces of time, and the diversity of its manifestations was evidence of its power to meet the range of human experience: 'For Christianity has many aspects: it has its imaginative side, its philosophical, its ethical, its political; it is solemn, and it is cheerful; it is indulgent, and it is strict; it is light, and it is dark; it is love, and it is fear' (p. 97). The density and variety that came with the passage of time were things to be valued.

How could one know that the doctrines that had grown up around the Jesus revealed in the gospel narratives were genuine developments of faith and not, as Protestants averred, the encrustations of popular superstition and priestly deception? This was the question Newman set out to answer in the *Essay on Development*. The most orginal part of his argument is his attempt to define how development in the intellectual sense could be identified: what were the signs of natural growth in an idea and what of corruption? He offered seven tests: 'Preservation of Type or Idea', 'Continuity of Principles', 'Power of Assimilation', 'Early Anticipations' (of later developments), 'Logical Sequence', 'Preservative Additions' (*'an addition which is conservative of what has gone before it'*), 'Chronic Continuance' (duration). These terms (especially 'type') and their systematic formulation recall the scientific classifications of the time, and suggest that Newman was thinking in terms of an organic development in ideas similar to that of contemporary biological evolutionists. He rejected the traditional supernaturalist notion of a Divine withholding, the so-called *disciplini arcani* or doctrine of reserve whereby truths were disclosed only as the human mind became ready to receive them, for the modern biological conception of an unfolding of coiled potential in interaction with environment. It is tempting to see Newman's 'development' as an anticipation of Darwinian evolution, but the more accurate comparison would be with Robert Chambers's *Vestiges of the Natural History of Creation* (1844), a virtually contemporary work which came to the conclusion that everything living had been designed 'to be developed from inherent qualities, and to have a mode of action depending solely on its own organization'.[43] Questions of influence are difficult to settle here; the 'development hypothesis' was in the air and Newman could well have encountered it in his reading, but the important point is that he chose to confront the Church's historical problem on modern grounds.

If Newman did not solve the problem of history it is because of the intrusion of his own history. The further one reads in the *Essay on Development*, the more apparent it becomes that what started as an objective consideration of a concept is turning into an exercise in apologetics on behalf of the current doctrines of the Roman Catholic Church and, therefore, on behalf of Newman's own decision to join that Church in the year the *Essay on Development* was published. Philosophy becomes theological self-justification. When he attempts to vindicate contentious doctrines by referring to 'the mind of the Church working out dogmatic truths from implicit feelings under secret supernatural guidance' (p. 418), the language virtually concedes the Church's right to make doctrine as it pleases, since only the Church has access to the 'implicit' and the 'secret'. This is an authoritarian outcome from exploratory beginnings, but is entirely typical of the oscillation between modernity and authority which is perhaps the defining characteristic of Newman's mind.

Pre-history

Around 1860 European geologists and archaeologists made the crucial breakthrough into human pre-history. There was plenty of evidence from the discovery of extinct mammals to push creation far beyond the traditional biblical 4004 BC, in which few now believed literally, but many were reluctant to make the connection with mankind. Archaeologists worked with a 'three-stages' model of primitive development based on the tools used by early humans, stone leading to bronze and then to iron. When two geologists excavating a cave near Torquay in 1858 discovered stone tools beside the bones of extinct animals they became sure that human beings had lived there in the remote past. Other geologists came and were similarly persuaded, including the leading geologist of the age, Sir Charles Lyell, who went on to write *The Geological Evidences of the Antiquity of Man* (1863) based on the Brixham Cave discoveries and others in Britain and France. Lyell's name gave respectability to the new Victorian science of anthropology.

Anthropology – the study of the origins and development of humankind – grew in the 1860s out of the confluence of evidence from various sources: local antiquarianism, archaeology, geological discoveries (some of them brought to light by railway-building), the work of the Ethnological Society on primitive tribes. What fused this material into the content of a developing science was the influence of evolutionary theory. Darwin concluded *The Origin of Species* (1859) with the cautious prophecy: 'Light will be thrown on the origin of man and his history.'[44] In 1871 he published *The Descent of Man* (from the higher primates). The transition from caution to intellectual acceptance of human evolution was a change of enormous significance, and it took place in a single decade. It meant that, for the intellectual community at any rate, the old 'degenerationist' myth of human origins in the Bible was replaced by a 'progressionist' myth based on contemporary science. This was not quite the unmixed blessing that it seemed at the time to progressives: although the biblical idea of a decline from an initial perfection ran counter to the evolutionary notion of development from simple to complex, it contained a cautionary tale about human fallibility. The evolutionary myth, the development hypothesis, tended to assume the superiority of the advanced to the simple, and where race was concerned this was a dangerous doctrine. Even those with the best of intentions could not help being influenced by the assumptions of their time, and there were others unhindered by good intentions.

Two different institutions contested for leadership of the new science in the 1860s. The Ethnological Society, founded in 1843 out of the old evangelical Aborigines Protection Society, retained some of the humanitarian impulses of its origin while moving towards a more intellectual attitude to race, and recruited from the ranks of established and now Darwinian scientists like T.H. Huxley. The young men who founded the breakaway Anthropological Society in 1863 were explicit racialists. Among their number were mavericks and cranks like the sinister Edinburgh anatomist Robert Knox, patron of the bodysnatchers Burke and Hare, and author of a book called *The Races of Men* (1850) in which he declared: 'With me race, or hereditary descent, is everything; it stamps the man.'[45] Rejecting the old slavery-abolitionists' belief that the negro was a 'man and a brother', Knox and others set about classifying racial differences according to pseudo-scientific categories of brain size and shape. They called themselves 'The Cannibal Club' and at their meetings used a gavel in the shape of a negro's head.[46] These wild men were absorbed and marginalised when the two societies merged under Huxley's influence into the Anthropological Institute in 1871; but even within mainstream and respectable anthropology, assumptions about the backward nature of primitive people persisted. In that engaging way Victorian books have of revealing their arguments in their subtitles, John Lubbock's *Pre-Historic Times* (1869) describes itself as being *illustrated by ancient remains, and the manners and customs of modern savages.* This approach to 'modern savages' is implicitly demeaning, just as the word 'savage' seems explicitly so today. Progressive evolutionism led Lubbock and those who thought like him to assume that mankind had evolved up a ladder of progress currently resting at white, European, industrial civilisation; those primitive peoples who had failed to take this main route of progress were not just different, as anthropologists would think today, or degenerate descendants of once higher races, as the degenerationists would have said, but 'living fossils' who could be studied for the light they threw on the pre-historic past. As they are now, so were we then.

Victorian anthropology was increasingly pulled away from its humanitarian roots in the Quaker–evangelical campaign for abolition of the slave trade towards an intellectual discipline based on the 'scientific' study of primitive peoples. But since an ideology of progress was inherent in the concept of science (see Chapter 3), anthropologists found it hard not to think of 'modern savages' as links in the evolutionary chain. They were to be studied carefully before history took them off, as a crumbling cliff might take away a fossil record, but not for themselves so much as for the light they shed on human origins long left behind. Also, since looking at modern savages was also contemplating one's distant ancestors, anthropology no less than other historical disciplines was influenced by contemporary preoccupations. If Edward Tylor (1832–1917) put religion at the centre of his *Primitive Culture* (1871) it may well be, as George Stocking has recently suggested, that he was concerned to legitimise his own loss of faith by tracing the origins of a slow but inevitable evolutionary path out of supernaturalism. If John McLennan (1827–81) chose to write on *Primitive Marriage* (1865), and to stress the role of matriarchy within it, it is likely that his choice of subject and the course of his argument were 'conditioned by the contemporary concern with problems of human sexuality and by the processes of social change affecting the institution of human marriage'.[47] The serious anthropologists deplored the racialism of the 'Cannibal Club', but their disapproving accounts of the habits of primitive people which could not be harmonised with development towards Victorian norms, and their assumption that these people belonged to the 'childhood of the race', contributed unwittingly to the climate of assumption in which end-of-century imperialism worked – namely that primitive peoples were 'children' who could be pushed around for their own good.

There is no conclusion to the nineteenth-century fascination with history and time for it is with us still; at the time of writing this, Stephen Hawking's *Brief History of Time* (1988) has been on the hardback bestseller list four years, long after most hardbacks have changed into paperback and begun their journey out of print. A conclusion to this chapter, however, may be taken from the writer who, besides Tennyson, was most burdened by the time-consciousness of the age. In Hardy's *A Pair of Blue Eyes* (1873) Stephen Knight finds himself clinging to a cliff-face and looking into the eyes of a trilobite fossil which had died millions of years before the advent of human beings. 'Time closed up like a fan before him', and he imagines the intervening stages of life: 'Fierce men, clothed in the hides of beasts' carrying 'huge clubs and pointed spears', cavedwellers, and 'behind them stood an earlier band'; then 'no man' but the mastodon and the megatherium, and on back to the lizards and the flying reptiles. Evolution runs in reverse, returning to the sea where 'the life-time scenes of the fossil confronting him were a present and modern condition of things' (ch. 22). Thus does Hardy dramatise the continuum that now ran from history through pre-history to those 'immense lapses of time' which 'had known nothing of the dignity of man'.

Notes

1. Mark Twain, '"Was the World made for Man?"' (1903), in *What is Man? and Other Philosophical Writings*, ed. P. Baender (Berkeley, California, 1973), p. 106. Quoted in Stephen Jay Gould, *Time's Arrow, Time's Cycle* (Cambridge, Mass. and London, 1987), p. 2.

2. See Tennyson's 'Parnassus' (1889) for the 'terrible Muses', and C. Ricks (ed.), *The Poems of Tennyson* (1969), p. 1410 for note to poem containing FitzGerald's remark which may have inspired it.

3. *Principles of Geology* (3 vols, 1830–33), I. p. 63.

4. 'The Representation of Time in Painting: A study of William Dyce's *Pegwell Bay*', *Art History*, I (1978), pp. 99–103.

5. *The Notebooks of Matthew Arnold*, edited by H.F. Lowry, K. Young, and W.H. Dunn (London and New York, 1952), pp. 409, 426, 430, 523.

6. *Essays of George Eliot*, edited by T. Pinney (1963), p. 214.

7. *Sartor Resartus*, edited by K. McSweeney and P. Sabor (Oxford, 1987), pp. 87–8.

8. *Life and Letters of T.H. Huxley* (2 vols, 1900), I, p. 237.

9. See *The Invention of Progress* (Oxford, 1989).

10. References are by Part, book, chapter, and page number to the World's Classics edition, edited by K.J. Fielding and D. Sorensen (Oxford, 1989); here Pt II, bk III, ch. 1, p. 409.

11. Centenary Edition, edited by H.D. Traill (30 vols, 1896–99), XXVII, 88.

12. Pt II, bk III, ch. 7, p. 453.

13. Pt I, bk I, ch. 4, p. 27.

14. Pt III, bk VI, ch. 7, p. 412.

15. Pt I, bk IV, ch. 4, pp. 139–40, 155.

16. Pt I, bk VII, ch. 9, p. 287.

17. Pt III, bk V, ch. 4, pp. 356–7.

18. For German influences see Rene Wellek, 'Carlyle and the Philosophy of History', *Philological Quarterly*, 23 (1944), 55–76.

19. Pt II, bk III, ch. 5, p. 441.

20. See *Time's Arrow, Time's Cycle* (Cambridge, Mass. and London, 1989).

21. *The Collected Letters of Thomas and Jane Welsh Carlyle*, edited by C.R. Sanders and K.J. Fielding (Durham, N. Carolina, 1970–), VIII, p. 135.

22. *History of England* (2 vols, 1889), I, ch. 6, p. 394.

23. 'A French Critic on Milton', *The Complete Prose Works of Matthew Arnold*, edited by R.H. Super (11 vols, Michigan, 1960–77), VIII, pp. 165–6.

24. 'Macaulay's Style', in *The Art of Victorian Prose*, edited by G. Levine and W.A. Madden (New York, 1968), pp. 127–53.

25. *Letters of Thomas Babington Macaulay*, edited by Thomas Pinney (6 vols, 1974–81), III, p. 252.

26. See Madden, 'Macaulay's Style', pp. 146–51.

27. 'History', *Edinburgh Review*, 47 (1828), 364.

28. *History of Civilisation* (2 vols, 1857–61), I, p. 266.

29. John Morley, *Life of Cobden* (2 vols, 1881), 429n.

30. *The Greek Heritage in Victorian Britain* (New Haven and London, 1981), p. 21.

31. Quoted in Christopher Newall, *The Art of Lord Leighton* (Oxford and New York, 1990), p. 59.

32. I am indebted here to the account of the tournament in Mark Girouard, *The Return to Camelot: Chivalry and the English Gentleman* (New Haven and London, 1981), ch. 7.

33. *Contrasts*, second edn (1841; reprinted Leicester, 1969), pp. iv–v.

34. Quoted in Alice Chandler, *A Dream of Order* (1971), p. 161.

35. *A Liberal Descent: Victorian Historians and the English Past* (Cambridge, 1981), p. 14.

36. *Ibid.*

37. T.B. Macaulay, *Critical and Historical Essays Contributed to the Edinburgh Review* (1872), p. 14.

38. *And When Did You Last See Your Father?: The Victorian Painter and British History* (1978), p. 149.

39. *Short Studies of Great Subjects* (2 vols, 1867), I, pp. 313, 302–3.

40. R.F. Clements, 'The Study of the Old Testament', in *Nineteenth Century Religious Thought in the West*, edited by N. Smart and others (3 vols, Cambridge, 1985), III, p. 124.

41. In [no editor] *Ideas and Beliefs of the Victorians* (1949), p. 151.

42. *An Essay on the Development of Christian Doctrine*, edited by J.M. Cameron (Harmondsworth, 1974), p. 100.

43. *Vestiges of the Natural History of Creation* (1844; Leicester, 1969), p. 359.

44. *The Origin of Species*, edited by J.W. Burrow (Harmondsworth, 1968), p. 458.

45. Quoted in P.J. Bowler, *The Invention of Progress: The Victorians and the Past* (Oxford, 1989) p. 109.

46. See G.W. Stocking, *Victorian Anthropology* (New York and London, 1987), p. 252.

47. *Ibid.*, p. 201.

Chapter 2
Religion: Reform, Rejection, Reconstruction

The religious life of this period was intense and disputatious, and its problematic presence can be felt wherever we look in nineteenth-century literature. From the comic clergyman in Dickens and Trollope, and their more serious counterparts in George Eliot, to the poetry of Tennyson, Arnold, Hopkins, and Clough; from the agnosticism of Hardy and Housman to the religious questing which underlies almost all Victorian autobiography; from the literature of orthodoxy in Newman to the 'Natural Supernaturalism' of Carlyle and Charlotte Brontë: the very pervasiveness and variety of religious experience in Victorian literature is a sign of its importance in the culture at large and, from one perspective, of its vitality. Thus T.H.S. Escott looked back from the Queen's Diamond Jubilee in 1897 and declared that 'the Victorian age is in fact above all others an age of religious revival'. He pointed to the reform of the clergy and organisation in the Church of England, its expansion overseas, the increased membership of all the churches; and he could have mentioned the churches built in the previous sixty years, for this was a heroic age of church building and restoration.[1]

And yet religion in Victorian Britain was also problematic in a way that it had not been before. The problems were both internal and external. Within the Church of England – the Established or State Church – there were the conflicts brought on by attempts to reform its structure in the 1830s, conflicts which precipitated the Oxford Movement and two decades of bad feeling between the Anglo-Catholic and the evangelical wings of the Church. In the 1840s the impact of continental historical criticism of the Bible started to make itself felt within the liberal wing of the Church, leading to public controversies of the kind that followed the publication of *Essays and Reviews* in 1860. There were the conflicts between the Established Church and the Dissenting or Nonconformist churches, between Church and Chapel, which became the principal focus for new nation grievances against the Establishment and so politicised religious debate that, as George Kitson Clark said, 'by the second quarter of the nineteenth century religion had received so political a shape, or politics so religious a shape, that it was for many people almost impossible to separate the two'.[2]

And looming over the clash of Church parties and interdenominational strife in the second half of the century was a challenge to the validity of religious belief itself, from scientific materialism in general and evolutionary biology in particular. The rejection of religious commitment and practice – militantly in atheism, wistfully in agnosticism, casually and by default in the growth of 'leisure' – was a symptom of the gathering tide of secularisation which belied the seeming buoyancy of church membership by 1900. 'God is dead,' the Madman declares in Nietzsche's *The Gay Science* (1882), 'And we have killed him.'[3]

Rejection of religious belief in the nineteenth century, however, was itself often a religious phenomenon, drawing upon the language and morality of Christianity, as Nietzsche observed in a penetrating, if brutal, comment on George Eliot in *The Twilight of the Idols* (1888):

> They are rid of the Christian God and now believe all the more firmly that they must cling to Christian morality. That is an English consistency; we do not wish to hold it against little moralistic females à la Eliot. In England one must rehabilitate oneself after every little emancipation from theology by showing in a veritably awe-inspiring manner what a moral fanatic one is. That is the penance they pay there.
>
> We others hold otherwise. When one gives up the Christian faith, one pulls the right to Christian morality out from under one's feet. This morality is by no means self-evident: this point has to be exhibited again and again, despite the English flatheads. Christianity is a system, a *whole* view of things thought out together. By breaking one main concept out of it, the faith in God, one breaks the whole: nothing necessary remains in one's hands.[4]

Newman would have agreed with these words (if not with their tone), as would leaders in the other churches opposed to theological modernisation. But the main current of religious thought in the nineteenth century flowed in the direction of what Nietzsche sarcastically calls the 'English consistency' of trying to rescue Christian morality from the departure or 'disappearance' of the Christian God, and – more widely – to reinterpret Christian doctrine in the light of disturbing new knowledge from science and biblical scholarship.[5] Hence the third term in the title of this chapter: reconstruction, which in the longer term has proved more characteristic of the period than either the 'loss of faith' or the bitter disputes of religious parties. Yet these parties are important, too, and discussion of Victorian religion cannot proceed without some awareness of their historic differences and contemporary strengths.

Religion in society, 1830–1890

In 1851 a religious survey was organised in conjunction with the usual decennial census. It was the only one of its kind and so provides a unique snapshot of church-going habits at mid-century. On a given Sunday in March 1851, and out of a total population in England and Wales of around 18 million, it was found that there had been 5,292,551 attendances at Church of England churches, 383,630 at Roman Catholic, and 4,536,264 at the main Nonconformist churches. These figures look healthy enough today, and at the time were seen to provide a triumphant vindication of Nonconformity's claim to equality with the Established Church. But they told a less certain story on closer inspection. When allowances were made for those who could not be expected to attend (the young, the sick, the old, their carers, and workers in necessary public services), and those who had attended more than once (since the census measured attendances not individuals), the national census agent came to the conclusion that the actual attendance figure was over five million souls short of what it would have needed to be to justify the claim that all who could go to church on Sunday, were going.[6]

These figures were, of course, disputed at the time, but their broad validity was not in question, nor were the implications. At a time when all the churches were energetically involved in missionary activity abroad, here was a vast mission-field at home. It was an irony which Dickens was exploiting contemporaneously in *Bleak House* (1852–53), where Mrs Jellyby devotes her life to the natives of Borrioboola-Gha and cannot see Jo the crossing-sweeper on her doorstep, who 'is not softened by distance and unfamiliarity; he is not a genuine foreign-grown savage; he is the ordinary home-made article' (ch. 47). The mission-fields were in the cities and in those areas where population had grown fastest as a consequence of industrialisation: Methodism had kept in touch with the earlier, pre-factory stage, and Roman Catholicism shepherded its largely immigrant flock carefully, but the Church of England was faced with the crisis of having to adapt an essentially pre-industrial, even medieval, parish structure to the new conditions. As *The Times* put it in 1853 (the year when the census results were published), the Church of England was 'the most paradoxical body in the world. It is, at the same time, the richest and the poorest; the most popular and the most exclusive':

> Its princely bishops, its magnificent cathedrals, its
> hospitable canons and zealous archdeacons, its comfortable
> incumbents, its parochial system, its village churches
> and devout congregations, all make up a whole which it
> wants but little poetry to convert into a very respectable
> anticipation of the new Jerusalem. . . . Unfortunately, some
> millions of the people of England have no more place in
> this Utopia than if they were subjects of the SULTAN or
> inhabitants of Bengal. A village becomes a manufacturing
> town, and swells into a city that numbers its hundreds of
> thousands, but the parochial system . . . has neither the
> resources, nor the independence, nor the organisation to
> supply the wants of so vast an increase.[7]

Somewhat overdrawn though this may be, it captures the dilemma faced by the Established Church in the first half of the century.

In one respect the census snapshot is misleading. By 1853 the Church of England had gone through twenty years of reform and upheaval: its architects were already building the needed city-centre churches, inequalities (of parish size, of clerical income) were being addressed, the calibre of the clergy had been significantly improved. Returning from thirteen years in New Zealand, Bishop G.A. Selwyn told a Cambridge congregation in 1854 that he had seen 'a great and visible change' in the Church since 1841: 'It is now a very rare thing to see a careless clergyman, a neglected parish or a desecrated church.'[8] Most significantly of all, although this was not evident in the 1850s, the Church of England succeeded in increasing its membership above the rate of population growth in the nineteenth century, while the Dissenting churches slipped below it after 1840.[9]

No one in 1830 would have predicted such revival in the fortunes of the Established Church, and in a sense this was only made possible by the tacit, piecemeal abandoning of its old hegemonic claims. At the time of the First Reform Bill the Church enjoyed a degree of political and spiritual control that it was widely perceived not to deserve, and when twenty-one of the twenty-nine bishops rejected the Bill's second reading in the House of Lords (six abstained), thus ensuring its defeat, it was inevitable that the spotlight of reform should turn on them. This revealed vast disparities of income: the ten wealthiest sees had an average annual income of £11,634, the wealthiest £22,305, whereas 3,500 vicars had to make do with less than £150 a year.[10] Pluralism, the holding of more than one living, and absenteeism were widespread, while the legacy of eighteenth-century spirituality, if one excludes the Evangelicals, was thin. There are many stories of pre-Victorian indifference and neglect. Desmond Bowen records the experiences of C. Kegan Paul:

> When he was a young curate at Bloxham near Banbury,
> he had a ninety-year-old vicar, who had been in the parish
> for fifty years. It was customary in the parish to have
> the Eucharist celebrated the required minimum of three
> times a year. In one celebration Kegan Paul remembers,
> upon the altar, which was covered by a dirty wine-stained
> cloth, there stood a loaf of bread and a dusty black bottle
> of wine which were to serve as the elements of the
> communion. When the prayer of Consecration was reached,
> to the horror of this pious curate, the vicar turned to the
> congregation to ask if anyone present had a corkscrew.[11]

When Charles Kingsley took up the living of Eversley in 1841, he found a cracked kitchen-bowl being used as the baptismal font, a broken chair leaning against the altar, and a dirty altar-cloth full of moth-holes. It would be wrong to build a picture of the pre-Victorian Church on details like these, but they indicate a neglect of ritual which, if it was at all widespread, helps to explain why the intense sacramentalism of the Oxford Movement held such a strong appeal for those who had been starved of it.

Tepidity was another vice of the unreformed Church. 'We have cherished contempt for sectaries [nonconformists]', Sydney Smith wrote in 1801 of his fellow-Anglicans' sermons, 'and persevered in dignified tameness so long, that while we are freezing common sense, for large salaries, in stately churches, amidst whole acres and furlongs of empty pews, the crowd are feasting on ungrammatical fervour, and illiterate animation in the crumbling hovels of Methodists'.[12] Of course there is another side to the story and Smith himself embodies it: his dates, 1771–1845, establish him as a man of the eighteenth century, and he can be seen as a real-life example of the kind of clergyman most admired by George Eliot: worldly and untouched by religious 'enthusiasm', but kindly, benevolent, tolerant of others' views, unostentatiously charitable – one thinks of Mr Irwine in *Adam Bede* (1859) and the Rev. Farebrother in *Middlemarch* (1871–72). Smith's own definition of the qualities desirable in a clergyman – 'discretion, gentle manners, common sense, and good nature'[13] – outlines an eighteenth-century ideal whose virtues a post-romantic, evangelising religious culture was not well placed to estimate justly.

Institutional reform of the Church was bitterly resented by High Churchmen who saw the Ecclesiastical Commission set up in 1835 as an unprecedented political interference in spiritual matters, and yet the legislation which flowed from the Commission's work in the next two decades only strengthened the Church internally and externally. Acts adjusting episcopal salaries and making provision for creating new sees (1836), for reforming pluralities (1838), and – most controversially – for redistributing income from cathedrals to parishes (1840), made possible the improvement of poor parishes and the creation of new ones. In his study of the sociology of nineteenth-century religion, A.D. Gilbert prints two tables which dramatically illustrate the structural transformations that took place within Anglicanism. The number of new churches built rose from 10 in the quinquennium ending in 1805, to 138 by 1830, to 360 by 1840, the first quinquennium of the Commission's activity, and to 401 by 1845. Secondly, the percentage of non-resident clergy in relation to all beneficed clergy dropped from 46.9 in 1810 to just over 30 in 1835, but to 9.5 in 1850.[14] When taken in conjunction with the steady overall growth in Anglican clergy throughout the period, these figures indicate a massive redirection of pastoral energy towards the needs of the new society. The spiritual springs from which that energy came will be discussed in the next section.

The 1851 Census confirmed what had long been asserted by opponents of the hegemonic claims of Anglicanism, that English religious life in the nineteenth century was effectively plural. In Scotland the Establishment – the Presbyterian Church of Scotland – had better claims to hegemony, until the Disruption of 1843 (over the issue of lay patronage) took a third of ministers and their congregations into the Free Church, because its parochial structure covered the whole country with something like equality of provision. The same could not be said of the Church of England: in Wales and in the new industrial towns and cities of the north and midlands, Dissent had taken root in the absence or neglect of the Establishment and dominated the local culture. The Census listed thirty different varieties of Nonconformity and in combination, it was reckoned, their membership outnumbered that of the Established Church. 'Old Dissent' comprised those groups with a long historical experience of resisting religious conformity: the Congregationalists, the Baptists, the Presbyterians (out of which group had sprung the Unitarians in the eighteenth century), and the Quakers. They had learned to live with their marginal status and were in a state of respectable decline until the advent of Methodism in the second half of the eighteenth century, when the itinerant preaching of the Wesleys and their followers brought an evangelical religion to the artisans and lower middle classes of the early industrial revolution. This 'New

Dissent', as it was called, led to recovery in Congregational and Baptist membership, and to the spectacular emergence (in 1795) of Methodism, the largest and most schismatic of Nonconformist groups. The fires of New Dissent were stoked in the pre-Victorian period, and after 1840 its growth-rate was to level off, taking a sharp decline at the end of the century.[15]

Dissent, Nonconformity, and Free Church are almost interchangeable terms, but taken in this sequence they fell into a series of ascending respectability: Dissent was raw and unreconciled, while Free Church proclaimed an unassertive independence and was increasingly the form adopted by Nonconformists (as in the title of the umbrella organisation set up in 1896, the National Council of Free Churches). It is hardly surprising they should have felt self-conscious in such matters. There was always the need for those outside the Established Church to shake off the insults that were added to the injury of their civic disabilities. In 1867, Matthew Arnold, a particular adept at the stylish insult, wrote:

> Look at the life imaged in such a newspaper as the
> Nonconformist, – a life of jealousy of the Establishment,
> disputes, tea-meetings, openings of chapels, sermons; and
> then think of it as an ideal of a human life completing itself
> on all sides, and aspiring with all its organs after sweetness,
> light, and perfection![16]

To which airy snobbishness there is the unanswerable riposte that if the culture of Nonconformity was impoverished by jealousy of the Establishment (always assuming that it was), the Establishment's own jealous exclusions were largely responsible. It is worth recalling that at the date of Arnold's writing Nonconformists were still liable to pay Church rates, and required to bury their dead according to Anglican rites if they wished to use the parish churchyard. Besides, such disabilities were only the tip of an iceberg of prejudice. As R.W. Dale wrote, replying to Arnold in 1870:

> The 'watchful jealousy' of the Establishment with which he
> reproaches us – whose fault is it? When farmers are refused
> a renewal of their leases because they are Nonconformists,
> when the day-school is closed against the child on Monday
> because it was at the Methodist Sunday School the day
> before, when in the settlement of great properties it is
> provided that no site shall be let or sold for a Dissenting
> chapel, and that if a tenant permits his premises to be
> used for a Dissenting service, his lease shall be void, can
> Mr Arnold wonder that we are 'watchful?[17]

The culture of Nonconformity, shaped as it was by long experience of slight and exclusion, is of the greatest importance to understanding nineteenth-century religion and politics. First, it was very various. Anglicanism contained many shades of opinion between High and Low Church, but nothing as wide as the gulf that separated the tolerant unitarianism of Mrs Gaskell's household from the earnest Calvinism of the Plymouth Brethren home in which Edmund Gosse grew up, and wrote about in his classic autobiography *Father and Son* (1907). Secondly, it was provincial, in the positive sense, each group having its particular area of concentration where it could exercise a distinctive local influence: the Quakers in Yorkshire, the Baptists in Bedfordshire, the Unitarians in Birmingham and Manchester, the Methodists in Leeds and the 'manufacturing districts' generally, the Calvinistic Methodists in north Wales. After the Municipal Reform Act of 1835, Nonconformists entered local government with an enthusiasm born of their exclusion, determined to reform it in the light of their political ideology. And that ideology, to come to the third distinctive feature of Victorian Nonconformity, was strongly individualistic. Just as their religion was based on the rights of the individual conscience to dissent from the demands of the State Church (and from the dissenting community itself, hence the tendency of Nonconformity to fragment), so their politics were shaped by distrust of state control and belief in free trade and individual effort. It is here, fascinatingly, that the religious culture and the secular merge in the formation of some key Victorian values, for the social philosophy of Nonconformity in its high Victorian phase is summed up by the titles of two books by men not known for their religious piety – Samuel Smiles's *Self-Help* (1859) and Herbert Spencer's *The Man Versus the State* (1884).

The third major grouping within nineteenth-century religion is Roman Catholicism. Its history as a denomination in the period is, from one point of view, a great success story. While Anglicans and Nonconformists fought bitterly over the Protestant flock, and worried about the millions missing from their churches, Catholicism experienced a steady growth in membership: in England and Wales it grew tenfold between 1780 and 1840, to some 700,000, and had doubled again by 1890, to around 1,400,000.[18] There are several reasons for this expansion, the chief being that Catholicism was the main beneficiary of Irish immigration in the nineteenth century. It benefited, too, in terms of publicity if not in numbers, from the dramatic conversions of prominent Anglo-Catholics like Newman; and it was able to consolidate these advances by reform in its organisational structure. The restoration of Catholic bishops to England in 1850 – to cries of 'Papal aggression' from Anglicans and Nonconformists – made national organisation possible for the first time since the Reformation, and in Henry Manning (1808–92) and Herbert Vaughan (1832–1903), successive Cardinal Archbishops of Westminster, Victorian Catholicism had two able administrators. But a price was paid for consolidation. Manning and Vaughan were both Ultramontane (literally 'beyond the mountains', meaning the Alps, therefore Roman, conservative, and centralising). The gentler indigenous Catholicism gave way in their hands to something more continental and triumphalist, and dogmatically conservative, as notoriously in the promulgation of the doctrine of papal infallibility after the Vatican decree of 1870.

Thus, by 1890 Catholicism seemed in a healthier state denominationally, if not intellectually, than the other Churches. Anglicanism had held its own only by abandoning, stage by stage, the legal privileges it once enjoyed as the State Church, and fighting in the open market, so to speak, for new members – a struggle in which it enjoyed a considerable advantage through its national parish network. But Nonconformity lost some of its *raison d'être* when there were fewer and fewer Establishment restrictions to dissent from; and as a Scripture-based religion it lost even more from the rise of historical biblical criticism. It was, indeed, a casualty of the historical tide which in 1830 it seemed to be riding so confidently. But having recognised that, one needs to go on to acknowledge what is perhaps the most remarkable fact of all about Victorian religion: the extent to which religious discourse tended to permeate other forms of intellectual and cultural discourse. We have seen it in Carlyle, employing biblical language to declare that the Bible was 'Hebrew Old-Clothes' (see Chapter 1); we shall see it again in the middle phase of Ruskin's art criticism, where *Modern Painters 2* interprets early Renaissance art by the lights of evangelical typology (Chapter 5) – a linking of art and religion which seems as quintessentially Victorian as Gladstone's religious conception of his political destiny. Even most of the unbelievers retained a religious seriousness and frame of mind after they had lost their faith, as the 'Crisis of Faith' section (p. 85) will show.

Evangelicalism and the Oxford Movement

'The Victorians inherited a great movement of the religious spirit', Owen Chadwick has written.[19] That movement was the evangelical revival of the eighteenth century. Our awareness of it is probably still coloured by the largely hostile picture of evangelical religion left by the Victorian novelists, a memorable gallery of sadists (Brocklehurst in *Jane Eyre*, Murdstone in *David Copperfield*), unctuous hypocrites

(Chadband in *Bleak House*), and careerists (Slope in *Barchester Towers*). All these examples come from novels published before *Adam Bede* (1859) and show by contrast the sympathetic originality of George Eliot in choosing for her Evangelical a beautiful young woman, Dinah Morris, preaching a religion of conversion to a gathering of rustics in the open air, at the end of the eighteenth century. The period, the setting, and the message are true to what might be called the heroic age of evangelicalism, when John and Charles Wesley and others took a simple gospel message to parts of the country where the Established Church was either faintly present or – for reasons of population change – not present at all. Methodism began as a movement within the Church of England, but the importance it gave to the role of the itinerant lay preacher, and the consequent disregard of parish boundaries in pursuit of fresh souls to convert, meant that separation was a constant threat, and duly took place after John Wesley's death in 1791 – but not before the revival had flowed through the old dissenting churches and left its permanent mark on the Established Church. Anglican evangelicalism became respectable and influential when it started to make converts among high society and the upper middle classes at the end of the century. With William Wilberforce (1759–1833), leader of the 'Clapham Sect' group of wealthy bankers and abolitionists, and then the great philanthropist Lord Shaftesbury (1801–85), the evangelical wing of the Church claimed the high ground of moral and social reform for much of Victoria's reign.

Evangelicalism is so often associated with joylessness in Victorian literature, with sabbath observance, temperance, and the disapproval of pleasure, that it is worth asking how it caught on in the first place. The simple but not the sole answer is that it offered the joy of the assurance of salvation now. To understand this one needs to think back into the state of mind where hell and everlasting punishment were spiritual realities: extreme Calvinists even believed that most of the human race had been predestined for hell since before the creation of the world. John Wesley was an Arminian, he believed in the availability of grace to all, but even so he found himself helpless beneath the burden of an overpowering sense of sinfulness. Eighteenth-century Anglicanism had many real virtues, but its characteristic posture of sociable deism had little to offer the soul *in extremis*. Its God remained behind the clockwork universe of Newtonian physics; He could not be reached. But the suffering God of the Gospels could be, if the Christian was prepared to acknowledge the depravity of mankind and throw himself on the mercy of God promised in Christ's atoning sacrifice. The result, for Wesley and thousands of others, was an experience of almost miraculous release, of the albatross of sin and guilt slipping from the neck, and in its place knowing the 'assurance' of salvation.

This conversion experience could be slow as well as sudden; it was the 'great change' at the heart of evangelical religion, and it issued in the 'seriousness' of manner and deportment which distinguished the convert.

The evangelical revival has traditionally been seen as an emotional, proto-romantic reaction against the worldliness of the eighteenth century and its prevailing doctrine of empiricism. D.W. Bebbington has suggested recently, however, that the opposite may be nearer the case, and that the revival was a product of the climate of Lockean empiricism, in that its appeal was to the reality of the conversion experience above dogma or doctrine: you were saved if you *knew* you were saved.[20] This would certainly explain the timing of the origin of the movement in the 1730s, too early to have been influenced by the Romantic movement gathering ground in Europe from the 1750s. Methodism built a communal structure on this experiential base: the various lectures and tea meetings sneered at by Arnold were means by which the faithful could reinforce their faith, and the scope given for lay activity in the church provided men – and, crucially, women – with a feeling of participation and belonging. Nor should the rich legacy of the Wesleyan hymn be forgotten, for it played an important part in giving these communities a sense of energy and joy.

But despite the aesthetic and emotional release of its hymns, evangelicalism was and remained a religion of the word. Preaching was fundamental to its devotional practice because it was through preaching that the individual soul was reached and converted; and conversion, the experience of 'the great change', was the heart of religious experience for the Evangelical. This could put a terrible strain on the individual conscience, especially for the young. How did one know the change had taken place? And how did one cope with the consequences if it had not? For one knew what those consequences were; preachers and writers of tracts made them terrifyingly clear:

> You may know a good deal about Christ, by a kind
> of head knowledge. You may know who He was,
> and where He was born, and what He did. You may
> know His miracles, His sayings, His prophecies, and
> His ordinances. You may know how He lived and how
> He suffered, and how He died. But unless you know
> the power of Christ's Cross by experience – unless
> you know and feel within that the blood shed on that
> cross has washed away your own particular sins, –
> unless you are willing to confess that your salvation
> depends entirely on the work that Christ did upon the
> Cross . . . Christ will profit you nothing. . . . You must

know His Cross, and His Blood, or else you will die in
your sins.[21]

There was a lot of spiritual bullying in the nineteenth century
and Evangelicals did their fair share ot it. If there was also a good
deal of hypocrisy, it was because such a talkative and declamatory
religion, operating with such limited counters (Christ, Cross, Blood,
Sin, Atonement), lent itself rather too readily to exploitation by the
specious rogue.

The Evangelical contribution to nineteenth-century culture was not
primarily intellectual but moral and emotional, and can be seen in the
great public campaigns against slavery or child labour, and perhaps
more enduringly in the middle-class home, the nursery of Victorian
values. 'I do not think that any one not being a fanatic, can regret
having been brought up as an Evangelical Christian': so wrote Frances
Power Cobbe (1822–1904), the journalist, campaigner for women's
and animal rights, and lifelong theist, in the chapter on 'Religion'
in her autobiography. 'I speak of the mild, devout, philanthropic
Arminianism of the Clapham School, which prevailed amongst pious
people in England and Ireland from the beginning of the century till
the rise of the Oxford movement, and of which William Wilberforce
and Lord Shaftesbury were successively representative.' Brought up to
think of God as 'the All-seeing Judge', her 'life in childhood morally was
much the same as it is physically to live in a room full of sunlight. Later
on, the evils which belong to this evangelical training, the excessive
self-introspection and self-consciousness, made themselves painfully
felt, but in early years there was nothing that was not perfectly
wholesome in the religion which I had so readily assimilated.' There is
a touching moment in this chapter when her father, reading the *Pilgrim's
Progress* to her older brothers and finding the seven-year-old Frances his
most attentive reader, gives the book to her, with an inscription dated
1830: 'This book, which belonged to my grandmother, was given as
a present to my dear daughter Fanny upon witnessing her delight in
reading it.' And from reading it so often the idea of 'Life a progress
to Heaven' was 'engraved indelibly on [her] mind'.[22] Here one sees the
enduring legacy of the evangelical upbringing: family piety and moral
purity, conscience (for good and ill), and the sense of life as a pilgrimage,
almost symbolically handed on from father to daughter. This is a far
cry from the thrashings of Mr Murdstone but is probably truer of the
generality of evangelical homes in the early nineteenth century.

In the severe but affectionate piety of such evangelical homes the
moral sense was rinsed clear, as it were, imparting a scrupulousness
to the individual's temperament which lasted through life and survived
changing opinions and diverging allegiances. In Frances Cobbe's case it

led her to question the morality of the dogmas she had been reared in, 'the dogmas of Original Sin, the Atonement, A Devil and eternal Hell' [p. 102], just as later in life she brought an evangelical earnestness to her great campaign against the horrors of animal vivisection. Newman, in the *Apologia Pro Vita Sua* (1864), said of the evangelical clergyman Thomas Scott, author of *The Force of Truth* (1779), that 'I almost owe my soul' to him, and he quotes two of Scott's maxims which can be taken as keys to his own progress from Evangelicalism to Roman Catholicism: 'Holiness rather than peace' and 'Growth the only evidence of life'.[23] 'Convictions change,' he said elsewhere, 'habits of mind endure'[24], and his own habit of mind was more deeply shaped by his evangelical upbringing than he perhaps realised. In Ruskin's autobiography, *Praeterita* (1885–89), the evangelical home is severe (he was thrashed when he cried) and spare (his only toys as a small child were a bunch of keys, a ball, a cart, and some wooden bricks), yet he derived from it the 'quite priceless gift of peace' and the habits of close, disciplined observation he brought later to the study of art. He would spend his time 'contentedly in tracing the squares and comparing the colours of [the] carpet; – examining the knots in the wood of the floor, or counting the bricks in the opposite houses; with rapturous intervals of excitement during the filling of the water-cart, through its leathern pipe, from the dripping iron post at the pavement edge'.[25]

Although the Clapham Sect Evangelicals were very involved in the world, the appeal of evangelical faith to the middle classes was partly that it offered a refuge from the world. The period of its expansion within the Church of England, from about 1780 to 1830, was a time of foreign wars, revolutionary thought, and rapid industrialisation and urbanisation: a potentially anarchic combination of developments. There was security in a faith which gave assurance of salvation in the world to come, and a rule of daily life that encouraged stabilising qualities of self-discipline, hard work, sobriety, temperance of speech (Ruskin recalled that he never heard his parents speak an angry word to each other, or scold a servant). The paradox is that these were qualities also well suited to success in business, and so drew the Evangelical into the sphere of worldliness, laying him or her open to the charge of hypocrisy. As Gladstone said, the Evangelical movement 'in lay life . . . harmonized very well with the money-getting pursuits'.[26] A stereotype of Victorian culture is the successful evangelical clergyman or businessman, sober-suited and serious, preaching the claims of another world while enjoying the fruits of this one.

In the first half of the century resentment against the Evangelicals built up in direct relation to the increasing visibility and vociferousness of their public campaigns. The fugitive virtue of the evangelical home was one thing; the same virtue grown militant and threatening to impose its will on the public by legislation was quite another. Evangelicals were the founders of the modern pressure group, and when from 1831 their various 'societies' came together for their annual May rallies at Exeter Hall in the Strand, 'Exeter Hall' became synonymous with an interfering sanctimoniousness. The societies did much good – in the work of the Anti-Slavery Society, the Royal Society for the Prevention of Cruelty to Animals (RSPCA), the Ragged School Union, the Sacred Harmonic Society, which made Exeter Hall the musical centre of London – and much harm; and no society did more harm to the evangelical cause itself than the Lord's Day Observance Society. Their deeply resented attempt to enforce an impossibly strict sabbatarianism on their fellow-citizens marked a turning-point in public perception of the movement: when crowds rioted in Hyde Park in 1855 against sabbatarian legislation their cause was thereafter tainted with the gloom of the Victorian Sunday. This is the context of Dickens's *Little Dorrit* (1855–57), and it has been suggested that the growing repressiveness of evangelical public opinion is the chief but unstated target of Mill's essay *On Liberty* (1859).[27]

The evangelical revival was a religion of the gospel and the sermon, the Oxford Movement of a rediscovered sense of the meaning of Church authority and ritual. They seem to be very different, and in fundamental aspects were, yet it is one of the more curious aspects of nineteenth-century intellectual history that several of those most deeply influenced by the movement came from Anglican evangelical homes. Newman of course was one of its leaders, and three of the four sons of William Wilberforce, 'the Liberator', went over to Rome after their experience at Oxford, as did their brother-in-law Henry Manning (1808–92). What made these men and others so susceptible to the appeal of Catholic and Anglo-Catholic religion? Mark Pattison (1813–84), who travelled the same journey but ended in agnosticism, wrote that he was attracted to the movement 'not by the contagion of a sequacious zeal, but by the inner force of an inherited pietism of an evangelical type'; a shared piety, what David Newsome calls 'the common pursuit of holiness', predisposed the mind.[28] Conscience, too, was an important common factor, at least in the case of Newman, for whom it was our chief evidence of the existence of God. There is also the impact of Romanticism on imaginations purified by evangelical discipline and therefore all the more likely to respond with intensity to appeals to the senses (think of Ruskin's rapture at the sight of the water-cart filling) and the imagination. Newman credited Scott's novels with awakening a feeling for the past which prepared the ground for the Oxford Movement. The writings of Wordsworth and Coleridge reaffirmed the mystery of the universe and our dealings with it, and the presence of this mystery in the human heart, so undermining the pretensions of rationalism.

Before considering the spiritual and intellectual character of the Oxford Movement, however, it is necessary to say something about the social and political context in which it arose; and this in turn requires a glance at Oxford in the 1830s. Contrary to what the technicolour lavishness of Matthew Arnold's famous encomium would lead one to expect ('Adorable dreamer, whose heart has been so romantic!', and so on), Oxford at this time was lethargic, exclusive, and intellectually narrow – provincial, even, to use one of Arnold's terms of dispraise.[29] It acted, intellectually, on what Pattison called the 'belief that all knowledge was shut up between the covers of four Greek and four Latin books. . . . The great discoveries of the last half century in chemistry, physiology, etc., were not even known by report to any of us', he said after the collapse of the Oxford Movement in 1845.[30] Dissenters were not allowed to matriculate at Oxford, whereas at Cambridge they could at least study the subjects in which they were not allowed to graduate, which was less of a handicap in the nineteenth century than it would be today. Dons could not marry without resigning their fellowships, and for most the best hope of marriage lay in acquiring a college living; their enforced and fretful monasticism did not create a natural social atmosphere. There were, of course, no women students. Thus, Oxford in the 1830s and 1840s was a thoroughly introverted community, socially, sexually, intellectually, theologically – a positive greenhouse in which plants could grow to heights not possible in the climate outside.

In this context, then, it is perhaps not surprising that Newman and his friends should have reacted in such an extreme way to the prospect of Church reform in the 1830s. He and Robert Wilberforce (1800–57) and Hurrell Froude (1803–36), all at one time fellows of Oriel, brought an evangelical severity to their High Church definition of the nature of the Church of England, and an evangelical sense of mission to defending it from state interference. They found a mentor and figurehead in John Keble (1792–1868), the Oxford Professor of Poetry between 1831 and 1841 and author of a collection of devotional poems, *The Christian Year* (1827), which rivalled *In Memoriam* as the poetic bestseller of the age. Their nominal leader in Oxford (which Keble left in 1836 to become his father's curate) was E.B. Pusey (1800–82), Professor of Hebrew, who spent two years in Germany and came back determined to save England from the perils of rationalism. Newman was the real leader, though, an energetic publicist for the group's views and an inspiring preacher from the pulpit of St Mary's. Taking a leaf (literally) from the Evangelicals' book, they published a series of tracts attacking the apostasy of the state in presuming to apply 'liberal' – i.e. rationalising and pluralistic – doctrines to the management of the Church, from which early grew their more enduring achievement: the reaffirmation of the Church's historical and spiritual identity in what they saw as a heretical age. They were called 'Tractarians' by their friends and 'Puseyites' by their enemies, the latter an unfortunately ugly word carrying suggestions of 'pus' and 'puce'.

The theology of the Oxford Movement grew out of their political situation, but it is useful to make a provisional distinction between the two and to bear in mind the hothouse conditions of early Victorian Oxford. There was not much Arnoldian sweetness and light about where clerical issues were at stake. When Renn Dickson Hampden (1793–1866) was appointed to the Regius Chair of Divinity in 1836 he was seen as a Whig appointment by a Whig prime minister, and a campaign of what can only be called persecution started against him. His offence was to have argued in a pamphlet that Dissenters be admitted to the university. Clerical opposition, led by Newman, took the unsavoury form of trying to read heresy back from the pamphlet into the theologically unexceptionable Bampton Lectures Hampden had given in 1832. Newman's *Elucidations of Dr Hampden's Theological Statements* (1836) accused him of relegating doctrine, 'or theological propositions methodically deduced and stated', beneath 'the simple religion of Jesus Christ, as received into the heart and influencing conduct'. Hampden was incredulous, hurt, and angry. 'I have done no wrong or unkindness to you, but on the contrary have always treated you with civility and respect', he wrote to Newman, accusing him of showing 'a fanatical persecuting spirit': 'I would readily submit to the heaviest charge of erroneous doctrine which your proud orthodoxy could bring against me, rather than exchange for your state of mind my conscious satisfaction at having neither willed, nor thought, nor done, any thing to hurt the feelings of a single person, by what I have written.' It is a strange example of the persistence of *odium theologicum* that Newman, who had himself behaved with such dignity and restraint after Kingsley's lunging tackle in 1864, could still in 1871 be calling Hampden's an 'atrocious letter'.[31]

Is is not the orthodoxy in Newman's 'proud orthodoxy' that is questionable but the pride, the haughty fastidiousness with which disagreeing fellow Christians were treated. On returning to England in 1833 and learning of the Reform Act, he wrote that he wanted to excommunicate Lord Grey and 'half a dozen more, whose names it is almost a shame and a pollution for a Christian to mention'.[32] He doubted whether he ought to sit down at table with Archbishop Whately, 'if I were in his neighbourhood'[33]; and he refused to sit at table with his brother Frank when Frank was a member of the Plymouth Brethren. If Dissenters were admitted to Oxford, how could a college tutor, he asked, 'look smilingly, and speak familiarly with those who have been baptised by strangers, and perhaps hold some deadly heresy?'

– as if Dissent were a terrible contagious disease.[34] But something is to be forgiven to those living in the heat of controversy, and no doubt there was provocation on the other side.

The Oxford Movement was not a movement in the modern sense of having an explicitly formulated 'programme' of action. It was a group of youngish, like-minded dons responding to a time of political crisis and in the process developing a fresh conception of the Church and of what devotional practice in it might be. They were not in any sense a clerical intelligentsia nor did they mean to be: their ideal was the by then slightly antiquated one of the unworldly High Church vicar ministering faithfully to a rural and implicitly south-of-England parish, like Keble at Hursley. Nor were they 'High Church' in the sense in which that was understood at Oxford in 1830, of 'high-and-dry' worldliness reacting with automatic violence to any challenge to the power of Establishment but offering no spiritual nourishment in return. Rather, they faced the questions their elders had forgotten to ask: where *did* authority in the Anglican Church lie and how could it be recovered in an age of liberalism? The answers took them back to the Elizabethan *via media*, the historical settlement by which Anglicanism retained Catholicism (the Apostolic Succession uncorrupted by the errors of Rome) while avoiding the Calvinistic extremes of the Reformation; and back to the seventeenth-century tradition of patristic scholarship, the study of the Church Fathers, and sacramental worship.

Recovering this 'Catholic' tradition in the church was essential to the Tractarian enterprise because it reopened the choked channels, as they saw them, leading back to the origins of Christianity. A Church that could claim direct descent from the Apostles had a historical security which Dissenters lacked; its sacraments, particularly the Eucharist, were conduits of grace flowing from the Fountainhead. Again and again in his writing Newman stressed the *reality* of what he worshipped. There was 'a visible Church, with sacraments and rites which are the channels of invisible grace', whereas evangelical religion, he told his brother Frank prophetically, had no such resources to survive the corrosive activity of the mind: 'till you see that the unconscious witness of the whole Church (as being a witness to an historical *fact*, viz. that the Apostle so taught), where attainable, is as much the voice of God . . . as Scripture itself, there is no hope for a clearheaded man like you. You will unravel the web of selfsufficient inquiry.'[35] The trouble with recovering the Catholic heritage of the Church is that it involved playing down and even criticising the Reformation, which inevitably brought upon the Tractarians the charge of Popery. Nothing did more to harm their cause than the posthumous publication of Hurrell Froude's *Remains* in 1838, where this most intemperate member of the group was revealed as having a hatred of the Reformation (he described it as 'a limb badly set' which 'must be broken again in order to be righted') and a morbid taste for private mortification. Once their opponents got wind of such practices as scourging, fasting, genuflexion, auricular confession, the label of effete Romanising began to stick.[36]

'Our effort . . . was wholly conservative', William Parker (1811–78) wrote, looking back on the movement. 'It was to maintain things that we believed and had been taught, not to introduce innovations in doctrine and discipline. . . . Our appeal was to antiquity – to the doctrine which the Fathers and Councils and Church universal had taught from the creeds.'[37] The Tractarians looked for support from the decisions of the Church Fathers and studied them carefully: getting 'back to the Fathers' is a constant refrain in Newman's life, and he kept seeing parallels between the current state of the Anglican Church and the decisions of the Councils of the Early Church. They also saw a parallel between their stand against liberalism and the situation of their English 'Fathers' of the seventeenth century, the Caroline divines who had stood by their king against the Puritans; and when accused of ritualism could point to the less visited sections of the Book of Common Prayer, where their practices were sanctioned. But their aims were not legalistic: they wanted to raise the sacramental awareness of their contemporaries out of the desire to restore mystery, a deeper reverence, to a religion in danger of being thinned out by too exclusive attention to the Bible and the Word. In the sacraments, Newman wrote in 1836, Christians receive the gospel 'in a temper altogether different from that critical and argumentative temper which sitting and listening engender'. As in the Primitive Church, 'the more Sacred Truths' were to be taught 'by rites and ceremonies'.[38] A 'Reserve' had to be practised in communicating religious knowledge, a holding back of analysis until the mind was prepared for it by a due reverence for the mysteries of faith.

Tractarianism as a movement lasted from 1833 to 1841, when Newman's ill-fated and ill-judged Tract XC, arguing the hospitality of the Anglican 39 Articles to Catholic interpretation, brought it to an end in a storm of controversy. His subsequent conversion to Rome in 1845 seemed to confirm what its opponents had always claimed about the movement. But Keble and Pusey and others remained within the Church, and their devotional legacy had a lasting influence. By recovering and reinterpreting an all but lost Anglo-Catholic tradition, they opened up a seam of spirituality which has enriched the Church ever since, and considering how recent was the memory of dusty altars and clergymen asking their congregations for corkscrews, this was a remarkable achievement. If their self-conscious ritualism was an offence to many – 'bowing to the east and curtsying to the west' was how Sydney Smith put it[39] – it also stirred depths of spiritual energy in others, inspiring them to found monastic religious communities dedicated to prayer, teaching, and work among the destitute of society. Their intellectual achievement was almost entirely backward looking and untouched by German influences, but by reviving the tradition of patristic scholarship they made the historic Church available again as a potential source of authority, to counterbalance a gospel religion becoming vulnerable to biblical criticism and a traditional naturalistic deism under challenge from contemporary science.

Newman and the Church

The trouble with the appeal to the Fathers is that it did not offer solid ground under Anglican feet either, or so Newman came to believe. The *Apologia* reveals a mind obsessed with the question of whether the Church of England was in schism or not, and even when allowances have been made for the apologetic, self-justificatory nature of that work, there is something excessive in the preoccupation: it betrays a character hungry for authority. Newman was not content with the Catholicity he and his fellow-Tractarians had recovered in Anglicanism, he had to press on in his study of the early Church Councils to find the genealogy of dogmatic orthodoxy; and having found it, he had to justify it to others, presenting them with a choice in either–or terms. There was to be no half-way house. He writes with relish of what he saw as the inevitable coming conflict between 'Catholic Truth and Rationalism': 'Then indeed will be the stern encounter, when two real and living principles, simple, entire, and consistent, one in the Church, the other out of it, at length rush upon each other, contending not for names and words, or half-views, but for elementary notions and distinctive moral characters.'[40] It is always a contest when religious opinions meet in Newman, and his appetite for the fight contrasts strongly with Tennyson and Arnold, in whose poetry the battle metaphor signifies spiritual weariness and disillusionment – the 'ignorant armies' clashing by night at the end of 'Dover Beach', the 'last weird battle in the west' where Arthur dies, friend fighting friend 'on the waste sand by the waste sea'.[41]

One might expect someone with Newman's orthodoxy and feeling for the 'drama of religion, and the combat of truth and error',[42] to have worked out a systematic rationalisation of his beliefs, but this is far from the case. His faith was dogmatic – in the traditional sense of being based upon the dogmas of the Church – but his approach to exploring the problems of faith was not. It was said of Newman in his own day that he had a mind unusually hospitable to the arguments of the sceptic: Huxley thought that a 'primer of heresy' could be culled from his writings. This is partly because he was a theologian with a low opinion of the claims of theology to provide logical proofs of the existence of God. He was not impressed by the traditional 'argument from design' summed up by William Paley in his *Natural Theology* (1802 – see Chapter 3), which deduced a benevolent Creator from the purposeful design of the natural world. Nor could he take any comfort from the spectacle of human history and society. 'If I looked into a mirror, and did not see my face, I should have the sort of feeling which actually comes upon me, when I look into his this living busy world, and see no reflexion of its Creator'; and then, in one of his characteristic surrenders of argumentative ground: 'Were it not for this voice, speaking so clearly in my conscience and my heart, I should be an atheist, or a pantheist, or a polytheist when I looked into the world.'[43]

The 'voice' is the voice of God speaking through the conscience. Newman is in the Romantic tradition of Coleridge and Schleiermacher in basing religious belief on the reality of feeling, the internal evidence rather than the external. No argument we can give for belief is as compelling, as real, as the argument of inner experience, the 'secret voice of conscience'.[44] No account we give of the mind's activity is as swift or instinctively sure as the operation of the mind itself, which Newman describes brilliantly in the metaphor of the mountain-climber:

> The mind ranges to and fro, and spreads out, and advances
> forward with a quickness which has become a proverb,
> and a subtlety and versatility which baffle investigation.
> It passes on from point to point, gaining one by some
> indication; another on a probability; then availing itself
> of an association; then falling back on some received law;
> next seizing on testimony; then committing itself to some
> popular impression, or some inward instinct, or some
> obscure memory; and thus it makes progress not unlike
> a clambering on a steep cliff, who, by quick eye, prompt
> hand, and firm foot, ascends how he knows not himself, by
> personal endowments and by practice, rather than by rule,
> leaving no track behind him, and unable to reach another.[45]

Newman's command of rhythm and his skill in introducing additions and quick changes of direction within the unfolding of his metaphor, almost convince us of the possibility that this sermon attempts to deny, that the reasoning process can be described.

This passage comes from Newman's 1840 sermon on 'Implicit and Explicit Reason' and makes a distinction which in different forms runs through all his writings on religion until his *Essay in Aid of a Grammar of Assent* (1870). We know more than we think we know, or can give an account of. 'All men reason . . . but all men do not reflect upon their own reasonings.' There is 'conscious and unconscious reasoning' and the latter is the mountain-climber in matters of faith. Faith is 'a reasonable process', it is not irrational, but equally it 'is not necessarily founded on investigation, argument, or proof', which can have the destructive tendency of imposing a cold formalism or encouraging irreverence:

> At best the science of divinity is very imperfect and inaccurate, yet the very name of science is a profession of accuracy. Other and more familiar objections readily occur; such as its leading to familiarity with sacred things, and consequent irreverence; its fostering formality; its substituting a sort of religious philosophy and literature for worship and practice; its weakening the springs of action by inquiring into them; its stimulating to controversy and strife; its substituting, in matters of duty, positive rules which need explanation for an instinctive feeling which commands the mind; its leading the mind to mistake system for truth. . . .[46]

Rule, system, science are here ranged against instinct, feeling, reverence, action in a quintessentially Romantic opposition. Explicit Reason is formulaic and mechanical, a scaffolding; Implicit Reason is quick and living, like the mountain-climber. So in matters of faith we should not expect to find 'certainty', which is a 'quality of propositions', but rest content with 'certitude', a receptive 'habit of mind' brought about by 'an *assemblage* of concurring and converging possibilities'.[47] He was later to use the analogy of a cable 'made up of a number of separate threads, each feeble, yet together as sufficient as an iron rod'.[48]

There is, unsurprisingly, a close connection between Newman's conception of the Church and his approach to questions of faith and reason. Speaking (as always) for himself, he wrote in *A Grammar of Assent* that 'our most natural mode of reasoning, is, not from propositions to propositions, but from things to things, from concrete to concrete, from wholes to wholes'.[49] What matters is the reality of living experience, a reality which Newman continually expresses in tactile and visual terms. Catholicity offered a 'Visible Church', with roots in history that could be traced back to the Apostles and therefore the living personality of Jesus, and sacraments with a tangible reality. Protestantism in so far as it diverged from Catholicity offered only the 'bubble of Bible-Christianity', always likely to be punctured by argument.[50] Someone who could be reasoned into faith could be reasoned out of it, and the aim of Newman's own reasoning – paradoxically – was to persuade his contemporaries to trust the impulses of conscience and memory which rationalism denied. He was in no sense a mystic: Christianity had to be justified in terms of its reality, or not at all. For, 'Revelation meets us with simple and distinct *facts* and *actions*, not with painful inductions from existing phenomena, not with generalized laws or metaphysical conjectures, but with *Jesus and the Resurrection*; and "*if Christ be not risen* . . . then is our Preaching vain, and your faith is also vain". Facts such as this are not simply evidence of the truth of the revelation, but the media of its impressiveness.'[51]

The historical import of Newman's *Essay on the Development of Christian Doctrine* (1845) has been discussed in Chapter 1 and here, by way of conclusion, I should like to say something about its auto-biographical dimension. He wrote the work on his Anglican 'deathbed', as he chose to call it, and there are moments when his handling of the argument is suffused with the emotion of this period. One such moment is his use of the river image to describe the Church's progress through history. The common assumption that a stream is clearest when close to its source does not apply to a religious body, he says, which gathers strength 'when its bed has become deep, and broad, and full':

> Its beginnings are no measure of its capabilities, nor of
> its scope. At first, no one knows what it is, or what it is
> worth. It remains perhaps for a time quiescent: it tries, as
> it were, its limbs, and proves the ground under it, and feels
> its way. From time to time, it makes essays which fail,
> and are in consequence abandoned. It seems in suspense
> which way to go; it wavers, and at length strikes out in one
> definite direction. In time it enters upon strange territory;
> points of controversy alter their bearing; parties rise and
> fall about it; dangers and hopes appear in new relations, and
> old principles reappear under new forms; it changes with
> them in order to remain the same. In a higher world it is
> otherwise; but here below to live is to change, and to be
> perfect is to have changed often.[52]

This is Newman at his greatest, master of a prose which is at once inevitable in momentum and exquisitely subtle and various in local discriminations; it mirrors a mind which combines an underlying certainty of belief with a quick responsiveness to the objections and difficulties involved in that belief. But there is more to it than that. Like the description of the river Oxus which forms the coda to Matthew Arnold's 'Sohrab and Rustum' (1853), this passage taps (whether consciously or not does not matter) Newman's deepest sense of himself and one of his most urgent needs. The Church struggling its way through history, wavering and then striking out in a 'definite direction', contending with 'parties' and 'controversy', changing yet remaining the same, is also Newman himself, the Anglican controversialist seeking to explain the Romeward flow of his life to himself and to others, and justifying its many changes in the spirit of Thomas Scott's aphorism from his Evangelical days: 'Growth the only evidence of life'.

Further, Newman's very identity seems bound up with finding the true Church, which explains why his autobiography is largely taken up with the record of that search and, conversely, why his writings on religion give such a strong sense of individual personality. The Church was always what mattered most to him. He would not have understood the (only partly) irreverent witticism that Jesus Christ came to bring the Kingdom of God but what came in its place was the Church. Newman's strength and his limitation was that he had a stronger feeling for the Church than for the Kingdom of God, where, if it exists at all, cardinals will surely have to sit at table not only with their schismatic Anglican brothers but also with Methodists, Baptists, Congregationalists and even – who knows? – the odd Quaker and Unitarian. That said, the Church was, and remains, something real, and by insisting on its reality and its availability to the doubting soul, Newman posed the dilemma of his century in the starkest terms: he at least could look Nietzsche in the eye. And his anticipation of a final showdown between Catholic truth and rationalism does not look like a bad prophecy of twentieth-century history, although from this standpoint (c. 1990) the revival of evangelicalism might surprise both camps.

The crisis of faith

Modern historians have been kind to the point of indulgence in their handling of the Oxford Movement. Contemporary observers could be less so: to Mark Pattison (admittedly an interested witness in view of the Tractarian past he wanted to repudiate) the eclipse of the movement was 'a deliverance from the nightmare which had oppressed Oxford for fifteen years'; in the light of the 1848 revolutions on the Continent 'it seemed incredible . . . that we had been spending years in debating any matter so flimsy as whether England was in a state of schism or no'.[53] One does not need to share Pattison's almost aggressive identification with intellectual modernity to see the force of that observation, nor be a Freudian to see how much the culture of Victorian Anglo-Catholicism owed to sexual sublimation. Young men from privileged backgrounds, whose most acute sense of sin was associated, it seems, largely with masturbation,[54] had their already developed feelings of physical shame exacerbated by an ethos which exalted the sanctity of denial. They learned to value fasting, and celibacy, and (for the more advanced) the masochistic satisfactions of the scourge: Gladstone, for example, would give himself a good whipping after his nocturnal 'missionary' visits to London prostitutes. At the same time their senses were stimulated by the colour and scents and music of High Church ritual. The energies denied in one direction flowed in another to charge with almost unbearable intensity the sensuousness of eye and ear one finds in Hopkins's poetry and in certain Pre-Raphaelite paintings. But a terrible price was paid by those like Christina Rossetti whose emotional lives were maimed by the impossible demands their religion made of their sexual natures. If the great evil of evangelicalism was bullying the conscience, that of tractarianism was teaching the Victorians to hate their own flesh.

By the 1840s, however, what was at issue was no longer the validity of Anglican orders, but for an increasing number of thinking people the validity of Christianity itself. The first phase of the Victorian 'crisis of faith' belongs to this decade. It is a striking fact that a significant number of intellectuals of the same generation (i.e. those born between about 1810 and 1820) but from different backgrounds began to doubt the truth of Christianity and, more significantly, its morality, and felt compelled to express these doubts publicly. In 1838 the Coventry Unitarian Charles Hennell (b. 1809) published *An Inquiry Concerning the Origin of Christianity*: this is the work which the young, Evangelical George Eliot (b. 1819) read in 1841 when she met Hennell's sister Cara, married to the free-thinker Charles Bray, as a result of which she started to lose her faith – if faith can be said to be lost in such a cause-and-effect way. (It says much for English provincial culture of the time, incidentally, and for Unitarianism, that they could produce a work which in all essential respects anticipates the findings of the German 'Higher Criticism' about discrepancies in the gospel narratives and their implications.) Frances Cobbe (b. 1822) was also from an evangelical home but moved much more slowly and painfully to Theism, as we shall see. J.A. Froude (b. 1818, brother of the Tractarian Hurrell) and Frank Newman (b. 1805) debated their spiritual problems noisily, in their then scandalous works *The Nemesis of Faith* (1849) and *Phases of Faith* (1850); Arthur Clough (b. 1819) and Matthew Arnold (b. 1822) more quietly, in their confessional poetry; all seem to have lost their faith, or had it deeply unsettled, in the 1840s. And lest the impression be given, as it is too often in histories of the subject, that suffering for religious doubt was confined to the intellectual middle classes, one should bear in mind the thousands of working–class men and women who joined secular societies and in doing so exposed themselves to economic discrimination much sharper than anything a doubting Oxbridge don had to suffer. During the six months when George Jacob Holyoake (1817–1906), founder of the Secularist movement, was imprisoned for atheism in 1841 – the last person in England to be so – his daughter died of hunger.

Why does 'doubt' make such a dramatic entry at this time? The traditional explanation is that intellectuals had their faith unsettled by developments in geology in the 1830s and by the application of new scientific–historical techniques to the study of the Bible, both of which had the effect of undermining the authority of scripture on which Protestantism was traditionally based. Certainly these developments, as we saw in the previous chapter, were important agents in the erosion of historical certainties, but they were not in themselves the main issues which disturbed the faith of first-generation Victorians. It has become increasingly clear that their objections to Christianity were overwhelmingly *moral* rather than scientific, objections to certain key doctrines of evangelical religion in which some had been reared but all had experienced in the religious culture of the time. The Atonement, chiefly, hell, everlasting punishment, original sin – a God who required the obedience of his creatures on those terms was a God who did not deserve worshipping, a primitive, barbaric Deity of whom Herbert Spencer wrote in his *Autobiography*:

> I had not at that time [c. 1840] repudiated the notion of a deity who is pleased with the singing of his praises, and angry with the beings he has made when they fail to tell him perpetually of his greatness. It had not become manifest to me how absolutely and immeasurably unjust it would be that for Adam's disobedience (which might have caused a harsh man to discharge his servant), all Adam's descendants should be damned, with the exception of a relatively few who accepted the 'plan of salvation' which the immense majority never heard of. Nor had I in those days perceived the astounding nature of the creed which offers for profoundest worship, a being who calmly looks on while myriads of his creatures are suffering eternal torments.[55]

But when he did perceive these things Spencer gave up whatever religion had descended to him from his Methodist grandparents, thereby exemplifying the familiar paradox of Victorian doubt: the moral sense turning on the evangelical doctrines which had helped to shape it.

What happened for this generation, in part, is that an elevated conscience and humanitarianism met the optimism of an age of reform to create a new mood of possibility. The early Victorian crisis of faith cannot be separated from a wider cultural conviction that the world could be improved and individual human beings with it. Expectation of reform suddenly made it possible to challenge Christianity's pessimistic view of human nature and the element of fear which had been one of its chief means of control. The response of the clergy to reform, the arrogance with which many of them continued to view the laity, and the bitterness with which they fought over what looked like slight matters of doctrine, forfeited much of the respect they used to enjoy. In this context it became possible to think the unthinkable and say the unsayable, and in doing so to feel the authenticity of what Tennyson called 'honest doubt'. Of course, there was another side of melancholy and loss, the 'eternal note of sadness' at passing faiths which Arnold heard in 'Dover Beach' (1853), but Tennyson's bracing 'There lives more faith in honest doubt, Believe me, than in half the creeds' is truer to the positive mood of the early Victorian doubter.[56] Writing in 1870, and employing the familiar metaphor of the ocean, J.A. Froude wrote of his generation's experience:

> The present generation which has grown up in an open spiritual ocean, which has got used to it and has learned to swim for itself, will never know what it was to find the lights all drifting, the compasses all awry, and nothing left to steer by except the stars. In this condition the best and bravest of my own contemporaries determined to have done with insincerity, to find ground under their feet, to let the uncertain remain uncertain, but to learn how much and what we could honestly regard as true, and believe that, and live by it. Tennyson became the voice of this feeling in poetry: Carlyle . . . in prose.[57]

For Froude's contemporaries did not abandon the search for a 'creed' (a potent word at this period) in abandoning the Christian creeds: they struggled to find a new one, and found it in secular religions like Comte's 'Religion of Humanity' (see below) or in various forms of theism. Again, the working-class radical was involved in this process of criticism and redefinition through the secular societies of the time: the first of these was set up in London in 1851 and some sixty societies were formed in the next decade, mainly in London and the industrial cities of the north.[58]

There is an important distinction that needs to be made between this generation of doubters and the next, those who read (or read about)

Darwin's *The Origin of Species* (1859). The increasing plausibility and comprehensiveness of a scientific, materialist explanation of reality, and the crucial breakdown of the traditional distinction between mankind and nature, took the wind out of Victorian ethical sails. The later mood lacks the energy and optimism of the earlier; it is marked by feelings of disinheritance, by resentment at the biological trap mankind now finds itself in, and by a compensating lyrical stoicism. Significantly, the word defining the new mood, agnosticism (coined by Huxley in 1869), is a negative, defining a state of 'not-knowing' that is passive rather than active. It is the difference between the moral optimism of George Eliot's early novels and the resignation of Hardy's.

What did the 'loss of faith' involve? The impression given by sensational religious novels, such as *Robert Elsmere* (1888) and other cassock-rippers of the period, is that it was rather like losing one's virginity: an irrevocable step attended by hysterical feelings of shame and guilt. The evidence of contemporary autobiography is less sensational and more interesting. Three accounts from different sexes and different stages of the period will give some idea of the variety of the experience. Charles Darwin (b. 1809) would be of exceptional interest anyway, as the discoverer of the theory of evolution by natural selection, and his loss of faith was of the gradual kind, accelerated by the death of his favourite daughter Annie in 1851. Frances Cobbe (b. 1822) offers a fascinating parallel and contrast to George Eliot in the way she shed her evangelical beliefs. Beatrice Webb, nee Potter (b. 1858), comes at the end of the period, late enough to have seen through what were in the 1840s the 'advanced' hopes of science as a substitute religion, but still hungering for some satisfaction for her deeply religious nature.

Darwin's father was unlike many parents of that period in being an enlightened and tolerant man, and it is obvious from the *Autobiography* (1887) that Darwin adored him. He seems to have grown up without any pressure to conform to a particular religious group or ideology, and his loss of faith was therefore untroubled by the rebellion against parental domination that Edmund Gosse, for example, recorded in *Father and Son* (1907). Left to make up his own mind, he proceeded slowly from a tepid conventional Christianity to a mild but complete agnosticism: 'The rate was so slow that I felt no distress, and have never since doubted even for a single second that my conclusion was correct.' The serenity of that sentence is somewhat ruffled, however, by the words that follow:

> I can indeed hardly see how anyone ought to wish
> Christianity to be true; for if so, the plain language
> of the text seems to show that the men who do not
> believe, and this would include my Father, Brother

and almost all my best friends, will be everlastingly
punished.
     And this is a damnable doctrine.[59]

That last sentence stands on its own and carries a charge of moral
outrage (and a bitter pun) felt nowhere else in Darwin's easy-going
memoirs. He goes on to offer reasons for agnosticism, in a dispassionate
manner, but this is the one moment when one senses he is really *moved*.
And what moves him is not just the thought that his beloved father
could go to Hell but, as J.R. Moore has suggested recently, perhaps the
memory of the death of his ten-year-old daughter Annie in 1851. While
his wife was at home having another child, Darwin was nursing his
dying daughter in Malvern and writing letters back describing Annie's
deteriorating condition. The experience of her suffering, his own
knowledge of the child's goodness and lovingness, and the outrageous
thought that she might be punished in the next life, were too much for
Darwin. He had the words 'A Dear and Good Child' defiantly inscribed
on Annie's tombstone.[60] So he, too, may be said to fall within the
category of the moral objectors to Christianity, even though he had no
contact with evangelicalism and seems otherwise to have had a painless
transition to unbelief.
     Frances Cobbe, on the other hand, was a deeply pious child who
responded intensely to the atmosphere of her evangelical home. Like one
of George Eliot's heroines she set herself high standards and punished
herself for not living up to them: 'I made all sorts of severe rules for
myself, and if I broke them, manfully mulcted myself of any little
pleasures or endured some small self-imposed penance.'[61] Her story
illustrates how much harder the loss of faith could be for a woman
than for a man, because, like George Eliot, she had to stay at home to
look after her widower father, under the iniquitous system that required
single daughters to remain in the family home as unpaid companions
to ageing parents. There was no escape from the moral pressure of
the religious home: sons could take their doubts to college or club,
daughters could only escape when they were sent away in religious
disgrace to stay with relatives, as happened to both women. Cobbe's
case was much harder than Eliot's, since she had initially no access to
modern books or to the kind of liberating freethinking circle that Eliot
found with the Brays and Hennells in Coventry; she had to work out
her faith with old tools like Gibbon on miracles, and her account is all
the more moving for that reason.
     Her doubts about the miracles started very early. At eleven she
surprised herself by questioning the plausibility of the miracle of the
loaves and fishes. Although she went through the usual evangelical
conversion experience at seventeen, doubts about the miracles returned

and with them questions about the historical and moral basis of Christianity:

> I had read very carefully Gibbon's XV and XVI chapters, and other books enough to teach me that everything in historical Christianity had been questioned; and my own awakening critical, and reasoning, and above all ethical, – faculties supplied fresh crops of doubts of the truth of the story and of the morality, and of the scheme of Atonement itself.' (p. 89).

Her account starts to assume a familiar pattern. The objections are 'above all, ethical' and yet the ethical imperatives remain. For four lonely years she struggled to reconcile religion and ethics, torn between having 'to accept a whole mass of dogmas against which my reason and conscience rebelled' and, in rejecting them, having 'as a necessary sequel, to cast aside the laws of Duty which I had hitherto cherished; to cease to pray or take the sacrament; and to relinquish the hope of a life beyond the grave' (p. 91).

She arrived at a point of disbelief in orthodox Christianity and agnosticism about the existence of God. Although she does not mention Carlyle, and may not at that stage have read *Sartor Resartus* (although she could have done, in 1840), she had obviously reached her 'Centre of Indifference' and it was followed by her version of 'The Everlasting Yea'. Just as Teufelsdröckh rediscovered his power to affirm watching the mountain-storm in the Alps, so Frances Cobbe found hers again after reading Shelley in the Irish countryside one 'sunny day in May'. Something stirred within her and she asked herself whether it was not possible to '"live up to my own idea of what is right and good? Even though there be no life after death, I may yet deserve my own respect here and now, and, if there be a God, He must approve me"' (pp. 92–3). Having made this recognition, she found she started to pray again.

> Of course, there was Christian sentiment and the results of Christian training in all I felt and did. I could no more have cast them off than I could have leaped off my shadow. But of dogmatical Christianity there was never any more. I have never from that time, now more than fifty years ago, attached, or wished I could attach, credence to any part of what Dr. Martineau has called the *Apocalyptic side of Christianity*, nor (I may add with thankfulness) have I ever lost faith in God. (p. 93)

There is not only Christianity in Cobbe's experience but also Romanticism (recovering the power of prayer recalls the Ancient

Mariner), a touch of Carlyle, and what Nietzsche and Newman would have seen as a timid sitting on the bank, a refusal either to jump into the river of dogma or walk away into the clear air of atheism. Cobbe exemplifies that moment in the Victorian religious consciousness when neither of these options satisfies the needs of individuals; far from being timid, she had the courage to declare and define her theism, and the half-way house she was one of the first to enter has become a very crowded building since.

When Beatrice Webb's *My Apprenticeship* was published in 1926, contemporaries who associated her with social investigation and a concern for the material conditions of the working classes were surprised to find how large a part the religious consciousness, as distinct from religious practice, had played in her life. The second chapter even had the early-Victorian-sounding title 'In Search of a Creed'. She exemplifies a later stage of doubt, although once again the starting-point was revulsion from the central evangelical doctrine of the Atonement: even at seventeen and newly confirmed (by 'a remarkably eloquent evangelical preacher'), she found the doctrine a 'stumbling-block, not because it struck me as irrational, but because it seemed to me immoral'; and she transcribed a diary entry of the time in which she says that the doctrine 'disgusts' her.[62] Her 'feeble hold on orthodox Christianity' went a year later, in 1876, loosened by 'the opening up of the religions of the Far East' and her simultaneous discovery of the 'religion of science' (pp. 82–3). The former is an ironic example of the Empire striking back: the missionaries took Christianity to the heathen, but the colonial administrators brought back the interests they had developed in Oriental religions. Beatrice Webb was introduced to Buddhism and Hinduism by one of them, Brian Hodgson (1800–95) the Orientalist, and they swept away her 'belief in the Christian Church and its Bible as the sole or even as the pre-eminent embodiment of the religious impulse in the mind of man'; she even, at the time, saw Buddha and his philosophy as 'logically and ethically superior to the Christ and the teachings of the New Testament', and found in Buddhist metaphysics 'a superficial likeness to the philosophy of modern science' (pp. 87–8).

Then traditional religion gave way to the religion of science, of which she became for a short while a disciple. 'The God was The Unknowable: the prophet was Herbert Spencer. Prayer might have to go, but worship would remain' (p. 90). But she found this a comfortless religion, 'bleak and dreary in sorrow and ill-health' (p. 96) – a realisation sharpened by the death of her mother. In a way that is similar to Cobbe's division between religious need and ethical rejection of Christianity, Webb found science 'bankrupt in deciding the destiny of man' and yet inescapable in any attempt at cosmic understanding: 'any avoidance of the scientific method in disentangling "the order of things" . . . spells superstition and usually results in disaster'. She found a way out of this dilemma in prayer: 'it is by prayer, by communion with an all-pervading spiritual force, that the soul of man discovers the purpose or goal of human endeavour' (p. 105). However, she could not explain to What or Whom she prayed, revealing only — with touching simplicity in so formidable an intellectual – the pleasure she took in sitting in St Paul's, 'with its still silent spaces', finding a wonderful restfulness in that House of God' (p. 320).

The image of Beatrice Webb sitting in St Paul's, drawing sustenance from an institution whose doctrines she rejects, is an apt symbol of the situation of the religious agnostic in the later nineteenth century; we seem already to be on the road that leads to the bicycle-clipped intruder of Larkin's 'Churchgoing' (1955). It prompts some concluding reflections on the nature of the Victorian crisis of faith. The first is that the challenge to orthodox Christianity was initially moral rather than scientific and may always have been primarily so, with science providing a rationalisation and justification rather than a cause. The latter receives some support from Susan Budd's study of the secularist movement: she found that in the biographies of 150 members of the movement between 1850 and 1950, ideas from geology, evolution, and biblical criticism were responsible for only three cases of loss of religious faith, and concludes that 'the revolution of scientific and theological thinking seems largely irrelevant'.[63] Nor would this be surprising. As Newman acutely points out in several places, men and women are swayed in these vital matters not by logic or theory but by instincts and emotions, and revulsion from the Atonement, Hell, and everlasting punishment was a very powerful emotion in the nineteenth century.

It was powerful because the period witnessed a decisive separation of the moral sense from the religious institutions which had once expressed it. Several reasons for this have already been suggested – the climate of reform, distaste for the party squabbles within and between the different churches, evangelical conscience turning on evangelical doctrine – but they exist within an overarching framework of historical consciousness. What damaged the authority of the Church in the nineteenth century were not the catapults of atheists and scientists, but the acid rain of historical relativism. Newman found that to be in history was to cease to be a Protestant; others found that to be in history was to question the exclusivity of Christian Revelation, to look around and beneath it, to explore its origins and relations with other religions, and to compare its value-system with that of others, sometimes not to the advantage of Christianity, as Beatrice Webb found. The growth of the Empire could only intensify this awareness of other faiths and other paths, and

Kipling's *Kim* (1901) is the great (and subversive) literary embodiment of that awareness.

By the same token, religious experience in this period should not be confined to what happened or did not happen in churches and synagogues. William James's *Varieties of Religious Experience* (1902) is a much better title for a study of Victorian religion than that old music-hall turn, Faith and Doubt. For belief was and is a matter of temperament: Darwin found it easy to shed his former beliefs because they were conventional and his was not a religious nature; but Cobbe and Webb, believing almost as little as Darwin, found it impossible to live without some object of worship and prayer. People did not stop being religious when they ceased believing in formal creeds. The religious temperament found other avenues for its expression: theism, science, socialism, even a walk in the hills or contemplation of the night sky. Such 'leakage' may have been regrettable to the orthodox, but it was inevitable, and no call to dogma was going to stem it: that was the problem, and the challenge, of modernity.

The challenge of modernity: *Essays and Reviews* and *Literature and Dogma*

By 1860 the British Protestant Churches were in a state of intellectual crisis, whether their members recognised the fact or not (and most did not). A religion traditionally based on the sufficiency of scripture was bound to come under threat when the authority of the Bible was challenged, on one side by moral objectors who condemned its God as a vengeful tribal deity, on the other by the erosions of historical criticism and the rise of a confident scientific materialism. How much of the Old Testament was true? How much of the New could be trusted? Pull on these threads and the old woollen jersey of faith started to unravel at an alarming rate. Then there was the problem of the miracles, not a new problem, certainly, but one to which modern science gave a chilly answer. 'That miracles have fallen into discredit is to be frankly admitted', Matthew Arnold wrote in the Preface to a cheap edition of his *Literature and Dogma* (1873), 'that they have fallen into discredit justly and necessarily, and through the very same natural and salutary process which had previously extinguished our belief in witchcraft, is to be frankly admitted also'.[64] Such candour took courage, and Arnold got away with it only because he was neither a clergyman nor a theologian – although his attempts at theological reconstruction were a good deal more interesting than those of the theologians, as we shall see.

Modernity was a particular challenge for the Free Churches, who not only tended towards an extreme of biblical literalism but also had made the Atonement the central doctrine of their faith. A profound conviction of sin, suddenly released by the discovery of the power of Christ's atoning sacrifice on the cross, had been the springboard for conversion in the heyday of the Methodist revival. Increasingly, however, the notion of substitutionary atonement – Christ dying for mankind as part of a bargain with God – lost its hold on the conscience, becoming an obstacle to belief rather than a help; Evangelicals of all denominations were faced with the difficult task of rethinking the bases of their faith. A slow shift from the Atonement to the Incarnation, from Christ's death to his humanity, took place; and some would say, to the dilution and eventual loss of what was most distinctive in nonconformism.[65] The transition to a historicised Bible was equally painful, although the famous and dramatic case of William Robertson Smith (1846–94) suggests that it need not have been so. Smith was a brilliant biblical scholar who became Professor of Hebrew at the Free Church College in Aberdeen at the age of twenty-four. He had studied in Germany and saw no incompatibility between the then not-very-new German methods of historical analysis and his Calvinist faith; nor did his superiors until his articles for the ninth edition of *Encyclopaedia Britannica* started to bring his views to a wider and more conservative Free Church readership. The entry on the 'Bible' (1875) gave particular offence because it questioned the accepted view of the authorship and sequence of the Old Testament books, suggesting that the Prophets preceded rather than followed the Law (Genesis to Deuteronomy) in order of composition. There followed a five-year campaign to deprive Smith of his chair, led by James Begg and the ultra-conservative Highland party in the Church, which was eventually successful at the 1881 General Assembly, by 423 votes to 245. The noteworthy feature of Smith's case is that he was censured for the influence his writings might exert rather than for their intrinsic heterodoxy; his superiors did not disagree with his views, for they realised their inevitability, but were prepared to throw him to the wolves in the interests of party unity.

There is everything to choose theologically, but not much morally, between Begg's campaign against Smith, and Newman and his friends' persecution of R.D. Hampden. Heresy-hunting is a disfiguring feature of nineteenth-century Christianity; it was the one activity sure to bring High and Low Church, Tractarians and Evangelicals, even Churchmen and Dissenters, into temporary alliance. Their targets were always the theological liberals, those known as 'liberal Anglicans' or more usually as the Broad Church. To this group belonged some of the most famous names of the period: Thomas Arnold (1795–1842), Frederick Denison Maurice (1805–72), and Richard Whately (1787–1863) in the first generation; A.P. Stanley (1815–81), Arnold's pupil and biographer, Benjamin Jowett (1817–93), Master of Balliol, and Frederick Temple (1821–1902), later Archbishop of Canterbury, in the second. The Broad Church was a tendency rather than a movement, and only became identified as a party within the Church when the publication of *Essays and Reviews* caused such an uproar in 1860.

As the name suggests, the movement was inclusive rather than exclusive: Thomas Arnold's *Principles of Church Reform* (1833) argued that membership of the Church should be available to all but Quakers and Roman Catholics; in this he followed Coleridge's vision of the Church of England as a truly national church, set out in *On the Constitution of Church and State* (1830). The Broad Church were unhappy with doctrines like 'the Atonement' and 'Everlasting Punishment', attempted to redefine them, and paid the price. F.D. Maurice, the group's leading if at times semi-detached theologian, lost his post as Professor of Theology at King's College, London, for seeming to suggest – the offending passage in his *Theological Essays* (1853) is not entirely clear – that perdition was not a place of punishment but a state of loss of the knowledge and love of God, and that salvation was always possible, as a condition of the very being of God. They were prepared to approach new developments in science and theology with an open mind; as Jowett said, 'the Christian religion is in a false position when all the tendencies of knowledge are opposed to it'.[66] And they could claim the period's greatest poet as a non-unionised member, for in many ways *In Memoriam* is the supreme Broad Church poem, with its respect for 'honest doubt' and the conclusions of science, its refusal to be bullied into credal orthodoxy, and its fundamentally historical and evolutionary conception of the religious instincts.

In an age of bitter sectarian rivalry it is pleasant to be able to record the spirit of ecumenism the Broad Church showed towards liberal Dissent, especially in their relations and interactions with that most despised of all denominations, the Unitarians. Coleridge was a Unitarian for fifteen years; Maurice's father was one, and his *Theological Essays* are addressed to the Unitarians. That fascinating exile from the security of orthodoxy, Blanco White (1775–1841), began as a Roman Catholic priest, converted to Anglicanism on coming to England, and became a secret Unitarian in 1818. As a fellow of Oriel between 1826 and 1831 he has the distinction of shaping the views of such influential Broad-Churchmen as Whately and Hampden (while at the same time playing the violin with Newman and teaching Pusey how to use the Roman breviary). Both groups held liberal attitudes to biblical criticism, were lukewarm on the importance of miracles to Christian faith, and

Plate 1. William M. Mulready, *Convalescent from Waterloo* (1822)

Plate 2. Ford Maddox Brown, *St Ives, AD 1630, Cromwell on his Farm* (1874)

Plate 3. William Dyce, *Pegwell Bay, Kent – a Recollection of October 5th 1858* (1859–60)

Plate 4. Sir Lawrence Alma-Tadema, *In the Trepidarium* (1881)

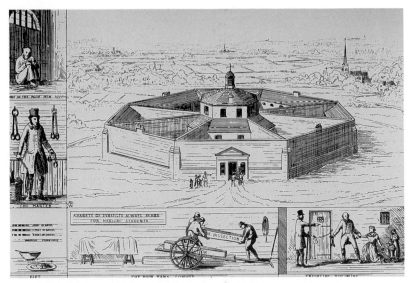

Plate 5. 'Modern Poor House', from Pugin, *Contrasts* (1836)

Plate 6. 'Antient Poor House', from Pugin, *Contrasts* (1836)

Plate 7. Julia Margaret Cameron, photograph of Sir John Herschel (1867)

Plate 8. John Martin, *The Deluge* (1826)

Plate 9. Sir John Everett Millais, *Christ in the House of His Parents (The Carpenter's Shop)* (1894–50)

Plate 10. Dante Gabriel Rossetti, *Beata Beatrix* (1864)

progressive on substitutionary atonement and everlasting punishment.

For a work that was to cause more furore in intellectual circles than almost any other book of the period apart from *The Origin of Species*, *Essays and Reviews* (1860) has a singularly unpromising title, and it can be difficult at this distance to see quite what all the fuss was about, so entirely have its main theological positions – on the relations of knowledge to religion and on the uses of biblical criticism – become a part of twentieth-century orthodoxy. Even by 1896 one of the contributors, Frederick Temple, was considered sufficiently safe to be made Archbishop of Canterbury. But thirty-five years earlier the editor, Henry Wilson, and Rowland Williams were tried for heresy in a Church court and convicted on two points of doctrine – for questioning the literal truth of the Bible and the doctrine of damnation. They appealed to the Judicial Committee of the Privy Council, which found in their favour in 1864 and awarded them costs (or as one wag put it, 'dismissed Hell with costs, and took away from orthodox members of the Church of England their last hope of eternal damnation'). But Pusey did not rest there, gathering 11,000 signatures to a declaration of Anglican clergy affirming the doctrines which had been questioned.

There were seven essayists of whom only one was a layman: Charles Goodwin. He contributed the collection's single essay on physical science, 'On the Mosaic Cosmogony', a critique of those scriptural geologists like Hugh Miller who were trying to reconcile geology with a more or less literal belief in the Book of Genesis. The one 'review' was by Rowland Williams of 'Bunsen's Biblical Researches', a densely allusive and unattractively written celebration of the German scholar's methods of historical enquiry. The second essay in the collection, it gave bite to the bland generalisings of Temple's opening essay on 'The Education of the World' about the progressive revelation of God through history: on his second page Williams struck the note that was to give most offence: 'We cannot encourage a remorseless criticism of Gentile histories and escape its contagion when we approach Hebrew annals; nor acknowledge a Providence in Jewry without owning that it may have comprehended sanctities elsewhere.'[67] In other words Christianity exists in history, its claims to Revelation may be supreme but cannot be exclusive, and its texts should be approached and interpreted in the same way as other ancient texts. And if the Bible is seen in this way, Williams goes on – following Coleridge and anticipating Matthew Arnold – it may be that what was fluid and poetic at source has hardened into doctrinal shapes it was never meant to take. 'Why may not justification by faith have meant the peace of mind, or sense of Divine approval, which comes of trust in a righteous God, rather than a fiction of merit by transfer?' Even Resurrection itself may 'mean a spiritual quickening. Salvation would be our deliverance, not from the life-giving God, but from evil and darkness, which are His finite opposites.'[68]

Williams's essay was the one to give most contemporary offence: it went even further down the demythologising road than Jowett's better-remembered 'On the Interpretation of Scripture' (the last essay in the volume), but Williams lacked Jowett's urbanity. The issues he raised were dealt with by Baden Powell, the Professor of Geometry at Oxford, in his essay 'On the Study of the Evidences of Christianity' – the only contributor to mention Darwin – and by his companion in heresy, Henry Bristow Wilson, the editor. In his essay on 'The National Church', Wilson drew attention to the results of the 1851 Census and opined that if five million people were absent from church on a Sunday, it was not because they had all read Strauss's *Life of Jesus* (1846) but because the traditional arguments for miraculous revelation and scriptural authority had broken down. They were now aware of the historical relativity of all religions and less patient with party and credal rigidity: 'the nearer we approach to the fountain head, the more definite do we find the statement of the Christian principle, that the source of religion is in the heart'[69] – and the nearer we come to the recognition (convenient of course to a Broad-Churchman) that the Early Church was 'multitudinist', tolerant of different parties. Finally, a more oblique mirror to the present was provided in Mark Pattison's more purely academic essay on 'Tendencies of Religious Thought in England, 1688–1750'.

None of these views was particularly original or new. Pusey, chief persecutor of the Essayists, had encountered them thirty years earlier when he studied under and was influenced by Johann Gottfried Eichhorn (1752–1827), the great liberal theologian at Göttingen (such spiritual wild oats had naturally been forgotten by 1860). But as in the case of Robertson Smith, what could be ignored in a learned journal became more threatening in book form, especially when the contributors seemed to be acting in concert, despite their denials in the Preface. And perhaps there is something to be said for the motives of their opponents, if not for their conduct. The thought of 11,000 Anglican clergy signing a petition in favour of everlasting punishment is not a pretty one, certainly, but it may be that the Essayists for their part did not, or could not, foresee the consequences of their position. For in effect what they were doing was surrendering Christianity to history. The metaphor of encrustation crops up in the volume: Wilson talks of the need to make distinction 'between the dark patches of human passion and error which form a partial crust upon [the Bible], and the bright centre of spiritual truth within',[70] and the implication is that the necessary scraping away will leave one with a hard stone or metal of supernatural Christianity. But what if the supernatural element itself proves vulnerable to the scraping process, and one is left with a purely 'natural', historicised Christianity? In their intolerant and dogmatic way, perhaps the opponents of *Essays and Reviews* realised this, even if the form their defence of supernatural faith took is unacceptable to us today.

It says something about the limitations of Victorian theology that the man who grasped the full significance of this situation was not a theologian but a poet and critic. Matthew Arnold published four volumes of theological writings in the 1870s: *St Paul and Protestantism* (1870), *Literature and Dogma* (1873), *God and the Bible* (1875), and *Last Essays in Church and Religion* (1877). There is a good deal of overlap between them, for Arnold was nothing if not a repetitive controversialist, but *Literature and Dogma* is the most daring and interesting of them; it contains the radical kernel of his religious views, and it was also, significantly, the most successful with his contemporaries, selling over 100,000 copies in various editions.[71]

Arnold's starting-point is the increasing failure, as he saw it, of supernatural dogmatic Christianity to retain its hold on the allegiance of either the intellectual classes or those he calls 'the masses'. It is seen to be at odds with the scientific temper of the age and to be losing in the struggle: 'our popular religion at present conceives the birth, ministry, and death of Christ, as altogether steeped in prodigy, brimful of miracle; – *and miracles do not happen*'. The contemporary need is 'to find, for the Bible, for Christianity . . . a basis in something which can be verified, instead of in something which has to be assumed'. In this task the 'received theology' of all the Churches and sects is no help; indeed, with its talk of a 'Personal Godhead' and its reliance on an elaborate metaphysics, orthodox theology was a major part of the problem.[72] If Christianity was to have a future it had to be able to look history and science in the eye, and Arnold's frequent use of words like 'verify' and 'experiment' indicate his intention to make it do so.

His first important insight – not original but developed with a clarity lacking in Coleridge and Maurice – concerns the nature of religious language. 'To understand that the language of the Bible is fluid, passing, and literary, not rigid, fixed, and scientific, is the first step towards a right understanding of the Bible.' It will save us from the errors of theological realism, of thinking that because the word 'God' has assumed a fixity in our minds this must imply a Personality. Rather, it is a literary term, ' a term *thrown out*, so to speak, at a not fully grasped object of the speaker's consciousness . . . and mankind mean different things by it as their consciousness differs' (pp. 152, 171). Men give this name to their instinct for conduct, which for Arnold is three-fourths of life:

> The idea of *God* . . . rests . . . not on a metaphysical
> conception . . . but on a moral perception of a rule of
> conduct not of our own making, into which we are born,
> and which exists whether we will or no; of awe at its
> grandeur and necessity, and of gratitude at its beneficence.
> This is the great original revelation made to Israel, this is
> his 'Eternal'. (p. 242)

This passage is as close as Arnold comes to saying that the instinct for conduct has the force of a *natural* instinct, and can therefore be read as a gloss on his better-known and much-derided definition of God as *'the enduring power, not ourselves, which makes for righteousness'* (p. 200). There are, of course, difficulties in identifying the religious instinct so closely with the moral instinct, but it provides Arnold with a verifiable basis, a basis in experience which can be known and appealed to; in this sense it is 'scientific'. 'Religion springing out of an experience of the power, the grandeur, the necessity of righteousness, is revealed religion, whether we find it in Sophocles or in Isaiah' (p. 195).

The essence of religious experience for Arnold is the 'happiness' and 'joy' which comes from acting in concert with the universal power which makes for righteousness. The core idea of the Old Testament is the discovery that *'righteousness tendeth to life'*, which is a 'great natural truth' (p. 195); that of the New is the 'secret' of Jesus – renunciation: 'He that will save his life shall lose it; he that will lose his life shall save it' (p. 201). These moral and psychological realities are the enduring bases of Christianity, and properly understood will ensure its future in a world increasingly dominated by the authority of scientific explanation. All else is *Aberglaube*, 'extra-belief', metaphysical hypotheses which belong to more primitive modes of thought and the human tendency to personalise deity. *'Man never knows how anthropomorphic he is'* (p. 184) was a saying of Goethe's that Arnold frequently repeats. In this category belong the notion of God as a person, 'the moral and intelligent governor of the universe' (p. 172); miracles, including Christ's resurrection and ascension; the Trinity (which Arnold mischievously compared to 'three Lord Shaftesburys' – a witticism deleted in later editions); the doctrine of the Atonement; and the three great historical creeds. Arnold did not want to destroy this metaphysical superstructure for those happy to believe it, only to persuade the unbeliever that a rejection of Christian metaphysics was not the same thing as a rejection of Christianity. There was an experiental truth to be discovered there which was deeper than dogma and more important.

Perhaps he went too far. It may be that the reconciliation he was attempting conceded to much ground to scientific naturalism, and did so because Arnold himself was deficient in feeling for religious experience. Conduct may be three-fourths of life, but it is less than three-fourths of religion, where ideas of the numinous and the transcendent appeal to needs which are deeper and less accountable than the morality of the Victorian gentleman. Arnold is easy to mock because of this, and the mockery of the orthodox is a way of setting aside the clarity with which he grasped and expressed the contemporary religious crisis, as no other of his contemporaries did. What he said of Maurice, that he 'passed his life beating the bush with deep emotion and never starting the hare' (p. 383), cannot be said of Arnold himself. The hare he started, the problem of theological realism in an age of science, was *the* religious problem of the later nineteenth century, and many of his contemporaries were grateful to him for bringing it at last into the open.

Moreover, it is a hare that has continued running into the twentieth century. Few people today are likely to accept Arnold's Victorian equation of religion with morality, or the equally Victorian optimism about the future of a Christianity reconstructed along these lines; but the problems he addressed – about the nature of religious language and the consequences of mankind's anthropomorphising tendency – have yet to be registered, let alone resolved, at the level of popular belief. When an Anglican bishop recently suggested that the main significance of Christ's resurrection might not lie in the historical miracle, he drew upon himself a storm of controversy more appropriate to 1870 than 1980. In this sense Arnold is the most modern of the Victorian writers on religion, refusing Newman's refuge in a historical Church and the liberal Anglican accommodation with a vaguely progressive evolutionism, cutting down to a layer where religion and science could meet in the authority of experience itself. For '[Christianity's] grandeur and truth are far best brought out *experimentally*; and the thing is, to make people see this' (p. 396).

Rejection and return: agnosticism and after

Matthew Arnold had his critics, but although his surrender of disputed ground was much more drastic than *Essays and Reviews*, none of them responded with the violence that the earlier volume attracted. Why? Partly it was because he was not a clergyman, but mainly because the whole climate in which religious issues were discussed (at least in England) had changed significantly by the 1870s. The *Essays and Reviews* affair had revealed the impotence of the Church courts, in that the Privy Council was not prepared to sustain ecclesiastical judgements of heresy: it was a victory for Newman's hated 'liberalism' and a demonstration of the declining political power of the Anglican Church. Gladstone's Liberal Government elected in 1869 went further down the same road, opening teaching fellowships at Oxbridge to non-Anglicans, shifting control of elementary education from the Church to the state by the 1870 Education Act, removing some of the historic disabilities of Nonconformists, and disestablishing the Irish Church.

A politically weakened Church Establishment found itself confronted by a newly confident and socially respectable kind of freethinker. Hitherto free thought had been easy to dismiss because of the suspicion that its proponents were not-quite-gentlemen involved with seditious working-class movements: the bogeyman figure of Thomas Paine (1737–1809) could always be invoked to show the association between atheism and republicanism. But the new freethinkers were not republicans but respectable scientists and men of letters, and they did not call themselves atheists but 'agnostics'. The change of name was crucial. This is T.H. Huxley's account of how he came by it:

> When I reached intellectual maturity and began to ask
> myself whether I was an atheist, a theist, or a pantheist,
> a materialist or an idealist, a Christian or a freethinker, I
> found that the more I learned and reflected the less ready
> was the answer, until at last I came to the conclusion that
> I had neither art nor part with any of these denominations
> except the last. The one thing in which most of these good
> people were agreed was the one thing in which I differed
> from them. They were quite sure that they had attained a
> certain 'gnosis' – had, more or less successfully, solved the
> problem of existence; while I was quite sure that I had not,
> and had a pretty strong conviction that the problem was
> insolvable. And with Hume and Kant on my side, I could
> not think myself presumptuous in holding fast by that
> opinion.[73]

Unlike atheism, agnosticism claims only not to know, and in this aligns itself with the tradition of British sceptical empiricism associated with Hume. This was a more respectable ancestry than Tom Paine or Voltaire. Moreover, it fitted the conditions of the new universe revealed by evolutionary biology – where the descent of mankind from the higher primates made it harder to discern a Divine parentage – and in turn derived authority from the gathering prestige of the new science. Many of Huxley's fellow-scientists were agnostics: it was almost a badge of belonging to a new intellectual élite.

The word was coined at a meeting of the Metaphysical Society in 1869, which is itself significant. The Metaphysical Society had been founded by James Knowles (1831–1903) in 1869, in an attempt to bring together the intellectual heavyweights of the day to discuss philosophical and theological issues. The membership, which was to be limited to fifty, included Tennyson, Gladstone, Huxley, Cardinal Manning, Bagehot, Froude, Frederic Harrison, Mark Pattison, John Tyndall the physicist, Leslie Stephen, Ruskin, and many other famous names. The fact that these leading clergymen, scientists, and men of letters (no women – sexual equality, like republicanism, was off the agenda) were prepared to meet once a month to discuss papers on topics like 'The Verification of Beliefs' (Henry Sidgwick, 1870) and 'The Soul before and after Death' (Cardinal Manning, 1877), is a sign that religious belief was now being called to account by the intellectual establishment. Many of these papers were published in such progressive magazines as *The Contemporary Review* and The *Nineteenth Century*, founded by Knowles in 1877. Suddenly theism was on the defensive and agnostic rebellion in the air. The note sounded in the famous line of Swinburne's 'Hymn to Proserpine' (1867) – 'Thou hast conquered, O pale Galilean, the world has grown grey from thy breath' – is defiant where Arnold and Tennyson had been plangent. In the 1870s there is a spate of books challenging the moral authority of the Christian world-view, of which Winwoode Reade's *The Martyrdom of Man* (1872), Leslie Stephen's *Essays on Freethinking and Plainspeaking* (1873), and Mill's *Three Essays on Religion* (1874) are only the better known. This is the context in which Hardy's agnostic vision was shaped, and the major novels he published in this decade – *Far from the Madding Crowd* (1874) and *The Return of the Native* (1878) – show the start of his movement away from Victorian pastoralism to the unconsoling natural universe of Darwin and Huxley.

Victorian agnosticism based itself on the assertion that, since nothing verifiable can be known about God, the only honest position was one of 'not-knowing', reverent or otherwise. The agnostics did not dispute other people's right to hold Christian beliefs, as an atheist might; they merely disputed the precision with which Christians purported to hold their definitions of deity and the rigour with which they enforced them as dogma – those who, as Leslie Stephen (1832–1904) memorably put it, 'defined the nature of God Almighty with an accuracy from which modest naturalists would shrink in describing the genesis of a black-beetle'.[74] But Stephen himself could be no less confident or dogmatic in asserting the empirical bases of his own position. In 1898 he wrote to William James after reviewing James's *The Will to Believe*: 'You infer that a man has a right to hold either the negative or the positive creed. My reply is that he has a right to hold *neither*. By Agnostic I do not mean a negative creed but an absence of all opinion; and that I take to be the only rational frame of mind.'[75] But, as James came to see, such rationalism was needlessly and ultimately self-destructively prescriptive, since it narrowed the basis of allowable experience as dogmatically as the religious had done. What was needed was a richer empiricism which recognised that religious experience could have its own validity. 'The only appeal is to experience,' Stephen had written, 'and to appeal to experience is to admit the fundamental dogma of Agnosticism.'[76] James's great 'Study in Human Nature', *The Varieties of Religious Experience* (1902), is, among many other things, a refutation of that statement.

Stephen was deficient in the imaginative sympathy necessary to understand the heights and depths of religious experience, or its poetry: he was too rational, as Arnold was too moral. T.H. Huxley was different; he had a genuinely religious nature which was never entirely reconciled to the scientific materialism with which he has become identified. He is an example of the agnostic as stoic and scientist, facing an indifferent universe with stoical courage and drawing comfort from science, not from science as vulgar 'progress' but as enduring, impersonal law. This agnostic faith is movingly expressed in the famous letter Huxley wrote to Kingsley after the death of his young son. At the burial he had been 'shocked' to hear the clergyman paraphrase St Paul's words: 'If the dead rise not again, let us eat and drink, for to-morrow we die.' Huxley repudiated this simple scheme of reward hereafter as the only basis of virtuous behaviour here. It was not the hope of immortality that had brought him 'redemption' from the sins of his youth, but something else:

> *Sartor Resartus* led me to know that a deep sense of religion
> was compatible with the entire absence of theology.
> Secondly, science and her methods gave me a resting
> place independent of authority and tradition. Thirdly, love
> opened up to me a view of the sanctity of human nature
> and impressed me with a deep sense of responsibility.[77]

There were many others at the end of the century who had come to feel also that a 'deep sense of religion' might be compatible with an absence of theology. Some, like William Hale White (1831–1913), found a refuge from religious doubt and narrowness in the pantheism of Wordsworth: 'God was brought down from that heaven of the books, and dwelt on the downs in the far-away distances, and in every cloud-shadow which wandered across the valley.'[78] Others attempted the harder task of re-establishing religious practice on humanistic grounds independent of Christianity. They were always a tiny minority, and

their efforts reveal how difficult it is to escape from the emotional and
psychological habits of a religious tradition that has been intellectually
rejected. Still, because they did seek some expression of the religious
instinct, and were not prepared to settle for the complacent negativities
of Leslie Stephen's kind of agnosticism, their story is an interesting
footnote in the spiritual history of the Victorians.

At the time the 'Religion of Humanity' seemed to be more than a
footnote: it was to be the religion of the future. Developed by the
French philosopher and sociologist Auguste Comte (1798–1857) as part
of his theory of Positivism (discussed in Chapter 4 below), it proposed
the replacement of God with Humanity as an object of worship. The
calendar was to be redrawn in thirteen lunar months, each named after
benefactors of humanity from Moses to Bichat (but excluding Christ),
and each day was to have its humanist 'saint'. Woman, as Madonna,
was to occupy a central place in worship, there was to be a secular
'priesthood' to serve the faith, and permitted forms of worship were
laid down in a *Catechism* – not for nothing was Comte accused of
promoting 'Catholicism without the Christianity'. Redemption was to
be found not in the reward of immortality but in knowing that one had
played a part, however small, in the upward progress of Humanity. In
the words of George Eliot's 'hymn', a favourite at positivist meetings
and church services:

> O may I join the choir invisible
> Of those immortal dead who live again
> In minds made better by their presence . . .

There is an echo here of the closing words of *Middlemarch*: 'the
growing good of the world is partly dependent on unhistoric acts;
and that things are not so ill with you and me as they might have
been, is half owing to the number who lived faithfully a hidden life,
and rest in unvisited tombs'.

Seen in the wider context of Comte's philosophy of positivism, the
Religion of Humanity played a significant part in shaping or confirming
the views of some of the chief humanists of the period, including
George Eliot and (with reservations) John Stuart Mill. But it translated
uncomfortably into religious practice. The main problems seem to
have been the liturgy, what and how much of it to have, and the
place of music in the 'service'. Newton Hall, home of the London
Positivist Society, formed a choir in 1883 and George Eliot's 'The
Choir Invisible' was set to music for it. Vernon Lushington composed
positivist hymns and Ethel Harrison, wife of Frederic, gathered these
and selections from the poets into an anthology, *The Service of Man*
(1890). Harrison (1831–1923) conducted marriage and funeral services,

drawing on Comte's *Catechism* and *The Book of Common Prayer*, but he later came to feel that the attempt to devise a formal liturgy had been premature and was the principal reason why the new religion had failed to catch on: 'the silly so-called services' had 'disgust[ed] educated and thoughtful men from taking Positivism seriously and [made] them (eg Times) treat us as a serio-comic sect, mumbling Catholic rites in a sordid hole.'[79]

A similar problem faced the Ethical Societies later in the century when they tried to translate their beliefs into ritual. Ethics, morality without religion, was a topical subject in the 1880s and 1890s, and Ethical Societies grew up, mostly in London, to provide communities of the like-minded where rationalists and philosophical Idealists could meet to hear lay sermons and debate moral and religious issues. In 1909 an Ethical Church was established in Bayswater. It had a choir – literally 'invisible' because it was hidden from the congregation in the upper of two semi-circular galleries – accompanying a 'service' consisting of anthems and hymns; these 'ethical hymns' were adaptations of traditional hymns and lyrics from the poets, set to music by a number of composers going back to Bach and Palestrina. There were two 'lessons', a period for prayer and meditation, and a discourse, followed by an anthem, a hymn, and some 'Dismissory Sentences' from William Blake. This took place in a building with a pulpit flanked by statues of the Buddha and Christ, and stained glass windows showing the figures of Elizabeth Fry, George Bernard Shaw, and St Joan. In 1923 a white marble column was placed in front of the lectern, inscribed with the words 'An Altar to the Ideal, the True, the Beautiful and the Good'. It comes as something of a surprise to learn that this Ethical Church survived until 1953.[80]

The Ethical Church and the Positivist Chapel are historical curiosities and it is easy to see what is wrong with them: the parasitical relation to traditional forms of worship, the overly optimistic faith in human nature and social progress, the making saints of modern individuals whose humanist sanctity would not survive the reading of a modern biography (better St Francis any day, one tends to feel, than George Bernard Shaw). Still, in their 'serio-comic' way these curious worshippers at a secular shrine had grasped an important truth about the decline of religion which the more respectable agnostics overlooked. One of the great historic functions of Christianity (or any other world religion) is to perform the rites of passage at the crucial stages of the individual's life – birth and marriage and death – and in doing so to dignify and integrate their passage through the world. A hundred years later modern so-called secular society is no nearer finding a replacement for that function, is indeed largely dependent still on the traditional forms, as the 'Weddings' page of any local newspaper abundantly demonstrates. The impulse to mock the Ethical hymn and the Positivist wedding-service should perhaps be tempered by recognition of this fact.

Nietzsche, to return in conclusion to one of Christianity's great accusers, spoke famously of the 'death of God' in the nineteenth century. A more accurate if less stirringly dramatic phrase might be the 'historicisation of God'. The combined effect of the successive waves of new thought and discovery – in historical scholarship, biblical criticism, geology, evolutionary theory, anthropology – was to dig out the foundations of the Judaeo-Christian religion and reveal it as a historical institution explicable by the same forces that were at work in other cultures shaping different faiths. The claim of Christianity to a special historical revelation took a battering from which it has never quite recovered. It has been customary to hear a dying fall in all this, the 'melancholy, long, withdrawing roar' of Arnold's 'Sea of Faith', but there were gains too. Anglican clergymen were much less powerful in 1900 than they were in 1800, but (perhaps for that reason) they were on the whole better informed, less arrogant, and more conscientious than in 1800; and they were more aware of the need for social mission. Nonconformists were in the throes of adjusting from the Atonement to the Incarnation, impelled by the increasing unacceptablity of the doctrine of substitutionary atonement to the modern conscience. If people were more aware of the relative character of individual religions, some had their beliefs strengthened by the knowledge of the richness and diversity of religious experience. Such knowledge, in turn, provided a better answer to science and agnosticism than dogma: nescience did not have the last word, for, as William James demonstrated, there *was* something known, and that was the variety of religious experience. This is arguably a healthier starting-point than the creeds and dogmas over which the orthodox fought such bitter and unsuccessful rearguard actions throughout the nineteenth century. In 1900 the Christian Church was no longer a great cathedral dominating the landscape and resenting any interference with its historic rights, but a City Church taking its place and its chance with other city buildings, and perhaps fulfilling its mission the more authentically as a consequence.

Notes

1. T.H.S. Escott, *Social Transformations of the Victorian Age* (1897), ch. 2.

2. *The Making of Victorian England* (1962), p. 162.

3. F.W. Nietzsche, *The Gay Science*, in *The Portable Nietzsche*, edited by Walter Kaufmann (New York, 1954), p. 95.

4. F.W. Nietzsche, *The Twilight of the Idols*, in *The Portable Nietzsche*, pp. 515–16.

5. The phrase 'disappearance of God' comes from J. Hillis Miller's book of that title, *The Disappearance of God: Five Nineteenth Century Writers* (Cambridge, Mass., 1963).

6. Census figures are from Owen Chadwick, *The Victorian Church*, I (1966), 365–6.

7. *The Times*, 22 June 1853, p. 4.

8. Quoted in A.D. Gilbert, *Religion and Society in Victorian Britain: Church, Chapel and Social Change, 1740–1914* (1976), p. 132.

9. *Ibid.*, pp. 28–9, 38–9.

10. Figures from Gerald Parsons (ed.), *Religion in Victorian Britain* (4 vols, Manchester, 1988), I, p. 18.

11. *The Idea of the Victorian Church* (Montreal, 1968), p. 53.

12. Quoted in Alan Bell, *Sydney Smith* (Oxford, 1980), p. 29.

13. 'Persecuting Bishops', *Works* (second edition, 1840), II, p. 5.

14. Gilbert, *Religion and Society*, pp. 130–1.

15. *Ibid.*, pp. 38–9.

16. *Culture and Anarchy*, ch. 1; see *The Complete Prose Works of Matthew Arnold*, edited by R.H. Super (11 vols, Michigan, 1960–77), V, p. 103.

17. *The Contemporary Review* (1870); quoted in *Victorian Nonconformity*, edited by J. Briggs and I. Sellers (1973), p. 107.

18. See Gilbert, *Religion and Society*, p. 46.

19. *The Victorian Church*, I (1966), p. 5.

20. *Evangelicalism in Modern Britain* (1989), pp. 50–60.

21. John Charles Ryle, 'The Cross'; quoted in G.P. Landow, *Victorian Types, Victorian Shadows* (1980), p. 17.

22. *Life of Frances Power Cobbe, as Told by Herself* (1904), pp. 81–5.

23. *Apologia Pro Vita Sua*, edited by D.J. DeLaura (new York, 1968), p. 17.

24. *The Letters and Diaries of John Henry Newman*, edited by C.S. Dessain and others, 31 vols (Oxford and London, 1961–84), XX, p. 236.

25. *Praeterita*, in *Works*, edited by E.T. Cook and A. Wedderburn (39 vols, 1903–12), XXXV, pp. 44, 21.

26. Quoted in Ian Bradley, *The Call to Seriousness* (1976), p. 156.

27. Bebbington, *Evangelicalism in Modern Britain* (1989), p. 106.

28. Mark Pattison, *Memoirs* (1885), p. 208; David Newsome, *The Parting of Friends* (1966), p. 14.

29. The encomium to Oxford is in the Preface to Arnold's first series of *Essays*

in *Criticism* (1865), the attack on provincialism in the essay in that volume on 'The Literary Influence of Academies'.

30. *Memoirs*, p. 257.

31. *Letters and Diaries*, IV, p. 83.

32. *Ibid.*, p. 32.

33. *Ibid.*, p. 27.

34. *Ibid.*, p. 210.

35. *Letters and Diaries*, V, p. 210.

36. For the homo-erotic ambience of Tractarianism see D. Hilliard, 'Un-English and unmanly: Anglo-Catholicism and homosexuality', *Victorian Studies*, 25 (1982), 181–210.

37. Quoted in Alec Vidler, *The Church at an Age of Revolution* (Harmondsworth, 1971), p. 53.

38. *Letters and Diaries*, V, 46.

39. Quoted in Hesketh Pearson, *The Smith of Smiths* (1934), p. 234.

40. *Apologia*, p. 28.

41. Tennyson, 'The Passing of Arthur', ll, 29, 92.

42. *Apologia*, p. 97.

43. *Ibid.*, p. 186.

44. *Fifteen sermons Preached before the University of Oxford* (1872), p. 33.

45. *Ibid.*, p. 257.

46. *Ibid.*, pp. 258–9, 262, 266.

47. *Apologia*, p. 29.

48. *Letters and Diaries*, XXI, 146.

49. *A Grammar of Assent*, edited by I.T. Ker (Oxford, 1985), pp. 213–14.

50. *Letters and Diaries*, XX, 465.

51. *Sermons*, p. 27.

52. *An Essay on the Development of Christian Doctrine*, edited by J.M. Cameron (Harmondsworth, 1974), p. 100.

53. *Memoirs*, p. 236.

54. Lest this seem a glib point, see *The Oxford Diaries of Arthur Hugh Clough*, edited by A. Kenny (Oxford, 1990), pp. lxi–lxii, and R.B. Martin, *Gerard Manley Hopkins: A Very Private Life* (1991), pp. 100–2.

55. *An Autobiography* (2 vols, 1904), I, 152.

56. *In Memoriam*, lyric xcvi.

57. *Carlyle's Life in London* (2 vols, 1884), I, p. 291.

58. See Susan Budd, *Varieties of Unbelief: Atheists and Agnostics in English Society, 1850–1950* (1977), p. 42.

59. Charles Darwin and T.H. Huxley, *Autobiographies*, edited by G. de Beer (1974), p. 50.

60. J.R. Moore, 'Why Darwin "gave up Christianity"', in *History, Humanity and Evolution*, edited by J.R. Moore (Cambridge, 1989), pp. 195–229; this reference pp. 218–20.

61. *The Life of Frances Power Cobbe* (1904), p. 86.

62. *My Apprenticeship* (1926), pp. 77, 79.

63. *Varieties of Unbelief* (1977), p. 123.

64. See *Dissent and Dogma* in *Complete Prose Works*, edited by R.H. Super (11 vols, Michigan, 1960–77), VI, p. 143.

65. As does, for example, R.J. Helmstadter in 'The Nonconformist Conscience', in *Religion in Victorian Britain*, edited by Gerald Parsons (1988), VI, pp. 61–95.

66. Quoted in Parsons (ed.), *Religion in Victorian Britain*, II, p. 195.

67. *Essays and Reviews* (1860), p. 51.

68. *Ibid.*, pp. 80, 81.

69. *Ibid.*, p. 160.

70. *Ibid.*, p. 177.

71. *Dissent and Dogma*, in *Complete Prose Works*, VI, pp. 453–4.

72. *Ibid.*, pp. 146, 150, 151.

73. T.H. Huxley, *Essays upon Some Controverted Questions* (1892), pp. 354–5.

74. *An Agnostic's Apology and other Essays* (1893; 1931 edition), p. 4.

75. Noel Annan, *Leslie Stephen, the Godless Victorian* (1984), p. 250.

76. *Agnostic's Apology*, p. 25.

77. L. Huxley, *Life and Letters of T.H. Huxley* (2 vols. 1900), I, p. 220.

78. *The Autobiography of Mark Rutherford* (11th edition, n.d.), p. 19.

79. Quoted by T.R. Wright in his *The Religion of Humanity* (Cambridge, 1986), p. 99, to whose excellent account of the movement I am indebted.

80. See I.D. MacKillop, *The British Ethical Societies* (Cambridge, 1986), pp. 121–2.

Chapter 3
Science: Re-Imagining the Universe

The nineteenth century saw the culmination and completion of the revolution in scientific thought which began with Copernicus and the destruction of the medieval earth-centred universe by Galileo's telescope in the seventeenth century. The key sciences of our period – astronomy and geology in the first half, evolutionary biology in the second – had the effect of immeasurably deepening contemporary understanding of the universe and mankind's place within it, but did so in terms that were still congruent with the mechanical philosophy of the seventeenth century, with Newton's gravitational universe and the empirical, 'commonsense' methodology associated with the name of Sir Francis Bacon. The joker in the pack of science, quantum physics, did not declare itself until the twentieth century, when particle physics started to undermine the stabilities of Victorian science. While they lasted, however, these stabilities gave the idea of science a confidence and a cultural authority which it had not had before and was not to enjoy in quite the same way again.

The authority which the idea of science enjoyed by the end of the century was hard-earned, however, and the story of its emergence is as much a part of the total picture as the development of individual sciences. There are many sides to the growth of the idea of science in the period. At the amateur level, science in the form of natural history was something of a national hobby among the middle classes. At the professional level, it was a cause to be fought for, through the modernising of the ancient universities, the struggle to establish science in education and win public finance for research, the drive towards the dignity of professional status. In the new industrial cities science, in the shape of the campaign for public health, was at the forefront of social reform. But it was over evolution that science made its most dramatic challenge to the existing intellectual order. With the growing acceptance of an evolutionary account of human origins after 1860, science became an increasingly confident and imperial ideology, laying claims to fields of human behaviour previously thought closed to it. From the structure of society to the workings of the subconscious mind and the nature of religious experience itself, 'science' was widely seen as the magic key that opened every door.

Victorian science: the social and institutional framework

Science as a cause was closely identified with the needs and ambitions of the new nation. When the British Association for the Advancement of Science (BAAS) was formed in 1831 its first meeting was held in York, not London, which was at least a symbolic gesture of solidarity with the activities of the many provincial Literary and Philosophical Societies of the time. Their dates of founding show how closely the cultivation of natural philosophy (as science was then called) was related to the Industrial Revolution in Britain: Manchester (1781), Derby (1783), Newcastle upon Tyne (1793), Birmingham (1800), Glasgow (1802), Liverpool (1812), Leeds (1818), Cork (1819), York (1822), Sheffield (1822). It is, as the historians of the BAAS say, virtually a roll-call of the major areas of the Industrial Revolution: 'Through the societies of the parvenu industrial towns, the early mill owners, merchants, capitalists, and engineers sought an intellectual rationalization and articulation of their experience.'[1] The BAAS was founded as a means of promoting the cause of scientific research and its application, and of raising public awareness of current scientific work, at a time when the metropolitan Royal Society was felt to be too aristocratic and too remote. Enlisting the commitment of provincial societies was an essential part of the enterprise, even if the management remained in the hands of the liberal-Anglican clergy and their leaders in the Cambridge, Edinburgh and Dublin professoriate. So their meetings were peripatetic: in the decade after York they went to, successively, Oxford, Cambridge, Edinburgh, Dublin, Bristol, Liverpool, Newcastle, Birmingham, and Glasgow; then Plymouth, Manchester, and Cork, before returning to York in 1844. It was at the 1860 BAAS meeting in Oxford that the famous encounter between T.H. Huxley and Bishop Wilberforce over *The Origin of Species* took place.

The provincial societies were – or had been – capable of real distinction in science. John Dalton (1766–1844) at Manchester was a scientist of international stature and importance, the discoverer of atomic weight. The Birmingham Lunar Society, founded in the mid-eighteenth century, numbered among its members James Watt (1736–1819), the inventor of the condensing steam engine, and his business partner Matthew

Boulton (1728–1809); Joseph Priestley (1733–1804), the chemist and theologian; Erasmus Darwin (1731–1802), grandfather of Charles and himself the author of a theory of evolution in verse; and Josiah Wedgwood (1730–95), the potter and canal builder. As their dates indicate, these were men of the eighteenth century, of an age of scientific universalism which was to give way to the inevitable specialisation of the nineteenth, and so cannot be considered typical figures of 1830. In two respects, however, their careers illustrate enduring features of provincial science. One is the close relation between science, technology, and 'manufactures'. They worked in close alliance with local industrialists (Watt and Boulton were themselves factory-owners) in the hope that their researches would have a practical application, and in many ways their influence can be seen in that monument to applied science, the Great Exhibition of 1851. The other was the link between provincial science and religious dissent in its various forms. Dalton was a Quaker, Priestley a Unitarian, Erasmus Darwin a deist. The provincial men of science were more likely to have been educated at a Scottish university or scientific institute, such as the Andersonian in Glasgow, or at one of the old Dissenting academies than at Anglican Oxbridge. The Dissenting tradition can also be seen in their faith in and commitment to the public lecture as a means of spreading scientific education more widely.

As bastions of the Anglican hegemony, Oxford and Cambridge were very resistant to the introduction of the 'progressive sciences'. Classics, mathematics, and at Cambridge theoretical (i.e. Newtonian) physics were felt to be sufficient for training the minds of Christian gentlemen. It was not until mid-century that an Honours School in Natural Sciences was set up at Oxford (1850) and a Natural Sciences Tripos at Cambridge (1851), and these were at first subjects to be studied only after a grounding in the more traditional curriculum. Degrees were, of course, confined to members of the Established Church. But it would be misleading to see the history of nineteenth-century science simply in terms of a struggle to shake off the dead hand of Anglicanism; this ignores the part played by reforming dons at Oxbridge as well as the contribution made by Anglican clergy (they were often the same people) in the early years of the BAAS. They shared the widespread view that what needed reform was the national educational system in England, to introduce science to the secondary school and to provide incentives for its study at a higher level in the form of marketable diplomas for students and secure careers for their teachers. Here the strongly provincial bias of practical science, with its empiricism and bias to the needs of industry, combined with the individualism and distrust of state control which were the historic legacy of nonconformity, worked against the setting up of national institutions for teaching and research of the kind to be found in such competitor nations as Germany. The old Mechanics' Institutes had tried to provide lectures and libraries for the working classes, but by 1830 these were moribund. It was only slowly, and under the influence of such powerful reformers as Prince Albert, that the scientific institutes were established and the structure of examinations and diplomas, necessary to provide incentives for study, put in place. Under his presidency the Royal Society of Arts conceived the plan that led to the Great Exhibition of 1851 and, in the enhanced publicity which this event gave to science and technology, initiated debates about the place of science in society. With his support the Royal College of Chemistry was founded in 1845, and ten years later the RSA set up exams for the Mechanics' Institutes, leading to diplomas which, it was hoped, would influence employers. In 1851 Owens' College, Manchester, was founded as an institution of specifically scientific higher education; it later became Manchester University. Between 1830 and 1850 the following specialist societies were formed: BAAS (1831), Entomological Society (1833), Botanical Society (1836), Microscopical Society (1839), Pharmaceutical Society, Chemical Society (1841), Ethnological Society (1843), Institution of Mechanical Engineers (1847). These are small but significant signs of a centrifugal tendency in early Victorian science; specialist societies tend to produce specialist journals, specialist journals to carry the results of specialist research, specialist research to be comprehensible only to other specialists in the field, and so scientists end up talking only to each other.

This was not yet the position in 1850 or even 1860. Against the neglect of science teaching at institutional level has to be set the huge appetite among all classes of society for scientific popularisations and collections of interesting facts about the world of nature. The work of Mary Somerville (1780–1872) is a case in point. Her *On the Connexion of the Physical Sciences* (1834) has been described as presenting 'a comprehensive picture of the newest researches and ideas in the physical sciences, calling to the attention both of specialists and of general readers much recent scientific work hitherto little noticed but subsequently important.'[2] It went through eight revised editions by 1849. A little down the intellectual scale, but serious, informative, and well written, were books like Gideon Mantell's *The Wonders of Geology* (1838; six editions by 1848), a popularisation of the uniformitarian views of Charles Lyell's *Principles of Geology* (1830–33), which came with an evocative frontispiece of a print by John Martin showing three iguanodons fighting in a primeval landscape. The more ambitious might have gone on to read Lyell, the less ambitious would be content with the large monthly periodicals which contained lengthy reviews of contemporary scientific works which were virtually digests of their contents, often supplemented by generous quotation. For all those who could not afford either the books or the reviews there were the summaries of scientific developments in works of useful knowledge like Charles Knight's *Penny Cyclopaedia* (begun 1836), *Chambers's Edinburgh Journal* (1832), and *Chambers's Educational Course* (1835).

It is a sign of the peculiarly English, or perhaps British, tradition of informed amateurism in the sciences – a tradition of which Charles Darwin is the supreme if also the last example – that the word 'scientist' should have been so late in coming and so long in establishing itself. The credit for coining it is usually given to William Whewell in his *Philosophy of the Inductive Sciences* (1840). Before that there had been 'natural philosopher' and after remained 'man [or gentleman] of science': both implied a backing off from the exclusive commitment to the material and experimental which 'scientist' seemed to imply – one to an older view which saw nature in a framework of philosophical considerations, the other to the detachment of the 'gentleman'. Huxley, for example, violently repudiated the new word.[3] Besides, 'amateurism' accurately describes the kind of interest that people of all classes took in the natural world. They explored it, often as a family outing, to collect specimens of plants, insects, fossils, seaweeds, anemones, which were then taken home to be put in a tank or a cabinet, catalogued, and explored under the microscope. It was for these enthusiasts that Philip Gosse (1810–88), the father in Edmund Gosse's autobiographical classic, *Father and Son* (1907), wrote books with titles like *The Romance of Natural History* (1860) and *Evenings at the Microscope* (1859).

The great monument to this enthusiasm is the Natural History Museum in South Kensington (1881–86), a terra-cotta witness to the importance of the sciences which transformed the Victorian intellectual landscape. It is not only that revolutionary theories in geology and biology were here being propounded, but also that these theories found an amateur audience that was unusually well prepared to comprehend them. The person who could read Mantell's *Wonders of Geology* had no difficulty in understanding Darwin, nor in perceiving the cosmological implications of his theory. It was precisely the human inferences to be drawn from these sciences which made them interesting, exciting, but also, in Tennyson's word, 'terrible'. The Victorians were not slow to draw those inferences.

There are two documents which convey something of the awesomeness which contemporaries found in Tennyson's two 'terrible muses', astronomy and geology. One is Julia Margaret Cameron's photographic portrait of Sir John Herschel (1792–1871), the great astronomer. More than anyone else, it has been said, Herschel 'represented the early Victorian ideal of the scientist'.[4] In addition to astronomy he wrote on chemistry, the theory of light, and the methodology of science, where his *Preliminary Discourse on the Study of Natural Philosophy* (1830) had a great influence on Darwin and Darwin's generation; he also made translations from *The Iliad* and the poetry of Schiller. Mrs Cameron did not treat her sitter with quite the reverence he was accustomed to from his peers, making him wash his hair beforehand and fluff it out to give a suitably 'wild' effect; and yet the resulting portrait (see Plate 7) captures both the man's intellectual distinction and the price he may have paid in attaining it. The strong contrast of light and dark suggests a man both inspired and haunted by the depths of space he has seen into.

The other is a passage from Darwin's *The Voyage of the 'Beagle'* (1845), recording his response to the spectacle of the rivers flowing down from the high Andes hills:

> The rivers which flow in these valleys ought rather to
> be called mountain-torrents. Their inclination is very
> great, and their water the colour of mud. The roar which
> the Maypu made, as it rushed over the great rounded
> fragments, was like that of the sea. Amidst the din of the
> rushing waters, the noise from the stones, as they rattled
> over one another, was most distinctly audible even from a
> distance. This rattling noise, night and day, may be heard
> along the whole course of the torrent. The sound spoke
> eloquently to the geologist; the thousands and thousands
> of stones, which, striking against each other, made the one
> dull uniform sound, were all hurrying in one direction.
> It was like thinking on time, where the minute that now
> glides past is irrecoverable. So was it with these stones; the
> ocean is their eternity, and each note of that wild music told
> of one more step towards their destiny.
>
> It is not possible for the mind to comprehend, except
> by a slow process, any effect which is produced by a
> cause repeated so often, that the multiplier itself conveys
> an idea, not more definite than the savage implies when
> he points to the hairs of his head. As often as I have
> seen beds of mud, sand, and shingle, accumulated to the
> thickness of many thousand feet, I have felt inclined to
> exclaim that causes, such as the present rivers and the
> present beaches, could never have ground down and
> produced such masses. But, on the other hand, when
> listening to the rattling noise of these torrents, and calling
> to mind that whole races of animals have passed away
> from the face of the earth, and that during this whole
> period, night and day, these stones have gone rattling
> onwards in their course, I have thought to myself,

can any mountains, any continent, withstand such
waste?[5]

This remarkable passage captures something of the austere and desolate
sublimity of a universe transformed by contemporary geology, as
Tennyson does in lyric 35 of *In Memoriam* (1850):

The moanings of the homeless sea,
The sound of streams that swift or slow
Draw down Aeonian hills, and sow
The dust of continents to be. . . .

The similarity is not accidental, for both Darwin and Tennyson are
contemplating the natural world through eyes alerted to the temporal
immensity of its processes by reading Charles Lyell's *Principles of
Geology* (1830–33), a work which rejected cataclysmic explanations of
changes in the earth's surface in favour of the longer-running natural
forces of erosion and sedimentation. Darwin had taken Lyell's first
volume with him when he left England in 1831; he picked up the second
in Montevideo in 1832, and the third in Valparaiso in July 1834, just
before his first excursion into the Andes. Lyell's work literally followed
him round the world and formed his understanding of natural processes
even as he observed them.
     It is this sense of a mind coming to terms with a changing perception
of the universe which the passage above communicates. The first
paragraph keeps within the semi-anthropomorphic discourse of traditional natural description, in which stones 'speak', find their 'eternity' in
the ocean, have a 'destiny' which takes them there. Although what they
describe is almost immeasurable, these words belong to a teleological
(having a purpose or final cause) discourse in which natural processes
can be talked about in the terms that human beings apply to their
own sense of life-pattern. But in the second paragraph this vestigial
anthropomorphism is virtually rubbed out. The reference to the hairs
on the head of the savage would seem to humanise the 'multiplier' but
in fact it does the opposite, suggesting how ignorant and arbitrary are
our attempts to measure such geological change. Darwin registers a
half-protest against the likelihood that the erosion he is witnessing could
possibly be the cause of profound geological change (Lyell's view) only
to answer himself by 'calling to mind that whole races of animals have
passed away from the face of the earth' while it was going on. The
first paragraph ends with 'destiny', the second with 'waste'; the passage
moves from the intimation of purpose to a recognition of the appalling
blindness, the mechanical relentlessness, of erosion.

'It was like thinking on time.' What we have here is not simply an act of record and observation but also an act of imagination. Darwin rises to the occasion, as it were, tries to convey the kind of universe in which such processes operate and, by implication, its significance for our understanding of biological change. If 'whole races of animals have passed away from the face of the earth' while these stones have been rattling down, then a vast womb of time has opened up for the formation of species. Thinking on time led him to the theory of evolution by natural selection.

From geology to evolution

In the 1820s, according to the biographer of Sir Roderick Murchison, the country gentleman who became a famous geologist, 'Such was the state of geological science at the time that a great work could be done by a man with a quick eye, a good judgment, a clear notion of what had already been accomplished, and a stout pair of legs.'[6] Part of the excitement of geology as an amateur pursuit was the real possibility of contributing to the development of a young science, hence that familiar figure on the early Victorian landscape, the palaeontologist, with his thick boots (almost as necessary as the 'stout pair of legs') and sharp geologist's hammer. What he – and sometimes she, for geology was one of the few sciences in which women could and did participate – would be looking for was fossils, the mineralized remains of dead organisms preserved in the layers of stratified rock formations. These objects were a subversive presence in the naturalist's cabinet, since they told of a universe infinitely older than the Book of Genesis seemed to allow. The successive layering of sediment took the geologist back millions of years. The fact that the petrified creatures found on cliff faces were marine animals spoke of enormous upheavals in the earth's surface. Again, it is Tennyson who captures the shock and wonder of contemporary discovery:

> There rolls the deep where grew the tree.
> O earth, what changes hast thou seen!
> There where the long street roars, hath been
> The stillness of the central sea.

> (*In Memoriam*, 123)

They were remains, most of them, of now extinct species, in a universe where, it was taught, God would abandon nothing that He had made.

The fossil record was evidence against the single act of creation in Genesis and for a much older universe in which species had grown up and become extinct, in a gradual progression from simple to more complex life forms.

At a time when many of the leading scientists were clergymen, or evangelical laymen like Hugh Miller, much energy in popular scientific writing went into attempts to reconcile the evidence of the rocks with what was then called the 'Mosaic Cosmogony', the account of the origin of the world in Genesis, which is the first book of Moses. The traditionally orthodox view was that propounded by Bishop James Usher of Armagh in the seventeenth century, that God had created the world in six days in 4004 BC. Few scientists believed that in 1830. The problem was rather how to accommodate the millions of years evidenced by the fossil record without destroying the authority of the Bible as Revealed Truth. Here the orthodox found what seemed to be a solution in the so-called 'catastrophist' theories of the great French anatomist, Baron Cuvier (1769–1832). In his *Essay on the Theory of the Earth* (1812) he proposed that the present state of the earth's surface was the result of a series of global cataclysms. The earth had been washed clean of species in a series of inundations, of which Noah's flood was the last, and repopulated by fresh creations or the migrations of such species as had survived. After each catastrophe there had been an advance in the complexity of organisms, leading up to the (relatively recent) creation of mankind.

Catastrophism saved the Mosaic account from the perils of literal interpretation, since these successive creations could be seen – with a certain manipulation of the written account – to precede the Six Days of Creation; alternatively, the Six Days could be seen to correspond to different phases of geological change. The theory also served for a while to save God from the deistic imputation of being a remote First Cause, the Great Initiator, against the gathering weight of evidence from biology, geology, palaeontology, that some form of development of species has taken place. When Hugh Miller defended his brand of catastrophism in *The Testimony of the Rocks* (1857) his foe was the 'development hypothesis':

> We cannot link on a single recent shell to a single extinct one. *Up* to a certain point we find the recent shells exhibiting all their present specific peculiarities, and beyond that point they cease to appear. *Down* to a certain point the extinct shells also exhibit all *their* specific peculiarities, and then they disappear for ever. There are no intermediate species, – no connecting links, – no such connected series of specimens to be found as enable us to trace a trilobite

through all its metamorphoses from youth to age. All geologic history is full of the beginnings and the ends of species, – of their first and their last days; but it exhibits no genealogies of development.[7]

The catastrophists were not cranks or bigots but serious scientists addressing what were at the time serious scientific problems – as Miller does here when he points to the absence of connecting links in the fossil record (a ghost which continues to haunt orthodox Darwinism). Their theories accounted for the violent upheavals in the earth's crust, which seemed inexplicable in terms of presently observable natural forces. But what if these upheavals – the sea-bed, for example, cresting in mountain ranges – could be explained in naturalistic terms? This was the case argued by Charles Lyell in his *Principles of Geology* (1830–33), a book which carried the conveniently explanatory subtitle: 'Being an Attempt to Explain the Former Changes of the Earth's Surface, by Reference to Causes now in Operation.' Lyell drew upon and developed the profound insight into geological processes advanced by the Scottish Enlightenment geologist James Hutton in his *Theory of the Earth* (1795): that the forces of erosion carry mud and stones to the sea-bed, where pressure builds up on the igneous rocks, leading to expansion and uplift and the formation of new land, which in turn is subject to erosion. The universe becomes a kind of machine, where, in Hutton's famous words, 'we find no vestige of a beginning, – no prospect of an end'.[8] Lyell argued for the uniform operation of these forces through time, hence the name 'uniformitarian' to describe his school. This is the view taken by Darwin in the passage discussed above.

There was a growing acceptance of uniformitarianism from the 1830s onwards and the corresponding decline of catastrophism helped both to shape the time-consciousness of the period and to weaken the prestige of the clergyman–scientist. But intellectual history should not belong only to the victors, and in the differences between the two schools there is an instructive historical contrast. Catastrophism had something in common with Romanticism – a sense of Apocalypse, of imminent revolutionary transformation. Its God might be terrifying and unpredictable, but He was continually in his Creation, and mankind was at the heart of it. There was a sequence to creation, a beginning and therefore an end: the Book of Genesis and the Book of Revelation were held together. Uniformitarianism offered a cyclical, self-renewing universe, accommodating but not demanding God as an explanation. The Great Interferer gives way to the Great Initiator. The difference is that between the violence and energy of John Martin's great painting *The Deluge* (1826) and the melancholy of Dyce's *Pegwell Bay*. In Martin's painting (see Plate 8) a terrified remnant crowd to a mountain-top to escape engulfment by the flood; in Dyce's (see Plate 3) the human figures wander on a desolate foreshore beneath the rocks that tell them of their cosmic insignificance. Here is one root of the melancholy which separates Victorian from Romantic culture.

Catastrophists and uniformitarians might dispute the age of the earth and the method of its formation, but the scientific establishment of the time – that is, the ruling Anglican professoriate in Oxbridge and London – were agreed on the fixity of species: that species were fixed, the product of individual acts of Divine Creation. To lose that certainty, to entertain the possibility of the mutability or transmutation of species (the idea that species might naturally adapt into other species without supernatural intervention), opened the door to seeing mankind in naturalistic terms as the inheritor of the animals rather than the angels. 'Evolution' in this sense was to be the import of *The Origin of Species*, but before the 1850s was chiefly associated with the work of the French naturalist Jean-Baptiste Lamarck (1744–1829). Lamarck was a 'transformist': he believed in the tendency of living organisms to develop into more complex forms through a process which is often treated as his discovery but in fact goes back to antiquity, the inheritance of acquired characteristics. Nature was purposive; its innermost processes encouraged the peaceful evolution of the higher animals from the lower, and rewarded individual success in adaptation with the passing on of desirable qualities to offspring.

Lamarck's ideas were very influential among the scientists, medical men, and intellectuals of the new nation in the 1820s and 1830s. As the first biologist to place mankind systematically within a natural rather than supernatural setting, he was an ally in their quarrel with the creationism of the Anglican–Oxbridge establishment. His view of nature as innately progressive gave intellectual weight to their campaigns for social and institutional reform, while the notion of the inheritance of acquired characteristics seemed to show that there was authority in nature for the efforts made by individuals and new social groups to better themselves.[9] It was a theory of evolution congenial to an individualistic, progressive view of human development, in contrast to Darwin's darker view of evolution by natural selection. And even when Darwin's theory seemed to have triumphed after 1860, it is arguable that Lamarck lived on in the way the bleaker implications of natural selection were overlooked in a progressionistic interpretation of the theory – for which, as we shall see, Darwin's own discourse gave some sanction.

The first British attempt to make explicit the link between geology and evolutionary biology which was implicit in Lyell's *Principles of Geology*, but which he was too careful to make in the early editions, came from a man outside the scientific establishment. Robert Chambers

(1802–71) was a self-made man, a successful Edinburgh bookseller and publisher with a keen amateur interest in geology. His knowledge of science was of that informed but essentially secondary kind to be found in the useful knowledge periodicals, such as *Chambers's Edinburgh Journal*, which had made his and his brother's fortune. Perhaps for this very reason, he felt able to attempt the synthesis of existing knowledge which more cautious scientists eschewed. His *Vestiges of the Natural History of Creation* (1844) is a characteristic product of new nation science: conceived in a provincial centre by a man whose affiliation was with secularists like George Combe (apostle of phrenology, the 'science' of locating human qualities in areas of the brain) rather than the Established Church, its account of natural history is rational and developmental, in keeping with a progressive view of human society. Chambers thought he saw in all the different sciences the operation of two 'laws':

> It is most interesting to observe into how small a field the whole of the mysteries of nature thus ultimately resolve themselves. The inorganic has one final comprehensive law, GRAVITATION. The organic, the other great department of mundane things, rests in like manner on one law, and that is, – DEVELOPMENT.[10]

Vestiges was a bold attempt to offer a new and comprehensive cosmology, and it immediately attracted the hostility of the scientific specialists – all the more so because the book proved so popular with the general reader, going through four editions in the first six months. It says something about the intensity of religious feeling at this period that all the editions before Chambers's death were published anonymously; it was more than his business was worth to be associated with a work that could drive the Professor of Geology at Cambridge to write: 'If the book be true, the labours of sober induction are in vain; religion is a lie; human law is a mass of folly, and a base injustice; morality is moonshine; our labours for the black people of Africa mere works of madmen; and man and woman are only better beasts!'[11] This often quoted response – made, it should be said, in a private letter – shows how intense contemporary resistance could be to the suggestion that mankind had evolved from the 'lower' animals.

The *Vestiges of Creation* is impressive in its scope and ambition but vulnerable in its detail. It begins with astronomy and the origins of the universe in the cooling of 'heated gaseous bodies' (the 'nebular' theory even then being discredited); moves on to geology and palaeontology, making the crucial link with biological development; and takes the story on through anthropology to the contested area of natural theology. In place of the notion of Special Creation, with God active in the formation of new species, Chambers discerns a 'law of development' (p. 196) at work in the world of plants and animals, propelling it on to ever more complex forms of organisation. This was heresy in 1844, and Chambers left a broad front on which he could be attacked; critics who did not want to take on his central point about the transmutation of species could criticise the inadequacy of his accounts of the origins of life or the mechanism of evolutionary change, both of which were indeed inadequate. Yet the intellectual over-reaching which the professional reviewers attacked was probably, when combined with the simplicity of Chambers's two 'laws', the source of its appeal for a general readership. They could sense that they were being offered a whole view of the origins and development of life on earth; what Chambers claimed as 'the first attempt to connect the natural sciences into a history of creation' (p. 388) was at least vigorous and consistent and easily grasped. It might be wrong in many places, and objectionable in its conclusions, but it was a refreshing change from the hothouse atmosphere of the scriptural geologists; in reading the book they could accustom themselves to the deplored 'development hypothesis' and see the evidence Chambers had gathered for it in his important chapter on 'The Hypothesis of the Development of the Vegetable and Animal Kingdoms'. There they were faced with the question which, presumably, Sedgwick had found so shocking: *is* it 'degrading' to think 'that any of the lower animals have been concerned in any way with the origins of man'?

> These creatures are all of them part products of the Almighty Conception, as well as ourselves. . . . All of them have had assigned to them by their Great Father a part in the drama of the organic world, as well as ourselves. Why should they be held in such contempt? Let us regard them in a proper spirit, as parts of the grand plan, instead of contemplating them in the light of frivolous prejudices, and we shall be altogether at a loss to see how there should be any degradation in the idea of our race having been genealogically connected with them. (pp. 233–5)

To a modern reader there is something so obviously humane in such an attitude that it is difficult to feel much sympathy for those who attacked it at the time. But it did have two rather chilling implications for even a sympathetic contemporary reader. The first is that God is pushed much further in the direction of a vaguely deistic First Cause. He is referred to throughout the *Vestiges* as the 'Almighty Conception', the 'Great Father', the 'Eternal One', the 'Divine Author', and so on. Such a universe exercised no special care for the individual:

> It is clear . . . from the whole scope of the natural laws, that the individual, as far as the present sphere of being is concerned, is to the Author of Nature a consideration of inferior moment. Everywhere we see the arrangements for the species perfect; the individual is left, as it were, to take his chance amidst the *mêlée* of the various laws affecting him. If he be found inferiorly endowed, or ill befalls him, there was at least no partiality against him. The system has the fairness of a lottery, in which every one has the like chance of drawing the prize. (p. 377)

The second implication was that mankind might not be the end of the line, that other higher (or different) types might evolve. Putting mankind back into nature and into an evolutionary scale thus imperilled not just the immortality of the soul, which was the objection of the orthodox, but the sense of the dignity and uniqueness of the individual which was the legacy of Christianity even for those who were losing belief in its supernatural sanctions. It was Tennyson's willingness to confront such anxieties in *In Memoriam* which made that work the representative poem of the early Victorian period.

The *Vestiges* was an important work in its day, but its day (*c.* 1845–60) did not long survive the publication of *The Origin of Species* in 1859, which put the idea of 'development' on an altogether more scientific footing. Chambers's contribution, it is usually said, was to put a crude idea of evolution into circulation, draw the theological fire, and so pave the way for Darwin's more circumspect formulation. There is some truth in this, but Chambers's contribution deserves a more positive expression: the science of the *Vestiges* may have been faulty in many places, but the book in its entirety gave the non-specialist, open- and fair-minded reader a sense of the existential feel of the development hypothesis. Chambers took the stopper off the bottle and the genie was not to be coaxed back in again.

Darwin and Darwinism

Charles Darwin (1809–82) knew the agony of bereavement in his private life, but in his public career as a scientist he was a singularly fortunate man. At Cambridge, reading for a career in the Church he did not want, he was taken up by the Professor of Botany, John Henslow, who recommended him for the naturalist's post on 'The Beagle'. That ship's five-year circumnavigation of the globe took him to just those places, like the Galapagos islands, where the geographical divergence of species could be observed, as well as providing him with a training in scientific observation and record which no university at that time could have offered. The Wedgwood fortune which came to him through his mother and his wife meant that he could devote his whole life to research without having to become a clergyman or get involved in the teaching and politics of university science. He was luckiest of all in the character of Alfred Russel Wallace (1823–1913), who developed a theory of evolution by natural selection as a result of observations in the Malay archipelago, and had drafted a paper on the subject in 1858 which would, technically, have scooped Darwin if it had been published in the normal course of events. It was only his humility, in sending the paper to Darwin, and his generosity, in allowing Darwin's friends to present papers by both of them to the Linnean Society, which preserved the originality of *The Origin of Species*: a more ruthless man might have wanted to write it himself. Finally, Darwin was fortunate in his friends, both those who acted as midwives to his greatest book and those, like T.H. Huxley, his 'bulldog', who defended it so effectively after publication. It is almost as if a special providence was at work to ensure that *The Origin of Species* should have been conceived, published, and defended in the most propitious way possible – which is ironic, since the import of the work was to replace providence with chance in the design of the universe.

What was Darwin's – and Wallace's – achievement? In essence, it was to marry the long perspectives of the geological record with a convincing theory of species change. Without the uniformitarian universe opened up by Lyell's geology Darwin would not have been able to imagine the concept of natural selection, as he himself admitted.[12] It is only a hypothesis and so theoretically open to challenge, but most subsequent work in genetics and biology has provided overwhelming evidence in its support. Darwin was led to it by two events in his life, the visit to the Galapagos islands on the 'Beagle' voyage and his reading of Thomas Malthus's *Essay on the Principle of Population* (1798). Malthus argued that population tended to grow geometrically (2,4,8,16,32,64) whereas the food supply grew only arithmetically (2,4,6,8,10), so that population growth always outstripped the means of subsistence unless checked by famine, disease, or 'parental restraint' (a solution middle-class reformers liked to preach to the lower orders while continuing to breed their own large families). Darwin saw the operation of Malthus's 'laws' in the wasteful procreativeness of the natural world. Allowed to breed freely, each species if left alone would soon choke the earth; it is only the struggle for the means of existence that ensures any stability or balance:

> Hence, as more individuals are produced than can possibly survive, there must in every case be a struggle for existence, either one individual with another of the same species, or with the individuals of distinct species, or with the physical conditions of life. It is the doctrine of Malthus applied with manifold force to the whole animal and vegetable kingdoms; for in this case there can be no artificial increase of food, and no prudential restraint from marriage. Although some species may be now increasing, more or less rapidly, in numbers, all cannot do so, for the world would not hold them.[13]

This recognition inspires Darwin to one of his most eloquent passages:

> In looking at Nature, it is most necessary to keep the foregoing considerations always in mind – never to forget that every single organic being around us may be said to be striving to the utmost to increase in numbers; that each lives by a struggle at some period of its life; that heavy destruction inevitably falls either on the young or old, during each generation or at recurrent intervals. Lighten any check, mitigate the destruction ever so little, and the number of the species will almost instantaneously increase to any amount. The face of Nature may be compared to a yielding surface, with ten thousand sharp wedges packed close together and driven inwards by incessant blows, sometimes one wedge being struck, and then another with greater force. (p. 119)

There is still something shocking in this conception of 'Nature', with its imagery of 'blows' violently striking the 'face', its metaphor of life as struggle and battle, and its ruthless, unpitying economy. That contemporaries reared on the gentle, restorative Nature of Wordsworth should have been shocked is not surprising; nor when they were told that the survivors of this struggle were those who had succeeded in inheriting and passing on variations of structure which enabled them to adapt more successfully to their environment. Given the 'great and complex battle of life', Darwin asks,

can we doubt (remembering that many more individuals
are born than can possibly survive) that individuals having
any advantage, however slight, over others, would have
the best chance of surviving and of procreating their kind?
On the other hand, we may feel sure that any variation in
the least degree injurious would be rigidly destroyed. This
preservation of favourable variations and the rejection of
injurious variations, I call Natural Selection. (pp. 130–1)

If Malthus gave Darwin insight into the ruthless economy of nature,
then his visit to the Galapagos islands provided dramatic evidence of
species change and its relation to geography and environment. Over
millions of years these barren volcanic islands had been seeded and
populated by stray plants and animals from the South American
mainland which, by the time of Darwin's visit, had changed into unique
species: huge tortoises, marine lizards which looked like small dragons,
mocking-birds and finches unlike any on the mainland. Moreover, these
species differed from island to island. The whole ecology of the place
was an argument against the fixity of species. The reality of organic
life, Darwin came to see, was adaptation and development under the
pressure of the struggle for existence. Only later did he work out the
engine of this process, natural selection.

Natural selection rests on three propositions: that organisms vary,
that their offspring can inherit these variations, and that the variations
may operate to the benefit of individuals in a world where many
more organisms are born than can hope to survive and reproduce.
It is an explanation of the process of species adaptation and therefore,
prospectively, of species change. As Darwin points out in his mild
opening chapter, breeders of domestic animals and plants assume the
inheritance of variations also. But what of origins? Could this theory
really account for the vast and intricate complexity of existing life? At
this point The Origin of Species could not help trespassing on the area of
natural theology. Like many middle-class Anglicans of his generation
Darwin had read William Paley's Natural Theology (1802) at university,
and been greatly impressed by it. Paley's was the classic expression of
the 'Argument from Design', the proof of God's existence from the
purposeful design of the universe: come across a watch when crossing
a heath and you would have to infer the existence of a watchmaker;
consider the complexity of the human eye in comparison with a
telescope – its adaptability to light, power of focusing, the way it
is protected by the eye-lid and the bone-socket – and the conclusion
must be, Paley argued, a 'cure for atheism'.[14]

The passage in The Origin of Species where Darwin attempts to
account for the evolution of the human eye is one of the most

daring in the book, for he must have known that he was sawing through one of the main planks of the Paleyan argument. It begins with characteristic but deceptive intellectual modesty. To suppose that anything so complex as the eye could be formed by natural selection seems 'absurd in the highest possible degree' (p. 217). It is hard for the imagination to encompass the infinitude of variations required for the movement from a simple to a complex eye. Yet crustaceans show gradations from the simplest optic nerve coated with pigment to eyes of some complexity, and why should this process of adaptation not be extended to the higher animals? It seems to baffle the imagination, and Darwin confesses that he has 'felt the difficulty far too keenly to be surprised at any degree of hesitation in extending the principle of natural selection to such startling lengths', but 'his *reason ought to conquer his imagination*' (p. 219, my italics), because the process can only be understood in terms of millions of minute changes. Paley's eye/telescope analogy is then introduced to show that natural selection could produce an eye superior to the telescope given enough time:

> We must suppose each new state of the instrument to be multiplied by the million; and each to be preserved till a better be produced, and then the old ones to be destroyed. In living bodies, variation will cause the slight alterations, generation will multiply them almost infinitely, and natural selection will pick out with unerring skill each improvement. Let this process go on for millions and millions of years; and during each year on millions of individuals of many kinds; and may we not believe that a living optical instrument might thus be formed as superior to one of glass, as the works of the Creator are to those of man? (p. 219)

The reference to 'the Creator' may be an attempt to appease the reader shocked by the implications of this reworking of Paley's famous analogy, for the truth is that these 'millions on millions of years' do not require a 'Creator', at least as anything more than a remotely initiating First Cause. If the process of natural selection can be seen operating, inexorably and without interruption, from the profound depths of time, then God becomes redundant as an explanation of species change. Previous 'evolutionary' theories had allowed for God because they had had no convincing mechanism of change: Darwin provided that. Mankind is hardly mentioned in *The Origin of Species* but the implications were obvious and soon spelled out – by Huxley in *Man's Place in Nature* (1863), by Lyell in his *Antiquity of Man* (1863), and by Darwin himself in *The Descent of Man* (1871).

The significance of this theory for human life and destiny was chastening. The poet A.E. Housman described it in terms of disinheritance: 'man stands today', he said in a lecture of 1892, 'in the position of one who has been reared from his cradle as the child of a noble race and the heir to great possessions, and who finds at his coming of age that he has been deceived alike as to his origin and his expectations'.[15] Conrad, more strikingly, saw the Darwinian universe as a machine:

> There is a – let us say – a machine. It evolved itself (I am severely scientific) out of a chaos of scraps of iron and behold! – it knits. I am horrified at the horrible work and stand appalled. I feel it ought to embroider – but it goes on knitting. You come and say: 'this is all right; it's only a question of the right kind of oil. Let us use this – for instance – celestial oil and the machine shall embroider a most beautiful design in purple and gold.' Will it? Alas, no! You cannot by any special lubrication make embroidery with a knitting machine. And the most withering thought is that the infamous thing has made itself: made itself without thought, without conscience, without foresight, without eyes, without heart.[16]

Conrad shows a more acute understanding of the radical element in Darwin's theory than did most of Darwin's contemporaries. Evolution by natural selection was not a theory about progress but about the machinery (and here Darwinian biology meshes with industrialisation) driving the development of life from simple to complex forms; it worked through random variations and towards no predetermined end. In the Age of Progress something so directionless was troubling, and what most Victorians understood by 'evolution' was really a blend of Darwin and the more progressive doctrines of Herbert Spencer (1820–1903). Spencer, whose ideas will be discussed in the next chapter, used the phrase 'Theory of Evolution' in his 1852 article on 'The Development Hypothesis' – seven years before *The Origin of Species* and at a time when it had not fully emerged from its older, embryological meaning.[17] In 1857 he published an article with the title 'Progress: Its Law and Cause' in which he argued that 'it is settled beyond dispute that organic progress consists in a change from the homogeneous to the heterogeneous'.[18] Spencer was confident that biological development was inevitably a matter of 'progress'; like modern biologists, Darwin was more inclined to be neutral.

The influence of Darwin on Victorian intellectual and cultural life is a vast subject, and there is space here to pick out only a few strands. The first is how easily *The Origin of Species* was absorbed, compared to the violence that had greeted the *Vestiges* fifteen years earlier. The growing momentum of developmental thinking in the 1850s was such that Darwin's contemporaries were more ready to give him a fair hearing. Contrary to the popular myth that *The Origin of Species* sprang evolution upon an unsuspecting world, and then went on to triumph after Huxley's defeat of Wilberforce at the 1860 BAAS meeting in Oxford, Darwin's was only one of various contending theories of evolution at the time, and was never 'triumphant' before 1900; it had to wait for Mendel's genetics to provide the clinching evidence. This is not to say that it was not seen at the time as a profoundly original and important work, giving evolutionism both scientific muscle and intellectual respectability, and providing an accessibly impressive demonstration of how the mind of a scientist worked.

Here there is a certain significance in the popular myth, for a second aspect of Darwin's influence is the part he played in the mythologising of science and consequently the impetus *The Origin of Species* gave to the process of institutionalising science as a secular profession in the later nineteenth century. That process needed a Darwin – needed, that is, a patently disinterested man and great scientist, someone not embroiled in the politics of Oxbridge and the BAAS, to propose a thesis which related scientific method to profound questions about origins and destiny which the intelligent lay reader could understand. *The Origin of Species* might be challenged on scientific grounds, but no one doubted Darwin's integrity and good faith, and only the most blinkered reader could fail to appreciate the seriousness of its intellectual ambition. 'There is grandeur in this vision of life', as the book's final sentence begins. It is here, perhaps, that the deeper symbolic significance of the famous Oxford BAAS meeting lies: not in the popular icon of Huxley – St George slaying the dragon superstition – but in the bishop's failure to respond with answering seriousness to the 'grandeur' of Darwin's vision. There was the modest scientist too shy to appear; the crowded room dominated by the clergy who had come to shout for their bishop; the bishop's persiflage as to whether his opponent was descended from a monkey on his grandmother's or his grandfather's side; and then, in the reverent tones of the writer in *Macmillan's Magazine*:

> Mr Huxley slowly and deliberately arose. A slight tall
> figure, stern and pale, very quiet and very grave, he stood
> before us and spoke those tremendous words. . . . He
> was not ashamed to have a monkey for his ancestor; but
> he would be ashamed to be connected with a man who
> used great gifts to obscure the truth. No one doubted his

meaning, and the effect was tremendous. One lady fainted
and had to be carried out. . . .[19]

What is remarkable about this account is how the roles have been
reversed. The bishop is worldly and insolent; Huxley has the austere
dignity of a Doctor of the Church.

Rightly or wrongly,[20] Wilberforce got the reputation of having
treated Darwin's theory with a scoffing frivolity which was all too
obviously 'Oxford'. The secular intelligentsia were weary of Oxford
and its power to resist those within and without who wanted to
modernise. There had been the wrangles of the Oxford Movement,
and the wrangles over the new Science Museum (opened in 1860 and
initiated by the BAAS meeting), and foot-dragging over university
reform in the 1850s. It must have seemed typical of the dominant
intellectual temper of the place that Matthew Arnold's inaugural lecture
as Professor of Poetry, 'On the Modern Element in Literature' (1857),
should have taken the form of arguing that the best way out of the
'modern dilemma' was to read the Latin and Greek classics. There were
many Anglican clergymen who could and did respond adequately to
The Origin of Species – Charles Kingsley was one – but the combination
of Wilberforce and Oxford was fatal. The ensuing secularisation of
science, no doubt inevitable in any case, took renewed energy from
this further breach in the Anglican hegemony.

If one turns from the institutional and cultural to the intellectual
context, the influence of Darwin, though vast, can perhaps be
summed up by saying that his theory put mankind back into nature,
implicitly denying the distinction which religion had traditionally set
up between humanity and the animals. Out of this came the feeling
of disinheritance which Housman expressed, and a growing sense
of the determining power of the environment over the individual.
Its characteristic literary manifestation is the late-nineteenth-century
movement known as 'Naturalism', in which the ideas of Schopenhauer
(1788–1860) combined with Darwin to produce the stoic determinism
of the fiction of Maupassant (1850–93) and Zola (1840–1902), and the
plays of Ibsen (1828–1906) and Strindberg (1849–1912).

Naturalism in its full continental severity never really established
itself in Britain, for reasons that say something about both the literary
culture and the nature of Darwin's own narrative. Recent criticism,
notably that of Gillian Beer and George Levine, has made us much more
aware of The Origin of Species as an imaginative narrative, comparable to
other forms of narrative like the novel. It too is a 'form of imaginative
history', concerned with beginnings and ends; it has a plot (although
not one the individual can influence, nor one with a predetermined
ending); and its significance, like that of a great novel, is 'essentially

multivalent'.[21] No concept in nineteenth-century English literature was more multivalent than 'Nature', and engagement with the phenomena of nature was at the heart of Darwin's enterprise. He inherited different but overlapping meanings. He was well-versed, as we have seen, in Paley's *Natural Theology*, with its argument from the design of Nature to the existence of God. He could hardly have avoided the 'Natural Supernaturalism' of Wordsworth and Carlyle. Like most Englishmen of his class he was familiar with the *Natura Naturans*, the Earth-Mother, of classical mythology. These associations, part-Christian and part-pagan, blow across his attempts to define the operations of the law of natural selection in more strictly scientific terms. His ambivalence shows in the irregular capitalising of Nature in the text and in the sudden spurts of lyricism when it almost becomes a providential agent:

> Under nature, the slightest difference of structure or
> constitution may well turn the nicely-balanced scale in
> the struggle for life, and so be preserved. How fleeting
> are the wishes and efforts of man! how short his time! and
> consequently how poor will his products be, compared
> with those accumulated by nature during whole geological
> periods. Can we wonder, then, that nature's productions
> should be far 'truer' in character than man's productions;
> that they should be infinitely better adapted to the most
> complex conditions of life, and should plainly bear the
> stamp of far higher workmanship? (p. 133)

Substitute 'God' for 'nature' here and it becomes plausible to speak of *The Origin of Species* as 'the last great work of Victorian natural theology'.[22] Or consider the many passages in which Darwin celebrates his delight at the profusion and fecundity of nature (the famous 'tangled bank' paragraph at the end, for example) – passages which would seem to be at odds with the bleakness of his argument. He participates in the ambivalence of his culture's discourse about nature. As in Hardy, whose work he influenced, it is a bleak site of evolutionary struggle and a place of generous and unending creativity. Out of such ambiguity comes a new natural theology, one which excludes or distances the traditional deity, but does not reintroduce Him in the clouds and hills and streams as Wordsworth had done. The new element is exhilaration in the perception of scientific law, which could be seen as evidence of God's purpose and design, as it was by Charles Kingsley in a letter which Darwin used in later editions of *The Origin of Species* to appease his theological critics[23]; or by Meredith in his great poem 'Lucifer in Starlight', where Lucifer escapes from hell only to be confronted and dismayed by the laws of the universe:

He reached a middle height, and at the stars,
Which are the brain of heaven, he looked, and sank.
Around the ancient track marched, rank on rank,
The army of unalterable law.

But to the agnostic temper such law was in itself a subject of reverence, with Nature replacing God as a source of religious feeling and consolation. To quote the last sentence of *The Origin of Species* in its entirety:

There is grandeur in this view of life, with its several
powers, having been originally breathed into a few forms
or into one; and that, whilst this planet has gone cycling
on according to the fixed law of gravity, from so simple a
beginning endless forms most beautiful and most wonderful
have been, and are being, evolved.[24]

The spread of science

The initial success of *The Origin of Species* makes 1859 a turning-point in the history of nineteenth-century science. Darwin provided a mechanism for evolutionary change which belonged to an altogether higher level of plausibility than anything that had gone before. That the bleaker implications of natural selection do not seem to have registered with most of his contemporaries owes something, as I have suggested, to the multivalence of the concept of Nature at the time, and something to the Victorian faith in progress. It is worth recalling that 1859 also saw the publication of Samuel Smiles's *Self-Help*, with its doctrine of self-improvement through effort. But the idea of a struggle for existence did strike a chord with contemporaries, who were used to high mortality rates, especially among the young; besides, they could see its applicability to a world of industrial competition and imperial expansion. The phrase 'survival of the fittest' was coined by Herbert Spencer, not Darwin, and by introducing a moral dimension to the more neutral conception of natural selection (only those survive who *deserve* to survive) it encouraged the application of a simplified evolutionism to the new social sciences.[25] In the 1860s and 1870s the science of anthropology, taking inspiration from Spencer's law of progress and Darwin's long time-scale, pushed through the theological barriers to talk openly of the emergence of mankind from the higher primates. This alliance of science and progress had its darker side, though, as we saw in Chapter 1. The idea that primitive peoples belonged to the 'childhood' of humanity was a sanction for interfering with their liberties – for their own good, of course. When that good coincided with the greater good of imperial expansion it was even better, and when it did not, the good of the more developed civilisations naturally had a higher claim.

The period from 1860 to 1900 was a time of unprecedented confidence in the power of science to solve the problems of life. Beatrice Webb (1858–1943) has a section of her autobiography called 'The Cult of Science' in which she looks back across the gulf of the Great War and finds it 'hard to understand the naive belief of the most vigorous minds of the 'seventies and 'eighties that it was by science, and by science alone, that all human misery would be ultimately swept away'. She put this 'almost fanatical faith' down partly to hero-worship: 'For who will deny that the men of science were the leading British intellectuals of that period; that it was they who were the self-confident militants of the period. . . who were routing the theologians, confounding the mystics, imposing their theories on philosophers, their inventions on capitalists, and their discoveries on medical men. . .?'[26] Another explanation is the religious reverence in which scientific law was held, especially at the moment of its discovery. Henry Adams (1838–1918) was living in London at the time when Darwin was being read and debated, and he writes in *The Education of Henry Adams* (1907) of how 'to other Darwinians – except Darwin – Natural Selection seemed a dogma to be put in the place of the Athanasian Creed; it was a form of religious hope; a promise of ultimate perfection.'[27]

An example of science's militant mood is the now-forgotten 'prayer-test' controversy of 1872–73, when the physicist John Tyndall (1820–93) published in *The Contemporary Review* an anonymous letter, believed to be by a London doctor, proposing that the efficacy of prayers for the sick be subjected to scientific testing. It suggested that an experimental ward might be set aside as the object of special prayer and its results over a period of time compared with past records and similar wards in other hospitals. In the ensuing furore, the eugenicist Francis Galton (1822–1911) came forward with statistical data he had been gathering which showed that those who had been the subject of public prayer, like the monarchy, lived no longer than other groups; indeed, that kings and queens died earlier than lawyers and military officers.[28] The anonymous writer was accused of atheism and impiety, but in fact his letter provides eloquent examples of the religion of scientific law discussed above; his objection to supernatural interference is really that it mars the moral beauty of a universe of undeviating law:

> There is no influence so soothing, none so reconciling to
> the chequered conditions of life as consciousness of the
> absolute stability of the Rock on which the physicist takes

his stand; who, knowing the intelligent order that pervades
the Universe, believes in it, and with true filial piety would
never suggest a petition for a change in the Great Will as
touching any childish whim of his own.[29]

At about this time Galton published his *English Men of Science: Their
Nature and Nurture* (1874), the result of elaborate questionnaires sent
to 180 leading scientists. Ostensibly a work of statistical objectivity,
the book celebrates the intellectual qualities of the scientist as implicitly
heroic, setting them within a framework which called not just for
reform but, in the concluding words, for 'the establishment of a sort
of scientific priesthood throughout the kingdom, whose high duties
would have reference to the health and well-being of the nation in
its broadest sense, and whose emoluments and social position would
be made commensurate with the importance and variety of their
functions'.[30]

Galton's phrase, 'scientific priesthood', unwittingly reveals the ambition
behind his otherwise cautious book, as it is behind the more enthusiastic
writings of Huxley and Tyndall, which was to challenge the *de facto*
priesthood for cultural leadership. This was partly the reason for the
campaign for the extension of science education in the nineteenth
century. The scientists' confidence came from the emergence, from the
1850s, of a world view which Frank Miller Turner has called 'scientific
naturalism'.[31] It was based on three theories which were taken in
combination to offer a sufficient explanation of life on earth: evolution,
usually in Spencer's Lamarckian formulation; atomic theory in Dalton's
'solid-ball' form; and the law of the conservation of energy, the First
Law of Thermodynamics, which held that the amount of energy
in the universe remains constant despite the various transformations
through which matter and energy may pass. Dalton's theory gave
solidity and regularity to matter, evolution implied the inevitability
of progressive development, and the First Law of Thermodynamics
seemed to ensure that the universe was a closed system, impermeable
by divine or miraculous intervention. Although it seemed 'advanced'
in 1870 it was not so much a modern view of the universe as the
culmination of the mechanical view which began with Newton and
Descartes. The development of the sciences for which Huxley and
Tyndall campaigned was to make it out of date well before the end
of the century. But, chastened and inspired by this universe of law, and
remembering the doctrinal squabbling that had disfigured the religious
life of the period, they propounded an ideal of science that was as much
moral as intellectual: as a pursuit detached, objective, value-free, offering
the ultimate, austere satisfaction of discovering what Huxley called 'the
rational order which pervades the universe'.[32]

It is not possible to think of the Victorian publicists of science without feeling a sense of historical irony. Their confidence in 'the rational order which pervades the universe' seems premature in light of the unpredictable world of modern quantum theory. Their faith in science as a force for good could not foresee the two-edged sword it has become in the twentieth century. Their belief – a noble aspiration when it was not an assertion of intellectual superiority – that science could be detached and value-free ignored the extent to which their own was permeated by the progressive values of the day. Above all, their confident naturalism drew upon the bank of religious feeling and religious language without knowing it did so.

The publicists of science were romantics, in short. They spoke eloquently for an undifferentiated 'science' in the hope of raising its cultural prestige and accelerating the introduction of 'Colleges of Science' throughout the country, and in this they were partly successful. But the consequence of reform in university and technical education was increasing specialisation, and specialisation undermined the synthesis of knowledge on which the confidence of the publicists rested. The most telling challenge to optimistic evolutionism, for example, came not from the Churches but from contemporary physics. Rudolf Clausius (1822–88) in Germany, and William Thomson (1824–1907), later Lord Kelvin, in Glasgow, developed a Second Law of Thermodynamics more sinister in its implications than the First: that heat passes in one direction only, from a warm to a colder body, so there is a continual diffusion and waste of useful mechanical energy – useful, that is, to mankind for life-sustaining purposes. When Kelvin applied this to the age of the sun he did so in ignorance of our modern knowledge of the thermonuclear processes which sustain and renew its energy output; he saw it as a cooling coal, which could not be more than a hundred million years old. 'As for the future,' Kelvin wrote in *Macmillan's Magazine* in 1862, 'we may say, with equal certainty, that inhabitants of the earth cannot continue to enjoy the light and heat essential to their life, for many millions of years longer, unless sources now unknown to us are prepared in the great storehouse of creation.'[33]

A hundred million years may seem a long time, but it was not nearly enough for the infinitely gradual process of descent by natural selection to have taken place. Such a drastically reduced time-scale effectively opened the door again to divine intervention. Darwin was deeply troubled by the implications of Kelvin's thesis as it was presented through lectures and articles in the 1860s, and it became 'an odious spectre' which made him adjust and shorten the time-scale for evolution through succeeding editions of *The Origin of Species*. Huxley's attempt to act as Darwin's bulldog on this issue proved less successful than it had been in the earlier debate with Wilberforce. Kelvin's time-frame seemed ineluctable: it did not disprove the theory of transmutation of species, but it seemed fatal to natural selection. [34] When he went on to reduce it to twenty million years, Darwinism was in crisis.

Kelvin's thesis had a further dimension. If the sun was a cooling coal whose extinction could be predicted by applying the Second Law of Thermodynamics, then the end of the world became imaginable. It would come by the gradual, irreversible waning of the sun's warmth and light – what was called the 'heat-death of the universe' – and, according to Kelvin, within a few million years. The prospect for the human race was a lingering extinction by cold, which seemed a poor outcome to the evolutionary ascent. Such a vision of the end of the world forms the climax to H.G. Wells's *The Time Machine* (1895), as the Time Traveller cycles on in a landscape gradually emptied of all organic life:

> The darkness grew apace; a cold wind began to blow in
> freshening gusts from the east, and the showering white
> flakes in the air increased in number. From the edge of
> the sea came a ripple and a whisper. Beyond these lifeless
> sounds the world was silent. Silent? It would be hard
> to convey the stillness of it. All the sounds of man, the
> bleating of sheep, the cries of birds, the hum of insects, the
> stir that makes the background of our lives – all that was
> over. As the darkness thickened, the eddying flakes grew
> more abundant, dancing before my eyes; and the cold of
> the air more intense. At last, one by one, swiftly, one after
> the other, the white peaks of the distant hills vanished into
> blackness. [35]

The Time Machine is also what Peter Morton has called a 'devolutionary nightmare', drawing upon late-Victorian fears about the degenerative potential in evolution. [36] The Time Traveller moves forward to the year AD 802,701 and comes upon a race of gentle beings, the Eloi, living a life of leisure in an Edenic Thames landscape; later he discovers that these effete creatures are in the power of the Morlocks, a cannibalistic race who live underground, emerging at night to feed off the Eloi they are 'farming'. Humankind has devolved downwards from its noon of promise in the nineteenth century, into two separate species. The moral of this part of the novel is a blend of Darwin, Huxley, and Samuel Smiles: struggle is necessary for creative development; to settle only for comfort and security is to decline.

The double pessimism of Wells's novel reveals the anxiety that was starting to cloud the scientific prospect by the 1890s. His teacher,

Huxley, never a naively optimistic evolutionist, took the occasion of his Romanes lecture on 'Evolution and Ethics' (1893) to caution against the ethical optimism implied by the phrase 'survival of the fittest'. The fittest were simply those best adapted to their habitat, not the morally best. A familiar point, but it is the stoic firmness with which the cosmic and the human are now separated that sets the tone of the essay in its time:

> the practice of that which is ethically best. . . involves a
> course of conduct which, in all respects, is opposed to
> that which leads to success in the cosmic struggle for
> existence. . . . Let us understand, once for all, that the
> ethical progress of society depends, not on imitating the
> cosmic process, still less in running away from it, but in
> combating it.'[37]

Huxley's opposition between the cosmic and the ethical and individual is exactly the stance adopted in Hardy's later novels *Tess of the d'Urbervilles* (1891) and *Jude the Obscure* (1895). Tess and Jude are evolutionary victims, registering their ethical protest against the cruelty of the cosmic process written into the institutions of their society, and bearing witness in their tragic destinies to the realisation, in Huxley's words, that 'the cosmic process has no sort of relation to moral ends' (p. 83).

With the establishment of large, modern research laboratories in the 1870s and 1880s, and the rise of specialist journals to cater for the co-operative enterprise of a growing scientific community, the 'hard' sciences like physics and chemistry started to pull away from a general readership. The mathematics required to understand physics became increasingly complex and the very foundations of the subject started to shift, away from Newtonian solidity towards the statistical and the predictive. The work of James Clerk Maxwell (1831–79) brought a new and unsettling sophistication to theoretical physics. Among much else (he predicted the discovery of radio-waves, for example) Maxwell argued that the laws of matter at the molecular level could have only a statistical validity, not mechanical certainty. Since neither they nor their encounters can be observed, he said in his 1873 paper on 'Molecules', 'molecular science teaches us that our experiments can never give us anything more than statistical information, and that no law deduced from them can pretend to absolute precision'.[38]

Hypothetically, the energy generated by the collision of gas molecules at a lower temperature could result in the passage of heat from the cooler to the warmer halves of a sealed cylinder, if a tiny intelligence (Maxwell's demon) was in there operating a frictionless shutter that let out only the faster-moving molecules from the cool side and let in only the slower-moving from the warm.[39] This theoretical reversal of the Second Law of Thermodynamics did not disprove the law, it simply demonstrated its statistical rather than absolute validity. Maxwell's demon is a gargoyle on the secular cathedral of Victorian science, and he looks forward to the imp of uncertainty at the heart of twentieth-century physics.

If physics in this period is a science which moved from the empirical to the theoretical, psychology tried to move in the opposite direction and place the study of mind on a properly 'scientific' basis. The attempt to develop what G.H. Lewes called a 'physiological psychology' – a biology of the mind – was controversial for the same reasons as descent by natural selection: it threatened to break down the traditional Christian distinction between matter and spirit, and by putting the individual back into nature, implicitly rejected a supernatural explanation of human origins and development.[40] Phrenology (or 'bumpology' as Sydney Smith called it) – the locating of individual moral and intellectual qualities in different areas of the skull – was its most popular early-Victorian form, and the traces of this pseudo-science can be found in the fiction of the period. (When Rochester in *Jane Eyre* tries to attract Jane's interest, for example, he invites her phrenological speculation, lifting his hair from his brow and revealing 'a solid enough mass of intellectual organs; but an abrupt deficiency where the suave sign of benevolence should have risen' [ch. 14].) Phrenology never succeeded in establishing itself as a reputable science, but in its way it was a clumsy step in the direction of the modern recognition that different faculties are controlled by separate areas of the brain. The movement was also something of a rallying-point for the disaffected scientists and medical men of the new nation; based in Edinburgh, and centred round the leading secularist George Combe (1788–1858), its affiliations were with social reform and natural (or no) religion, unlike the mood of Anglican compromise prevailing in the BAAS. Chambers of the *Vestiges* belonged to Combe's circle.[41]

Herbert Spencer started out as a phrenologist, and in his work psychology is absorbed into the mainstream of nineteenth-century evolutionary thinking. It will be recalled that he had already worked out a theory of evolution before Darwin, and his *Principles of Psychology* appeared in 1855, four years before *The Origin of Species*. He was the first to offer a fully evolutionary psychology: that the mind is formed in the process of adjusting to its environment, and cannot be studied apart; and that it inherits through the nervous system the legacy of its predecessors' adaptations. These insights were arrived at speculatively, without any practical demonstration, and yet they proved fruitful. In 1879 the first laboratory was set up by Wilhelm Wendt in Leipzig, and psychology was on its feet as an experimental science.

When Beatrice Webb read the psychological works of Spencer and others in the 1880s, she found it a depressing experience. 'Instead of the exact descriptions of the actual facts of individual minds. . . I seemed to find nothing but arbitrary definitions of the mind in the abstract, which did not correspond with the mental life of any one person'; whereas 'for any detailed description of the complexity of human nature, of the variety and mixture in human motive, of the insurgence of instinct in the garb of reason. . . I had to turn to novelists and poets'.[42] What they could offer was insight into the operations of the unconscious mind, and here the Romantic poets and essayists were far in advance of the scientists. Wordsworth's sense of the 'dark/Inscrutable workmanship that reconciles/Discordant elements' in the growth of the personality, making them 'cling together/In one society', enabled him to see and portray the significance of the seemingly trivial and inconsequential.[43] They recognised the importance of what Freud was later to call 'dream-work': Coleridge in his three great visionary poems, De Quincey in his exploration of his drug-induced dreams and nightmares in *Confessions of an English Opium-Eater* (1822). 'The machinery for dreaming planted in the human brain was not planted for nothing', he wrote in the sequel, *Suspiria de Profundis* (1845). 'That faculty, in alliance with the mystery of darkness, is the one great tube through which man communicates with the shadowy.'[44] Well before Freud and Proust, De Quincey offered a beautiful image of the layering of experience in the memory: the mind as a palimpsest on which successive writings have been inscribed and seemingly obliterated, but capable of recovery by some great shock to the system:

> Yes, reader, countless are the mysterious handwritings of
> grief or joy which have inscribed themselves successively
> upon the palimpsest of your brain; and, like the annual
> leaves of aboriginal forests, or the undissolving snows
> on the Himalaya, or light falling upon light, the endless
> strata have covered up each other in forgetfulness. But by
> the hour of death, but by fever, but by the searchings of
> opium, all these can revive in strength. They are not dead,
> but sleeping. . . . In some potent convulsion of the system,
> all wheels back into its earliest elementary stage.[45]

Interest in the workings of the unconscious grew in sophistication through the century. Mesmerism, a semi-occult form of hypnosis, became respectable in Britain when the fashionable physician John Elliotson (1791-1868) began a series of public hypnotic demonstrations in 1837. As physician to Dickens, Wilkie Collins, and Thackeray (whose

Pendennis is dedicated to Elliotson), he was sure of a sympathetic audience, and mesmerism became something of a middle-class parlour game in the 1840s. Unlike phrenology, hypnotism held out real scientific possibilities, and when put on a proper experimental footing by the French neurologist Jean-Martin Charcot (1825–93) it exerted a formative influence on his most famous pupil, Freud. The trance-like states induced by mesmerism raised the question of how far the conscious mind was master in its own house. By mid-century it was being suggested that the unconscious might be an equal or even a dominant partner in mental activity. In 1853 W.B. Carpenter (1813–85), the physiologist, introduced the concept of 'unconscious cerebration', the hidden activity of the mind and its behaviour in states of suspended consciousness like sleep, hypnosis, and drunkenness. The suggestion that the unconscious might act in opposition to the conscious self was a source of moral anxiety, but it had creative possibilities: Wilkie Collins and Dickens used it to dramatic effect in their 'sensation' novels *The Moonstone* (1868) and *The Mystery of Edwin Drood* (1870). But how responsible was the conscious mind for the behaviour of the unconscious? 'We commit in dreams acts for which we should weep tears of blood were they real', Frances Power Cobbe wrote in 1870, 'and yet never feel the slightest remorse'. In attempted explanation she offered the image of the horse and the rider for the relations of conscious to the unconscious mind; sleep releases the horse from its bit and allows it to gallop free, but it remains the case 'that the dreaming brain-self is not the true self for whose moral worthiness we strive, and for whose existence after death alone we care'.[46]

Frances Cobbe's separation of a 'true self' from a potentially anarchic 'dreaming brain-self' may seem naive to our post-Freudian perspective; out of such divisions, after all, came the rigidities and frustrations that were to produce the psychoses which the first psychoanalysts treated. Freud would have had little patience with her characteristic and not ignoble aspiration to 'higher' behaviour. He lies just over the horizon of this book and one cannot help seeing the Victorian discussion of the unconscious in the light of his fierce determination to break down the barriers set up by the conscious mind, to rob it of its pretensions to nobility by reducing human motive to primitive instincts. But lest one gives the misleading impression that Freudian psychiatry was a goal of enlightenment towards which the Victorians were fumbling, it is worth pointing out how historically conditioned his own vision was. In 1804 Jean-Paul Richter prophetically described the unconscious as an 'inner Africa, whose unknown boundaries may extend far away'.[47] The Freudian unconscious has a lot in common with late-Victorian images of Africa, as both the home of 'lower' races to be tamed and a place of licentious temptations. It is no accident that the imperial claims of

Freudian psychoanalysis should arise at the same time as the 'scramble for Africa' and European imperial expansion before the Great War. His famous statement about the 'id', the storehouse of instinctual energy in the unconscious, that 'where id was, there ego shall be', has a ring of the missionary promising his home society that he will supplant the witch doctor and the tribal chieftain, while his very low opinion of the satisfactions of civilisation suggests that it would not be surprising if the missionary went native.

Conclusion: literature and science

This is a particularly rich period for studying the interrelations of literature and science because the revolutionary sciences, geology and evolutionary biology, were comprehensible to the layperson in a way that modern physics is not. Their profound cosmological implications were soon grasped and debated, and absorbed into the imaginative bloodstream of the culture. It was not a one-way street. Tennyson read Lyell and Chambers and translated their writings into a thrilling poetry of cosmic process; Huxley and Tyndall quoted Tennyson (by far the poet most frequently quoted by the scientists); and Huxley ended 'Evolution and Ethics' with a ringing quotation from 'Ulysses'. Aesthetic boundaries were not fixed: Ruskin (1819–1900) could make his study of geology the foundation of his theory of painting, while Tyndall could end *Heat Considered as a Mode of Motion* (1863) with a celebration of the imaginative power of science: 'presented rightly to the mind, the discoveries and generalisations of modern science constitute a poem more sublime than has ever yet addressed the human imagination. The natural philosopher of to-day may dwell amid conceptions which beggar those of Milton.'[48]

The issues of science, the questions it asks, and the ways it chooses to answer them, cannot be separated from the assumptions of the culture at large. So the rapid cultural assimilation of evolutionary geology and biology can be seen as part of the larger tide of historicism which, as I suggested in the first chapter, was flowing through this period from the start. Nature, like the Time-Spirit in Carlyle's *French Revolution*, was larger than the individual and indifferent to his needs; but (unlike Carlyle's cyclical vision) her movement was linear, it might be progressive, and in the exploration of its steady sequence there was both moral discipline and religious consolation. That at least was the view of the writer who applied the method and ideology of science most thoroughly to her novels, George Eliot:

> The great conception of universal regular sequence, without
> partiality and without caprice – the conception which is the
> most potent force at work in the modification of our faith,
> and of the practical form given to our sentiments – could
> only grow out of that patient watching of external fact,
> and that silencing of preconceived notions, which are urged
> upon the mind by the problems of physical science.[49]

The grand impersonality of scientific process, 'without partiality and
without caprice', has modified 'faith' by removing the possibility of
supernatural intervention but has left a different faith in its place, the
knowledge that we live in a universe whose rules will be applied with
absolute justice. If we have lost the hope of heaven, we have lost also
the demeaning fear of arbitrary schemes of salvation and damnation,
and the human creature can stand upright for the first time in history.
And so science in George Eliot's novels comes to take the place once
occupied by providence or destiny, as she explores the 'universal regular
sequence' by which moral outcomes are inevitably generated by moral
actions.

George Eliot wrote these words in 1865 in the *Fortnightly Review*,
which her partner George Henry Lewes (1817–78) was currently
editing. The importance of Lewes in encouraging and supporting
her career as a novelist is, of course, his chief claim on posterity,
but his own career and scientific work are of more than marginal
significance, if only because they illustrate so well the literary context
of mid-Victorian science. Lewes was the most many-sided of Victorian
intellectuals – a novelist and dramatist (without distinction), the author
of a history of philosophy and the standard nineteenth-century life of
Goethe, and a writer of admired reviews for all the advanced Victorian
journals: his four essays on 'Mr Darwin's Hypotheses' (1868) attracted
the approval of Darwin himself, who wrote encouraging Lewes to make
them into a book.[50] But Lewes aspired to being more than an intellectual
middle-man and, whether driven by unconscious feelings of emulation
or not, spent the last two decades of his life attempting to uncover the
physiological basis of the mind. He made many visits to laboratories
in Germany and set up his own at home, where hundreds of frogs had
their brains experimented with, the 'results' of these experiments going
into what he hoped would be his surviving monument, the synthesis of
physiology and psychology which he called *Problems of Life and Mind*
(5 vols, 1874–79). The work is indeed a monument, but a monument
to the presumptions of an imperialist scientific ideology which looked
to giving 'science' the inclusiveness of a theology.

Lewes was the kindest and most generous of men but one cannot read
without revulsion that, for example, one of his frogs (called 'Froggie')

died of starvation after living without its brain for several months.[51] And one understands John Forster's sense of outrage when Lewes in an otherwise sympathetic review-essay of the first volume of Forster's *Life of Dickens* (1871) compared Mr Micawber to one of those 'frogs whose brains have been taken out for physiological purposes, and whose actions henceforth want the distinctive peculiarity of organic action, that of fluctuating spontaneity'.[52] There is a self-admiring scientism about such remarks, an air of being up with the latest discoveries, which grates now as much for its datedness as for its complacent acceptance of the cruelties of vivisection. The signs are that George Eliot was rather embarrassed by Lewes's garden-shed experiments but her novels also have their rhetoric of scientism, the references to electric batteries, tissue exploration, and so on. Ruthless exposer of egoism though she was, her authorial comment is sometimes touched with a kind of intellectual hubris which she may well have learned from Lewes, who wrote at the end of his last essay:

> When Science has fairly mastered the principles of moral relations as it has mastered the principles of physical relations, all Knowledge will be incorporated in a homogeneous doctrine rivalling that of the old theologies in its comprehensiveness, and surpassing it in the authority of its credentials.[53]

The title was 'On the Dread and Dislike of Science'. Like many later victims of the search for a 'homogeneous doctrine', Lewes's lobotomised frogs had good reason to dread the new religion of Science.

Notes

1. J. Morrell and A. Thackray, *Gentlemen of Science* (Oxford, 1981), p. 12.

2. E.C. Patterson, *Mary Somerville and the Cultivation of Science, 1815–40* (Boston, The Hague, Dordrecht, Lancaster, 1983), p. x.

3. See S. Ross, 'Scientist: The Story of a Word', *Annals of Science*, XVIII (1962), pp. 65–85.

4. S.S. Schweber, 'Scientists as Intellectuals: The Early Victorians', in *Victorian Science and Victorian Values: Literary Perspectives*, edited by J. Paradis and T. Postlewait (New York, 1981), p. 20.

5. *The Voyage of the 'Beagle'* (1845 edition), pp. 316–17.

6. Quoted by Lynn Barber in *The Heyday of Natural History* (1980), pp. 184–5.

7. *The Testimony of the Rocks* (Edinburgh, 1857), Lecture V, p. 201.

8. *Theory of the Earth* (Edinburgh, 1795), p. 200.

9. See here A. Desmond, 'Lamarckism and Democracy', in *History, Humanity and Evolution*, edited by J.R. Moore (Cambridge, 1989), pp. 99–130.

10. *Vestiges of the Natural History of Creation* (1844; Leicester, 1969), p. 360.

11. Quoted C.C. Gillispie, *Genesis and Geology* (New York, 1959), p. 165.

12. See *More Letters of Charles Darwin*, edited by F. Darwin and A.C. Seward (2 vols, 1903), I, pp. 177.

13. *The Origin of Species*, edited by J.W. Burrow (Harmondsworth, 1966), p. 117.

14. W. Paley, *Natural Theology* (13th edition, 1811), ch. 3, p. 33.

15. 'Introductory Lecture' (1892), in *Collected Poems and Selected Prose*, edited by C. Ricks (1989), p. 272.

16. *Joseph Conrad's Letters to R.B. Cunninghame Graham*, edited by C.T. Watts (Cambridge, 1969), p. 56; letter of 20 December 1897.

17. See here P.J. Bowler, 'The Changing Meaning of "Evolution"', *Journal of the History of Ideas*, 36 (1975), 95–114.

18. *Essays* (2 vols, 1901), I, p. 10

19. Quoted by Tess Cosslett in *Science and Religion in the Nineteenth Century* (Cambridge, 1984), pp. 151–2.

20. It may be wrongly: see J.V. Jensen, 'Return to the Wilberforce–Huxley Debate', *British Journal for the History of Science*, 21 (1988), 161–80.

21. Gillian Beer, *Darwin's Plots* (1983), p. 9.

22. J. Durant, 'Darwinism and Divinity: a Century of Debate', in *Darwinism and Divinity*, edited by J. Durant (Oxford, 1985), p. 16.

23. Kingsley wrote: 'I have gradually learnt to see that it is just as noble a conception of Deity, to believe that He created primal forms capable of self-development into all forms needful *pro tempore* and *pro loco*, as to believe that He required a fresh act of intervention to supply the *lacunae* which He himself had made. I question whether the former be not the loftier thought.' See 1959 Variorum Edition of *The Origin of Species*, pp. 167–8.

24. *The Origin of Species*, pp. 459–60

25. For a discussion of the relations between evolution and anthropology see P.J. Bowler, *The Invention of Progress: The Victorians and the Past* (Oxford, 1989).

26. *My Apprenticeship* (1926), pp. 130–1.

27. *The Education of Henry Adams* (1907; 1928 edn), ch. XV, p. 231.

28. See S.G. Brush, *The Temperature of History* (New York, 1978), pp. 78–84.

29. *The Contemporary Review*, XX (1872), p. 770.

30. *English Men of Science: Their Nature and Nurture* (1874), p. 260.

31. See *Between Science and Religion: The Reaction to Scientific Naturalism in Late Victorian England* (New Haven, 1974), ch.

32. 'The Progress of Science' (1887), in *Collected Essays* (9 vols, 1893–94), I, p. 60.

33. 'On the Age of the Sun's Heat', *Macmillan's Magazine*, V (1862), p. 393.

34. See the discussion of 'Darwinism on its Deathbed' in Peter Morton, *The Vital Science: Biology and the Literary Imagination 1860–1900* (1984).

35. H.G. Wells, *The Time Machine*, in *Selected Short Stories* (Harmondsworth, 1958), ch. 11, pp. 77–8

36. Morton, *Vital Science*, p. 112.

37. *Collected Essays*, vol. IX (1894), pp. 81–3.

38. *Nature*, VIII (1873), 437–41; p. 440.

39. See M. Goldman, *The Demon in the Aether: The Story of James Clerk Maxwell* (Edinburgh, 1983), ch. 10.

40. See L.S. Jacyna, 'The Physiology of Mind, the Unity of Nature, and the Moral Order in Victorian Thought', *The British Journal for the History of Science*, XIV (1981), 109–32.

41. See J.A. Secord, 'Behind the Veil: Robert Chambers and *Vestiges*', in *History, Humanity and Evolution*, edited by J.R. Moore (Cambridge, 1989), pp. 165–98.

42. *My Apprenticeship*, pp. 137–8.

43. *The Prelude* (1850), I, lines 352–5.

44. *Confessions of an English Opium-Eater and Other Writings*, edited by G. Lindop (Oxford, 1985), p. 88.

45. *Ibid*, pp. 145–6.

46. 'Unconscious Cerebration', *Macmillan's Magazine*, 27 (1870), p. 523.

47. Quoted in L.L. Whyte, *The Unconscious Before Freud* (1967), p. 133.

48. John Tyndall, *Heat Considered as a Mode of Motion* (1863), p. 433.

49. George Eliot, 'The Influence of Rationalism', *Fortnightly Review*, I (1865), p. 55.

50. See Rosemary Ashton, *George Henry Lewes: A Life* (Oxford, 1991), pp. 244–5.

51. *Ibid*, p. 242.

52. 'Dickens in Relation to Criticism', *Fortnightly Review*, XVII (1872), pp. 141–54; *Dickens: the Critical Heritage*, edited by Philip Collins (1971), p. 574.

53. 'On the Dread and Dislike of Science', *Fortnightly Review*, NS, XXIII (1878), p. 815.

Chapter 4
The Life of Ideas and the Culture of Politics

In January 1841 Sir Robert Peel formally opened a new Library and Reading Room in his Tamworth constituency. His speech described the organisation of the library and its practical usefulness to the working-class readers for whom it had been designed: there they would find information about farming methods and modern technology, and an introduction to the new world of science which would be for them both morally elevating and, in worldly terms, socially advancing. Books on theology and politics were to be excluded because of their potential divisiveness. In other words, Tamworth was to be a typical early-Victorian Mechanics' Institute, providing the kind of 'hard' utilitarian information that would help to make its users the self-helping employees which their employers desired, but not the relaxing reading which, as it turned out, was what most of them really wanted: works of biography and travel, and most of all fiction, and newspapers.[1] This new library would be forgotten today (it closed in 1874) had Peel's speech not inspired John Henry Newman to write his famous series of letters to *The Times* which has become known as 'The Tamworth Reading Room'. It is a forceful reaffirmation of a religious attitude to knowledge at a time when secular, utilitarian attitudes were gaining ground.

In essence, Newman's objections to Peel's speech were twofold: he resented the exclusion of theology and religious writing from the library, and he disagreed with the moral claims being made for secular knowledge:

> I consider . . . that intrinsically excellent and noble
> as are scientific pursuits, and worthy of a place in a
> liberal education, and fruitful in temporal benefits to the
> community, still they are not, and cannot be, *the instrument*
> of an ethical training; that physics do not supply a basis, but
> only materials for religious sentiment; that knowledge does
> but occupy, does not form the mind; that apprehension of
> the unseen is the only known principle capable of subduing

> moral evil, educating the multitude, and organizing
> society . . . .[2]

Huxley or George Eliot, as we saw at the end of the previous chapter, had a more sanguine view of the inspirational power of scientific 'law', but Newman was writing earlier, and his target is an ideology rather than science as such. Although 'The Tamworth Reading Room' is addressed to Peel, its scorn is reserved for the 'Useful Knowledge' movement initiated by that Whig uncle of Victorian reform, Henry Brougham (1778–1868). A co-founder of the *Edinburgh Review*, a campaigner for national education independent of denominational control, and a key figure in the founding of the secular University of London, Brougham was at the centre of the campaign against the Anglican hegemony in the early nineteenth century. Newman is fighting from within the hegemony, defending its moral claims against what he calls '*Broughamism*', a satirical compound of Bentham's utilitarian ethics and Brougham's utilitarian approach to education. And education is the larger context of the argument: the hidden issue in Newman's essay is contemporary debate about what part the Church should play in national education (for until 1870 'National' schools were Anglican schools), and how valid a secular education could be.

At this distance it may seem difficult to see what all the fuss was about. Why should not working men and women (and Newman's mockery of the library's accessibility to women is one of the unworthier moments in his argument) have a place of peace and quiet to which to retire from the noise, overcrowding, and sheer drudgery of their lives? And why not exclude works of religious and political controversy when these matters were the cause of so much of the noisy divisiveness of contemporary life? As an Oxford gentleman, Newman would have had little understanding of the first question, and as a considerable controversialist himself, he had little sympathy with the second. But he was on stronger ground when it came to the moral claims of the Useful Knowledge movement. 'Knowledge is Power' was their slogan, by which they meant the power of factual and scientific knowledge: to Newman such knowledge had 'no power of persuasion':

> The heart is commonly reached, not through the reason,
> but through the imagination, by means of direct im-
> pressions, by the testimony of facts and events, by history,
> by description. Persons influence us, voices melt us, looks
> subdue us, deeds inflame us. Many a man will live and die
> upon a dogma: no man will be a martyr for a conclusion.
> (p. 178)

He did not foresee that the heart and the imagination might be profoundly stirred by the terrible order of the Darwinian universe, but his point against 'Broughamism' sticks: that its claim to the morally improving character of utilitarian knowledge could not be sustained if it failed to reach the depths of human nature that religion appealed to – in particular, the imagination. This was the weak point in the Useful Knowledge movement, that it distrusted the imagination: hence the reluctance to allow light reading on the shelves of Mechanics' Institutes. Knowledge was to be absorbed passively, not possessed imaginatively; and it was to be the kind of knowledge, practical and scientific, that makes good mechanics.

This small episode is a reminder (if any is needed) of how intensely politicised early Victorian intellectual life was. Newman's letters were addressed to a once and future Tory Prime Minister, and attacked a former Whig Lord Chancellor; they were a calculated intervention in the contemporary debate about cultural leadership. But what the episode reveals are the weaknesses on both sides. Newman is shown to be unsympathetic to the recreational needs of the new industrial poor, and unaware that the Anglican hegemony now needed adapting as well as defending if it was to survive in the new conditions of the 1840s. 'Broughamism' emerges as equally indifferent to the recreation of the poor when not practical and scientific, its dogmatic secularism leading – in Newman's view, at any rate – to an impoverished view of human need and human possibility. Both offer panaceas – return to dogmatic Christianity, reform through self-improvement – which did not begin to meet the needs of industrial Britain in the 1840s. It is now necessary to look more closely at the constituent elements of Broughamism: the 'Scotch Knowledge' which Brougham and others influenced by the Scottish Enlightenment brought to England, and the utilitarianism which is commonly associated with the writings of Jeremy Bentham.

The march of mind: Scotch knowledge and English utilitarianism

In thinking about the condition of British intellectual life in 1830, it is helpful to keep two important historical factors in mind. The first is the intellectual narrowness and social exclusiveness of Oxford and Cambridge – a familiar theme in this book which needs no further elaborating. The second is the impact of the French Revolution in first stimulating and then, after the Terror, severely checking British republicanism, and the effect of the ensuing Napoleonic Wars in cutting off a generation from continental travel and direct encounter with foreign thought until about 1820. Reform was frozen and the natural party of moderate reform, the Whigs, ossified in the postures of the 1790s. The threat of conquest and invasion was used by the Tory government to justify repressive social legislation. At this period the confident voice of reform came not from London but from Edinburgh, in the shape of the *Edinburgh Review* (founded 1802), the originator of the most influential medium of intellectual debate in the nineteenth century. Its politics were Whig-progressive, contemptuous alike of the democratic fervours of popular radicalism and the resistance to civil and religious liberty of the then Lord Chancellor, Lord Eldon (1751–1838). 'On domestic subjects', Bagehot said, 'the history of the first thirty years of the nineteenth century is a species of duel between the Edinburgh Review and Lord Eldon'.[3]

To Walter Bagehot, banker, editor of *The Economist* and influential political commentator, the vigour of the *Edinburgh Review* came from its roots in a different intellectual tradition, one which encouraged wide-ranging thought on a variety of matters rather than intensely focused concentration on a few:

> it cannot be doubted that, as a preparation for the writing of various articles, the system of Edinburgh is enormously superior to that of Cambridge. The particular, compact, exclusive learning of England is inferior in this respect to the general, diversified, omnipresent information of the north; and what is more, the speculative, dubious nature of metaphysical and such like pursuits tends, in a really strong mind, to cultivate habits of independent thought and original discussion. (p. 22)

What was the 'system of Edinburgh' (or Glasgow, or Aberdeen), and what is its significance in the formation of Victorian intellectual life? It was a system of education by professorial lecture in which students were encouraged to see knowledge as the study of man as a social being. Law, history, philosophy, economics were not kept separate as they are today, but brought into relationship. A charismatic figure like Dugald Stewart (1753–1828) might be the Professor of Moral Philosophy at Edinburgh, but he would lecture on psychology, logic, ethics, politics, and political economy (economics). And as E.S. Dallas wrote in a review of Stewart's Collected Works in 1858, there was 'a practical tendency [in] all his observations. If he was a philosopher he was also a man of the world and of society.'[4] The range and urbanity of these men were a stimulus to extra-curricular debate, carried on in student societies like the Speculative Society in Edinburgh, where issues of history, politics, legislation, and literature were debated. This was an environment likely to produce reforming intellectuals with an appetite for what we would now call the social sciences, and a bias towards the practical and the everyday. To quote Dallas again, 'the whole of Scottish metaphysics is a protest against metaphysics . . . . its leading principle is an appeal to "common sense" '.[5]

'Scotch knowledge' was vigorous and wide-ranging in scope, and in the doctrine of Political Economy, with which the Scottish school was particularly associated, its proponents seemed to have discovered the justifying economic theory of industrial society. History played a part in ensuring that the Scots intellectuals who shared these ideas should meet the sons of the Whig nobility who would later be able to advance their careers in Parliament, law, and the civil service. The Napoleonic Wars had closed off continental Europe for the traditional grand tour, and several young noblemen were sent instead to Scottish universities, where they would reside with the professor and finish the first stage of their education before going on to Oxbridge. Three Victorian Prime Ministers took this route, the future Lords Melbourne, Palmerston, and John Russell. Ambitious young Scots lawyers and medical students were able when young to make the friendships that would later provide entry to the aristocratic centres of political influence, while even an abbreviated list of the famous names who studied under a man like Stewart shows how widely his influence touched the political life of the period: Lords Palmerston, Ashburton, Lansdowne, John Russell, Brougham, Cockburn, as well as the founding spirits of the *Edinburgh Review*, Francis Jeffrey, Francis Horner, and Sydney Smith. The Scottish Enlightenment tradition gave these men a long-range, progressive view of historical development and so encouraged them to think commonsensically about legislative reform, to practise religious liberalism, to distrust the hysteria of religious denominations and political sects, and to put a perhaps excessive faith in the power of knowledge as a means of individual and social improvement.

With the exception of James Mill (1773–1836), father of John Stuart, the Scots-educated reformers were Whigs, working for change within the traditional framework of the balanced constitution of monarch, aristocracy, and people: they did not look for democracy in the modern sense but for adjustments in the balance which would reflect the growing commercial power of the middle classes. That is what the 1832 Reform Act was about. Mill looked for something much more radical. He was one of the leaders of a group of intellectuals and reformers called 'Benthamites' or 'utilitarians' but who are probably defined most precisely by the term his son gave them: 'philosophic radicals'. They were radical because they wanted to change society at the root, and philosophic because they wanted to educate their countrymen into an understanding of the 'laws' on which a new society should be built. These 'laws' were, for their time, shockingly materialistic, and had two main components: the utilitarian ethics of Jeremy Bentham (1748–1832), and the doctrine of Political Economy, derived from Adam Smith's *Wealth of Nations* (1776), seasoned with Malthus's population theory, and cooked by the economist David Ricardo.

'Nature has placed mankind under the governance of two sovereign masters, *pain* and *pleasure*. It is for them alone to point out what we ought to do, as well as to determine what we shall do. On the one hand the standard of right and wrong, on the other the chain of causes and effects, are fastened to their throne.' Thus the famous opening words of Bentham's *Introduction to the Principles of Morals and Legislation* (1789).[6] There is a certain fitness in the fact that they appeared in the year of the outbreak of the French Revolution, creature of the French *philosophes*, for Bentham was an English *philosophe* and his philosophy of utility has the boldly simplifying confidence of the Enlightenment behind it. Mankind is a pleasure-seeking and pain-avoiding species, and any attempt to legislate for their happiness must begin and end, Bentham thought, by recognising this fact and applying what he called the 'principle of utility': 'By the principle of utility is meant that principle which approves or disapproves of every action whatsoever, according to the tendency which it appears to have to augment or diminish the happiness of the party whose interest is in question: or, what is the same thing in other words, to promote or to oppose that happiness' (p. 65). Once grasped, the principle of utility rendered redundant the various ethical concepts by which people masked their egoism, such as '*Moral Sense*', '*Common Sense*', '*Rule of Right*', '*Natural Justice*' (pp. 78–9). With these confusing notions aside, legislators could get down to creating the conditions in society which individuals sought in their private lives. Just as the individual wanted to maximise pleasure and minimise pain, so the business of the state should be to facilitate, in the famous phrase coined by Joseph Priestley, 'the greatest happiness of the greatest number'.

The 'interest of the community', for Bentham, was simply 'the sum of the interests of the several members who compose it' (p. 66). The only way to ensure that these interests were adequately represented was in a Parliament elected by universal suffrage at frequent intervals. Otherwise, men and women would find their interests imposed upon by the sinister traditional institutions of society: the Church, the aristocracy, and the tribe of lawyers who kept them in power by weaving an obfuscating web of legislation around them. The first task of the Benthamite reformer was to clear away that web with the broom of utility; the second was to replace the lawyer with the administrator as the agent of reform. If it is hard to understand how theories as crude as Bentham's could have inspired a political movement, one explanation is that it gave a greatly enhanced prestige to the civil servant and the public official (both Mills were administrators in the East India House). Another reason was the exhilaration of knowing one belonged to an embattled and virtuous minority. The Benthamites were not only alienated from their natural enemies, the Tories and the Church of England, but also from their potential allies in the Whig camp, many of whom were ambitious lawyers seeking a political career through aristocratic patronage. In 1824 they set up their own journal, the *Westminster Review*, as a 'utilitarian' alternative to the Whig *Edinburgh Review*.

There were, however, two subjects on which the younger Whigs and the small group of philosophic radicals tended to agree: the power of education to reform society, what in slogan form was popularly called the March of Mind, and the doctrine of Political Economy. The latter was derived, like Darwin's theory of evolution, from the population theory of Thomas Malthus. The tendency of population is always to grow faster than the production of food, unless held back by famine, disease, or contraception. Ricardo's 'iron law of wages' dictated – or so it was held at the time – a natural, just-above-subsistence price for labour. When population rises a fall in wage-rates inevitably occurs. When population falls as a result of the ensuing famine, wage-rates may rise, but only temporarily, for increased prosperity leads to the abandonment of parental restraint, an increase in population follows, and the grim see-saw dips downwards again.

It must be said in historical retrospect that there was no evidence for the machine-like regularity the political economists claimed for their theories; but it looked 'scientific', it seemed to fit the boom-and-bust conditions of labour-intensive capitalism, and it satisfied two powerful instincts of the Victorian middle classes: puritanical austerity and economic individualism. If the political economists were right, there was little point in interfering with these laws. So one has that strange conjunction in the radical mind of political reformism and economic determinism which is one of the hardest parts of the period to penetrate sympathetically.

Benthamism is often talked about as if it were synonymous with *laissez-faire* economic theory, and certainly the two attitudes of mind often went together. But there was always a potential conflict between them. In both theory and practice, the principle of utility allowed a degree of *dirigisme* which the orthodox political economist deplored. This is well illustrated in the career of the sanitary reformer Sir Edwin Chadwick (1800–90). As one of Bentham's most zealous disciples, he drafted the 1834 Poor Law Amendment Act and was so vigorous in enforcing its deterrent objectives when secretary to the permanent commission that he was known as the most hated man in England. Yet, applying the same principles, he produced the great 1842 *Report on the Sanitary Condition of the Labouring Population*, which is one of the cardinal documents of nineteenth-century social reform. Chadwick's subsequent work in public health led him to see that more, not less, central control and finance was required. The sewers beneath the great industrial cities are the arteries of a new body-politic which Victorian tax- and rate-payers helped to create once their eyes had been opened by men like Chadwick. *Laissez-faire* could not have done this, and nor did any government of the time believe that it could.

The best critique of Bentham's philosophy is John Stuart Mill's essay on that subject, which will be discussed in the next section; that, in turn, can be seen as part of a delayed response to a devastating attack on the elder Mill's theory of government made by Macaulay in the *Edinburgh Review* of 1829. This is such an important episode, in what it did for the confidence of the philosophic radicals and what it revealed about contrasting assumptions in the reformers' camp, that it is worth examining briefly. At issue were two different theories of government and two different methods of reasoning, the deductive and the inductive, or the *a priori* and the empirical. James Mill's *Essay on Government* (1820) was an encyclopaedia article which became a political pamphlet in the 1820s; it argued, in the Benthamite tradition, that there was a 'science' of government which could – indeed must – be derived from the known 'laws' of human nature, these being the universal tendency to seek pleasure and avoid pain. From these premises, and in a drily syllogistic manner which permitted few concrete historical instances, Mill proceeded to prove that representative (male) democracy was the only safe form of government.

Macaulay's review had its own political context, namely the struggle for leadership in the era of reform and a desire to see off a radical group who were challenging the intellectual and historical foundations of progressive Whiggism. So it begins with a few well-placed insults at these Malvolios of contemporary intellectual life; they are 'schoolmen', Mill is 'an Aristotelian of the fifteenth century, born out of due season', attempting to write 'an elaborate treatise on Government, from which, but for two or three passing allusions, it would not appear that the author was aware that any governments actually existed among men'.[7] He goes on to demonstrate how Mill's theoretical propositions about the irreconcilability of monarchy and aristocracy, for example, are contradicted by the evidence of history, and he exposes how thin and unsatisfactory the utilitarian conception of 'interests' was. The demolition is so well done, the affirmation of the inductive over the *a priori* method of reasoning so conclusive, that one overlooks how self-serving this confident empiricism is. Democracy is tainted with the fanaticism of schoolmen, so when it is invoked as a possibility it is in terms of a nightmare future when 'a few lean and half-naked fishermen . . . divide with owls and foxes the ruins of the greatest of European cities' (p. 122). Empiricism is in league with government by interest groups who know best, for 'the higher and middling orders are the natural representatives of the human race. Their interest may be opposed, in some things, to that of their poorer contemporaries, but it is identical with that of the innumerable generations which are to follow' (pp. 122–3).

The 1832 Reform Act was brought about by people who thought like Macaulay, and who for their part saw it as a victory over Tory reaction and Benthamite utopianism. The philosophic radicals, their confidence shaken by attacks like Macaulay's, were stranded between compromising with Whig reformers in Parliament and losing constituency support by siding with more extreme groups like the Chartists outside.[8] But in one sense they had the last word, for the issues they raised about democracy and the individual's relationship to the state were to dominate political thought and debate in the next sixty years. Furthermore, although James Mill may have failed to educate more than a handful of his contemporaries, he did educate his son, and it was through his son's writings that the legacy of utilitarianism was transformed into that most characteristic of Victorian ideologies, liberal individualism.

John Stuart Mill: the evolution of a Victorian liberal

If one can bypass for a moment the famous education and mental crisis, there is much in John Stuart Mill's *Autobiography* (1873) which parallels a work antithetical to it in spirit and outlook, Newman's *Apologia Pro Vita Sua* (1864). Both are histories of opinion rather than acts of intimate confession, written by men who began in the severity of sects (Benthamism, Evangelicalism) and never shook off that severity, despite the story they tell of moving into wider intellectual waters. Both write with confidence in the knowledge that the story of their opinions is uniquely representative of major developments in contemporary intellectual life: the path from philosophic radicalism to liberalism, the pilgrimage from Oxford to Rome. Both record a coming to rest in early middle life in positions of apparently contented intellectual security, Newman in the arms of the Catholic Church, Mill in his marriage to Harriet Taylor (one is tempted to say 'in the arms of Harriet Taylor', but that suggests a carnality which seems to have been absent from their highminded union). By about 1840, if we are to believe the *Autobiography*, the thirty-four-year-old Mill had come to the end of his intellectual development: 'I have no further mental changes to tell of.'[9]

Of course, the education and its aftermath cannot be bypassed, for they have become a legendary stopping-place in any account of nineteenth-century intellectual life. John Mill had 'no remembrance of the time when [he] began to learn Greek', but thought it must have been about the age of three.[10] Between then and starting Latin at eight he read a number of the Greek prose classics, including Herodotus, Xenophon, and the first six dialogues of Plato. He also read extensively in ancient and modern history, but 'this was a voluntary rather than a prescribed exercise' (p. 29); and he also read and enjoyed *Don Quixote, The Arabian Nights*, and *Robinson Crusoe*. At eight he started on the Greek poets as well as learning Latin, and by twelve he had read *The Iliad* and *The Odyssey*, plays by the Greek dramatists, all Thucydides, and Aristotle's *Rhetoric*. Mill was required not only to be word-perfect himself but to pass on this knowledge to his younger sisters, and the story goes that if anyone failed their father's evening interrogations they all went to bed supperless.

Thus far James Mill had given his son a thorough if premature (by about ten years) grounding in the traditional classical education. Now at the age of twelve he was started on logic, with Aristotle's *Organon* and a drilling in 'syllogistic logic' which gave him skill, he later felt, in 'dissecting a bad argument' (p. 37). This was followed by Plato and training in the Socratic method, and then at thirteen by a course on political economy, which John Mill learned so well that his father was later able to use his son's notes when writing his *Elements of Political Economy*. At fourteen he went abroad to spend a year in the French home of Jeremy Bentham's brother, where he developed an interest in French politics and continental thought that was to be lifelong. John Mill was a modest man, and when he said that his education had given him 'an advantage of a quarter of a century over my contemporaries' (p. 44), he was not boasting.

Much nonsense is talked about the ill-effects of James Mill's system. His son insisted that it was not 'an education of cram' (p. 45), that he had learned to understand what he had been taught, and had been grateful all his life for learning how to dissect a bad argument and prosecute a good one. There is also Raymond Williams's point that when he read a criticism of James Mill's system he always felt like adding a marginal note: 'Yet the system, after all, produced John Stuart Mill.'[11] The deficiencies in the system were not that it was fact-crammed, or even that it asked too much of John Mill (that is how he saw it, anyway), but that it lacked love and affection, that it cut him off from the companionship and pursuits of his contemporaries, and most of all that it had made him prematurely analytical. So when the crisis came at the age of twenty, and he asked himself whether he would really be made happy if the reforms he had learned to work for were realised, he discovered that he would not. 'At this my heart sank within me: the whole foundation on which my life was constructed fell down' (p. 112). This mood of depression, of feelinglessness, which Mill illustrates by quoting Coleridge's 'Dejection Ode', lasted for many months and was only lifted when reading in Marmontel's *Memoirs* of the young boy's reaction to the death of his father, Mill found himself in tears. This moment of involuntary release – comparable to the Mariner's release when blessing the water snakes in *The Ancient Mariner* – lifted the gloom, and Mill found further 'medicine for [his] state of mind' (p. 121) in the work of another Romantic poet, Wordsworth. His tears at Marmontel's account of a father's death have an obvious root in his own feelings of loyalty, aggression, and guilt towards his overbearing father.

Mill traced his nervous breakdown, as it would be called today, back to an imbalance in his education, which 'had made precocious and premature analysis the inveterate habit of [his] mind' (p. 115). What was needed was a rediscovery of the importance of feeling: 'The maintenance of a due balance among the faculties, now seemed to me of primary importance. The cultivation of the feelings became one of the cardinal points in my ethical and philosophical creed' (p. 118). This realisation began to influence his thinking on philosophy and society, and it received a profound confirmation when in 1830 he met and fell in love with Harriet Taylor, who was then and remained for the next twenty years a married woman. The father dominates the first part of the *Autobiography* with his 'masculine' intellect and forcefulness; Harriet presides over the rest, an embodiment of noble, 'feminine' feeling and a symbol of Mill's victory over the elements in his upbringing which had brought about the mental crisis. If his praise of her virtues now seems excessive, it is partly because of the gratitude he felt to her for bringing him the affection and companionship denied in his childhood.

In the next fifteen years we can see Mill reappraising his radical inheritance in the light of these experiences and of the reading he was doing in contemporary thinkers. Much of this work was done in the form of reviews for periodicals and is marked by a new interest in, and sympathy for, the historical consciousness. Mill never forgot the mockery his father had received from Macaulay for presuming to discuss historical development in terms of 'universal laws', and he realised that Macaulay's empirical approach, while only superficially 'objective', was always able to summon up a rich texture of anecdote and example to trump any more theoretical approach. Did this mean that a 'science' of history and government was doomed to failure? Mill was reluctant to surrender this doctrine of utilitarian faith, and he saw that it would need to be historicised to survive. There might not be unchanging 'laws' of human nature, as his father had supposed, but there might be laws of historical development. About 1830 he started to read the writings of Claude Henri Saint-Simon (1760–1825), the founder of French socialism, and of his followers, who included Comte. Mill was immediately attracted to their division of history into 'organic' periods, when men and women were held in the sway of a controlling belief, and 'critical' periods, when the belief started to lose its hold over their minds, their behaviour, and their modes of social organisation. Christianity had been such an 'organic' period, but a 'critical' phase had set in with the Reformation and reached a crisis with the French Revolution. There was nothing very new in the perception of the present as a time of transition and crisis, but the Saint-Simonians put it in the context of a historical dynamic.

Auguste Comte (1798–1857) took the task of systematisation a good deal further. Positivism, the philosophy with which his name is associated, is both an interpretation of past history and a prognosis of future progress based on a 'positive' synthesis of all human activities in a new science of society – a kind of sociology with wings. It was based on his law of the three stages: that societies, institutions, and sciences pass through a 'Theological' phase, when all phenomena are understood in relation to a supernatural power; a 'Metaphysical', when they are interpreted in the light of abstract laws and principles; and the 'Positive', when they are finally revealed in their true reality by the only method which carried authority in the nineteenth century – the inductive method of scientific observation. But the Positive stage had not yet been achieved; there was work to be done in extending the methods of science into the human sphere, and synthesising physical, natural, and human science into a new master-science of sociology. Once this had been done, however, and the 'law' of humanity's development been consecrated by the Religion of Humanity (see Chapter 3 above), mankind would have the key to progress.

It is not hard to see why Comte and the Saint-Simonians appealed to Mill at this time of upheaval in his intellectual and emotional development. As he wrote in the *Autobiography*:

> This doctrine harmonized well with my existing notions,
> to which it seemed to give a scientific shape. I already

regarded the methods of physical science as the proper
models for political. But the chief benefit which I derived
at this time from the trains of thought suggested by
the St Simonians and by Comte, was, that I obtained a
clearer conception than ever before of the peculiarities
of an era of transition in opinion, and ceased to mistake
the moral and intellectual characteristics of such an era,
for the normal attributes of humanity. I looked forward,
through the present age of loud disputes but generally
weak convictions, to a future which shall unite the best
qualities of the critical with the best qualities of the organic
periods . . . . (pp. 132–3)

The last sentence shows Mill's willingness to reconcile, if not to
synthesise, opposing concepts and ideas. So in the 1830s and 1840s
we find him starting to explore the truths of human nature and society
inherent in conservative writings which, as a young radical, he had seen
dismissed out of hand by his father; extending his interest, too, into
kinds of writing, like poetry, for which they had had no time. In 'The
Two Kinds of Poetry' (1833) he explores the possibility that there might
be a kind of thought-in-feeling in poetry as valid as the philosopher's
search for truth; and in an 1838 essay on Alfred de Vigny he develops
a distinction between the 'conservative' and the 'radical' types of poet,
concluding that while the greatest will combine aspects of both, 'there
is a perpetual antagonism between these two; and until human affairs
are much better ordered than they are likely to be for some time to
come, each will require to be, in a greater or less degree, tempered by
the other'.[12]

Mill's receptivity to conservative ideas in the later 1830s owes
something to his friendship with disciples of Coleridge like John Sterling
and F.D. Maurice, and takes the characteristic form of trying to
'temper' his radical inheritance with the best insights of their tradition.
This process of tempering is at its most impressive in the two,
linked essays on 'Bentham' (1838) and 'Coleridge' (1840). These men
were 'the two great seminal minds of England in their age', and
their achievements were complementary: 'to Bentham it was given to
discern more particularly those truths with which existing doctrines
and institutions were at variance; to Coleridge the neglected truths
which lay *in* them'.[13] Bentham had brought a new, essentially scientific
approach to the problems of legislation; by breaking every subject
down into its smallest constituent parts and reclassifying them in
the light of the utility principle, he had made reform possible: 'He
found the philosophy of law a chaos, he left it a science' (p. 75).
But his philosophical reach had been fatally crippled by his boyish

temperament ('He was a boy to the last'), and by the narrow limits of his understanding of human motivation, which showed no imagination for disinterested conduct in any of its forms. Coleridge comes across as a radical conservative, looking for the truths that lay within institutions rejected as corrupt by reformers; for 'the very fact that any doctrine had been believed by thoughtful men, and received by whole nations or generations of mankind, was part of the problem to be solved, was one of the phenomena to be accounted for' (p. 100). Mill is particularly taken with the argument in Coleridge's *On the Constitution of Church and State* (1830) in favour of a national clerisy, which he interprets in a secular sense as providing opportunity for informed intellectuals to lead opinion and keep society in contact with its past.

In the background of Mill's sympathy for Coleridge's organicism and attraction to the idea of a clerisy is a growing ambivalence towards the workings of democracy, another article of Benthamite faith inherited from his father. James Mill had been a democrat for largely negative reasons, as a safeguard from the tyranny of interest groups, and in particular the tyranny of aristocracy. His son felt the moral force of the democratic ideal but feared something else, the tyranny of public opinion and its power to enforce a general mediocrity. Reviewing Alexis de Tocqueville's *Democracy in America* (1835) in 1840, he concluded rather pessimistically that America was a mirror in which a Britain without its aristocracy could be seen: it was '*all* middle class', a society reduced to uniformity by commercialism, and therefore requiring a counterpoise in the shape of some institutionalised form of clerisy which would sustain 'an opposite order of sentiments, principles of action, and modes of thought'. These would be 'an agricultural class, a leisured class, and a learned class'.[14]

An 'opposite order': Mill's liberalism, as it grew out of his father's radicalism, is characterised by a strong theoretical commitment to the virtue of hearing the other side – not in a spirit of easy tolerance (though tolerance is important), and not in order to arrive at a compromise or a synthesis, but in a mood of moral and mental discipline. The progressive intellectual keeps himself and his society fit through a continual willingness to see the weaknesses in his own side and do justice to the strengths in his opponent's case. If he can, he will assimilate these strengths; but if he cannot, he will still honour them and struggle to ensure that the conservative case is heard at its best. And he will pay particular attention to the criticism which the conservative makes of the radical case, since that is the last thing which the radical is likely to hear or attend to – as Mill well knew from growing up in a radical sect. Such strenuous open-mindedness is what distinguishes liberalism from the single eye of radicalism.

On Liberty (1859), is, with the *Autobiography*, Mill's best-known and most enduring work, and the one which most fully sets out the desirability of a society that is intellectually plural. Its basic assertion is simple (too simple, some have said): 'that the sole end for which mankind are warranted, individually or collectively, in interfering with the liberty of action of any of their number is self-protection'.[15] The liberty to be guarded by this 'principle' comprises freedom of thought and expression, 'liberty of tastes and pursuits . . . of doing as we like', and freedom for individuals to combine 'for any purpose not involving harm to others' (p. 71). The argument is conducted with an urgency born of Mill's conviction that 'the tendency of all the changes taking place in the world is to strengthen society, and diminish the power of the individual' (p. 73), and that in Britain the most pressing danger came from the power of public opinion in the newspapers to squeeze out individuality and enforce a dull uniformity: this is not, it must be said, how many of his contemporaries saw the situation. Individuality is not only a good in itself but contributes to the good of society as a whole:

> In proportion to the development of his individuality, each person becomes more valuable to himself, and is, therefore, capable of being more valuable to others. There is a greater fullness of life about his own existence, and when there is more life in the units there is more in the mass which is composed of them. (pp. 127–8)

For all his theoretical insistence on the value of richness and diversity, however, there remains something abstract in Mill's conception of individuality, and the talk of 'units' and 'mass' here reveals how hard he found it to escape from the mentality he had criticised in Bentham ('Bentham's idea of the world is that of a collection of persons pursuing each his separate interest or pleasure'). Mill's sense of society in *On Liberty* is atomistic and negative, and the work's affirmation of the rights of the individual is expressed in terms of an extreme divorce between the individual and society. There is little if any feeling for the ways in which a rich individuality might be nourished by custom and tradition, and this thinness at the roots leads to a corresponding élitism: 'No government by a democracy or a numerous aristocracy . . . ever did or could rise above mediocrity, except in so far as the sovereign many have let themselves be guided (which in their best times they always have done) by the counsels and influence of a more highly gifted and instructed *one* or *few*' (p. 131).

The limitations of Mill's liberalism are evident in his handling of education. He objects to the setting up of a state system on the grounds that it would be 'a mere contrivance for moulding people to be exactly like one another', which if successful would establish 'a despotism over the mind, leading by natural tendency to one over the body'. At the same time children must learn to read, and he proposes that they should have to attend public examinations in a series of ascending complexity to ensure basic literacy and numeracy; if they failed, the father 'might be subjected to a moderate fine, to be worked out, if necessary, by his labour, and the child might be put to school at his expense' (p. 177). A proposal so doctrinaire and despotic reveals a breathtaking ignorance of the reality of working-class life. One can only conclude that Mill's consciousness of his own over-education left him with little awareness that under-education might be worse.

Mill's resistance to state education marks *On Liberty* out as a document of the first phase of Victorian liberalism, when individuality had to be rescued from society rather than developed within it. The fact that there are still and perhaps always will be societies which oppress the individual gives the book its enduring relevance. So, too, do its arguments in favour of eccentricity, freedom of association, minority rights, and free speech, which need defending even (or perhaps especially) in societies which think themselves to be free. But it is not simply a document in the public realm, and one can speculate that it may also have held an unconscious autobiographical significance for Mill himself. In the setting out and development of its main assertion of liberty his father would have found much to approve. But even James Mill might have picked up the note of rebellion in his son's advocacy of heterodox opinion, although he would not presumably have traced it back to his educational regime. We can, however, in passages like this:

> Supposing it were possible to get houses built, corn grown,
> battles fought, causes tried, and even churches erected
> and prayers said by machinery – by automatons in human
> form – it would be a considerable loss to exchange for
> these automatons even the men and women who at present
> inhabit the more civilized parts of the world, and who
> assuredly are but starved specimens of what nature can and
> will produce. Human nature is not a machine to be built
> after a model, and set to do exactly the work prescribed
> for it, but a tree, which requires to grow and develop itself
> on all sides, according to the tendency of the inward forces
> which make it a living thing. (p. 123)

Mill too aspired to being a living tree rather than a Benthamite machine, and the idea of development 'on all sides' was the impetus behind his own intellectual journey and his distinctive legacy to Victorian liberalism.

The culture of politics

Mill's most substantial contributions to political debate are his essay *On the Subjection of Women* (1869), which argues for reform of their legal situation and voting rights on the same terms as men, and his *Considerations on Representative Government* (1861). The latter gives political flesh to the concerns of *On Liberty* and reflects Mill's new commitment to a contemporary reform which Trollope hated: a civil service chosen by competitive examination. Legislation was to be proposed by a legislative commission of experts drawn from a bureaucratic élite, which Parliament should be able to debate and reject but not amend in detail. The suffrage should be limited to those who could read and write, and minority opinion institutionalised by proportional representation. The ballot should be open rather than secret, since willingness to defend one's vote was a necessary part of Mill's essentially educative conception of democracy. It staked out a position of 'advanced liberalism' which, like much that Mill wrote, presupposed a greater appetite for self-development in the individual citizen than most possessed, then or now.

The insights of cynicism were denied to Mill, but they help to make Walter Bagehot's *The English Constitution* (1867) the classic analysis of the realities of political power in mid-Victorian Britain. Worldly-wise, witty, cynical, anti-theoretical – and with a touch of the complacency that often accompanies these qualities and was typical of the economic prosperity and declining radicalism of the 1860s – Bagehot is the Lord Chesterfield of constitutional history. Just as Chesterfield exposed the Augustan 'art of pleasing' by revealing its hidden motivations, so Bagehot opened up the ornately decorated clock face of the English constitution to reveal the inner mechanism. The clock works, and works well, but there is little relation between its workings and the various 'literary' (i.e. theoretical) explanations given. Bagehot is refreshingly free from the pompousness of Burke and Macaulay on constitutional matters, and he sees the Mills's search for a science of politics as putting the cart before the horse. Forget the fiction that England was governed by the Queen in Parliament. Forget the theory of the three estates – Monarch, Lords, and Commons – and the balanced constitution. Admire by all means, for they are admirable, the symbolism and pageantry of state occasions. But do not imagine that any of these things explains the success of the English constitution. The clock is driven by the weights of deference and hidden power, the '*efficient* parts' behind the '*dignified*'.[16]

England, in fact, is a 'disguised republic'. The monarch is important: as symbolic head of society she is intelligible to the many and removes that post from political ambition; she is a focus for religion and a mirror for morality. But she no longer rules, although she may advise the real rulers. Nor do the aristocracy in the House of Lords rule. They symbolise the stability of land, which carries a prestige higher than that of money, but their chamber is ill-attended and selected on principles too narrow to attract ability. Monarch and aristocracy constitute the 'dignified' part of the constitution: their function is to encourage and satisfy the attitude of 'deference' to rank which is the hidden spring of the system. The 'efficient' part is the House of Commons: there the emergence of ability is guaranteed (for Bagehot) in almost Darwinian terms. Whereas monarchs and nobles inherit, the leaders in Parliament have to struggle in a testing open market which ensures that those who rise to the top will be individuals of exceptional and varied abilities.

> They will have had to conduct the business of Parliament
> so as to satisfy it; they will have to speak so as to satisfy
> it. The two together cannot be done save by a man of very
> great and varied ability. The exercise of the two gifts is
> sure to teach a man much of the world; and if it did not,
> a Parliamentary leader has to pass through a magnificent
> training before he becomes a leader. (p. 117)

These 'leaders', assembled in Cabinet, constituted the real machinery of government.

Government by men like these was in the interest of all, however inadequately their interests were reflected in the composition of Parliament. Bagehot's limitations – which were partly the limitations of his class and period – show in his complacent attitudes to extending the franchise. Adult male suffrage would make this form of government impossible, he writes, but that is not what most people want: they are happy with the present arrangements. As for the exclusion of the working-classes, since they 'contribute almost nothing to our *corporate public opinion* . . . the fact of their want of influence in Parliament does not impair the coincidence of Parliament with public opinion' (p. 176, my italics). Still, appearance requires that 'their advocates should be heard as other people's advocates are heard', otherwise the House of Commons 'will not *look* right' (p. 181). The idea that considerations of justice might be involved in this issue does not weigh with Bagehot:

'corporate public opinion' is what counts, and he is unaware of, and unconcerned by, the extremely narrow range within which it operated – that it largely excluded women, for example, most of the population outside London and all of it outside 'England', and the contemporary social classes from the small shopkeeper down.

Bagehot's complacent acceptance of the limits of the political nation coexists with a radical scepticism about its mode of operation. There is nothing in Carlyle or Dickens more devastating in its implications than Bagehot's description of the English constitution as a *'theatrical show* of society', a pageant of great men and beautiful women and conspicuous wealth.

> There is in England a certain charmed spectacle which imposes on the many, and guides their fancies as it will. As a rustic on coming to London finds himself in presence of a great show and vast exhibition of inconceivable mechanical things, so by the structure of our society, he finds himself face to face with a great exhibition of political things which he could not have imagined, which he could not make – to which he feels in himself scarcely anything analogous.
> (p. 248)

And so while the rustic gapes open-mouthed at the spectacle, he fails to see where real power lies:

> The apparent rulers of the English nation are like the most imposing personages of a splendid procession: it is by them the mob are influenced; it is they whom the spectators cheer. The real rulers are secreted in second-rate carriages; no one cares for them or asks about them, but they are obeyed implicitly and unconsciously by reason of the splendour of those who eclipsed and preceded them.
> (p. 249)

Perhaps the brilliance of Bagehot's metaphor here concedes, like Chesterfield's letters, rather more than even he meant to give away, for its implications are revolutionary. If most of the English people are a kind of country bumpkin imposed upon by the mere show of society, then the task of the radical reformer must be to expose the glitter of the show and awaken the bumpkin to his real strength – which is what Marx wanted to do.

Bagehot contributed at least three insights of permanent value to the understanding of British political society. One is the notion of deference, the respect which royalty and aristocracy attract from those below them in the social scale. Another is his distinction between the dignified and the efficient parts of the constitution, which later analysts have placed differently but still found useful in understanding the workings of constitutional monarchy. The third, bound up with deference, is his awareness that imagination and emotion play a much larger part in determining attitudes than the utilitarian rationalism of a Mill ever allowed. 'As yet the few rule by their hold, not over the reason of the multitude, but over their imaginations, and their habits; over their fancies as to distant things they do not know at all, over their customs as to near things which they know very well' (pp. 250–1). But only 'as yet'; he feared that any considerable extension of the franchise would destroy the mystique on which the system depended, and his introduction to the 1872 edition is pessimistic about the consequences of the 1867 Reform Bill which had enfranchised the urban working class: 'As a theoretical writer I can venture to say, what no elected member of Parliament, Conservative or Liberal, can venture to say, that I am exceedingly afraid of the ignorant multitude of the new constituencies' (p. 281).

Although *The English Constitution* is an enduring classic of political thought, its usefulness as a guide to the political nation is greatest for the period between the First and Second Reform Bills, 1832 and 1867. Gladstone's 1868 government worked to a new agenda with a new generation, and on his own admission Bagehot was happier with those he called the 'pre-'32 statesmen' (p. 269). Like Trollope, he found it hard to imagine a world not ruled by men like Lord Palmerston. So far from being a limitation, however, Bagehot's awareness of the power of aristocracy is his chief contribution to illuminating the context in which the political novels of Disraeli and Trollope were written and read. Local government was different, but the culture of national politics before 1870 was profoundly aristocratic. Not only were cabinet members and prime ministers drawn disproportionately from the landed classes, the whole rhythm of politics was dictated by the London 'season' and the shooting season which followed it. Aristocratic assumptions governed the elections of MPs. It was an expensive business getting elected if one did not have an aristocratic or other patron, since votes had to be bought. When he contested the Yorkshire constituency of Beverley in the 1868 election Trollope was told by his agent: 'You won't get in. I don't suppose you really expect it. But there is a fine career open to you. You will spend £1000, and lose the election. Then you will petition, and spend another £1000. You will throw out the elected members. There will be a commission, and the borough will be disfranchised. For a beginner such as you are, that will be a great success.'[17] This proved to be a quite accurate prediction of the course of events at Beverley, except that Trollope managed to escape with losses of 'only' £400.

It cost money to get into Parliament and it cost money to stay there. MPs were unpaid in the nineteenth century; the only hope of a salary came with government office. The dilemma of the politician without money, pulled in opposite directions by political ambition and financial need on the one hand, and principle on the other, is the subject of Trollope's *Phineas Finn* (1867–69). His disillusioning experience at Beverley darkens his portrayal of political life in its successor, *Phineas Redux* (1873–74). But Trollope did not want the modern solution to these problems, salaried MPs elected by secret ballot, any more than a civil service meritocracy. He clung to an ideal of gentlemanly disinterestedness as superior to the professionalisation of government, and embodied it in the figure of that 'very noble gentleman',[18] Plantagenet Palliser.

The importance of the ideal of the gentleman in mid-Victorian political culture can hardly be exaggerated. Put crudely, it was a concept that aristocrats had been brought up to honour and the new public schools were putting in the grasp of the middle classes, and so formed a ground on which both could meet with dignity. Not being the preserve of a single caste, it was open to negotiation and therefore to appropriation from below: the new professional classes – doctors, civil servants – could claim it, wealthy manufacturers could buy it for their sons in the public schools, Samuel Smiles ended *Self-Help* (1859) by offering 'The True Gentleman' as the goal of character to which the self-helper should aspire. That Plantagenet Palliser might not have recognised the village youth reading his Smiles as a gentleman did not matter: the important thing is that it was an agreed cultural goal which facilitated the incorporation of a new élite within the old structure, giving social dignity and self-respect to the new generation of professional men Britain needed to administer an increasingly complex society at home and an expanding empire abroad. Considered in this light, the Victorian redefinition of the gentleman was an extremely successful enterprise, since it harnessed the traditional elements of honour and disinterestedness to the Victorian values of work, self-discipline, energy, and perseverance. The Victorian middle classes made gentlemanliness into an ethic of honest administration.

The rhetoric of gentlemanliness prevailed in the House of Commons, where the convention of referring to one's opponent as 'the honourable gentleman (or lady) opposite' survives to this day. It is a 'dignified' part of the system which was also highly 'efficient'. An unseemly dispute could usually be terminated by an appeal to a common code, as Palmerston did in 1852 when he made a conciliatory speech reminding his followers that 'we who are Gentlemen on this side of the House should remember that we are dealing with Gentlemen on the other side'.[19] The code reached out to the clubs and salons in London where 'society', journalism, and politics met in a tight little world which set firm limits to political debate. One writer in 1881, seeking to explain why the socialism of Marx had failed to take on in the country that had provided him with all his data, put it down to the fact that in England 'there is no democratic or revolutionary opposition, organized or speculative. The course of politics has long run very smooth; none of the questions of the day have forced the fundamental principles of the existing system into popular debate; there has been no abstract philosophical discussion of them of any deep-reaching kind.'[20] It was extraordinarily difficult to get an issue like women's suffrage discussed in Parliament at all. Working-class suffrage was discussed, but only in terms of minimal concessions, and the system was heavily weighted against the election of a working man to Parliament.

If the code of the gentleman (and the lady) dominated Westminster, then an ethos of respectability was at work behind attempts to reconstruct working-class political culture after the disappointments of Chartism in the 1840s. These focused on the trades unions, which had always been vulnerable to trade depressions and accusations of lawlessness (unions were secret societies that committed their members to violent acts) and economic illiteracy (unions could do nothing to alter wages, which were determined by the laws of the market). But men like Robert Applegarth (1834–1925) did much to change the public perception of unionism. By developing large amalgamated unions from local roots – by 1870 his General Union of Carpenters and Joiners had ten thousand members and over two hundred and thirty branches[21] – he and others like him were able to offer their members some elementary social security benefits as well as the usual strike pay. More importantly, they set an example of legality and constitutionalism, and – in Applegarth's impressive witness to the Royal Commission on Trades Unions set up in 1867 – articulate moderation. Respectable unionism won its legal rights in the 1870s, and by doing so created the conditions in which a new political force, the Labour Party, could be born.

One can read Trollope and Bagehot and overlook the fact that there was another political culture beyond Westminster, in the municipal life of the cities and towns. The Municipal Reform Act of 1835 created great opportunities for the energetic local reformer, and although the political rhetoric of reform was in favour of individualism and financial retrenchment – the state reduced to a 'nightwatchman' role – the practice often proved rather different. The public health problems created by industrialisation could not be cured by sticking-plaster, and their solution required amounts of public money not allowed for in classical economic theory. Progress, in the shape of public libraries, museums, parks, cost money; some of it came from local magnates turned philanthropist, like Andrew Carnegie in Scotland or the Rowntree family in York, but most had to come from the rates. There were possible careers of satisfying local achievement through helping to institute these reforms, but the pull of Westminster was always there for the very ambitious. The classic case is Joseph Chamberlain (1836–1914), who as Mayor of Birmingham from 1873 to 1876 developed what was known as 'gas and water socialism', using the profits from the utilities he had taken into municipal ownership to finance an ambitious scheme of urban improvement. At the age of forty he went into Parliament and rose to become the leader of the imperialist wing of the Liberal Party. It is one of the many ironies of history, however, that the sanitary reforms and slum clearances he helped to implement in Birmingham have lasted longer than the British Empire around which his national reputation was based.

Democracy, the state, and socialism

The nature of democracy and the wisdom or otherwise of extending the franchise were the issues which exercised the political nation in the 1860s. The debate took place within what are considered today very narrow, even élitist, limits: the modern principle of one-person, one-vote was remote from all but the most radical imaginations. Even the Chartists, who three times brought their petition for reform to Westminster (in 1839, 1842, and 1848), had asked only for universal *male* suffrage, and no government was prepared to concede even that until 1918. At bottom was a fear of the 'residuum', the landless labourers and migrant poor who, it was felt, might become an overwhelming force if stirred up by some unscrupulous demagogue. Consequently, extensions of the franchise were tied to property and the payment of rates – to the £10 householder in 1832, then to all urban householders in 1867, then to county householders in 1884. By the end of our period two out of three adult males had the vote, but it was around the enfranchisement of the majority of the urban working class in 1867 that the most anxious debate centred. Disraeli's Bill of that year, and Gladstone's first Liberal government elected on the new franchise in 1868, were widely felt to mark a decisive turning-point in Victorian politics.

    To some it was a simple matter of 'Shooting Niagara' (1867), as Carlyle called it in an essay of that title; but his reaction can be discounted as an old man's hysteria. Matthew Arnold looked at the Hyde Park riots which followed the Home Secretary's injudicious decision to ban a meeting of the Reform League there in 1866, and saw in them the 'anarchy' implicit in Mill's philosophy of 'doing as one likes'

(*Culture and Anarchy*, 1869). But what strikes one in retrospect is how groundless were the fears of the pessimists; the disenfranchised were more patient and more constitutional in their expectations than Carlyle or Marx thought possible. The post-Reform Bill Parliaments did not 'shoot Niagara' but completed the business of 1832; the significance of Gladstone's ministry of 1868–74 lies not in what it did for the working class but in its consolidation of the power of the middle classes. The new nation at last came into its inheritance. A potentially unstable coalition of old Whigs, right-wing and advanced liberals, radicals, and Nonconformists at last enacted away most of their religious and civic disabilities. More controversially, since it clashed with advanced liberal nostrums of the minimal state as well as with nonconformist suspicion of Anglican influence, the 1870 Education Act took the first step towards setting up a national, publicly funded system of education in England and Wales.

Gladstone's 1868–74 reforming administration was a turning-point because it looked both back, to the redressing of historic civil grievances, and forwards to the inevitable outcome of reform in an enlarged role for the state. Education exemplified the dilemma for classical liberals: to build on the existing denomination-based system meant leaving too much power with the Established Church, but creating a non-denominational system meant raising taxes and thus making the nightwatchman state work by day as well as by night. It was the circle which Chamberlain had tried to square in Birmingham with his 'municipal socialism'. The reality was that reform and reduced public expenditure were incompatible: Gladstone's dream of abolishing income tax was as fanciful as Trollope's Plantagenet Palliser's scheme for decimal coinage. Liberalism could only develop by growing out of the horror of the state action it had inherited from the political economists.

Discussion of democracy was energised by contemporary anxieties, among which may be mentioned fear of swamping by 'numbers' (what Carlyle called 'swarmery'), fear of the tyranny of public opinion (Mill), and fear of the loss of high cultural standards. 'The difficulty for democracy is', Matthew Arnold wrote, 'how to find and keep high ideals'. The sentence comes from Arnold's essay on 'Democracy' of 1861, which is in many ways the most measured and perceptive contribution to the debate. He does not rant like Carlyle but recognises that the coming of democracy is an inevitable development which, 'like other operations of nature, merits properly neither blame nor praise'.[22] It is, in fact, one manifestation of '*the modern spirit*', that 'irresistible force, which is gradually making its way everywhere, removing old conditions and imposing new, altering long-fixed habits, undermining venerable institutions, even modifying national character . . .' (p. 29)

Arnold's tolerant historicism enables him to recognise simultaneously that the age of aristocracies was passing, that its passing was inevitable, but that democracy has something of great importance to learn from the old order. Anticipating Bagehot in his use of the word, he sees that the aristocracy no longer command the 'deference' which their 'high feeling, dignity, and culture' (p. 13) used to inspire in those below them. The danger for democracy lies in becoming '*Americanised*' when it loses the elevating example of nobility and culture which, at its best, aristocracy provided.

> Nations are not truly great solely because the individuals composing them are numerous, free, and active; but they are great when these numbers, this freedom, and this activity are employed in the service of an ideal higher than that of an ordinary man, taken by himself. Our society is probably destined to become much more democratic; who or what will give a high tone to the nation then? That is the grave question. (p. 18)

Arnold's answer – one that no 'advanced liberal' could have accepted – is the state, defined as a nation's 'ideal of high reason and right feeling, representing its best self, commanding general respect, and forming a rallying-point for the intelligence and for the worthiest instincts of the community' (p. 19). It is at this point that Arnold the professed liberal becomes Arnold the conservative, and one begins to see him in a tradition of conservative–liberal thought going back to his father's, Thomas Arnold's, idea of a National Church and to Coleridge's clerisy. His essay evades the central problem of how such a state could be created in the world of contemporary politics, a problem that is redefined but brought no nearer solution when 'Culture' takes over from the 'State' in *Culture and Anarchy*. But Arnold's failure to deal with praxis invalidates neither his long-range historical analysis nor his critique of dogmatic individualism. He saw, for example, that Mill's free market in opinions offered no guarantee as to quality: 'It is a very great thing to be able to think as you like; but, after all, an important question remains: *what* you think' (p. 24). Indeed, his essay can be seen – like *Culture and Anarchy* where the chapter heading 'Doing as One Likes' comes from *On Liberty* – as partly a reply to Mill.

It is also a pondering upon the implications of the most influential discussion of democracy before 1860, Alexis de Tocqueville's *Democracy in America* (1835, 1840). Arnold's pejorative use of 'Americanise' shows a pessimistic interpretation of what in that book is a much more finely balanced assessment. Tocqueville (1805–59) saw the movement towards equality and democracy as inevitable, and approached America as a mirror in which the democratic future could be seen: 'I confess that in America I saw more than America; I sought there the image of democracy itself, with its inclinations, its character, its prejudices, and its passions, in order to learn what we have to fear or to hope from its progress.'[23] The fascination of America for European liberals like Tocqueville and Mill was that it was a society which had grown up without an aristocracy, and without the complicated entanglements of international relations which involved European societies in wasteful wars. America had gone further down the road of privatising individual life, and because the 'principle of enlightened self-interest' had there taken the place of traditional loyalties and motivations, American society could be seen as a kind of experiment in *laissez-faire*. This is what worried Arnold and attracted Mill.

Tocqueville saw in America a society where people behaved as if they were equal, and accounted for this not in terms of popular suffrage but of popular self-government at the local level. The United States had carried the principle of political decentralisation much further than any previous society. Provincial self-government might be more untidy and less efficient than government by an administrative élite, but because it involves each citizen as a citizen 'the feeling he entertains towards the state is analogous to that which unites him to his family, and it is by a kind of selfishness that he interests himself in the welfare of his country' (p. 94). And since there was no hidden agenda set by an élite, the greatest happiness of the greatest number was the principle deciding legislation. The dangers of democracy on the American model corresponded to its virtues: the poor calibre of representatives at national level; the 'despotism of the majority'; the tyranny of public opinion in a society without counterbalancing institutions of authority; the relative lack of independence of mind and freedom of discussion.

Mill wrote of Tocqueville that 'between aristocracy and democracy he holds the balance straight, with all the impassibility of a mere scientific observer'.[24] This is true, and all the more remarkable in Tocqueville's case because he was himself a member of the French *petite noblesse* whose grandfather and aunt had been guillotined during the Terror. But British discussion of democracy is haunted by the idea of aristocracy, as if by some great player past his best who no longer fits into the team plans. For Carlyle in 'Shooting Niagara' the true and best leaders were 'the unclassed Aristocracy by nature'.[25] Mill looked at Tocqueville's America and saw the English middle class, in its restlessness and upward mobility and commercialism, and looked for 'a great social support for opinions and sentiments different from those of the mass. The shape which that support may best assume is a question of time, place, and circumstance; but . . . there can be no doubt about the elements which must compose it: they are, an agricultural class, a leisured class, and a learned class' (p. 198). Mill's 'learned class' is Coleridge's clerisy again, and it is difficult to see how his 'agricultural class' would be very different from a landed aristocracy. Arnold's 'apostles of culture' in *Culture and Anarchy* are aristocrats of the spirit. Although he claims for them a commitment to 'the *social idea*' and to 'equality', the voice of an embodied culture often seems to speak in tones of aristocratic disdain:

> The people who believe most that our greatness and
> welfare are proved by our being very rich, and who most
> give their lives and thoughts to becoming rich, are just
> the very people whom we call Philistines. Culture says:
> 'Consider these people, then, their way of life, their habits,
> their manners, the very tones of their voice; look at them
> attentively; observe the literature they read, the things
> which give them pleasure, the words which come forth out
> of their mouths, the thoughts which make the furniture of
> their minds; would any amount of wealth be worth having
> with the condition that one was to become just like these
> people by having it?[26]

Arnold is prepared to call the *de facto* aristocracy 'Barbarians', but his 'we' addresses and attempts to create an alternative élite who would leaven the lump of democracy. When taken in conjunction with his jibes at Dissenters in *Culture and Anarchy*, and the ludicrous suggestion that they should consider joining the Established Church, it was a rhetoric more likely to alienate than persuade the philistines (the middle classes). In many ways the plainer treatment of the issues in 'Democracy' is more convincing today.

Arnold complained in *Culture and Anarchy* that 'we have not the notion, so familiar on the Continent and to antiquity, of *the State*' (p. 117). Not the notion perhaps, but the reality was steadily growing within the body of a society whose progressive rhetoric was of *laissez-faire* and minimal government. 'At the very time when the minimal, decentralized, regulatory, *laissez-faire* State of the entrepreneurial ideal was consolidating itself as the norm of political theory, the expanding, centralized, bureaucratic State of modern times was coming into being in administrative practice.'[27] What may be called the Victorian informa-tion explosion, the mass of data about the new society coming from the statistical societies and the decennial census returns, put a pressure on anti-interventionist ideology which only the very committed could resist. As we have seen in the case of Edwin Chadwick, public health was often the issue which converted administrators and politicians to positive action, since sanitary reform yielded such dramatic results. The establishment of professional civil and foreign services, selected by merit rather than patronage, and the development and consolidation of the modern professions, created in effect a modern clerisy whose interests could not be entirely identified with any of the traditional classes (upper, middle, and working). In conjunction with the clergy proper they formed an important and increasingly influential social group. Partly because professionalisation distanced them from the market-place, and partly because many of them had a direct interest in the efficient administration of a modern state, they no longer shared the urgency of their parents' faith in economic individualism.

There was one unequivocal spokesman for *laissez-faire* liberalism in the later Victorian period. Herbert Spencer (1820–1903) is a kind of eccentric uncle in the house of modern liberalism, just as likely to embarrass his nephews and nieces by revealing the primitiveness of his social views as by exposing the barbarism of theirs, for he was a strong opponent of imperialism at a time when the Liberal Party was starting to flirt with the idea. In *The Man versus the State* (1884) he accuses the modern Liberal of being essentially a Tory, for he has acquiesced in the steady growth of restrictive legislation in the last quarter-century. The fact that the examples he gives are largely in the areas of health and safety at work, weights and measures regulation, children's employment, and regulation of working hours, does not deter him from drawing the conclusion from this regulation that 'in so far as it has been extending the system of compulsion, what is now called Liberalism is a new form of Toryism'.[28] Worse, it will lead to the 'coming slavery' of socialism. We are taken down a toboggan ride which begins with Factory Acts and municipal libraries, and ends via increased taxes and bureaucracy in a nightmare world of socialist tyranny:

> It would need but a war with an adjacent society, or some
> internal discontent demanding forcible suppression, to at
> once transform a socialistic administration into a grinding
> tyranny like that of ancient Peru; under which the mass of
> the people, controlled by grades of officials, and leading
> lives that were inspected out-of-doors and in-doors,
> laboured for the support of the organisation which
> regulated them, and were left with but a bare subsistence
> for themselves. (p. 42)

It takes a fevered imagination to envisage how this Orwellian world could come about from setting up a municipal library, and the weakness in Spencer's argument is that he fails to distinguish between the kind of legislation that makes working conditions safer, trading standards more honest and accurate, industry therefore more efficient, and legislation which encroaches on the citizen's liberty of action. But for Spencer the distinction was probably not important; his faith in the doctrine of *laissez-faire* was total because it was underwritten by the 'laws' of nature. As the man who coined the phrase 'survival of the fittest', he saw any attempts to interfere with the evolutionary process in society as a tampering with 'laws' which, if left alone, would ultimately work towards progress. There would be suffering, but Spencer saw that as inevitable; there would be more suffering, amounting to the enfeeblement of the whole species, if the state stepped in to artificially protect the unfit, and he quotes a passage from his earlier *Social Statics* (1851) which includes the following:

> Note, further, that their carnivorous enemies not only remove from herbivorous herds individuals past their prime, but also weed out the sickly, the malformed, and the least fleet or powerful. . . . Meanwhile, the well-being of existing humanity, and the unfolding of it into this ultimate perfection, are both secured by that same beneficient, though severe discipline, to which the animate creation at large is subject: a discipline which is pitiless in the working out of good: a felicity-pursuing law which never swerves for the avoidance of partial and temporary suffering. The poverty of the incapable, the distresses that come upon the imprudent, the starvation of the idle, and those shoulderings aside of the weak by the strong . . . are the decrees of a large, far-seeing benevolence. (p. 67)

In 1884 Spencer disclaimed the 'teleological' (i.e. Providential) implications of this passage but nothing else: perhaps only a man without close human ties could have written it.

Spencer's 'Social Darwinism', as it came to be called, met with an enthusiastic reception in America from 1860 onwards, where his evolutionary ethic was interpreted as a justification for 'Robber Baron' capitalism. In Britain he was something of a nightmare from which second-generation liberal intellectuals were trying to awake. Their task was to rescue liberalism as a political philosophy from the 'pitiless discipline' of waste he had celebrated. It was also to construct a more positive conception of liberty than Mill's. Both tasks required a more creative approach to the idea of the state than classical liberalism had taken. In the writings of T.H. Green (1836–82), L.T. Hobhouse (1846–1929), and others, the reforming legislation which Spencer had deplored was justified for creating the conditions in which individuals

could develop their humanity and by doing so make a richer contribution to society as a whole. It might be an infringement of liberty in
the abstract to reduce the daily working hours of women in factories
from fourteen to ten, but a woman working fourteen hours a day
had effectively little time or energy left to use her liberty. So with
elementary education and public health. 'Every injury to the health of
the individual is,' Green said in 1881, 'so far as it goes, a public injury.
It is an impediment to the general freedom; so much deduction from our
power, as members of society, to make the best of ourselves.' Society
was therefore justified in setting certain limits to freedom of contract
and in enforcing sanitary regulations. As to compulsory education:

> Without a command of certain elementary arts and
> knowledge, the individual in modern society is as
> effectually crippled as by the loss of a limb or a broken
> constitution. He is not free to develop his faculties. With
> a view to securing such freedom among its members it
> is as certainly within the province of the state to prevent
> children from growing up in that kind of ignorance which
> practically excludes them from a free career in life, as it
> is within its province to require the sort of building and
> drainage necessary for public health.[29]

This switch in Liberal thinking from a hands-off individualism to a
wider concept of individuality as citizenship was accompanied by
a reappraisal of the Spencerian/Darwinian conflict-model of social
evolution. In his essay on 'The Ethical Basis of Collectivism' (1898)
Hobhouse questioned whether competition was the nature of advanced
organisms like human societies, citing the family as a prime example of
co-operation in nature. There are echoes of Arnold's 'best self' as well
as Romantic organicism in his assertion that the 'true conception of an
organic society is one in which the best self of each man is and is felt
to be bound up with the best life of his fellow-citizens'.[30] The 'organic'
metaphor – limp though it may be now from sociological over-use –
affirms a positive reciprocity between individual and environment, and
therefore a positive (if cautious) approach to state action: in Michael
Bentley's nice metaphor, the individual is 'not so much an impermeable
brick out of which a "society" might be built in the manner of a wall
as a soluble crystal dependent for its consistency and usefulness on the
medium that surrounds it'.[31]

    In the case of someone like Hobhouse, advanced liberalism is talking
over the garden-fence to Fabian socialism. As a friend of Beatrice and
Sydney Webb, as the first Professor of Sociology at London University,
and as the author of a book on *The Labour Movement* (1893), Hobhouse

illustrates the part played by liberalism in shaping the character of British socialism, which has traditionally been parliamentary and libertarian. (Perhaps this should be narrowed to 'English' socialism, for its Scottish version has shown a dark strain of sympathy with totalitarianism, as a dip in the collected poems of Hugh McDiarmid will demonstrate.) The first working-class members of Parliament – miners – entered as Liberals in 1874. Socialism as a political ideology and incipient movement does not make itself felt until the 1880s. In the 1840s and 1850s there had been the Christian Socialists, it is true, but that was an essentially paternalistic movement led by middle-class Christian reformers like F.D. Maurice and Thomas Hughes (1822–96), and lacked the grass-roots involvement to sustain it. Only in Germany was there a developed socialist movement, and according to John Rae in his 1881 article on 'The Socialism of Karl Marx and the Young Hegelians', this had made little impact in Britain, where 'the writings of Marx are hardly better known . . . than those of Confucius'. His explanation is that British socialism is not 'revolutionary': 'the working classes are preoccupied with the development of trades unions, of friendly societies, and of the great co-operative movement, from which . . . they not unwarrantably expect great results. Revolutionary Socialism is therefore quite foreign to the present temper of the English mind.'[32] The first English edition of *Das Kapital* did not appear until 1887.

The father of the 'great co-operative movement' which Rae mentions is usually taken to be the Welshman Robert Owen (1771–1858), the factory owner and inspirer of the early co-operative societies. Yet it can be argued that the social experiment by which Owen is best known, the cotton mills at New Lanark, belongs just as plausibly to the history of enlightened capitalist paternalism as to the history of socialism. Owen had a Rousseauistic faith in the shaping power of environment, and when he took over the management of his father-in-law's mills he was determined to put this faith into action by reforming every aspect of his workers' lives: their working and housing conditions were improved; a shop was opened to sell them food at reasonable prices; their children under ten were taken from the factory and either looked after in a nursery (thus allowing the mothers to work) or educated in a school which was also a kind of community centre where evening lectures and dances were held; and the environment was given a 'village' character with a green in front of the school, landscaped paths, and gardens where the workers could grow their own vegetables. Recreation was important and Owen, a secularist, spared his workers and their families the horrors of the traditional Scottish Presbyterian sabbath. The experiment worked, or so Owen claimed in his influential *A New View of Society* (1813); the 2,000 inhabitants were greatly improved under the new regime: 'Drunkenness is not seen in their streets, and the children are taught and trained in the institution for forming their character without any punishment. The community exhibits the general appearance of industry, temperance, comfort, health, and happiness.'[33] The venture also made increased profits for Owen and his financial backers.

New Lanark belongs to the pastoral phase of British industrialisation. Beautifully situated on the banks of the upper Clyde, whose waters powered the mills, its village-like character encouraged Owen to find a solution to post-Napoleonic War social distress in the idea of small 'Villages of Cooperation' for the unemployed. These were never realised successfully, partly through lack of government support, partly because of the difficulty that attends all attempts to create co-operative communities within a competitive society. When the co-operative movement took off later in the century its founding members compromised with the profit motive to the extent that the Rochdale Pioneers, when drawing up their historic constitution in 1844, allowed for the paying of a dividend to members. The co-operative and labour movements drew much inspiration from Owenite example, but deferred his Utopian hopes in favour of creating a working-class mutual-aid system within society, which would provide some basic welfare provision as well as food, and would work with the trades union movement for the gradual transformation of society from within. Like the gradualism of the Fabian Society which provided much of the intellectual leadership of the early Labour Party, theirs was a long-range and peaceful socialism. Revolutionary socialism looked for the violent and 'inevitable' overthrow of the bourgeoisie by the industrial proletariat predicted by Marx; every riot in an industrialised country proved a false dawn, and the revolution came belatedly in the one European country where, in terms of the Marxian analysis, the catalyst conditions did not exist: feudal Russia.

There is no more remarkable and yet representative account of the transition from classical liberalism to democratic socialism than that given by Beatrice Webb in her autobiography, *My Apprenticeship* (1926). Her family background was an archetypal new nation genealogy: grandparents who had risen from humble origins to employer status – 'Nonconformists in religion and Radicals in politics, they both became, after the 1832 Reform Act, Members of Parliament, intimate friends of Cobden and Bright, and enthusiastic supporters of the Anti-Corn Law League.'[34] Her father graduated in law from the new London University, of which one grandfather, a Unitarian, had been a founder. After losing his family fortune in the financial crash of 1847–48, her father recovered it, and more, as a successful timber trader; and in becoming a wealthy entrepreneur he dropped both the radicalism and the unitarianism, switching in the 1860s to conservatism. 'As a citizen of the British Empire my father bred true to the typical political development of Victorian capitalism' (p. 8). Herbert Spencer was a close family friend; some of the most moving passages in the autobiography concern her affection for this 'good old man' who had given her his time and attention when no one else did in her childhood, but whose social and political views she could not share.

Beatrice Webb reminds one of a George Eliot heroine, like Dorothea Brooke in *Middlemarch*: she was born into privilege and longed to improve the world, and she brought to the task religious energies no longer satisfied by traditional Christianity. But the autobiography reveals her to be much tougher than Dorothea Brooke. Through her father and Herbert Spencer she was exposed to the hard logic of *laissez-faire*; through the visits she made, incognito, to the Lancashire mill town her family had come from, she experienced the 'religious socialism of the dissenting communities' (p. 166), and realised that their almost pastoral balance of chapel and co-op could not last. The new socialism must be able to answer the one and retain the communal warmth and powers of self-government of the other. The turning-point in her career came when Webb joined Charles Booth (1840–1916) to work on his pioneering survey of poverty in London. Booth recognised, and Webb through working with him, that the constant exchange between the individualists and the socialists rested on *a priori* assumptions on both sides; and he set out to establish the facts of poverty in London by a scientific combination of quantitative analysis (based on census and school attendance figures) and qualitative description (based on home visiting). The seventeen volumes of *Life and Labour of the People in London* (1903) put the description and analysis of urban poverty on a new plane of statistical sophistication: they revealed that while the majority of the working population was living in some degree of security, thirty per cent – or over a million people – lived in a state of poverty.

Webb believed that Booth's work had been responsible for the 1908 Old Age Pensions Act, as well as other welfare legislation, but she saw his method of sociological analysis as being even more important. His 'sociological science', based on breadth of data and depth of analysis, made him 'the boldest pioneer . . . and the achiever of the greatest results, in the methodology of the social sciences of the nineteenth century' (p. 247). The time was up for the grand systematisers like Comte and Marx and Spencer, and Booth's researches had exposed the inadequacy of private philanthropy; the social reformer's task now was a *fin de siècle* Benthamism – to provide and analyse the essential data. And since the data revealed the failure, as Webb saw it, of the 'gigantic and cruel experiment' (p. 344) of the Industrial Revolution, what must take its place is the managed society of socialism. In the final chapter, 'Why I

Became a Socialist', she describes the stages by which she abandoned her hopes of curing social evils by controlling 'the economic activities of the landlord and the capitalist' (p. 391), and her discovery of the potential for social justice in the co-operative and trades union movements: 'It was . . . by the recognition that the essential feature in the co-operative movement was not the advantages that it brought in the way of economical housekeeping and the thrifty accumulation of continual small savings, but the invention of a new type of industrial organisation – the government of industry by the community of consumers, for their common benefit as consumers – that my difficulties were removed' (p. 393). Here in a nutshell is the difference between advanced liberalism and socialism at the end of our period. Reforming liberals were prepared to go as far as what Charles Booth called 'Socialism in the arms of Individualism', believing that 'our Individualism fails because our Socialism is incomplete' (p. 254). Socialism looked for 'the invention of a new type of industrial organisation'.

Empire and Utopia

Between 1846, when Peel fell from office over the repeal of the Corn Laws, and 1874, when Disraeli at last came to power with a viable majority, the Conservative Party enjoyed only two short periods in office. For much of that time their leaders had their hands full keeping their ship united and afloat on a current that seemed to be running strongly with free-trade liberalism. But in the 1870s the current changed, and Disraeli managed, in Robert Blake's words, 'to acquire for the Conservatives a monopoly in the partisan expression of a new *Zeitgeist* – the inchoate, half-romantic, half-predatory emotions and ideas inspired by the idea of empire during the last quarter of the nineteenth century'.[35] It is not easy to account for such changes in the *Zeitgeist*. The British Empire had been steadily growing since the sixteenth century: why did people suddenly awaken to its importance in the 1870s? A combination of factors would seem to be responsible. There was the Indian Mutiny of 1857–58 and the shock waves it sent out, a violent reminder of the fragility of the British presence in the subcontinent and the need for a justifying ideology of possession. Then there was the excitement of living in the golden age of African exploration, when the Dark Continent was being opened up by a succession of heroic European explorers. The narratives they wrote of their travels were real-life versions of Rider Haggard's *King Solomon's Mines* (1885), stories of incredible survival in alien environments spiced with danger and controversy. Livingstone's *Missionary Travels and Researches in South Africa* (1857) was a tremendous bestseller; it was followed by a series of books in the 1860s about the search for the source of the Nile: *The Lake Regions of Central Africa* (1860) by Richard Burton (1821–90), *Journal of the Discovery of the Source of the Nile* (1863) by John Hanning Speke (1827–64), and *The Albert N'yanza* (1866) by Samuel Baker (1821–93), each offering different solutions to what was then a vexed and fascinating question.

If stories of exploration created interest in Africa, a moral sanction for the European attitude of superiority to other, more primitive races was provided by the intense and unprecedented missionary activity of the period.[36] Honest doubt may have been all very well for troubled intellectuals at home but the missionaries who went to Africa and India had few doubts about the superior truth of Christianity or the superiority of European civilisation, and they had the backing of an unclouded public opinion and plentiful funds. Their task enjoyed the cultural prestige reflected from the legendary life and death of David Livingstone (1813–73), the first European to cross Africa from coast to coast and the discoverer of the Victoria Falls. The Livingstone we know today is a more complex and interesting figure than his contemporaries saw – a hard, unclubbable man, an unsympathetic husband and parent, driven at the end less by zeal for the gospel than by a passion for finding the source of the Nile, but redeemed by his concern for his Africans and their love for him. To his contemporaries he was a sanctified hero of self-help: the Blantyre millhand with the Latin grammar propped up on the loom, the poor boy who became a doctor, went to Africa and came back to the acclaim of all from the Queen downwards; who returned despite increasing ill-health and travelled on against the advice of friends and the last-minute discovery by Stanley; who was found dead praying on his knees by his African servants and brought back by them to the coast, where the body was taken to England and a hero's funeral in Westminster Abbey. So exemplary-seeming a life was bound to inspire hagiography, as it did, and give life to a whole genre of missionary biography.

' "I beg to direct your attention to Africa," ' Livingstone told his audience in the Cambridge Senate House in 1858. ' "I know that in a few years I shall be cut off in that country, which is now open; do not let it be shut again! I go back to Africa to make an open path for commerce and Christianity." '[37] He had envisaged the alliance of 'commerce and Christianity' as something which would prove of mutual benefit to the Africans and the Europeans, but the path which the missionary and the explorer opened was soon overrun by the would-be imperial powers in the desperate 'Scramble for Africa' of the 1870s and 1880s. By 1884, when the German Chancellor Bismarck set up the Congress of Berlin to decide on the partitioning of Africa, Africa had become an issue in European power-politics, and the concern for the bodies and souls of the Africans (which the missionaries had exhibited, however tactlessly) now took second place. Far from being a triumphalist notion, in consequence, there is much truth in the paradox that British imperialism as an idea was born looking over its shoulder, the creature of anxiety rather than of confidence – anxiety about economic decline brought on by the slump of 1873, about industrial challenge from America and Germany, about the rise of Germany as a European power, about the intentions and vast potential of Russia, about safeguarding the sea and overland routes to India, about competing spheres of influence in Africa. In the lectures which make up his book *The Expansion of England* (1883), J.R. Seeley, Professor of History at Cambridge, tried to make his countrymen aware that they inhabited a sleeping giant. 'We seem, as it were, to have conquered and peopled half the world in a fit of absence of mind.' But they failed to see that this 'Greater Britain' of English-speaking peoples was a potential great power that might 'take rank with Russia and the United States in the first rank of state, measured by population and area, and in a higher rank than the states of the Continent'.[38] There was a choice to be made ('incomparably the greatest question which we can discuss') between this Greater Britain and becoming a middle-rank European power, below Germany 'and scarcely equal to France' (p. 18).

Greater Britain (1868) is the title of a book by the Liberal politician Sir Charles Dilke. Imperialism divided the Liberal Party, attracting the support of leading figures on the 'progressive' wing, like Joseph Chamberlain and the future Prime Minister H.H. Asquith (1852–1928). The old Radical, Cobdenite, Free Trade wing of the party resisted the siren call of Empire, to their eternal credit; Herbert Spencer wrote piercingly of the connections between imperialism, militarism, and slavery (see below). Gladstone, too, was more aware of the dangers of imperial expansion than the advantages, and set them out in an article of 1877 in *Nineteenth Century* replying to the Liberal lawyer E.V. Dicey (1832–1911). At issue was the annexation of the Nile delta to secure the Suez Canal, which in turn was believed to be necessary to protect the passage to India. Gladstone objected to expansions of the existing Empire because they 'are rarely effected except by means that are more or less questionable, and that tend to compromise British character in the judgment of the impartial world'; because 'we already have our hands too full' abroad and should be tending to problems at home; and because Britain lacks the population to sustain a world-wide Empire.[39] For Gladstone India was not the jewel in the crown – Queen Victoria had been made 'Empress of India' by Disraeli the previous year – but a drain on the exchequer, and the justification for the British presence there was firstly moral, that it should be seen to benefit the Indian people. Besides, would the stoppage of the Suez Canal be a disaster? It would mean a loss of trade, but the sea-route to India round the Cape of Good Hope would be fast enough for all military purposes. The occupation of Egypt would be additionally 'a very dangerous experiment on the common susceptibilities of Islam' (p. 159). The historical irony is that the pace of events during Gladstone's next government forced him to act against his principles and annex Egypt in 1882, with historical consequences that his article had only too presciently foreseen.

'The root and pith and substance of the material greatness of our nation lies within the compass of these islands;' Gladstone wrote, 'and is, except in trifling particulars, independent of all and every sort of political dominion beyond them' (p. 153). Dicey set out the alternative Greater Britain thesis. Unroll the map – invariably the first move in imperialist rhetoric – and you will see how much of it is coloured red: 'The United Kingdom, with an area of 120,000 square miles and a population of thirty-three millions, rules over eight million square miles of the globe's surface and two hundred million of the world's inhabitants.'[40] He makes the increasingly familiar comparison with the Roman Empire, a fateful analogy which aroused notions of 'mission' and 'manifest destiny' (Dicey uses both) already planted in middle-class minds by study of the classics. The British Empire has come about by accident rather than conscious design, and like some successful evolutionary variation is the result of 'a certain instinct of development inherent in our race' (p. 296). Dicey does not disguise the racial basis of his imperialism.

> To say that our Empire is 'bone of our bone, and flesh
> of our flesh' is not to express an opinion, but to assert a
> fact. So long as Englishmen retain at once their migratory
> instinct, their passion for independence, and their
> impatience of foreign rule, they are bound by a manifest
> destiny to found empires abroad, or, in other words, to
> make themselves the dominant race in the foreign countries
> to which they wander. (p. 297)

Dicey disagreed with Gladstone about the financial burden of Empire, but even if it were true the Empire would still be worthwhile as a great exercise-ground for English energies. 'The energies of our race, the qualities which have made these islands what they are, find their scope, nutriment, and development in the work of colonising new lands, administering foreign governments, and ruling over less masterful races. Greater Britain serves as a safety-valve for Great Britain' (p. 299).

Not all imperialists held Dicey's instrumental attitude to 'less masterful races', but late-Victorian imperialism would not have been possible without a belief in 'manifest destiny' and the superiority of Western civilisation: it might have defects, he said, but 'no man not given to paradox can question its superiority to that of the other quarters of the globe' (p. 300). Strange, then, but not surprising, that these expressions of cultural confidence and racial superiority should carry with them an undertow of sadness. The trouble with the Roman analogy is that it cut both ways; empires fall as surely as they rise, and a nation embarked on an imperial course is locked into that inevitable rhythm. Manifest destiny is also tragic destiny. Even Dicey's bullish article contains reflections like this: 'Everything in this world, empires, races, creeds, is destined to pass away; and if the probable durability of the kingdoms of the earth could be estimated by any actuarial process, I doubt the first or even the second place in calculated longevity being assigned to Great Britain . . .' (p.298). Or as Kipling put it more eloquently:

> Far-called, our navies melt away;
> On dune and headland sinks the fire;
> Lo, all our pomp of yesterday
> Is one with Nineveh and Tyre! . . .
> ('Recessional', 1897)

One of the most important consequences of Empire was the focus it returned on the home country. If imperial expansion was justified in terms of racial superiority – or at least superior racial efficiency – what was it in the character of the English that equipped them for their Roman task? Imperialism awakened a new sense of Englishness. To anyone not English-born there is a piquant ambivalence in the way 'English' and 'British' are used in the literature of and about imperialism. It is always 'the British Empire', as if to spread whatever opprobrium might attach to imperialism, but the genius is that of 'England' – a mythical/historical entity combining mongrel roots with buccaneering enterprise (Drake, Raleigh, and other of Froude's 'forgotten worthies') and deep pastoralism. Imperialism both inspired and was justified by a new sense of English racial identity: the drive outwards was also a drive inwards and backwards, to discover an essential rural England untouched by the machine. The emotional heart of Empire did not belong to politicians or even to its apologists, but to Puck of Pook's Hill, Kipling's pastoral spirit of Sussex history. On the one hand the ideology of Empire was promoted at a popular, mythic level in the boy's stories of G.A. Henty (1832–1902) and the patriotic poems of Sir Henry ('Drake's Drum') Newbolt (1862–1938); on the other, an equally mythic England of the village was being created in works like *A Shropshire Lad* (1896) by A.E. Housman (1859–1936). In Kipling the imperial and the racial-pastoral are combined: the story of England's history which Puck tells to Una and Dan in *Puck of Pook's Hill* (1906) and *Rewards and Fairies* (1910) is the genealogy of the 'manifest destiny' which had taken the young servants of Empire, the colonial administrators and engineers, to India in his earlier stories.

Dicey insisted that 'the existence of the British Empire is a fact and not a fancy' (p. 294). True, but it was also a fancy, in the sense of being a dream of escape from the humdrum realities of modern urbanised society. No doubt the work of the imperialist on the ground was as hard and as thankless as Kipling's early stories show it to have been, and only a cynic would want to belittle the idealism that fed their dream of Empire. But a dream is what it was; the lure of Empire for the British upper and middle classes was that its service offered a long holiday from reality on a global playground where they could enact the fantasies inspired by a classical education, and become the Romans of the modern world. Rome was a dangerous example, for as Gladstone reminded a Midlothian audience in 1879, the Roman 'mission' had been 'to subdue the world', being 'a State whose very basis it was to deny the equal rights, to proscribe the independent existence, of other nations'.[41] Empire was a dangerous dream for the home society also, since it encouraged militarism and the sacrifice of the individual to the group and the cause. No one saw the drift of these developments more clearly than Herbert Spencer in his last essays. In 'Imperialism and Slavery' (1902) he attacked his own country for its conduct in the Boer War, deploring the military force used to subjugate the Boers, and pointing out that such imperial adventures were expensive and enslaving for the imperial power itself: 'So long as they continue to conquer other peoples and to hold them in subjection, they will readily merge their personal liberties in the power of the state, and hereafter as heretofore accept the slavery that goes along with imperialism.' His remarkable essay on 'Re-Barbarization' (1902) draws attention to the spread of militarism in contemporary life. Its spirit has infested modern culture in surprising but, he argues, related ways: there is the Salvation Army, with its military ranks and battle hymns and *War Cry*; the rise of school cadet corps and their encouragement by Anglican headmasters; the new appetite for stories of battles and conquering generals; the growth of professional sport and the space given to it in the newspapers.

It was all very strange to a man of Spencer's generation who could remember the peaceful hopes of mid-century. Nothing illustrated 'the utter change of social sentiment' more clearly than a recent decision that 'the Great Exhibition of 1851, which was expected to inaugurate universal peace, should be commemorated in 1901 by a Naval and Military Exhibition: an anti-militant display having for its jubilee a militant display!'[42] In cultural terms, it is the difference between (say) the anti-militarism of *Vanity Fair* (1847–48), or the domesticity of *David Copperfield* (1849–50), and Kipling's *Stalky & Co.* (1899) to which Spencer refers without naming as the work of an author who 'in depicting school-life, brings to the front the barbarizing activities and feelings and shows little respect for a civilizing culture' (p. 131). 'Re-Barbarization' is a prophetic essay and deserves a place in any anthology of the voices prophesying war before 1914.

Yet, Marx would have said, what did Spencer expect? Was not imperialism and the aggression it involved already implicit in the cut-throat capitalism he had advocated? The doctrine of the 'survival of the fittest' could extend beyond individuals and companies to nations and races, and was so extended by apologists for empire. The problem of empire was the problem of capitalism. And the problem of capitalism, for those appalled by its waste and injustice, was the relentless engine of competition, which in the economic and social field was what the machine of natural selection was in the biological. There were successful efforts to alleviate the economic struggle for existence in the nineteenth century – the co-operative movement was one, the model industrial villages built by paternalist employers another – but most attempts to question the 'laws' of political economy, the workings of the engine, were dismissed as ignorant and misguided. The British critique of industrialism is therefore overwhelmingly moral and humanitarian. When Ruskin made his brave attempt to redefine political economy in the *Cornhill* articles which became *Unto this Last* (1862), he was so violently attacked that the editor, Thackeray, was forced to stop serialising them. One contemporary found it 'intolerable that a man whose best performances are deformed by constant eruptions of windy hysterics should be able to avail himself of the pages of one of our most popular periodicals for the purpose of pouring out feminine nonsense, in the language which women would have far too much self-respect to employ, upon so grave a subject as political economy'.[43]

Karl Marx (1818–83) realised that any effective critique of industrial capitalism would have to confront the question of political economy. Despite the subsequent failure of his prophecies and the collapse of the political systems which attempted to establish them, his potency as a social thinker derives from the way his writings yoked together two of the most powerful ideologies of the century: Romanticism and Science. The Carlyles and the Ruskins had the first, and the Herbert Spencers the second, but Marx was the first social theorist to capture the prestige of the scientific methodology from the half-baked 'science' of the Victorian economists and mount it on the Pegasus of prophecy. The revolutionary transformation of society is not just something to be wished after and longed for, which was the dream of Utopian socialists, but something which *must* come because it is an inevitable outcome of the scientific development of the modern body politic.

Another way of putting it is to say that Marxism is the product of an intellectual marriage between Hegelian idealism and Darwinian science. From Hegel Marx inherited a teleological vision of philosophical and historical development whereby mind, or spirit, worked its way through a series of self-correcting oppositions – the famous 'dialectic' – to a final state of complete freedom and self-consciousness. He came to reject Hegel's idealism but not his structure of explanation. Darwin, to whom Marx had wanted to dedicate the first volume of *Capital*, opened his eyes to the biological struggle for existence which lay beneath and around the social. However, Darwin's evolutionary machine was not going anywhere in particular; but Marx's was. As the *Communist Manifesto* (1848) has it:

> The essential condition for the existence, and for the sway
> of the bourgeois class, is the formation and augmentation
> of capital; the condition for capital is wage-labour.
> Wage-labour rests exclusively on competition between the
> labourers. The advance of industry, whose involuntary
> promoter is the bourgeoisie, replaces the isolation of the
> labourers, due to competition, by their revolutionary
> combination, due to association. The development of
> Modern Industry, therefore, cuts from under its feet the
> very foundation on which the bourgeoisie produces and
> appropriates products. What the bourgeoisie, therefore,
> produces, above all, is its own grave-diggers. Its fall and the
> victory of the proletariat are equally inevitable.[44]

Modern history has shown that there was nothing 'inevitable' in this development, and Marx's 'therefores' assert a logical and scientific progression for which there was no evidence. He is revealed, in fact, as a victim of the nineteenth-century mythologisation of science. In a curious way, he has more in common with Herbert Spencer than might at first seem likely. Both men held an austere view of the possibilities of capitalism: in Spencer it is welcomed for its evolutionary discipline, in Marx deplored for its cruelty, but neither thinker was able to imagine that capitalism might have powers of growth to deal with the problems thrown up by its workings. It is this adherence to a scarcity theory of economic life which limits both men to an essentially nineteenth-century political economy.

In the writings of Marx and Engels 'Science' and 'Utopia' stand opposed as reality and illusion. There is a good case, however, for seeing Marx as a Utopian writer blinded to his utopianism by the myth of scientific objectivity. Mircia Eliade discusses Marxian communism along these lines in his study of the encounter between contemporary faiths and primitive religions, *Myths, Dream, and Mysteries* (1967), noting its combination of the 'myth of the Golden Age . . . at the beginning and the end of History' with 'a truly messianic Judaeo-Christian ideology', in which the proletariat plays the role of the suffering Redeemer who defeats the Antichrist (the bourgeoisie) in a final conflict between Good and Evil. What is remarkable in Marx's case, he observes, is that in distinction from other nineteenth-century philosophers of history, he proposes 'an *absolute goal of History*'.[45]

Viewed in these terms, it is perhaps not surprising that Marxism succeeded where Comte's 'Religion of Humanity' failed. Comte offered the trappings of the old religion, but the altar was empty. Marx accepted all the implications of secularisation, but his altar, metaphorically speaking, was not empty. In place of Jesus was a suffering proletariat and a message of redemption through history. It was a message with a powerful appeal for a guilt-ridden, religion-less middle class. Arnold Toynbee addressed the poor in 1883 as follows:

> We – the middle classes, I mean, not merely the very rich –
> we have neglected you; instead of justice we have offered
> you charity, and instead of sympathy we have offered you
> hard and unreal advice; but I think we are changing. If you
> would only believe it and trust us, I think that many of us
> would spend our lives in your service. You have . . . to
> forgive us, for we have wronged you; we have sinned
> against you grievously – not knowingly always, but still
> we have sinned, and let us confess it; but if you will forgive
> us – nay, whether you will forgive us or not – we will
> serve you, we will devote our lives to your service, and we
> cannot do more.[46]

This is the language of religious confession and dedication, and may help to illustrate the context of guilt and idealism in which Marxism took root – not simply as another variant of socialism but as a secular religion inspired by a Utopian vision.

The politics of gender

In recent years the proletariat's place on the cross had increasingly been taken by the woman, as feminist scholarship has first rediscovered the extent of women's wrongs in the nineteenth century and then gone on to reinterpret all areas of Victorian culture in the light of them. The second stage of this process has passed well beyond an interest in the woman-as-rebel to an interest in woman-as-other, a suppressed voice heard in the distortions of the male culture's attempts to ventriloquise it, whose very unfixedness makes it a radical adversary of the fixtures of 'patriarchy'. The focus has shifted, to take a literary analogy, from Jane Eyre, the vociferous rebel with conventional expectations, to Jane Fairfax in *Emma*, whose opaque otherness eludes and therefore challenges the conventional social categories. We have become much more aware of what is being said in the silences and exclusions of female experience, and of what female stereotypes (the Angel in the House, the Fallen Woman, the Madwoman, the Siren, the Criminal) reveal about the needs and uncertainties of the Victorian male. It is now evident that there is a double 'politics of gender' at work in the period: an outer struggle for women's legal and political rights, and the inner struggle of both men and women to cope with the demands of powerful but failing cultural stereotypes.

The legal situation of women before the passing of the 1882 Married Women's Property Act is summed up with characteristic force by Frances Cobbe in the title of one of her essays at the time, 'Criminals, Idiots, Women, and Minors' – these being the classes of people considered unfit for most legal and all political rights at the time.[47] Until 1882 a woman's money and property passed into the control of her husband when she married, unless a prior settlement had been made. The justification was that a woman could have no interest separate from that of her husband; they were, in the words of that legal Bible, Blackstone's *Commentaries*, 'one person in law', and 'the very being or legal existence of the woman is suspended during the marriage, or at least is incorporated or consolidated into that of her husband'.[48] Women's political emancipation could not proceed before their legal emancipation, since, if they were married, the law effectively denied them independent action outside the home. Reform in this area was difficult because, as Mill and Cobbe saw, it ran into opposition that was all the more powerful for not being entirely rational. 'So long as an opinion is strongly rooted in the feelings,' Mill observed at the start of *On the Subjection of Women* (1869), 'it gains rather than loses in stability by having a preponderating weight of argument against it'.[49] Cobbe saw that where legislation for marriage was concerned, masculine sentiment would always be more powerful than considerations of justice – 'the sentiment entertained by the majority of men on the subject; the ideal they have formed of wedlock, the poetical vision in their minds of a wife's true relation to her husband'.[50]

The 'poetical vision' of marriage was encouraged by the endings of thousands of novels, by highly popular books of wifely instruction like

Mrs Ellis's *The Women of England* (1838, and much reprinted), and by such classic expressions of elevated domesticity as Coventry Patmore's *Angel in the House* (1854–63) and the lecture 'Of Queen's Gardens' in Ruskin's *Sesame and Lilies* (1865). Underlying most of these works is the assumption that men and women occupy separate but complementary 'spheres', which come together in marriage to complete the lack in the other. 'Each has what the other has not: each completes the other, and is completed by the other: they are in nothing alike, and the happiness and perfection of both depends on each asking and receiving from the other what the other only can give.'[51] Ruskin's idealised vision of marriage is essentially a modern form of chivalry, in which the husband goes out into the hardening world to do battle with foes and the wife waits at home ready to bind up his wounds:

> The man, in his rough work in open world, must encounter
> all peril and trial; – to him, therefore, must be the failure,
> the offence, the inevitable error: often he must be wounded,
> or subdued; often misled; and *always* hardened. But he
> guards the woman from all this; within his house, as ruled
> by her . . . need enter no danger, no temptation, no cause
> of error or offence. This is the true nature of home – it is
> the place of Peace; the shelter, not only from all injury, but
> from all terror, doubt, and division.[52]

As for education, a woman ought to have only so much as to allow her to encourage her children and enter sympathetically into her husband's pursuits; and she must at all costs avoid the 'dangerous science' (p. 127) of theology.

Given the assumptions of the time, Ruskin's is not an undignified vision of married life, it just bore little relation to the reality of sexual relations or contemporary society. Nor is this surprising. Ruskin's own six-year marriage to Effie Gray was unconsummated and had ended in annulment for impotence in 1854: he was in no position to offer advice to others – though, being Ruskin, this did not deter him. His idealised image of marriage takes no account of the fact that for the great majority of Victorian women, i.e. the working class, there was not a choice between work and home but, if they were lucky, between different kinds of labour, while for the middle-class wife even a comfortable home was usually a place of labour of a different but no less exhausting kind: the treadmill of the yearly pregnancy. As to the sorrow which women of all classes and in all ages before our own have known from high infant mortality rates, we can only glimpse it today in the grief of Third World mothers, but it was an omnipresent reality for even the most prosperous Victorians. When he was Dean of Carlisle the future Archbishop of Canterbury, Archibald Tait and his wife lost five daughters in one scarlet fever epidemic in 1856. The children were aged between one and ten, and their deaths took place in little more than a month, between 6 March and 10 April.

The notion of separate spheres also helps to explain the opposition to the extension of women's rights in the nineteenth century. It is difficult now to put ourselves in the frame of mind of the many women, by no means all unintelligent or reactionary in other matters, who felt that getting the vote would threaten domestic and national stability, and who were prepared to fight against franchise reform. But there were powerful ideological assumptions at work. At a time when the right to vote was related to the voter's presumed ability to exercise it wisely, women were felt to be at the mercy of their biology; menstruation, pregnancy, child-rearing, and the menopause were unsettling (and little understood) female phenomena, likely to make women unreliable in the polling-booth; and there was no lack of prestigious, conservative doctors willing to say so in public. Victorian science, progressive in matters of religion, was less so when it came to gender. The 'advanced' findings of evolutionary anthropologists taught that the differences in cranial shape between men and women showed the inferior capacity of the female mind.[53] It followed, the argument went, that women's strengths were emotional rather than logical, sympathetic and domestic rather than rational and worldly; and that for them to enter the public domain of political debate was to risk losing their countervailing power, which could best be exercised in the home. As the signatories to Mrs Humphry Ward's 1889 'Appeal Against Female Suffrage' put it:

> While desiring the fullest possible development of the
> powers, energies, and education of women, we believe
> that their work for the State, and their responsibilities
> towards it, must always differ essentially from those of
> men, and that therefore their share in the working of the
> State machinery should be different from that assigned
> to men. . . . To men belong the struggle of debate and
> legislation in Parliament; the hard and exhausting labour
> implied in the administration of the national resources
> and powers; the conduct of England's relations towards
> the external world; the working of the army and navy;
> all the heavy, laborious, fundamental industries of the
> State. . . . In all these spheres women's direct participation
> is made impossible either by the disabilities of sex, or by
> strong formations of custom and habit resting ultimately
> upon physical difference, against which it is useless to
> contend.[54]

This 'Appeal' appeared in the June 1889 issue of *Nineteenth Century* and carried the signatures of the wives of such prominent Liberals of the day as T.H. Green, Leslie Stephen, Frederic Harrison. T.H. Huxley, Walter Bagehot, Matthew Arnold, and others, indicating that anti-suffragism was then far from being considered the reactionary cause that it seems today. The issue also contained a protest form against female suffrage which women readers were invited to complete and return, in the flattering knowledge that 'the deliberate opinion of the women readers of *Nineteenth Century* might certainly be taken as a fair sample of the judgment of the educated women of the country, and would probably receive the sympathy and support of the overwhelming majority of their fellow countrywomen'. Some 1,500 of them did.[55] Publishing their names and addresses in a subsequent issue of the journal must have seemed a crushing rebuttal of the reply to the 'Appeal' made by the suffragist Millicent Fawcett.

This episode is usually seen as a high-water mark of the resistance to women's rights in the nineteenth century, but, as is often the case, in the moment of triumph the Achilles' heel of anti-suffragism was exposed. Mrs Ward's signatories stood revealed as women in comfortable circumstances, some titled, most known through their husbands' achievements rather than by their own: as their opponents were quick to point out, they had no need of the vote. Moreover, she was appealing to a shrinking constituency: her 'fair sample of the judgment of the educated women of the country' did not take into account the views of a younger generation liberated by the educational reforms which were starting to offer at least the prospect of a decent secondary and university education to women in the later nineteenth century. When she formed the Women's National Anti-Suffrage League in 1908, Mrs Ward got a much rougher ride and Mrs Fawcett got her revenge, defeating her old adversary in public debate by 235 votes to 74.[56]

In retrospect it can be seen that the anti-suffragists made a fetish of the vote. Reforms admitting women to higher education, and to the administration of School Boards and Boards of Poor Law Guardians – both of which Mrs Ward and other anti-suffragists supported – were soon demonstrating the intellectual equality which the 'separate spheres' ideology denied. Nor was it lost on contemporary observers that the vigour of her campaign belied its message that women were essentially unfit for public life. If it is hard to feel much sympathy for the anti-suffragists, however, one can feel some for the uncertainties that lay beneath the surface of their campaign – the hesitations of women confronted with the new freedoms opening up in the second half of the century. As more and more middle-class women went out to work, they learned to enjoy something of the independence and camaraderie that working-class women had long known in the factory, but leaving the home could also mean loneliness, and pursuing an active career clashed with the passive stereotype of femininity and risked taking a woman, especially a woman not confident of her marriageability, out of the established routines of middle-class match-making.

The problem for men was in a sense the reverse of this. The active career which tempted women disturbed many men, for various reasons. The association of domestic virtue with passivity made the active woman threatening. The thought that women might have access to the secrets of the trade seemed to challenge the mystique on which masculine professional prestige depended, and the first female aspirants to a medical degree were fiercely and indeed unscrupulously resisted.[57] Then, the emergent figure of the independent woman challenging for space on traditional male territory threatened what one can call the existential pact between the sexes. Arising out of Romanticism is the concept of the woman as the guarantor of the selfhood of the man – Heathcliff calling Cathy his 'soul' in *Wuthering Heights* (1847), the speaker in Matthew Arnold's 'Dover Beach' making his plea for mutual love against the crowding confusion of the world:

> Ah, love, let us be true
> To one another! for the world, which seems
> To lie before us like a land of dreams . . .
> Hath really neither joy, nor love, nor light . . .

But if the woman is going to live in the 'world' on the same terms as the man, her countervailing power will be lost. This is such an important change, historically, that it is not surprising that men should have resented the forces which brought it about, in so far as they understood them.

Another disturbing feature of the movement for women's rights was that it started to expose the double standards by which many men lived. The 'social evil', as prostitution was called, was tacitly accepted as a necessary concomitant of late marriages and annual pregnancies, men's sexual needs being considered more urgent than these limits satisfied. But when Parliament in the 1860s passed a series of Contagious Diseases Acts, requiring the registration of prostitutes in garrison towns and allowing their compulsory medical examination by the police if suspected of venereal disease, a national campaign was mounted against them, led by the redoubtable Josephine Butler (1830–1906). Support for this campaign grew larger and lasted longer – the Acts were not repealed until 1886 – than the framers of the Acts could possibly have imagined. The reason was that the Acts were not a single issue confined to feminists, but involved questions of individual liberty and double standards (why should soldiers and sailors not be inspected, since their health was the cause of the legislation?), and drew different groups, from the social libertarian to the respectable lady who objected to legal recognition of prostitutes and secretly feared that she might one day be a victim of the police herself.

To say that the twenty-year campaign against the Contagious Diseases Acts opened up the female body to public discussion is perhaps going too far, but it contributed substantially to the demystification of sexual relations for those women it involved and influenced. With the publicity given to contraception by the Bradlaugh–Besant trial of 1877–78, and the slow but steady development of work outside the home in 'respectable' and fulfilling careers like nursing and teaching, the choice for most middle-class women at the end of the century was no longer between production-line motherhood and being a governess or an idle spinster. At the same time marriage remained the goal of most women in all classes. The problem for men and women was therefore different: for women it was a question of knowing how far to take their new freedoms, for men of reconciling women's new knowledge and freedom with what they had learned to expect of womanhood.

Notes

1. For a full discussion of this episode see Wendell V. Harris, 'Newman, Peel, Tamworth, and the Concurrence of Historical Forces', *Victorian Studies*, 32 (1989), 189–208. I am generally indebted to Harris's account of this episode for historical information.

2. 'The Tamworth Reading Room', in *The Evangelical and Oxford Movements*, edited by Elisabeth Jay (Cambridge, 1983), p. 185.

3. 'The First Edinburgh Reviewers', *Literary Studies* (2 vols, 1911), I, p. 10. The Scottish contribution to early nineteenth-century English thought is the subject of Anand Chitnis's book, *The Scottish Enlightenment and Early Victorian English Society* (1986), to which I am generally indebted here.

4. 'Scottish Philosophy', *The Times*, 1 April 1858, p. 6.

5. *Ibid.*, p. 6.

6. John Stuart Mill and Jeremy Bentham, *'Utilitarianism' and Other Essays*, edited by A. Ryan (Harmondsworth, 1987), p. 65.

7. *Edinburgh Review, 49* (1829), 161–2.

8. On this point see W.E.S. Thomas, *The Philosophic Radicals* (Oxford, 1979), pp. 441–2.

9. *Autobiography*, edited by J.M. Robson (Harmondsworth, 1989), p. 169.

10. *Ibid.*, p. 27.

11. *Culture and Society 1780–1950* (Harmondsworth, 1961), p. 70.

12. 'Alfred de Vigny', *Collected Works of John Stuart Mill*, edited by J.M. Robson and others (33 vols, Toronto and London, 1963–91), I, p. 469.

13. *Mill on Bentham and Coleridge*, edited by F.R. Leavis (1950), p. 40.

14. *Collected Works*, XVIII (1977), pp. 167, 198.

15. *On Liberty*, edited by G. Himmelfarb (Harmondsworth, 1974), p. 68.

16. *The English Constitution*, introduction R.H.S. Crossman (1963), p. 61.

17. *An Autobiography* (1953), pp. 257–8.

18. *Ibid.*, p. 156.

19. Quoted in Robert Blake, *Disraeli* (1966), p. 336.

20. John Rae, 'The Socialism of Karl Marx and the Young Hegelians', *The Contemporary Review*, XL (1881), 586.

21. See Asa Briggs, *Victorian People* (Harmondsworth, 1965), ch. 7.

22. *The Complete Prose Works of Matthew Arnold*, edited by R.H. Super (11 vols, Michigan, 1960–77), II, pp. 17, 7.

23. *Democracy in America*, edited by P. Bradley (2 vols, 1945), I, p. 14.

24. *Works*, XVIII, p. 56. This quotation comes from Mill's 1835 review of Tocqueville's first volume.

25. *Collected Works* (30 vols, 1895), XXX, p. 21.

26. *Complete Prose Works*, V, pp. 97–8.

27. Harold Perkin, *The Origins of Modern English Society 1780–1880* (1969), p. 319.

28. *The Man versus the State* (1884), p. 17.

29. Quoted in Robert Eccleshall, *British Liberalism* (1986), p. 182.

30. *International Journal of Ethics*, VIII (1898), 145.

31. *The Climax of Liberal Politics* (1987), p. 78.

32. *Contemporary Review*, XL (1881), 586.

33. *A New View of Society*, edited by V.A.C. Gatrell (Harmondsworth, 1969), pp. 126–7.

34. *My Apprenticeship* (1926), p. 2.

35. *The Conservative Party from Peel to Thatcher* (1985), p. 128.

36. See Geoffrey Moorhouse, *The Missionaries* (1973).

37. *Ibid.*, p. 131.

38. *The Expansion of England* (1909 edition), pp. 10, 19.

39. 'Aggression on Egypt and Freedom in the East', *Nineteenth Century*, 11 (1877), pp. 149–66; p. 151.

40. 'Mr. Gladstone and Our Empire', *ibid.*, pp. 292–308; p. 294.

41. *Midlothian Speeches* (1879), p. 127.

42. *Facts and Comments* (1902), pp. 121, 128.

43. *The Saturday Review*, X (1860); quoted in *Ruskin: the Critical Heritage*, edited by J.L. Bradley (1984), p. 274.

44. *The Marx–Engels Reader*, edited by R.C. Tucker (New York, 1978), p. 483.

45. *Myths, Dreams, and Mysteries* (New York, 1967), pp. 25–6.

46. Quoted in Beatrice Webb, *My Apprenticeship*, pp. 182–3.

47. 'Criminals, Idiots, Women, and Minors: Is the Classification Sound?', *Fraser's Magazine*, LXXVIII (1868), 777–94.

48. Quoted by Phillip Mallett in his essay on 'Women and Marriage in Victorian Society', in *Marriage and Property*, edited by E.M. Craik (Aberdeen, 1984), pp. 159–89; p. 162.

49. *Collected Works*, XXI (1984), p. 262.

50. Cobbe, *loc. cit.*, p. 787.

51. *Works*, XVIII, p. 121.

52. *Ibid.*, p. 122.

53. See 'Huxley and Woman's Place in Science: The 'Woman Question' and the Control of Victorian Anthropology', in *History, Humanity and Evolution*, edited by J.R. Moore (Cambridge, 1989), pp. 253–84. For a history of the anti-suffrage movement, see Brian Harrison, *Separate Spheres: The Opposition to Women's Suffrage in Britain* (1978).

54. *Nineteenth Century*, 25 (1889), 781–8.

55. *Loc. cit.*, p. 788.

56. See John Sutherland, *Mrs Humphry Ward* (Oxford, 1990), p. 303.

57. Elizabeth Garrett Anderson (1836–1917) was a pioneer of the cause of medical education for women. Rejected by the main teaching hospitals in England and Scotland, she acquired a qualification through a loophole in the regulations of the Society of Apothecaries, which was subsequently quickly closed; for long she remained the only woman admitted to membership of the British Medical Association. But the inspiration of her example, and the success of the hospitals for women she helped to found, gradually opened the way for women in the medical profession.

Chapter 5
The Arts in an Industrial Age

Of all areas of Victorian cultural achievement, the one that has taken longest to rehabilitate is that which is loosely and somewhat unsatisfactorily called 'the arts' – painting, music, architecture, sculpture. Perhaps this is not surprising. The period's output in these fields was so huge, and so eclectic in style and uneven in quality, that it was impossible for rediscovery to move confidently on a broad front. The process of revaluation was not helped by what might be called the thin blue line of aesthetic snobbery running from Matthew Arnold through Wilde, Pater, and the Aesthetes to Bloomsbury, for whom 'Victorian' was almost synonymous with bad taste. If any single figure may be said to have turned the tide of appreciation it would be Sir John Betjeman, who made the British public aware of the virtues of Victorian architecture at the time when their city planners were pulling it down wholesale. Now there is an intellectual climate much more willing to do justice to Victorian architecture and painting, and positively enthusiastic in discovering the aesthetics of a technological age, from railway building to photography. But one damaging label persists, at least among students of literature: that the Victorian middle classes were 'philistine'.

For this Matthew Arnold must take some of the blame. He had the public-schoolboy's eye for a nickname and 'philistine' was a telling one to use in the knockabout comic mode of works like *Culture and Anarchy* (1869) and *Friendship's Garland* (1871). 'Philistine' conjured up images of lumbering Goliaths brought low by elegant sling-shots from the nimble Davids of the cultural élite, but the label really conflates two separate accusations, one of which is manifestly untrue: that most of the Victorian middle classes were Bounderby-like, hostile and indifferent to higher culture, and that when they were not, the objects of their admiration were inferior. Arnold was unable to see the inadequacy of the first charge because his own concept of 'Culture' was too literary, classical, and backward-looking: 'the best that *has been thought* and *said* in the world'. He had little understanding of what was culturally enriching in, for example, the reading aloud of novels by the family fireside, the networks of music-making that linked the parlour song to the choral society via the church choir, the collecting of prints made available by the new technological processes mentioned in the Introduction, the opening up of municipal art galleries to a new public, even the art of the music-hall. One hates to talk like a quantity surveyor in these matters, but there is no doubt that more, and more varied, 'cultural' activity was pursued by more people in the nineteenth century, relative to the total population, than ever before. When the Art Treasures Exhibition was held in Manchester in 1857 – the first of its kind, incidentally, and one that exhibited photography along with modern and classical paintings – over a million visitors of all classes came to see it. The question of quality is, of course, a separate matter.

The Manchester Exhibition also dispels the idea that the new nation industrialist was an uncouth provincial like Arnold's Mr Bottles in *Friendship's Garland*. It was conceived and brought to fruition by a committee of merchants, industrialists, and professional men. One of them was a cotton magnate, James Watts, whose country house contained paintings by Rubens, Holbein, and Gainsborough; there he entertained Prince Albert when the Consort came north to open the exhibition. Another, Thomas Fairbairn, commissioned Holman Hunt's now-famous Pre-Raphaelite painting, *The Awakening Conscience*, and had it shown at the exhibition.[1] Men like these were the patrons of contemporary painting, architecture, and music; and they took the initiative in setting up the buildings, the athenaeums and institutions, which themselves survive as distinctive expressions of Victorian culture. The Manchester Royal Institution, now the Art Gallery, was designed for a local committee of business and professional men by Sir Charles Barry (1795–1860), who went on to design the Athenaeum in that city at the same time, 1837 onwards, as he started work on the London Reform Club. Manchester may have been exceptional, as the home of the 'Millocracy', but it was far from unique. The 'provincial' civic pride of many leading industrialists provided a focus and a stimulus for the cultural life of their cities which had not been there before, and because they were drawn to the art of the present, there is a good chance that poor, condescended-to Mr Bottles might have been rather better informed about contemporary developments in the arts than was Arnold himself.

If he was better informed it was partly because he had read Ruskin (1819–1900). The first volume of *Modern Painters* (1843) is a bold and brilliant book, and must have been exhilarating to read at the time. Whereas later critics like Arnold and Pater were to bind culture to classical sources again, here was a young critic prepared to tell his readers that the classical painters they had been taught to venerate were inferior, in truth to nature, to a living painter in their midst,

Turner. There are other criteria than truth to nature, of course, but this fitted the mood of a new middle-class public which had been brought up on Wordsworth, were reading the realistic novels of the day, becoming aware of photography as a medium, and feeling the stirrings of national pride. If Ruskin seemed at times dogmatic, then his dogmatism was supported by the most convincingly detailed analyses of painting and natural phenomena that they had ever read. *Modern Painters 1* was an act of aesthetic enfranchisement for an insecure new public, and it is to the centrally important figure of Ruskin that we must now turn.

Modern Painters and early Victorian aesthetics

One of Ruskin's earliest memories was of standing on the sofa and preaching a short sermon beginning 'People, be good'.[2] It was a prophetic action in more senses than one because he was to spend much of the rest of his life lecturing his countrymen on the same theme, and the temperament revealed in his writings is often bossy, opinionated, arbitrary in judgement, and (in areas where an art critic can ill afford to be so) profoundly prudish. Yet he is also the greatest art critic in the language, and his importance in the history of nineteenth-century aesthetics rests securely on the fact that he single-handedly rescued the reputation of a major English artist, and in doing so created the conditions of taste in which the Pre-Raphaelite movement could grow. Like most of the Victorian sages he benefits from selection, but no slicing of the *œuvre* can excise the moralism. Nor should it try to, for the interpenetration of art and morality is the strength of Ruskin's criticism and was a chief reason for its popularity with the early Victorian public.

When *Modern Painters 1* appeared in 1843 the currently fashionable forms of paintings were the narrative genre tradition associated with Sir David Wilkie, William Mulready, and Sir Edwin Landseer (see Introduction), and the historical genre which had been revived by the government-sponsored competition for artists to provide murals for the Palace of Westminster, rebuilt after the great fire of 1834 (see Chapter 1). Both rested on a consensual 'realism' of an intensely literary kind, for which Trollope – perhaps appropriately – provides the neatest definition in his prescription that a novel 'should give a picture of common life enlivened by humour and sweetened by pathos'.[3] Beside such domesticated realism, J.M. Turner (1775–1851) was bound to seem odd: a great painter, perhaps, sublime in his effects, but undisciplined, wild. Ruskin set himself passionately to the task of proving that Turner was the reverse of wild, but a disciplined artist who understood the kinetic forces of nature much better than any other painter of the time. Turner was Ruskin's Wordsworth, and a quotation from Wordsworth prefaces each volume of *Modern Painters*.

First, however, there is an apparent incongruity to be faced. Ruskin in his father-figure relation to the Pre-Raphaelites is known to have encouraged them in their almost painful attention to the minutiae of detail in nature, yet in the case of Turner he was celebrating an artist whose characteristic effects seem at first glance *im*precise – great swirling masses of colour in which people and objects (railway trains, tug boats) lack clarity of what Ruskin called 'realization'. Perhaps the incongruity is never quite resolved – nor does it matter that it should be – but Ruskin's answer goes to the heart of his aesthetic: that Turner is in fact truer to the facts of nature than earlier, ostensibly more 'realistic' landscape painters like Constable, because he brings out the inner forces and energies which shape the surface of the natural world. In addition, the critic who would understand Turner must be something of a geologist, botanist, mineralogist, and meteorologist: Ruskin was all these things and saw no incompatibility between them and a taste for the sublime. In this he differed from Wordsworth, about whom Ruskin famously said that 'he could not understand that to break a rock with a hammer in search of crystal may sometimes be an act not disgraceful to human nature, and that to dissect a flower may sometimes be as proper as to dream over it'.[4] Ruskin was both a 'dissector' and a 'dreamer', and he taught his readers that painting could be approached with something of the precision they were used to bringing to botanising. So he will affirm 'the uncertainty' (of colour in nature) captured in Turner's painting, 'the palpitating, perpetual change', and then demonstrate the point by inviting the reader to

> pick up a common flint from the roadside, and count, if
> you can, its changes and hues of colour. Every bit of bare
> ground under your feet has in it a thousand such; the grey
> pebbles, the warm ochre, the green of incipient vegetation,
> the greys and blacks of its reflexes and shadows, might
> keep a painter at work for a month, if he were obliged
> to follow them touch for touch: how much more when
> the same infinity of change is carried out with vastness of
> object and space.[5]

Precision and infinity, science and the sublime, meet in Ruskin's writings, and the didacticism is reassuring as well as stern, for his examples are nearly always taken from objects observable on a day's walk in hilly country.

The five volumes of *Modern Painters* may be said to complete the unfinished business of English Romanticism. Ruskin did for Turner what Coleridge did for Wordsworth – demonstrated the aesthetic logic in an artist hitherto considered wildly visionary. The first volume was published when he was only twenty-four and he was soon revising it and apologising for its 'hasty execution and controversial tone' (he had claimed, for example, that Turner was the greatest painter who had ever lived). There is a case, however, for seeing it as the most original and, in a sense, most enduring of the five, for it is here that Ruskin displays, in passages of brilliant analysis of Turner's paintings, the grounds of authority for his later aesthetic prescriptiveness. His theories were built upon the idea of truth to nature he found in Turner, and their theologising in subsequent volumes is no longer so convincing to a post-Darwinian reader as it was to contemporaries, whereas the original defence retains its freshness of discovery and iconoclasm. An additional reason for appreciating the first volume is its openness to the modern: 'All classicality, all middle-aged patent-reviving, is utterly vain and absurd; if we are now to do anything great, good, awful, religious, it must be got out of our own little island, and out of these very times, railroads and all.'[6] Perhaps championing a painter who created the great *Rain, Steam and Speed – the Great Western Railway* made Ruskin more sympathetic to the energies of the machine than he was later to become. It certainly made *Modern Painters* an important background influence on the emergence of a popular taste for painters like W.P. Frith (see below), who developed a new democratic narrative style concentrating on contemporary subjects.

Ruskin begins *Modern Painters* by making a distinction between mere 'imitation' in art, a quality appealing to the lower pleasures of recognition and requiring a high degree of finish for its success, and 'Truth', a moral quality related to our understanding of what is true in nature. Great landscape art is that which gives us a sense of the power and mystery and eternal changefulness of nature, and Ruskin found little evidence of these in the old masters – by which he meant Poussin, Claude, and the Dutch landscape painters. They had finish, and of course great respectability, but no colour or energy: 'I much doubt if there be a single *bright* Cuyp in the world.'[7] But in Turner:

There is not a stone, not a leaf, not a cloud, over which
light is not felt to be actually passing and palpitating before
our eyes. There is the motion, the actual wave and radiation
of the darted beam: not the dull universal daylight,
which falls on the landscape without life, or direction,

or speculation, equal on all things and dead on all things; but the breathing, animated, exulting light, which feels, and receives, and rejoices, and acts, – which chooses one thing, and rejects another, – which seeks, and finds, and loses again, – leaping from rock to rock, from leaf to leaf, from wave to wave – glowing, or flashing, or scintillating, according to what it strikes; or, in its holier moods, absorbing and enfolding all things in the deep fulness of its repose . . . but still, – kindling or declining, sparkling or serene, – it is the living light, which breathes in its deepest, most entranced rest, which sleeps, but never dies.[8]

There had never been art criticism like this in English before. By verbal accumulation, participial adjectives and verbs, syntactical repetition, and most of all by the control of rhythm subtly exercised over that long (and here shortened) second sentence, Ruskin achieves an answering energy to the energy of light in Turner's paintings. The cliché lying embalmed in the literary theory of the day, 'truth to Nature', is brought startlingly to life in this and other passages of *Modern Painters* and given a new force of moral meaning. Ruskin taught his contemporaries to look up at the skies (in the section 'Of Truth of Skies'), to respond to the architectural depth of clouds and the drama of their changing formations, to delight in sunrise and sunset; in 'Of Truth of Earth' we are taken from the sublime of the mountains ('the bones of the earth') to the stones at their foot, and told that the small is of as much significance as the sublime. Always the point of reference is Turner, in whose paintings these 'truths' are made manifest.

Ruskin had little difficulty in reconciling the 'Romantic' and the scientific in his writings, but the theological posed certain problems when he went on to develop his aesthetic in later volumes of *Modern Painters*. One of the many similarities between Turner and Wordsworth was that Turner in his art was more pantheistic than specifically Christian: the energies in his paintings can be seen as religious but only in the Wordsworthian sense of expressing 'something far more deeply interfused'.[9] But Ruskin was an Evangelical Anglican and his hero's pantheism was not enough for him. The second volume of *Modern Painters* (1846) is more theoretically ambitious and more theologically decided – the effort to link the two resulting in the development of his influential theory of 'types', the seeing in nature of 'types' or 'symbols' of Divine truths. 'There is not any organic creature,' he wrote, 'but, in its history and habits, will exemplify or illustrate to us some moral excellence or deficiency, or some point of God's providential government, which it is necessary for us to know'.[10] This essentially static and allegorical view of nature is at odds with the

Romantic vitalism of Turner, and was to provoke a crisis in Ruskin's thinking when it clashed with the discoveries of modern geology.

The theocentric theorising of *Modern Painters 2* was inspired by an important intervening development in Ruskin's life: he read a book by the French critic Alexis Rio on *The Poetry of Christian Art* (1836), and inspired by its praise of the Italian Primitives, he made a visit to Italy (for the first time without his parents) to explore their work. Rio's view was that the High Renaissance had been a sunset rather than a dawn, in which the pure religious art of Giotto and Fra Angelico had become extinguished in the move to a more sophisticated, secular art, beginning with Raphael. Ruskin's enraptured discovery of Fra Angelico (*c.* 1400–55) in Florence, and then of the religious art of the historically later Tintoretto (1518–94) in Venice, made a profound impact on him, comparable to the discovery of the 'pagan' Turner which had inspired the first volume. Now he sought to develop an aesthetic that would include the truth of Turner's landscape and the religious truth of the Italian Primitives and Tintoretto. The task was to find a moral and religious basis for a theory of beauty. He begins by making a distinction between 'the mere animal consciousness of the pleasantness' of beauty, which he calls 'Aesthesis', and 'the exulting, reverent, and grateful perception of it' which he calls 'Theoria', taking the word from Aristotle and using it to mean 'contemplation'. Without the moral and religious awareness of the 'Theoretic Faculty', 'the sense of beauty sinks into the servant of lust'. (Ruskin's exaggerated fear of an easy slide from sensuousness to lust is what I meant earlier by his profound prudishness.)

In the colder, more dogmatic argument of *Modern Painters 2*, good taste has become a manifestation of holy living and its acquisition an 'analogy to, and in harmony with, the whole spirit of the Christian moral system'.[11] The waywardness of beauty now has to be disciplined by consciousness of God. Ruskin makes a distinction between two aspects of beauty comparable to the distinction between the animal 'Aesthesis' and the moral 'Theoria': there is 'Vital Beauty', which he calls 'the appearance of felicitous fulfilment of function in living things', and 'Typical Beauty', which is the quality in exterior phenomena which 'may be shown to be in some sort typical of the Divine attributes'.[12] And so the sublime is baptised: the delight we take in the spectacle of distant water beyond open ground is not allowed simply to communicate its sense of 'something far more deeply interfused', but must become a 'type' of 'infinity', and from there the road into Evangelical orthodoxy runs as straight as a ray of the setting sun: 'It is of all visible things the least material, the least finite, the furthest withdrawn from the earth prison-house, the most typical of the nature of God, the most suggestive of the glory of His dwelling-place.'[13]

Beauty is perceived instinctively, but contemplation ('Theoria') of our impressions makes us aware that what we perceive as beauties are embodiments of Divine attributes. Thus were Romanticism and religious orthodoxy reconciled in an unstable synthesis – unstable, because when Ruskin lost his evangelical faith he came to realise that his typology had been a subjective projection of values *upon* phenomena rather than a discovery of them *within* phenomena.

Ruskin did not of course discover typology, which is a long-established and even rather primitive mode of inscribing and interpreting meaning in a work of art. But the conjunction of his celebration of the Italian Primitives with his attempt to develop a theory of typology was to be crucially influential in the formation of the Pre-Raphaelite movement. As Professor Landow has pointed out, it was the second volume of *Modern Painters* which excited the imaginations of Holman Hunt and Millais: Ruskin's analysis of the typological symbolism in Tintoretto's *Annunciation* seems to be have been particularly influential.[14] Noting the unusual setting of the event in the forecourt of a dilapidated and deserted palace, Ruskin had drawn attention to the way the light in the left foreground was angled up to highlight a clean square stone in the middle of a crumbling column. 'This, I think, sufficiently explains the typical character of the whole,' he wrote. 'The ruined house is the Jewish dispensation; that obscurely arising in the dawning of the sky is the Christian; but the corner-stone of the old building remains, though the builder's tools lie idle beside it, and the stone which the builders refused is become the Headstone of the Corner.'[15] What excited Hunt and Millais about this reading was the possibilities it seemed to hold out for enriching the tradition of narrative realism in which they were working: a 'symbolic realism' would be a means of embodying layers of significance (and for them, specifically religious significance) not available to the literalism of the daguerrotype and early photograph. How this was achieved will be discussed in the next section.

The first volume of *Modern Painters* gave Ruskin's middle-class readers the excitement of discovering that great art could be and was being created by their contemporaries; the second developed a theory of art which spoke in their language, the language of biblical knowledge, evangelical theology, and Romantic feeling. In the decade which passed before the publication of the third and fourth volumes in 1856, however, Ruskin changed: he turned his attention to the more 'social' art of architecture, in works like *The Seven Lamps of Architecture* (1849) and *The Stones of Venice* (1851–53), and he began to lose his faith, if not in God, then in the exclusiveness of the Christian Revelation, and he lost his earlier confidence in the moral sufficiency of landscape. His loss of faith and doubts about landscape had the effect of hobbling the development of the aesthetic set out in the earlier volumes. *Modern Painters 3*, subtitled 'Of Many Things', disavows any intention 'to pursue the inquiry in a method so laboriously systematic' as before,[16] which was making a virtue of necessity. There may be no loss in this for a modern reader, even a gain, for the volume contains much fine writing as well as some of his most enduring theoretical statements, such as the discussion of the Grotesque in chapter 8 and 'Of the Pathetic Fallacy' in chapter 12. There is also a certain drama in knowing, as we do now, that Ruskin was struggling with his previous certainties. But the effect can be disconcerting. The moral rhetoric goes on undiminished ('People, be good') and it takes time to realise that we are being told slightly different things – that there is validity in pagan mythology, for example, or 'gloom' as well as 'glory' in mountains – and that these do not fit easily with the premises of the earlier volumes. 'Do I contradict myself?', Ruskin might have replied with Whitman, 'Very well then I contradict myself.'[17] But what is allowable in a poet is less so in a theorist of art, and the question remains whether the five volumes of *Modern Painters* add up to more than the sum of their splendid parts.

If they do, their shape may be found in the curve they describe – with some unevenness – from an origin in evangelical romanticism to a destination in tragic humanism, with Turner as the touchstone and focus of Ruskin's changing values. Landscape is the starting-point and end of *Modern Painters*: at first an unquestioned good and source of value – pictorial, moral, and spiritual – the 'Moral of Landscape' (*Modern Painters 3*, ch. 17) is increasingly worried over as Ruskin comes to terms with its changing historical imaginings and implications for mankind, and it ends as 'The Dark Mirror' (Pt IX, ch. 1) of *Modern Painters 5* (1860), where his intellectual reversal is declared in the humanistic affirmation

> that all the power of nature depends on subjection to the human soul. Man is the sun of the world; more than the real sun. The fire of his wonderful heart is the only light and heat worth gauge or measure. Where he is, are the tropics; where he is not, the ice-world.[18]

The Ruskin who wrote these words had abandoned Christianity and Wordsworthian pantheism; he could no longer look at a highland landscape without seeing behind the picturesque to the dead ewe in the burn, the poverty of the man and boy fishing in it, the butterfly trapped on the surface and seized by the fish.[19] His awareness of the cruelty of the evolutionary universe goes hand in hand with his discovery of the sufferings of the poor and the cruelty of the doctrines of Political Economy, which he was soon to attack in *Unto this Last* (1862). The progress is towards the human and the social in every area: from the empty to the peopled landscape, from biblical typology to universal symbolism, from God-in-nature to God-in-man. In this sense *Modern Painters* does indeed have a coherence beneath its contradictions and sideways wanderings. But even the contradictions are of value, for they are a sign of a mind continually involved with the most important questions of all: the relationship between the art of the past and the art of the present, and the relation of both to the realities of the modern world.

Past and present in Victorian painting: Pre-Raphaelitism and after

'You are to be in all things regulated and governed,' said the gentleman, 'by fact . . . You are not to have, in any object of use or ornament, what would be a contradiction in fact. You don't walk upon flowers in fact; you cannot be allowed to walk upon flowers in carpets. You don't find that foreign birds and butterflies come and perch upon your crockery; you cannot be permitted to paint foreign birds and butterflies upon your crockery . . . You must use . . . for all these purposes, combinations and modifications (in primary colours) of mathematical figures which are susceptible of proof and demonstration. This is the new discovery. This is fact. This is taste.' (ch. 1)

And this is Dickens in *Hard Times* (1854), making fun of the Department of Practical Art, which had been set up in 1852 under his friend Henry Cole (1808–82) to improve the quality of British design. It is perhaps leaning too heavily on an incidental comic moment (the man from the ministry does not appear again) to point out that Cole in his capacity as the director of the recently formed Museum of Manufactures (1852) was committed to the twin aims of 'the improvement of taste in design, and the application of fine art to objects of utility'[20] – flowers *and* facts, you might say. But flowers versus facts is more fun, and it fits into a familiar Romantic antithesis in *Hard Times* between the machine on the one hand, and poetry, fancy, feeling, on the other. And yet that Dickens makes the joke at all in a novel of this date is evidence that the relationship between art and modernity is becoming problematic. Move the debate on fifty years and 'combinations and modifications (in primary colours) of mathematical figures', i.e. abstract art, might be the height of fashion, and flowered carpets and wallpaper the reverse. 'Taste' in the 1850s was shifting ground as traditional forms and modern technology entered into the long and unfinished process of negotiation which has continued down to the present. It is a typical paradox of the time that the designer who probably put more flowers on Victorian walls than anyone else was William Morris (1834–96), a man who hated industrialisation but who was able to spread his anti-modern, medieval designs only because his modern factory made it possible.

In the arts, as in so much else, the Victorians were people in transition: anxious inheritors of romanticism's confident expansiveness who felt, quite rightly, that their ancestors had lived in a simpler world. Their problem was making artistic sense of the unprecedented in human history, and it is hardly surprising if there was an element of trauma in their response, a reaching for the usable past to mediate the threatening present. Very few Victorian works of art capture the present with the energetic welcome of Turner's *Rain, Steam, and Speed*, where the glowing heart of the engine rushes towards the spectator along the diagonal of the rainswept viaduct. Much more typical would be St Pancras Railway Station in London (1868–74): there the largest train shed ever built was fronted by the largest Gothic hotel, designed by George Gilbert Scott (1811–78). One can interpret such juxtapositions as evidence of a kind of cultural schizophrenia in the period, a violent divorce between 'art' and 'utility' with art requiring the clothing of the past to keep it undefiled by the smoky present.[21] A less melodramatic view would be that Gothic ennobled the present, or was felt at the time to do so, and that the important distinction to make in approaching a period so historically eclectic as this is not between styles of the past and present, but between uses of the past which took account of present realities and those which did not – those which were merely escapist.

Some such distinction, certainly, is needed in approaching the achievement of the Pre-Raphaelite movement. There can never have been a significant movement in painting that was so intensely literary and historical. Ford Madox Brown (1821–93), the oldest and never fully paid-up member, began his career with historical paintings on national themes which reflect the influence of the German 'primitive' Nazarene school and the interest in historical subjects inspired by the Westminster murals competition: romantic/nationalistic moments from Britain's past like *The Execution of Mary Queen of Scots* (1840) and *Wycliffe Reading his Translation of the Bible to John of Gaunt* (1847). Shakespeare, Keats, and Tennyson provided material for some of the most famous works by the painters and sculptors who formed the original Pre-Raphaelite Brotherhood in 1848. Out of Shakespeare's plays came (among others) *Puck* (1847) by the sculptor Thomas Woolner (1825–92); *Ferdinand Lured by Ariel* (1849) and *Ophelia* (1852) by John E. Millais (1829–96);

Claudio and Isabella (1853) by William Holman Hunt (1827–1910); *Twelfth Night* (1850) by Walter Deverell (1827–54). Shakespeare and Tennyson provide the subject for Millais's *Mariana* (1851), while the poems of Keats, especially his narrative poems 'Isabella' and 'The Eve of St Agnes', were the inspiration for Millais's *Isabella* (1849), Hunt's *Eve of St Agnes* (1848) and *Isabella and the Pot of Basil* (1867), and *The Eve of St Agnes* (1856) by Arthur Hughes (1832–1915). In fact, if one includes paintings on Biblical subjects and religious allegories, like Hunt's *The Light of the World* (1853), in the category of the historical, the first and most creative phase of Pre-Raphaelitism, the decade or so from 1848, could almost be said to be creating more from the past than from the present. It is notable, however, that Brown, Hunt, and Millais combined their interests in the historical with a commitment to painting contemporary life. So what was the Pre-Raphaelite movement, and what was it about it that made this strange combination of the literary, the historical, the biblical and allegorical, and the contemporary, seem challengingly modern in 1848?

First and foremost, it was a movement of young men. When the original Pre-Raphaelite Brotherhood (PRB) was formed in Millais's house in 1848, Millais himself was only nineteen, Hunt twenty-one, and the other moving spirit, Dante Gabriel Rossetti (1828–82), twenty. With his Italian blood, Rossetti may have been responsible for the secret society element and the use of the initials 'P.R.B.' on canvases, which as much as anything was responsible for the hostility their work attracted initially. To these three central figures were added four others to make up the magic figure of seven: Woolner the sculptor, F.G. Stephens (1828–1907) the art critic, the painter James Collinson (1825–81), and Dante Gabriel's civil servant brother William (1829–1919). Collinson was the oldest, at twenty-three. In the background were older painters like Ford Madox Brown and William Dyce (1806–64) who were working along the same lines and provided inspiration.

They were united more in what they disliked than in any detailed programme of their own: their programme was their dislike and when that cooled they went their separate ways. Whether or not they had read *Modern Painters* (Hunt had read the books and he passed the message to Millais), they were living in the new atmosphere of ideas which Ruskin had created, when it suddenly became possible to throw off the dead weight of the classical rules on which they had been force-fed at the Royal Academy Schools. 'Why should the highest light be always on the principal figure?', Hunt recalled asking Millais in 1848. 'Why make one corner of the picture always in shade? For what reason is the sky in a daylight picture made as black as night? . . . and then about colour, why should the gradation go from the principal white, through yellow to pink and red, and so on to stronger colours?'[22] This was 1848, after all; governments were being overthrown all over Europe; why should the dead hand of Sir 'Sloshua' Reynolds lie for ever over the teaching of painting in England? (This was the name they gave to the first President of the Royal Academy, Sir Joshua Reynolds (1723–92), a liberating genius in his day but by the 1840s associated with all that was restrictive and conventional in the running of the Academy.)

The Pre-Raphaelite Brotherhood picked up their label without any specific hostility to Raphael – and, its critics would say, without much knowledge of him either. His work was seen at the time (again the influence of Ruskin) to mark a turning-point from an older kind of painting which may have lacked the technical sophistication of the moderns, but more than made up for it in sincerity of feeling. The PRB wanted to get back that quality of freshness and sincerity. 'Sincerity' is now a virtually discredited term in modern criticism, since it leads to a confusion between intention and execution. The view tends to be Oscar Wilde's, that (at least in aesthetic matters) 'a little sincerity is a dangerous thing, and a great deal of it absolutely fatal'.[23] Certainly the sincerity that took Holman Hunt to the Holy Land, there to purchase the poor goat which he painted by the Dead Sea as *The Scapegoat* (1856), was fatal – for the painting as well as the goat. But in its old-fashioned way it still seems the best word to describe what motivated the Pre-Raphaelites at their best. The originality of the movement lay not so much in subject-matter, for both archaism and a realistic treatment of the contemporary were already trends in the painting of the period, but in the intensity with which they approached their subjects, and in the technical means used to translate intensity of vision into intensity of colour and detail.

Intensity of colour, which is what first strikes one in comparing Ford Madox Brown or the early Millais with their contemporaries, was achieved by ignoring the 'rules' of chiaroscuro and gradation of light, and painting directly on to a wet white background with small brushes. This was slow work, a race against the drying of the white, and made slower by that meticulous attention to the smallest detail which is the second most striking characteristic of Pre-Raphaelite painting. The lengths to which the PRB were prepared to go to achieve authenticity of detail are legendary. Sitting – or rather floating – for Millais's *Ophelia*, Lizzy Siddal posed in a bath kept from freezing by lamps underneath; even so the lamps went out, she caught a bad cold, and her father threatened to sue Millais if he did not pay the doctor's bills.[24] For his *Wounded Cavalier* (1856), William Shakespeare Burton (1824–1916) had a hole dug in the ground so he could portray the ferns around the dying figure more accurately.[25] But no one took thoroughness and authenticity further than Ford Madox Brown in painting *The Last of England* (1856). 'To insure the peculiar look of *light all round*, which objects have on a dull day at sea,' he wrote in a catalogue note, 'it was painted for the most part in the open air on dull days, and when the flesh was being painted, on cold days.' And by cold he meant cold: he began his out-of-door sittings with snow on the ground and finished when it was 'intensely cold, no sun, no rain – high wind, but this seemed the sweetest weather possible, for it was the weather for my picture & made my hand look blue with the cold as I require it in the work, so I painted all day out in the garden'.[26] There is something characteristically naive but admirable in his belief that only by exposing himself to the cold could he create the effect of cold.

The typical Pre-Raphaelite painting (if there is such a thing) is marked, then, by a luminosity of colour spread more or less evenly over the whole composition, and by a particularity of detail crowding to the very edge of the canvas. The corollaries are a flattening of perspective, the forgoing of the concentration of focusing which gradated lighting provides, and a proliferation of detail: like the Victorian novel, you get what you pay for, and then some. There is another technical similarity with the fiction of the day in the painters' use of symbolism to enhance and deepen the effect of realism. A Pre-Raphaelite painting will stand in relation to realistic genre painting as (say) Dickens does to Trollope. The point can be illustrated with reference to one of the most famous of all these works, Millais's *Christ in the House of His Parents* (1849–50), sometimes called *The Carpenter's Shop*, which is of particular interest because it drew a famously philistine review from Dickens himself.

In Millais's painting (see Plate 9) the young Christ is showing a cut in his palm to his mother and father. To say that he occupies the centre of the picture is true only in the sense that he stands in the middle of the group, his presence lightly emphasised by the curve that sweeps upwards from the foot of Mary's dress through their hands and along Joseph's arm. Otherwise he has to compete for our attention with the carpenter's assistant on the left, the flock of sheep outside the door, the figures of St Anne (Mary's mother) and Joseph, young John the Baptist carrying a bowl of water, and generally with the clutter of the ordinary carpenter's shop where Millais worked on the painting – planks of wood and tools on the walls, shavings on the floor. The painting draws you into its detail, and yet standing back reveals another feature of composition: the arch which the other figures make around Jesus and his mother, emphasised by the arched window in the back wall on the right. Perhaps it was the implicit Tractarianism of this grouping that worked subconsciously on Dickens, for his reaction in 'Old Lamps for New Ones' (15 June 1850) is curiously contradictory. On the one hand he associates the PRB with the archaising tendency in the time, 'the great retrogressive principle' which would return science and literature to their less developed past, while on the other Millais is attacked because his painting is too developed along the line of realism: Podsnap-like he objected to the 'hideous, wry-necked, blubbering, red-headed boy, in a bed-gown', to the figure of Mary 'so horrible in her ugliness, that (supposing it were possible for any human creature to exist for a moment with that dislocated throat) she would stand out from the rest of the company as a Monster, in the vilest cabaret in France' and so on. 'Wherever it is possible to express ugliness of feature, limb, or attitude, you have it expressed. Such men as the carpenters might be undressed in any hospital where dirty drunkards, in a high state of varicose veins are received. Their very toes have walked out of Saint Giles's.'[27]

It is sad to find the author of *Oliver Twist* writing like this (and one hopes that the respectable Millais *père* did not read it, for he was the model for Joseph), but revealing also. Dickens invokes the names of all the genre painters of the day and invites them ironically to banish from their minds 'all religious aspirations, all elevating thoughts; all tender, awful, sorrowful, ennobling, sacred, graceful, or beautiful associations' (p. 237). Painting in his eyes had to be idealised, and the violence of his and others' reaction is the clearest sign that Pre-Raphaelitism was different from what had gone before. But he was wrong about *Christ in the House of his Parents*: the relationship between Mary and Jesus here is indeed 'tender', and the painting *is* 'religious', in a double sense. First, it makes extensive use of prefigurative symbolism. The cut in the child's palm has come from the nail in the wood which St Anne is reaching to remove; the red of blood is echoed in the clothes of Joseph and Anne, and in a single red flower by the door. Against the wall on the left is what looks like the bottom half of a cross, the sheep outside remind us of Christ the Good Shepherd, and the water so anxiously carried by John the Baptist on the right looks forward to Christ's baptism and the start of his ministry.

But Millais's painting is 'religious' in another, less mechanical way, which links together the subject, the treatment, and the world of 1850. Timothy Hilton has written of the 'democratization of holiness' in early Pre-Raphaelite painting,[28] and there is no better example than this. Christ is restored from idealisation to the world of work and the humble realities of a carpenter's shop, and he is shown as vulnerable to these things, leaning towards his mother for comfort in the way that any child would. His head scarcely rises above the level of the door on which the adults are working; his mother has to kneel to comfort him. This is a Christ in whom contemporaries could see their own children and, bare-footed as he is, the children of the poor – not the haloed idealisation they had become used to. What was so shocking was the reminder that Christ had himself been a vulnerable child, and a poor child. It is strange that Dickens did not see this, for his own art had similar sympathies and he makes a comparable use of prefigurative symbolism to deepen the effect of realism.

In its first phase, Pre-Raphaelitism was associated with religious subjects and techniques of representation, but it is only in Hunt's work that this remains a continuing preoccupation. His *Finding of the Saviour in the Temple* (1860) is a 'Protestant' answer to Millais's painting: the young Christ looks confidently out at us, stepping firmly away from his mother's protecting embrace. When he turns to a contemporary subject in *The Awakening Conscience* (1854), which Hunt had originally titled 'A still small voice', the scene of the kept woman's rising from her lover's chair is packed with symbolic detail of entrapment by sin and possible redemption. But religion is not really the central Pre-Raphaelite theme, despite the impression given by the frequent reproduction of these paintings. If there is a thread running through their choice of literary texts and contemporary subjects, linking Millais's Ophelia to Rossetti's obsessive portraits of Jane Morris, it is love. Not passion, for passion requires movement and Pre-Raphaelite paintings are notoriously static, but love as longing, as unfulfilled or thwarted or expectant desire. Only occasionally do they portray love that is companionable or fulfilled; Ford Madox Brown (an exception to this as to many generalisations about the movement), shows it in *The Last of England*, where the couple on the emigrants' boat hold each other's right hands with a natural familiarity, while with her left the mother clasps an infant's hand which is peeking out of her cloak. The paradigm figures of Pre-Raphaelite desire are Juliet and Ophelia, and their literary derivatives and modern analogues: Keats's Madeline and Isabella, Tennyson's Mariana and Lady of Shallott – young women whose sexuality encounters obstacles which are in varying degrees maiming. It is remarkable how frequently these figures appear in Pre-Raphaelite painting, to the exclusion of all the other subjects, including female types, which they could have taken from past literature.

An unkind judgement would be that the Pre-Raphaelites were drawn to this kind of threatened, girlish woman because they were themselves immature and sentimental, and perhaps there is some truth in this. But it ignores the degree of intensity in these paintings – intensity of detail, and even more the piercing intensity of colour which is, of course, lost in monochrome reproduction. The luminous reds, blues, violets, and purples, seemingly lit up from within, as Ruskin said of Turner's clouds, give a directness of emotional presence to these women, whether it is Millais's Mariana stretching her back in weariness or the girl turning aside with tears in her eyes in *April Love* (1855) by Arthur Hughes (1832–1915). Indeed, such intensity and depth of colour is what is usually understood as 'Pre-Raphaelite'. The observer cannot be neutral, as with the genre picture; the furnishings of desire and longing challenge us to respond, demand that we look at these figures from the literary past with the eyes of the present, just as Millais had done with Christ in the carpenter's shop. We are given images of young women oppressed by authority and vulnerable to their feelings, and invited to see present realities in them: Mariana is a Shakespearian character and a full-bodied young woman, feeling the frustration of unused powers; the face which the girl turns up to the kiss of the threatened Huguenot in Millais's painting (1852) is bright with fear and intense commitment; the drowned Ophelia has her contemporary counterparts in the fallen women of paintings like Spencer Stanhope's *Thoughts of the Past* (1859). Not all Pre-Raphaelite images of women stress their vulnerability, obviously, but sympathy for their vulnerability, awareness of what they endure through the inhibitions and prohibitions of society, a sense of desires unmet or desire misused, are powerful sources of feeling in the paintings of the movement.

There may be other, biographical and historical, reasons why many of the women in these paintings should affect us as they do, whether in terms of their sexual vulnerability or their erotic power. The Pre-Raphaelites differed from earlier painters in the extent to which they were prepared to depart from the conventional studio model and seek out the beautiful young women they called 'stunners'. These were usually to be found in the working class, since no respectable girl – with the exception of the painter's own family, naturally, of which Millais made considerable use – would be allowed to visit a painter's studio unchaperoned: when Dickens's daughter Kate modelled for the girl of Millais's *Black Brunswicker* (1860), she not only came with a chaperone but posed with a lay-figure rather than a live male model. No such proprieties stiffened the posture of Fanny Cornforth, a blacksmith's daughter, or the barmaid Annie Miller, both of whom worked as prostitutes and had a relaxed attitude to displaying their bodies. Ford Madox Brown found the inspiration for his best-known female figures in an uneducated country girl, Emma Hill, whom he made pregnant and eventually married. Dante Rossetti was obsessed first with Lizzie Siddal, the most respectable (an ironmonger's daughter) and tragic of these women, and then with Jane Morris, the daughter of a stable groom.

The painters of the movement were young and idealistic, and they were caught between traditional middle-class assumptions about what constituted respectability in a woman and their attraction to the freshness, vitality, and malleability of their lower-class models. Marriage with these women had become a possibility; it was in the air – the hero of Clough's contemporary epic *The Bothie of Toper-na-Fuosich* (1848) marries a crofter's daughter – and for this very reason they attempted to 'improve' their models to prepare them for middle-class life. Brown tried to polish Emma's manners before he married her; Holman Hunt dithered about marrying Annie Miller and subjected her to a course of self-improvement which she finally rebelled against because he failed to offer the carrot of marriage. The most complex of these cross-class relationships is Rossetti's with Lizzie Siddal. Lizzie was different. Not only did she come from the fringes of the lower middle class but she had a social and artistic sensitivity that the others lacked; she did not need coaching in manners and she possessed a real artistic gift, which to his credit Rossetti encouraged. Their relationship began in discipleship on her part and idealisation on his: Lizzie was to be Beatrice to his Dante, a symbol of unattainable purity who would inspire and redeem the earthbound artist. She held out for marriage, knowing it was her only security in her precarious situation; he put it off for various reasons until it was almost too late. As Lizzie struggled against the destructive myth in which Rossetti had wrapped her, falling into ill-health and laudanum addiction, he turned to Annie Miller and Fanny Cornforth for the sexual satisfaction which his imagination did not allow Lizzie to give him. Eventually he married her – out of sympathy for her ill-health, it has been said – in 1860, when she was thirty. Two years and a stillborn child later she was dead of laudanum poisoning, possibly self-administered. The story is open to many interpretations, but on any reading it is a paradigm of the ambiguous relationship the Pre-Raphaelite painters had with the lower-class women who inspired their work, and helps explain the urgency in their portrayal of fallen women and the tenderness tinged with guilt in their imagination of the vulnerable and the betrayed.[29]

Rossetti's monument to Lizzie is *Beata Beatrix* (1864–70; see Plate 10), arguably his greatest and most mysterious painting, and a work which illustrates as well as any the transition from the first to the second phase of Pre-Raphaelitism. Here Lizzie-as-Beatrice is seated, head tilted back, eyes closed, a look of cold ecstasy on her face, while a red dove drops a white poppy on her lap. Her head is flanked by two figures, who have traditionally been identified as Dante and Love. On the right is a sundial in a pool of light, its shadow falling on 9, the hour of Lizzie's death and possible suicide. The sundial is phallic in shape,[30] and aimed like a field-cannon at the look of ecstasy on the girl's face. Technically, the painting is a turning-away from the clear line and crowding precision of detail in early Pre-Raphaelitism: the background figures are very indistinct, and the girl's hair and dress seem perfunctorily done. Only those areas on which light falls approach the detail we would expect, and these are the poppy (source of the laudanum that caused her death), the dove (traditionally white, but here stained with the red of passion and death), the girl's pale face, and the sundial. By bringing these features into conjunction, the light insists on their symbolic reading:

this is a painting about the relations between love and death. But it does not 'read out' with the moral clarity of earlier Pre-Raphaelite painting. What are we to make of that phallic sundial? A symbol of time and a commemoration of the hour of her death, yes; but in conjunction with the other highlighted features, also a symbol of male desire and its destructiveness, pointing to a pale face whose dying ecstasy (or is it pain?) is more sexual than spiritual. Passion brings death for this most vulnerable of Pre-Raphaelite heroines, as the red dove brings the pale flower. *Beata Beatrix* is not really about Dante's Beatrice but about Dante Gabriel's Lizzie, and commemorates, along with her death, his understanding of his own responsibility for it.

Beata Beatrix marks the turning-point in Pre-Raphaelitism, when an art of clear line, accurate detail, and publicly available symbolism gives way to an art of mood, dream, and esoteric symbolism. Even before Lizzie's death (and perhaps in part responsible for it) Rossetti had turned from the *jeune fille spirituelle* to the large, fleshly women with whom he is chiefly associated – buxom bar-room blondes like his sometimes housekeeper and mistress Fanny Cornforth, and then, with increasing obsessiveness, Jane Morris, the tall, dark-ringletted, cupid-lipped, sultry-looking wife of his friend William Morris. With a sumptuousness of colour that is more Venetian than Florentine, Rossetti painted these ladies, already well-furnished by nature, in the richest of furnishings: flowers, silks and furs, Morris wallpaper. The effect is toothsome but ultimately monotonous, for what is communicated is an obsession rather than a subject. Jane Morris is Venus, and Proserpine, and Mariana, and Guinevere, and the Blessed Damozel, and – one feels – she could have been Tess of the D'Urbervilles and Deirdre of the Sorrows too, had Rossetti lived to paint them. The narrative frameworks implied by the titles are largely pretexts for Rossetti to resume his caressing attention to Jane Morris's lovely long neck, with the dark curls always swept aside to reveal it, his attempt to capture the unrevealed meaning in the large dark eyes and rich, unsmiling lips. The face is painted again and again but remains a mystery; the narrative contexts are merely settings for this inscrutable jewel.

Yet the mystery, the inscrutability, the dream-like languor, the falling-away of narrative as an important element in pictorial conception – these were just the qualities to endear Rossetti's paintings to the later Aesthetic movement, who were bored with story-telling in painting, and even more bored (as was Rossetti) with Ruskin's moralising and geologising. And a quality of dream unites the productions of Pre-Raphaelitism's second phase, in the 1860s, when Rossetti formed another trio, with the younger William Morris (1834–96) and Edward Burne-Jones (1833–98). They tried, and failed, to paint Arthurian murals on the new walls of the Oxford Union; they were more successful in setting up the art-design firm of Morris, Marshall, Faulkner & Co., which was in time to produce the medievalised furnishings associated with the name of William Morris down to the present day. Perhaps this is fitting: Morris belongs more vitally to the history of design than the history of art. His uncritical and unhistorical medievalism was the inspiration for his important campaign for the preservation of ancient buildings, and produced one of the Utopian classics in the language, *News from Nowhere* (1890), but in poetry and drawing it remains irredeemably and monotonously escapist. Paradoxically, despite all Morris's energetic socialism, the spark of engagement with the contemporary world which gives the first phase of Pre-Raphaelite archaism its vitality has gone. Dream-feeling and a complete lack of engagement with the contemporary also characterise the work of Burne-Jones, although his paintings have their own kind of strange power and he feels his way towards some of the problems which aestheticism tried to deal with. His female figures share the languor which seems to have afflicted late Victorian art like a sleeping-sickness. In the classicists like Lord Leighton and G.F. Watts, as we saw in Chapter 1, naked and rosy-bottomed young women are portrayed lounging, swimming, or sleeping in postures redeemed from the erotic by the respectability of classical associations and allegory. Burne-Jones's are usually more clothed – there are a few nudes or glimpsed bottoms – but there is a dream-like character to the whole composition which is not present in the classicists' sunlit languor. The eighteen young women coming down the semi-circular staircase of his *The Golden Stairs* (1880) are almost identical in look and dress, and each carries a musical instrument. One can imagine an allegorical title that would have reconciled this vision to the contemporary expectation of some narrative meaning – 'The Spirit of Music Descending from Heaven to Earth', perhaps – but Burne-Jones refused it deliberately, offering in effect a symbolist painting which invited varying individual interpretations. His haunting *The Depths of the Sea* (1887) has a narrative pretext, a mermaid drowning a naked young man, but its structure taps psycho-sexual fears: high and narrow, the painting shows the drowned man being dragged by the woman down a long column of underwater rock, while on her face is a look of predatory menace which would not be out of place in a painting by Aubrey Beardsley – not surprisingly, for Burne-Jones was one of Beardsley's great heroes.

The literariness and relative coherence of Pre-Raphaelitism means that the movement tends to command a disproportionate attention in accounts of nineteenth-century painting, as perhaps it has done here. This being so, it is important to keep the following considerations in mind: that the movement in its first phase was, in many ways, not so much a departure from, as a necessary revitalising of, a dominant genre tradition which by 1850 had declined into sentimentality and insipidity; that there was a strong realistic impulse within it committed to the sympathetic portrayal of contemporary life; and that this impulse was also at work more widely in other painting of the period. The linking figure is Ford Madox Brown. There are relatively few paintings which actually celebrate the work by which the new society was built, but Brown's famous *Work* (1852–65) is one, showing a team of navvies digging up a Hampstead street, benignly surveyed by 'brain-workers' in the form of Carlyle and F.D. Maurice. *Iron and Coal* (1855–60) by William Bell Scott (1811–90) is another, perhaps even more impressively so since it portrays work in the forge of a Newcastle shipyard.

Brown also portrayed the casualties of contemporary society in the emigrant couple of *The Last of England* (1855) and the unmarried mother of his unfinished '*Take your Son, Sir*' (1851–57), thrusting her new-born illegitimate child at the viewer/father in a parody of the Madonna and Child. There is *The Stonebreaker* (1857) by Henry Wallis (1830–1916), in which an exhausted or possibly dead labourer lies slumped in a twilit rural landscape – one of the most moving of all Victorian paintings. Concern for the sufferings of the poor inspired the artists who worked for the illustrated weekly paper, the *Graphic*, founded in 1869. Luke Fildes (1843–1927), contributed a sketch 'Houseless and Hungry' to the first issue, and it grew into his magnificent frieze (the pun is unintended, but appropriate) of the poor queuing for a free bed in the depths of winter, *Applicants for Admission to a Casual Ward* (1874). Hubert von Herkomer (1849–1914), who illustrated *Tess of the D'Urbervilles* for the *Graphic* – not very well, it has to be said – specialised in paintings of Chelsea pensioners and old women in workhouses, and prison is the setting of one for *Newgate – Committed for Trial* (1878) by Frank Holl (1845–88), a powerful painting focusing on the predicament of the wives and children of the imprisoned men.

Most Victorian painting, however, turned away not only from social problems but from the characteristic 'outer' life of the society, choosing to concentrate on the events and rituals of family life, and dealing with the poor much as it did with animals – whimsically, and with an eye for the humour and pathos of every situation. An exception should be made for W.P. Frith (1819–1909) who, while still recognisably in the genre tradition stemming from Hogarth, showed more of his energy and appetite for variety than most of his contemporaries. It is fitting that details from *Ramsgate Sands* (1854), *Derby Day* (1856–58), and *The Railway Station* (1862) should so often be chosen to illustrate the covers of modern reprints of Victorian novels: there is a similar panoramic sweep and interest in the variety of individual types. At the same time, it is revealing that Frith was one of the first painters to turn to photography for help, asking a photographer to go about Epsom on

Derby Day and take 'as many queer groups of people as he could'.[31] Photography was the coming art/science of the day, and we are only now beginning to recognise its true importance.

Photography

In August 1835 a country gentleman of easy means and keen scientific interests – a man in circumstances very similar to Darwin's, in fact – succeeded in producing a crude photographic negative of a latticed window in his ancestral home, Lacock Abbey. His name was William Henry Fox Talbot (1800–77) and he is usually credited with being the 'Father of Photography', although that title might also be claimed for Louis Daguerre (1789–1851), who had developed a means of producing images directly on to a copper plate coated with a sensitised silver solution. But Talbot's 'negatives' (the name was coined by Sir John Herschel the astronomer) had one great advantage over the 'daguerrotype' in that copies could be made from them, and once the chemical problems of speeding up and fixing the negatives had been solved, the future belonged to Talbot's 'calotypes', as they were called in the early days (from the Greek *kalos*, meaning beautiful). Discovered on the threshold of the Queen's reign, photography is the most characteristic of Victorian media: it brought together science and art in a novel way, was realistic, inescapably contemporary, incipiently democratic, and promised victory over the Time-Spirit which haunted the age. In 'its power of rendering permanent that which appears to be as fleeting as the shadows that go across the dial', Sir Frederick Pollock told the Photographic Society of London in 1855, it ensured that 'nothing that is extraordinary in art, that is celebrated in architecture, that is calculated to excite the admiration of those who behold it, need now perish; but may be rendered immortal by the assistance of Photography'.[32]

Photography expanded rapidly, in direct relation to improvements in technology. It took Talbot half-an-hour to get his image of the window in 1835; twenty-five years later Herschel was dreaming aloud about the snapshot, the action picture taken at speeds of one-tenth of a second; by 1890 the snapshot had arrived and photographers like Paul Martin (1864–1944) were taking shots of the seaside which capture the movement of waves breaking and children playing. (Moving water in early Victorian photography tends to look like the froth on a glass of stout.) As the technology improved, cameras became smaller, easier to use, cheaper, and therefore accessible to more and more people. If photography remained a middle-class pastime for most of this period, photographic prints and reproductions found their way into working-class homes, and the family-group photograph became available to the respectability-seeking working class to an extent that the traditional oil portrait had never been. Photography was democratic in other ways. As a new medium it did not come weighed down with tradition and precedent. There were at that time no schools to enforce rules, no approved models to copy, no binding hierarchy of subjects and themes, no Matthew Arnolds telling you that the productions of the present could never hope to rival those of the past (there was no past for photography), no Ruskins telling you what to paint. This state of affairs was immensely liberating and helps to explain the energetic variety of Victorian photography.

In fact, it is not quite true to say that photography had 'no past', for there was the past of pictorial representation and this raised the question of the new medium's relationship to it. Was photography an art or a science, and if an art, what responsibilities did it have to the pictorial tradition? Very broadly speaking, one can divide the Victorian photographers into those who saw their task chiefly as that of recording the contemporary scene for themselves or for the customers who gave them specific commissions, and those who were in varying degrees aware of a pictorial tradition and of the need to establish photography in relation to it. If this distinction seems to valorise the would-be artist at the expense of the recorder, it is not meant to. Take the case of Robert Howlett (1831–58), the photographer hired by Frith to provide material for *Derby Day*. He was a hard-working professional photographer whose early death may have been caused by over-exposure to the chemicals used in developing: not a man who could afford to pick and choose his projects, in other words. One of these commissions was to record the stages in the construction of Isambard Kingdom Brunel's steamship, *The Great Eastern*, out of which came the famous portrait of Brunel standing in front of the ship's launching chains (see Plate 11). If any single photograph can be said to capture the essence of that entrepreneurial moment in Britain's industrial history, it is surely this, with the great engineer standing like some cocky Artful Dodger in front of the huge, menacing links which, however, his confident posture still manages to dominate. But this masterpiece was taken on the run, not carefully composed in a studio; its greatness owes something to skilful positioning and gradations of light, but most to an opportune capturing of man and moment which is the special grace of photography and which need owe little or nothing to 'artistic' ambitions in the medium. It would be a great mistake to assume that the High Art tradition (of which more below) was necessarily identical with creativity in this medium.

Scientific developments in chemistry made for increasing speed of exposure and precision of detail, but no more than in the history of painting or poetry can sophistication be equated with progress. Some of the finest examples of nineteenth-century photography are to be found at the outset, in the work of the Scottish partnership of David Octavius Hill (1802–70) and Robert Adamson (1821–48). Starting out with the intention of providing photographs for Hill's epic painting of the ministers who left the Church of Scotland in the Disruption of 1843, they soon turned to general photography and in the four years of their partnership, from 1843 to 1847, produced what has been estimated at some 3,000 photographs, the majority of them portraits.[33] Hill and Adamson worked in calotype, deliberately choosing it over the greater precision of daguerrotype because the coarseness of the paper negative produced a depth of darkness in the print and correspondingly dramatic contrasts of dark and light. This suited the portraiture of charismatic and controversial public figures, and it produced even more remarkable results with Newhaven fishwives, who, not owing their portraits to long-forgotten ecclesiastical squabbles, come across with a rare universality. Their portrait of Mrs Hall (Plate 12) is beautifully composed, the light funnelling up from the base of the striped skirt to the face and bonnet, and the half-averted face looking down the angle of light to the right-hand corner, while the hands seem to push away the empty basket even as they hold it. In the dual movement of the head and hands there is suggested a modesty, a vulnerability before the camera, but the strong contrasts of black and white, meeting in the woman's only partly revealed face, convey also an impression of dignity and undeclared power, hinted at in the strong nose, firm but kindly mouth, shaded eyes, and black hair. This is not the fishwife of the genre painter, who would play her allotted role in a pantomime choreographed for middle-class reassurance, but one individual, Mrs Hall, who both submits to and resists the intrusion of the camera. The strong contrasts of the calotype create the impression of individuality in depth – as they do in Rembrandt, the painter with whom the early photographers were most frequently compared.

The discovery of the wet colodion process of mid-century enabled light-sensitive chemicals to be fixed on glass, and the glass negative soon took over from the calotype. The name 'photography' was coined by Herschel in 1839 and supplanted the charmingly literal 'sun-pictures'; by the 1850s it had become a craze, helped on by the Great Exhibition and others, and by the enthusiasm of Prince Albert. In 1853 the Photographic Society was set up with Roger Fenton (1819–69) as its moving spirit and first secretary. Fenton's own working life as a photographer (he was also a qualified lawyer) was limited to a ten-year period between 1852 and 1862, in the course of which he produced a greater range of distinguished work than any other Victorian photographer. He was for a while photographer-in-residence at the British Museum, recording its historical artefacts; he went to the Crimean War as a commissioned photographer (although none of his pictures get very close to the action); he did portraits of the Royal children for Prince Albert, who was an influential patron; and for himself – he was another of these Victorian gentlemen of independent means – he photographed cathedrals, country houses, and landscapes. In both his own *œuvre* and his work for the Photographic Society, Fenton sought to establish photography as a medium of realistic if 'poetic' contemporary record; he does not seem to have been much in sympathy with the movement toward allegory and genre which came in at the end of the 1850s as a means of elevating the medium.

Despite this, attempts have recently been made to recruit Fenton for the High Art tradition by detecting biblical typology in some of his landscapes.[34] Whatever the merits of this approach and the validity of its inferences – and typology looks increasingly like the Victorian equivalent of modern Freudianism in that every bush can be made to seem a bear – it is not on those grounds, surely, that the artistic claims of photography are to be founded. If the medium's intellectual seriousness is to be based on the fact that it can be 'read' like a Pre-Raphaelite painting, then its aesthetic inferiority is implicitly conceded, since no photograph can compete with the colour, texture, or volume of a painting. It is in what Victorian painting did not or could not do that the aesthetic opportunities and justification lay – in the graininess of the everyday. Photography recorded the whole range of contemporary life, from the eminent Victorians to the children in the industrial streets, from cathedrals and castles to train sheds and slums. The fact that few of these things found a place in the painting of the period does not in itself make photography an art, although the breadth of the contemporary photographic record may help us to see what was inadequate in the traditional art of the time. It is as a medium of interpretation as well as record that photography can approach the status of art. From the start, photographers experimented with effects of light and shade and with differences of focus; they altered the negative in processing, or touched it up, or – and this was a cause of much controversy – superimposed one negative on another in printing. These were all manipulations of the exact in the interests of interpretation. Photography becomes an art, one could say, when a basically naturalistic medium is so shaped by the vision of the photographer that a unique fusion of subject, medium, and imaginative temperament takes place. Such fusions were and are rare, but when they happen, in Howlett's Brunel or Julia Margaret Cameron's portraits, they illuminate the contemporary as nothing else can.

Unfortunately, if understandably, this is not how many serious Victorian photographers saw it. Having been brought up to revere the Italian and Dutch masters and to admire the Victorian genre painters, men like Oscar Rejlander (1813–75) and Henry Peach Robinson (1830–1901) tried to make photography a High Art by turning it to the subjects hallowed by pictorial tradition – allegorical figures and groups, sentimental genre studies, affecting deathbeds, characters and scenes from Shakespeare, Scott, Keats, and Tennyson. The idea was to elevate this poor relation by introducing it to better company than could be had by looking out of the window. Aesthetic dignity was to be found not in developing the intrinsic qualities of the medium, which must always give it a disposition towards the present, but by aligning it extrinsically with the conventions of a supposedly superior pictorial tradition. The result is all too often a heavy falling between stools, *tableaux vivants* unredeemed by colour and looking like the faded prints of a local dramatic society production in an old newspaper.

Julia Margaret Cameron (1815–79) had a foot in both camps. Her idealising nature and lifelong friendship with the painter G.F. Watts inclined her to the High Art side; at the start of her career in 1864 she wrote to Herschel: 'My aspirations are to ennoble Photography and to secure for it the character and uses of High Art by combining the real and Ideal and sacrificing nothing of the Truth by all possible devotion to Poetry and beauty.'[35] But she had too strong a feeling for the actual to be comfortable with the literary subjects and *tableaux vivants* of the High Art movement, and when she turned her hand to them, in illustrating Tennyson's *Idylls of the King*, the results are by common consent among the weakest, most wooden in all her work. Her genius was for the close-up. She is the first modern photographer in that she grasped the possibilities of filling the whole frame of a picture with the subject's head and exploiting effects of chiaroscuro within it. In the Herschel portrait (Plate 7), the face comes towards the viewer with a look of searching intensity: the brilliance of the light on his hair and the left side of his face, by throwing everything but the glint in his right eye into shade, gives us a feeling of the depths of space through which the great astronomer has travelled – like Wordsworth's Newton, 'Voyaging through strange seas of Thought, alone'.[36] The downward fall of light in the portrait of Carlyle (Plate 13) emphasises the severe lines from nose to mouth; the eyes remain in shadow, and the slight blurring of the head outline only adds to the impression of ferocity in the old prophet. This is the one contemporary portrait of Carlyle to make you feel his *unsettling* power. On the other hand Julia Jackson – Mrs Cameron's niece and mother of Virginia Woolf – is photographed with her head turned to one side, the light falling on her profile so as to bring out the delicacy of her features and the fineness of her neck.

These portraits and others succeed in her stated aim of combining 'real and Ideal': Herschel is a supreme type of the scientist, Carlyle is the contemporary-as-prophet, Julia Jackson woman and Madonna.

In Julia Cameron's portraits the woman and the moment met. Because she lived near Tennyson on the Isle of Wight during her creative phase, she had access to his large circle of friends among the writers and intellectuals of the period; and because she had that English upper-middle-class confidence that will not take no for an answer, she would cajole and bully the eminent into surrendering their dignity in the cause of her art, as they would not have done in a professional studio. Like Tennyson, most of them would groan and submit, shivering in her greenhouse studio as she developed the negatives in the coal-hole. She was well aware of the distinction of the poets, painters, and scientists she photographed, and her bossy, untidy informality created just the right atmosphere for capturing the individual behind the reputation: here, too, she is the first of the moderns. Her moral and religious allegories are not to everyone's taste, but in her portraits of the famous, and in some of her studies of young women and children, she left behind a sizeable album to support the claim that she was indeed the greatest of the Victorian photographers.

Architecture

The most remarkable building of Queen Victoria's reign was the huge glass exhibition centre erected in Hyde Park to house the exhibits of the 1851 Great Exhibition, which *Punch* aptly dubbed the Crystal Palace. Seen from the air it presents the appearance of a kind of inverted cathedral, where the high, barrel-shaped structure in the centre is the transept and the portions on either side form an enormous, 1848-foot-long nave. And there have been many, then and since, who have seen it as a symbol of the inverted values of Victorian Britain, a monument to materialism and complacency. But to do so is not only unhistoric but also unfair. If the Crystal Palace is a monument to anything it is to the daring and ingenuity of Victorian technology, and to the imagination of Joseph Paxton (1801–65) who, as the Duke of Devonshire's gardener and factotum, is said to have sketched out its design on a piece of blotting-paper during a meeting of the directors of the Midland Railway. The objects in the Great Exhibition may have been grossly material in their heaviness and over-decoration, but the building which housed them was antithetical: constructed from Paxton's design out of the materials he had used in building the huge conservatory at Chatsworth, glass and cast iron, the Crystal Palace was light and airy and evanescent; it could be and was taken down and erected elsewhere. No previous building had demonstrated such ultimate functionalism.

In retrospect, the Crystal Palace points to the road *not* taken by nineteenth-century architects and has become a standard reference point in modern discussion of the Victorian 'battle of the styles'. If this was an Age of Progress, then should not modern architecture be displaying a distinctive style to suit, one which used the technology and building materials of the day to create a domestic architecture appropriate to the heroic achievements of the railway age? Some contemporaries asked this question and wondered aloud about the beauty of the present. 'What can be more pleasing, in its place, than the light iron roof, with its simple, yet intricate supports of spandrels, rods, and circles at Euston Square, or the vast transparent vault and appropriate masses of brick-work at King's Cross? What "fine art" that we could have time to understand on a Railway journey could equal the beauty of the throbbing engines, or the admirably calculated reticulation and intersection of the iron lines at some great junction?'[37] This is the poet Coventry Patmore, reviewing Ruskin's writings on architecture in 1854. Such views were heresy to Ruskin: he ridiculed the contemporary preoccupation with finding a new style, asserting the authority of the traditional models and the desirability of architects having a thorough grounding in them before daring to contemplate innovation of any kind. The outcome of the debate was a victory for Ruskin and those who thought like him, in the sense that the daring use of cast iron and glass to be seen in the Crystal Palace and the great London train sheds failed to translate itself into a distinctive Victorian 'style'. Or, it might be more accurate to say, the Victorians reached a typical compromise in combining historical models with modern technology: their style was revivalism.

Before considering the various aspects of nineteenth-century revivalism it is worth asking why architects found it so difficult to escape from the models of the past. Granted that no new style is ever created overnight, or is ever entirely new, the extent of Victorian dependence on Gothic or neo-classicism still calls for some explanation. Ruskin's influence is part of the answer, but he was influential only because there were deep uncertainties which needed the reassurance his steam-rollering moralism provided. The first uncertainty was the burden of choice; as the architect Gilbert Scott observed in 1856, he and his colleagues had read too much art-history:

> the peculiar characteristic of the present day, as compared
> with all former periods, is this, – that we are acquainted

Plate 11. Robert Howlett, photograph of Islambard Kingdom Brunel

Plate 12. David Octavius Hill and Robert Adamson, photograph of Mrs Elizabeth Hall (1840s)

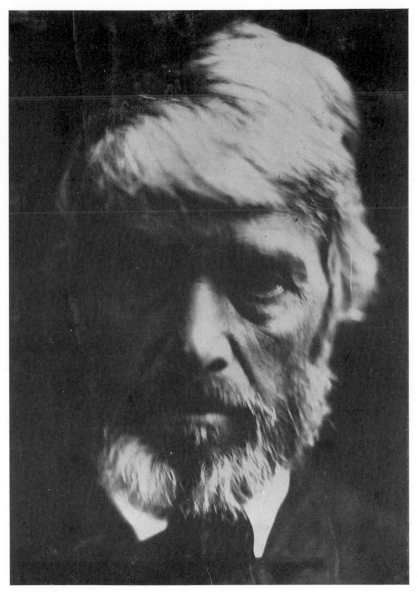

Plate 13. Julia Cameron, photograph of Thomas Carlyle (1867)

Plate 14. Interior of the Reform Club, Pall Mall

Plate 15. Interior of the University (Science)
Museum, Oxford, from Eastlake (1872)

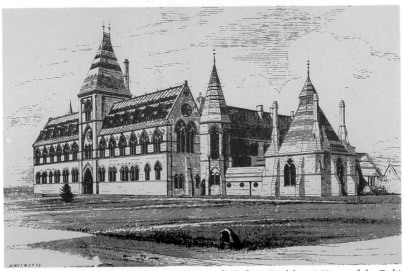

Plate 16. The University (Science) Museum, Oxford, from Eastlake, *A History of the Gothic Revival* (1872)

Plate 17. Perycroft, an example of Charles Voysey's Vernacular architecture

Plate 18. Tissot, caricature of Matthew Arnold, from *Vanity Fair*, 11 November 1871

MAUDLE ON THE CHOICE OF A PROFESSION.

Maudle. " HOW CONSUMMATELY LOVELY YOUR SON IS, MRS. BROWN ! "

Mrs. Brown (a Philistine from the country). " WHAT ? HE'S A NICE, MANLY BOY, IF YOU MEAN THAT, MR. MAUDLE. HE HAS JUST LEFT SCHOOL, YOU KNOW, AND WISHES TO BE AN ARTIST."

Maudle. " WHY SHOULD HE BE AN ARTIST ? "

Mrs. Brown. " WELL, HE MUST BE SOMETHING ! "

Maudle. " WHY SHOULD HE BE ANYTHING ? WHY NOT LET HIM REMAIN FOR EVER CONTENT TO EXIST BEAUTIFULLY ? "

　　　　　　[*Mrs. Brown determines that at all events her Son shall not study Art under Maudle.*

Plate 19.　George du Maurier, 'Maudle on the choice of a profession', from *Punch* LXXX,12 February 1881

with the history of art . . . It is reserved to us, alone of
all the generations of the human race, to know perfectly
our own standing-point, and to look back upon a perfect
history of what has gone before us, tracing out all the
changes in the arts of the past as clearly as if every scene
in its long drama were re-enacted before our eyes. This is
amazingly interesting to us as a matter of amusement and
erudition, but I fear is a hindrance rather than a help to us
as artists.[38]

Here – yet again – is the oppressive historicism of the age. The second
uncertainty was a feeling of unworthiness in relation to the achievements
of the past. Better to work within established traditions and use their
respectability to authenticate one's own, than to risk stylistic novelties
which might reveal one's parvenu status. Victorian architects failed to
break through to a distinctive style because they were too respectful of
their predecessors: they lacked the oedipal impulses of modernism.

What Victorian architecture lacks in coherence, however, it more
than makes up for in variety – variety of styles, and variety within
styles. Revivalism was not a static phenomenon but involved a continual
development: new materials were adapted to traditional forms, and
building styles responded quickly to changes in the climate of opinion.
People were more conscious than they are today of the ideological
implications of architectural style. When the series of buildings that
now constitute the Government Offices in Whitehall was mooted,
the Whig Lord Palmerston was Prime Minister and he favoured a
classical style over the 'Tory' Gothic plans of Gilbert Scott; despite
intensive lobbying by Scott and his supporters, his plan failed to win
the competition. Then Palmerston fell from power in February 1858,
and Lord John Manners (the nominal leader of the Young England
movement of the 1840s) became First Commissioner of Works in
Derby's short-lived administration. Scott was given the job only to
find Palmerston back in office in 1859, determined that the great public
offices of the world's most powerful nation should not be built in
what he considered the gloominess of Gothic. In the end Scott had
to acquiesce and design the Foreign Office in the Renaissance style
favoured by Palmerston.

The battle of the styles was not as sharp at the start of the period
as it was to become in the 1850s. Sir Charles Barry (1795–1860),
although a Renaissance Revivalist at heart, could enter the competition
to design the new Houses of Parliament in 1835 and win it with
a plan that satisfied the requirement that the only allowable styles
were Gothic and Elizabethan. The famous perpendicular skyline did
not satisfy a medieval purist like Pugin, who described it to a friend

as 'All Grecian, Sir: Tudor details on a classical body',[39] but it gave a tremendous fillip, as the competition's terms were intended to do, to Gothic as a *national* architecture. At the same period (1839–40) Barry was innovating in a quite different direction by rejecting the Greek Revival style favoured by Regency architects for public buildings, and turning to the Italian Renaissance palazzo style for the Reform Club in Pall Mall (Plate 14). These two remarkable buildings embody different aspects of the contemporary sense of historical destiny. The Reform Club, as the name suggests, was a club for the new men enfranchised by 1832, the radicals and manufacturers who were not made welcome at the home of aristocratic Whiggery, Brooks's, and so designed a building that would express the vigour and independence of their class. Westminster asserted the continuity of present with past.

The Reform Club bears a little closer scrutiny, for it too combines past and present in a completely satisfying way. Barry took from the Italian *palazzi* he admired the notion of a central tiled courtyard or saloon with an upper gallery and colonnade, off which the main rooms led. In Italy the courtyard would have been open, but by enclosing it with a skylight (see Plate 14) he achieved an effect of great volume and spaciousness, a meeting-place for the new liberals that was both informal and dignified – an appropriate embodiment of their aspirations to be the merchant-princes of their time. It was also comfortable in the best 'modern way, with gas lighting and a 5-horsepower steam engine housed beneath the Pall Mall pavement which pumped hot and cold water through the building and powered a system of central heating and ventilation: warm air entered the rooms of the club through disguised holes in the cornices and ceiling decorations, and the whole building was ventilated through outlets in the glass roof. The Reform Club expresses a significant moment in architectural history and an important phase in British political history: it is one of the great buildings of the nineteenth-century.[40]

The revised classicism of Barry's public buildings in Manchester and London, his Renaissance classicism, was seen at the time as a 'progressive' style. The case of Gothic was a little more complex. In *A History of the Gothic Revival* (1872) Charles Eastlake pointed to the paradox of Victorian Gothic: 'At first it may seem strange that a style of design which is intimately associated with the romance of the world's history should now-a-days find favour in a country distinguished above all others for the plain business-like tenour of its daily life. But this presents a paradox more obvious in a moral than in an historical sense.'[41] Historically, Perpendicular or 'pointed' Gothic could be seen as the true current of national architecture running from the middle ages through the Tudors and Elizabethans until artificially dammed by the importing of continental neo-classicism in the seventeenth and eighteenth centuries; by reclaiming it, as the terms of the competition for the new House of Commons explicitly did, modern Englishmen could rediscover their heritage. To that extent Gothic was a style whose time had come again. But morally, Gothic had associations with the old religion which were inconvenient (to say the least) for Protestants of the nineteenth century. Pugin's intemperate Catholicism did not help the cause of Gothic. The temperate, scholarly work of the Camden Society, founded by Cambridge dons in 1839, did much for the history and preservation of existing Gothic buildings; but the results of their work – published in their journal *The Ecclesiologist* – tended to focus attention on those external features of church building, such as the decoration of altar screens, which had become associated in the popular mind with the doctrinal and liturgical antiquarianism of the Oxford Movement. In its first phase, 1830–55, Gothic church architecture was High Anglican architecture to the average Protestant, and looked upon with corresponding distrust. 'They saw mischief lurking in every pointed niche,' as Eastlake wittily puts it, 'and heresy peeping from behind every Gothic pillar' (p. 268). The national and the spiritual meanings of Perpendicular Gothic were potentially at odds, and perhaps only in a public building could it be quite acceptable. Perhaps Pugin was right, too, in seeing the new Houses of Parliament as a subtle compromise, 'Tudor details on a classic body'.

Church building was highly visible in the early years of Victoria's reign because of money made available by Parliament and then the Ecclesiastical Commissioners to build Anglican churches for the new population growing in new areas. Perpendicular Gothic was a popular choice: it was fashionable, it was spiritual, it was 'national', and depending on the extent of decoration required, it did not need to be either expensive or offensive to Broad Church sensibilities. The very structure of such a building embodied the awakened spirituality of the age: the skyward thrust of spire and pinnacle expressed the urge to escape the materialism in which their predecessors had sunk, the long and narrow nave focused attention on the altar rather than the pulpit, at a time when Anglicans were becoming more aware of the sacramental dimension of their religion. Varying degrees of formal division (between nave and chancel, where the altar was situated) and decoration (in the elaboration of altar screens, pillar carvings, etc.) were explored through the pages of *The Ecclesiologist*, and once decided on, established how 'high' a new Anglican church was going to be. There was a good deal of pedantry and ecclesiastical snobbery in the early Victorian Gothic revival, but much genuine idealism too; this was a chance to start again and create a new housing for a rediscovered spirituality.

In the 1850s an important development in the theory of Gothic took place: Ruskin entered the debate. He had little sympathy for the old Anglo-Norman Perpendicular style that had been promoted by Pugin as the true tradition. Ruskin knew Venice well, and admired the Italianate Gothic of St Mark's and the Doge's Palace. In *The Stones of Venice* (1851–3) he introduced them to a public which had hitherto been accustomed to see them as the unremarkable products of a decadent civilisation. He has been credited with 'Protestantising' Gothic; the truth is rather that he universalised it, seeing Venetian Gothic as the expression of the life of a whole society, and offering it, in the famous chapter 'On the Nature of Gothic', as a passionately felt alternative to modern industrial civilisation. 'Previous apologists for the Revival', Eastlake observed,

> had relied more or less on ecclesiastical sentiment, on historical interest, or on a vague sense of the picturesque for their plea in its favour. It was reserved for the author of 'The Stones of Venice' to strike a chord of human sympathy that vibrated through all hearts, and to advocate . . . those principles of Medieval Art whose application should be universal. (p. 278).

By opening the somewhat narrowly ecclesiastical character of early Victorian Gothic to continental styles, by advocating the decoration of windows and doors and capitals with elaborate carving, by encouraging architects to exploit different colours and textures of stone, and by turning attention to civic and secular building, Ruskin was a major influence on the formation of High Victorian Gothic (1850–70), of which these are all distinctive features.

Ruskin was not much interested in the practicalities of architecture, but there is one building in which he was closely involved from the start and which reflects his influence in many ways, and this is the Oxford Science Museum, begun in 1855 and left not quite finished in 1860. The architects, the Irish firm of Woodward and Deane, were chosen with more than half an eye on Ruskin's approval, and they seem to have been more than half willing to design a building that would express his principles. From the front (Plate 16) the building shows an amalgam of several styles: English Gothic on the ground floor, Italianate on the first floor, a Flemish roof with dormer windows and wedge-shaped tower, all contained within the firm frame that Ruskin admired in Venetian Gothic. To the side the laboratories are separately housed in a building shaped like the Glastonbury kitchen, adding a touch of the English picturesque Gothic which either softens or distracts from the firmness of the main building, depending on taste. The mouldings of the windows and door were elaborately carved in stone depicting the variety of plant and animal life, and the theme was continued in the building's interior. There (Plate 15) a tiled quadrangle was roofed in glass supported on iron pillars, and the nature theme is pursued in the decorations at the top of the columns and in the carved capitals on the first floor. Statues of famous scientists occupy the bays on the ground floor. Seen from this angle it is a curious hybrid, part cathedral, part railway station; a visual expression of confidence in the stability of the relations between nature, art, and science – most ironically so, for the first scientific gathering it housed was the meeting of the BAAS in 1860, during which Huxley and Wilberforce had their famous clash over Darwin's *The Origin of Species*.

Does the stylistic eclecticism of the Oxford Museum work? That is the problem with High Victorian Gothic generally. The Crystal Palace had its integrity (a glass showcase for the Railway Age), the Reform Club has its integrity (a Renaissance building for men of the new industrial Renaissance), but where is the unifying idea behind this amalgam of Flemish town hall, Venetian palace, railway station Gothic, and medieval picturesque? Michael Brooks was plausibly suggested that it needs to be 'read' in its totality, rather like a Pre-Raphaelite painting, with particular attention to the decoration (the carvings, the statues, the murals in the lecture rooms); the Oxford Museum is, he argues, 'the first example of an important Victorian architectural genre – the Illustrated Building', and its text is the Ruskinian message, Nature as Revelation.[42] This may well be true (although one wonders how the Glastonbury-kitchen-laboratories fit into the picture, and the answer is that they do not, being an inconvenient accessory to the main sermon in stone), and if it is, the building reveals a deep incompatibility between the nature of Gothic and the meaning of science. Ruskin's text was out of date before the museum was finished, and, like so many Victorian attempts to reach permanence in an age of change, it made little allowance for developments in the study of nature. The decorative took precedence over the practical, but before long the laboratories were going to have to come in from the kitchen and the statues (metaphorically speaking) go out to the lumber room.

As public rather than ecclesiastical architecture, High Victorian Gothic displays the strengths and weaknesses of Woodward and Deane's Oxford Museum: these are above all *large* buildings, noble in conception, elaborate and meticulous in detail, ambitious in their eclecticism, but too dependent on the corset of historical style: the living forces of the present move uncomfortably within them, dwarfed by the scale and by the past, like the men and women in Plate 15. Palmerston's resistance to Gilbert Scott's Gothic showed a true instinct beneath the prejudice: neo-classicism was a more fitting style for Whitehall, and in fact the majority of public buildings in the nineteenth century were in the neo-classical form. Nor, for that matter, did neo-classicism become entirely eclipsed as a style of Church architecture either, as the distinctive temple-like churches of Alexander 'Greek' Thomson (1817–75) in Glasgow demonstrate.

In the 1870s a small but significant reaction started to set in against the grandiose pretensions of neo-classicism and High Gothic. The Vernacular Revival, as it is called, was part of a larger awakening to the virtues of regional life, of the homely and the local, which took place in the later nineteenth century. There are the regional novels of Thomas Hardy; the growth of a serious interest in folksong, initially in Wales and Scotland, and later in England; a new respect for traditional crafts and materials; a revulsion from the urban, the large-scale, the mechanical. The roots of this development lie in a consciousness of accelerating change: people start to appreciate traditional things when modernity threatens to take them away, and behind the Vernacular Revival was a growing disenchantment with the Machine Age which the Great Exhibition had celebrated so uncritically. A key text here is 'On the Nature of Gothic' in Ruskin's *The Stones of Venice*. Fruitfully self-contradictory as ever, Ruskin argues there that the accuracy of detail which he had demanded of artists elsewhere in his writings (in *Modern Painters*, for example) was a vice in architecture, because it was a sign of mechanical finish. Now that industrial processes could turn out thousands of identically finished objects, the sign of life in art of any kind was *imperfection*: 'It seems a fantastic paradox, but it is nevertheless a most important truth, that no architecture can be truly noble which is *not* imperfect.' Imperfection means life, and life means change; and the workman who has been able to express his individuality, even at the cost of error, will create a living, changing, life-giving artefact as the more accurate factory-hand will never do. Gothic is the architecture of imperfection. So far, Ruskin may seem only to be adding his bit to the battle of the Goths and the classicists. What was revolutionary about 'On the Nature of Gothic' was the violence of his polemic against industrialisation ('It is not, truly speaking, the labour that is divided; but the men: – Divided into mere segments of men – broken into small fragments and crumbs of life . . .') and his three rules for modern design:

1. Never encourage the manufacture of any article not absolutely necessary, in the production of which *Invention* has no share.
2. Never demand an exact finish for its own sake, but only for some practical or noble end.
3. Never encourage imitation or copying of any kind, except for the sake of preserving records of great works.[43]

William Morris read these words while an undergraduate at Oxford and they changed the direction of his life, turning him from a conventional career in the Church to become the founder of the Arts and Crafts movement. He was to commemorate his debt to Ruskin by producing a Kelmscott Press edition of 'On the Nature of Gothic'. It became a canonical text of British socialism and was widely sold to working people in penny-pamphlet form. Ruskin inspired Morris to design wallpapers and furnishings using colourful organic shapes and natural materials, and Morris, with his enormous energy, inspired his contemporaries to turn away from the over-decoration of High Gothic and see beauty in simplicity. His ideal was a Cotswold village. Although not an architect himself, he was a powerful enemy of vandalising 'renovations' and in 1877 founded the first architectural preservation society, the Society for the Protection of Ancient Buildings.

The phrase 'Arts and Crafts' became current when an Arts and Crafts Exhibition Society was formed in 1877 in reaction against the drive to professionalisation within the Royal Institute of British Architects, which wanted to make architecture a closed shop like law and medicine. Its founding members were pupils of the prolific Richard Norman Shaw (1831–1912), craftsmen of various skills, and Morris himself. Their aim was to keep architecture in touch with craft materials and skills, and these were displayed in their annual exhibitions. The Society provided an intellectual forum and meeting-place for the architects of the Vernacular Revival. The movement begins with the home that Philip Webb (1831–1915) designed for William Morris in 1859, and ends with its absorption into Modernism in the work of Frank Lloyd Wright (1869–1959), but its heyday was the period from 1880 to 1910 in the buildings of such architects as W.R. Lethaby (1857–1931), Charles Voysey (1857–1941), Charles Rennie Mackintosh (1868–1928) and Charles Robert Ashbee (1863–1942). Architecture is the most moralistic of artistic enterprises, and the values of Vernacular were never better summed up than by Charles Voysey in his statement that 'simplicity, sincerity, repose, directness and frankness are moral qualities as essential to good architecture as to good men'.[44] Such qualities are best realised in the house rather than in the country mansion. *The English House* (1904–05) was the title of the admiring contemporary study of the movement by Hermann Muthesius, an architect attached to the German Embassy: he was most struck by Vernacular's lack of display, its comfort, simplicity, and quiet individualism, in contrast to the self-conscious stylishness of German architecture. Vernacular, in fact, was the architecture of Englishness.

Vernacular came out of Low Gothic, out of the informal country vicarages designed by those giants of High Gothic, William Butterfield (1814–1900) and George Edmund Street (1824–81). The influence can be seen in the steep roof and pointed arches of Webb's home for Morris, the Red House (so-called because of the red bricks used), and in Charles Voysey's lingering fondness for the flying buttress. But the essential character of the Vernacular Revival was its willingness to revive and try to adapt other styles of national architecture: the 'Old English' with its timbered upper storeys, mullioned windows, and tall brick chimneys; the 'Queen Anne', the red-bricked, sash-windowed architectural equivalent of the pastiche Augustanism of Thackeray's *History of Henry Esmond* (1852). Sometimes the synthesis of styles is achieved and something pure and original emerges, as in several of Voysey's buildings (see Plate 17); at others we seem close to suburban 'Tudorbethan'. But successful or not, Vernacular belongs with that double movement of national consciousness discussed in the previous chapter, whereby a Roman expansion overseas is accompanied by the re-discovery of a sustaining myth of rural England, the home of Puck and the Shropshire Lad. Classicism was the style for the new Romans abroad, Vernacular for their retirement homes at Pook's Hill.

Music

'Das Land ohne Musik,' the Country without Music, was the title of a book about Britain by Oscar Schmitz (1914), and it has become a familiar definition of British musical achievement between Henry Purcell (1659–95) and Sir Edward Elgar (1857–1934). As with all such generalisations, it depends on what is meant by 'music' and what is meant by 'Britain'. If music is understood in the formal, classical sense of orchestral performance (symphonies and concerti) and grand opera, then British musical life was hampered by a failure to develop the institutions that would have fostered it and by willingness to rely (as the British car buyer does today) on imported German models – Handel in the eighteenth century, Beethoven, Mendelssohn, and Wagner in the nineteenth. There was no tradition of patronage by the aristocracy of native talent comparable to that in Germany, and neither they nor the middle classes identified themselves with the movements of musical nationalism taking place in Germany, Russia, Czechoslovakia, and elsewhere. Grand opera was, by aristocratic tradition, Italian opera; Covent Garden was the Royal Italian Opera House until 1892, and the practice was to translate operas in all languages, including Wagner's, into Italian. This was not the way to encourage a national operatic tradition. Taking their lead from the nobility, the middle classes did not sufficiently respect or reward the professional composer and musician. Several careers which began in promise ended in the grind of teaching and performing to make ends meet. This is what seems to have happened to William Sterndale Bennett (1816–75) and even to a career so outwardly successful as that of Hubert Parry (1848–1918), and it might well have happened to Elgar himself had it not been for the determination of his wife: at one point the greatest English musician since Purcell was composing on paper that Alice Elgar had ruled for him.

For the performer who was not a star, life was hard and uncertain; engaged on a concert-by-concert basis, he or she had to eke out a living by teaching in homes where they were considered as little better than dancing teachers. George Eliot provides a vivid picture of a musician's professional pride colliding with middle-class snobbish amateurism in *Daniel Deronda* (1876), where the – admittedly exceptional – Herr Klesmer exposes the shallowness of the heroine's musical standards in a scene of brutal honesty, and later marries the daughter of the Arrowpoint family in the teeth of their opposition to his foreignness. He and Catherine Arrowpoint share a dedication to music which in the novel is a symbol of useful work in a lazy, corrupt society. Unfortunately most middle-class Victorians saw things the other way round. It took a foreigner (like Klesmer) to found the first professional orchestra in Britain, Charles Hallé (1819–95), and he did so in Manchester where, again, there was a significant immigrant community to support his concerts. Hallé appointed his musicians by the season and so was able to raise standards of performance; by keeping admission prices as low as possible, with special cheap seats at the back of the hall for the working classes, he did much to expand the audience for classical music; and by touring to other British cities he encouraged the taste which led to the formation of similar orchestras in other major cities. Hallé always looked to encourage English music and could find little of it about, but his achievement was to start creating the conditions in the 1860s for the national renaissance that came at the start of the twentieth century.

There are other kinds of music, however, and other ways of looking at the musical achievement of Victorian Britain. England came very late to the folk-song revival. The first collection of English folk-song, William Chappell's *The Ballad Literature and Popular Music of the Olden Time*, was published in 1855. The Folk Song Society was not founded until 1898. The equivalent enterprise for Scotland had begun a century earlier. James Johnson's *The Scots Musical Museum* started to appear in 1787 and contained many old Scottish songs which Burns had collected and 'repaired'. By 1850 these had long been in the European bloodstream, to the extent that their existence, and the example of Burns in travelling the land collecting words and music, was a major influence in the growth of musical nationalism. Religion took the place of nationalism in the musical life of nineteenth-century England. When Wagner went to hear Handel's *Messiah* at Exeter Hall, the London centre of Nonconformity, he concluded: 'I got to know the true spirit of English musical life there. It is closely intertwined with the spirit of English Protestantism . . . attendance at [Handel's *Messiah*] is considered the equivalent of going to church.'[45]

The Victorian age was a great period of hymn-writing in the Church: it was a part of the reconstruction of Anglican spiritual life and went with the church building and liturgical reform. *Hymns Ancient and Modern* first appeared in 1861. Nonconformity's corresponding period was the eighteenth century, when Isaac Watts (1674–1748), Charles Wesley (1707–88), and John Wesley (1703–91) left an even richer body of hymns which were of profound importance in the formation and sustenance of Nonconformist religion. The chapel was often the only centre of social life for the new industrial poor and hymn-singing helped to promote a sense of community. The variety, tunefulness, and sheer power of *The Messiah* and other oratorios made them a natural extension of musical activity, allowing the singer some of the musical pleasures of opera without, as Wagner shrewdly saw, losing the religious sanction necessary to the puritan temperament. The local employer, sensing the communally binding power of music, would often encourage the local choral society and the works band, and these survive today in parts of Wales and the north of England.

In London, the respectable went to Covent Garden but a more vital form of vocal music was to be heard in the music halls, which by 1860 numbered over thirty and rapidly spread to the rest of the country, adapting to local traditions of song and humour in the process. Cocky, sentimental, 'naughty', and patriotic by turns, the music-hall song may have lacked the sophistication of operetta, but it kept in touch with the realities of contemporary life better than the often lugubrious parlour-song. Who would not rather listen to 'My Old Dutch' than 'The Lost Chord', to 'Burlington Bertie – from Bow' than 'Come into the Garden, Maud'? No apologies or historical adjustments are needed to enjoy 'My Old Dutch': it has the sentiment stiffened by folk-experience of Burns's 'John Anderson my Jo, John'. 'The Lost Chord' is an art-song and invites comparison with other art-songs, like German *lieder*: it is not necessarily a failure, within its own terms the song may even be a success, and it is still to be heard on programmes like 'Your 100 Best Tunes'. But as with so many other Victorian parlour-songs, it never quite shakes off the antimacassar.

'The Lost Chord' sold half-a-million copies in its first twenty-five years and was the creation of Arthur Sullivan (1842–1900), who also wrote 'Onward, Christian Soldiers', several oratorios and orchestral pieces, and, of course, the music for the comic operettas produced at the Savoy Theatre with the libretti by W.S. Gilbert (1836–1911). The Savoy Operas – from *Trial by Jury* in 1875 to *The Gondoliers* in 1889 – are the most successful musical products of the age, if success is to be measured by survival. They may not be great music or even great operetta, but as Michael Kennedy says, 'they were the up-market apotheosis of the two musical forms with which the majority of the British people were familiar and to both of which Sullivan contributed – the hymn-tune and the drawing-room ballad'.[46] Their continuing popularity says something about the survival of a middle-class habit of mind which was formed in the nineteenth century. As for great music, that had to wait for Elgar and *The Dream of Gerontius* (1900): it came at the end of the century, in the oratorio form that had been so widely employed by Victorian composers, but with one significant difference from the oratorios Wagner heard at Exeter Hall. Elgar was a Catholic, and in basing his oratorio on a poem by Cardinal Newman, he was breaking with the long Protestant tradition going back to Handel.

The aesthetic resistance

'*All art constantly aspires towards the condition of music*', wrote Pater in his essay on 'The School of Giorgione' (1877).[47] It is one of the more amusing ironies of Victorian culture that aesthetes like Pater seem to have cared more for the dignity of music than the musicians themselves. They cheerfully subordinated music to the narrative-cum-moralistic demands of the hymn or the parlour-song, while the Aesthetes wanted to subordinate narrative to music. Music was their symbol of an art in which there was no divorce between form and matter, style and subject:

> For while in all other kinds of art it is possible to
> distinguish the matter from the form, and the under-
> standing can always make this distinction, yet it is the
> constant effort of art to obliterate it. That the mere matter
> of a poem, for instance, its subject, namely, its given
> incidents or situation – that the mere matter of a picture,
> the actual circumstances of an event, the actual topography
> of a landscape – should be nothing without the form,
> the spirit, of the handling, that this form, this mode of
> handling, should become an end in itself, should penetrate
> every part of the matter: this is what all art constantly
> strives after, and achieves in different degrees. (p. 86).

The 'mere matter' of a poem or painting: there is the note of provocation, with its corollary assertion that the tendency of art was to 'become an end in itself'. Pater's readers were so used to literary, narrative, and allegorical art, where subject predominates over form, that any declaration of formalism like this was bound to seem shocking, and the hint that art might tend to become an end in itself (Pater does not say that it was) was positively decadent. Formalism was a threat to the union of art, morality, and nature which Wordsworth and Ruskin had forged for them.

The year in which Pater's article appeared, 1877, saw the opening of the Grosvenor Gallery in London, the first of the independent galleries which, by exhibiting a greater selection of modern painting, came to undermine the authority of the Royal Academy. The Pre-Raphaelites had resented the power of the Royal Academy, but they all looked to its summer exhibition as the chief testing-ground and market-place for their paintings, and in due course several of them became its stalwarts. The Grosvenor soon became associated with the new Aesthetic movement – the Aesthete Bunthorne in Gilbert and Sullivan's *Patience* (1881) is 'A greenery-yallery, Grosvenor Gallery, Foot-in-the-grave young man' – because of the row over an experimental painting, *Nocturne in Black and Gold* (1877), by a young American-born painter and flamboyant Aesthete, James McNeill Whistler (1834–1903). The gallery's proprietor had exhibited this quasi-impressionistic work alongside paintings by safer, more established artists, and it was violently attacked by Ruskin in one of his *Fors Clavigera* letters, who intemperately declared that he had 'seen, and heard, much of Cockney impudence before now; but never expected to hear a coxcomb ask two hundred guineas for flinging a pot of paint in the public's face'.[48] Whistler sued for libel.

The Ruskin–Whistler law-suit is rich in symbolism. It is sad that Ruskin, whose own career as an art critic had begun with an eloquent defence of the seemingly 'formless' Turner, could no longer extend patience and sympathy to another experimental painter thirty years later. The trial was a test of the degree of formalism an English jury were prepared to tolerate in their painting, but even more was it a test of Ruskin's authority. The outcome was a Pyrrhic victory for Whistler – a farthing's damages and legal expenses that ruined him. But the combination of Whistler's wit at the trial and Ruskin's failure to attend was fatal for Ruskin's reputation with a younger generation of artists and writers. Henry James may be allowed to speak for them: 'Mr. Ruskin's language quite transgresses the decencies of criticism, and he has been laying about him for some years past with such promiscuous violence that it gratifies one's sense of justice to see him brought up as a disorderly character.'[49]

The time was ripe, in fact, for a challenge to Ruskin's authority. He had become a 'disorderly character' because of what we can now see as a crumbling in the foundations of his aesthetics: he had lost his Evangelical certainty in the 1850s and nature was now starting to fail him under the impact of evolution and industrialisation, but he had not lost the habit of moralising. His immense prestige blocked the asking of overdue questions about art's relation to the Darwinian universe, to science, to religion, to contemporary developments on the continent (the first Impressionist exhibition in Paris was in 1874), and – not least – to art itself. Painting differs from literature in the degree to which there is a legitimate and substantial satisfaction to be obtained from the non-representational – from colour and patterns of colour, the texture and shape of materials, formal patterning, the effect of light on different surfaces, and so on. Victorian painting had lost touch with these more purely 'aesthetic' pleasures in the dominance of narrative, and Whistler's most challenging work was a reminder of them. When he called his famous painting of his mother *Arrangement in Grey and Black: Portrait of the Painter's Mother* (1872), he was provoking his contemporaries to think about the formal elements in painting. It is the conjunction of the abstract and the familiar in the title that is disturbing. How can one approach one's *mother* as an 'Arrangement in Grey and Black'? Most interpreters have settled for the second half of the title, although even that causes problems – a less maternal mother would be hard to find in nineteenth-century painting. But if the work is seen in the context of its full title it becomes an exercise in the problematics of formalism, an invitation to the viewer to explore the ways he or she constructs meaning when faced by the unfamiliarly familiar.

The Aesthetic movement was a mixture of straightforward rebellion against Victorianism, new theorising, and extravagant posing – all meeting in unstable fusion in the symbolic rise and fall of Oscar Wilde (1854–1900). Its landmarks are the aggressive paganising of Swinburne's *Poems and Ballads* (1866), the fastidious paganising of Pater's *Studies in the Renaissance* (1873) and *Marius the Epicurean* (1885), Wilde's *Critic as Artist* (1891) and *The Portrait of Dorian Gray* (1890), Gilbert and Sullivan's *Patience* (1881), and Wilde's trials. More West-End than Left-Bank as an intellectual movement, it suffered the West-End's revenge when Mr Justice Wills gave Wilde the hardest sentence the law allowed.[50] Yet the roots of Wilde's dandyism and of Pater's aesthetics are in the elegant, proto-aesthetic posturings of Matthew Arnold. If this seems an unfamiliar way of looking at Arnold, consider the figure in Tissot's contemporary cartoon for the magazine *Vanity Fair* (Plate 18), with its nonchalant posture and smile verging on the supercilious. Arnold's legacy to the Aesthetic movement was, firstly, his Hellenism, but more importantly his poising of 'Culture' *against* the middle classes and a way of talking about their lives and beliefs that could be both 'superior' and witty. At times he seems only a dancing-pump away from Wilde, as when, for example, he observes that 'Dissent, as a religious movement of our day, would be almost droll, if it were not, from the tempers and actions it excites, so extremely irreligious'.[51] There is also the deadly dart of the 'philistine' label, which the Aesthetes were to adopt as synonymous with middle-class taste. Finally, in 'The Function of Criticism at the Present Time' (1865) and elsewhere, Arnold rescued the *idea* of criticism as an autonomous activity, subsidiary to but not necessarily less valuable than the creative, from its current low esteem and from a clutter of other activities. This crystallising out of criticism as an activity in itself was an essential preliminary to the development of what Pater called 'aesthetic criticism', and Wilde's *Critic as Artist* can be seen as a typical carrying to extremes of Arnold's position.

There is, however, one crucial difference between Arnold and Pater. He did not suffer from the epistemological uncertainties – doubts about the grounds of his knowledge – which Pater knew as a student of contemporary psychology. When Arnold writes in 'On Translating Homer' (1861) that 'the business of criticism is to see the object as in itself it really is', he believes that there is something 'out there' to be known which criticism can grasp and clarify. Walter Pater (1839–94) quotes these words in his Preface to *The Renaissance* and at once gives them a sharp turn inwards: '"To see the object as in itself it really is," has been justly said to be the aim of all true criticism whatever; and in aesthetic criticism the first step towards seeing one's subject as it really is, is to know one's own impression as it really is, to discriminate it, to realise it distinctly.' This is a decisive utterance in the history of nineteenth-century aesthetics because it amounts to a declaration that what matters is the temperament of the critic. Pater goes on:

> The objects with which aesthetic criticism deals – music, poetry, artistic and accomplished forms of human life – are indeed receptacles of so many powers or forces: they possess, like the products of nature, so many virtues or qualities. What is this song or picture, this engaging personality presented in life or in a book, to *me*? What effect does it really produce on me? Does it give me pleasure? and if so, what sort or degree of pleasure? How is my nature modified by its presence, and under its influence? The answers to these questions are the original facts with which the aesthetic critic has to do; and, as in the study of light, of morals, of number, one must realise such primary data for one's self, or not at all. (p. xxix).

If this passage is read with the last sentence removed it seems intensely narcissistic; it could even figure in one of George du Maurier's lampoons and cartoons of the Aesthetes in *Punch* (see Plate 19). Put it back in and one is aware of a different discourse: 'facts', 'study of light', 'data' – these belong to the language of science. Pater is not saying, as Wilde does, that cultivating one's temperament and impressions is a pleasing exercise in hedonism, but that these are the only *data* of which the critic can be sure. In this he shows himself a true child of the Victorian scientific revolution.

Pater's doctrine of impressionism derives from a Heraclitan feeling for the inevitable passing of all things reinforced by evolutionary theory, the implications of which he quickly grasped. 'Modern thought is distinguished from ancient by its cultivation of the "relative" spirit in place of the "absolute"', he wrote in his essay on Coleridge (1866), observing that Coleridge's life had been 'a disinterested struggle against the application of the relative spirit to moral and religious questions'. A doomed struggle, however, because as he observes: 'The moral world is ever in contact with the physical; the relative spirit has invaded moral philosophy from the ground of the inductive sciences.' The modern human being is a complex creature, constantly influenced by forces of environment and heredity – 'remote laws of inheritance, the vibrations of long past acts reaching him in the midst of the new order of things in which he lives' – and by 'the character of the age':

> It seems as if the most opposite statements about him were alike true; he is so receptive, all the influences of the world and of society ceaselessly playing upon him, so that every hour in his life is unique, changed altogether by a stray word, or glance, or touch. The truth of these relations experience gives us; not the truth of eternal outlines effected once for all, but a world of fine gradations and subtly linked conditions, shifting intricately as we ourselves change; and bids us by constant clearing of the organs of observation and perfecting of analysis to make what we can of these. To the intellect, to the critical spirit, these subtleties of effect are more precious than anything else.[52]

There are no religious or moral absolutes; we are changing creatures in a world which is constantly changing. The response of previous Victorian sages (for in his way Pater is a sage also) to this condition had been Carlyle's renunciation or Arnold's resignation. Pater's is a disciplined paying of attention to what passes. For him aestheticism is a discipline, a science of sensation; not swinish indulgence or living for the moment, but a 'constant clearing of the organs of observation and perfecting of analysis'. It has its own morality too, which is not so very different from that found in the novels of Henry James: highly developed creatures have a duty to respond adequately to the richness of their experience, and in the quality of their response, their capacity to register and interpret 'subtleties of effect', lies their existential justification.

But the subtleties proved too much for Pater's senior colleagues at Oxford, when expressed in the famous 'Conclusion' to *The Renaissance*. There they read that 'success in life' was to 'burn always with this hard, gemlike flame', and that 'not the fruit of experience, but experience itself, is the end', and concluded, understandably perhaps, that this Fellow of Brasenose was a danger to his young charges. Pater responded to the atmosphere of criticism by removing it from the second edition. What his critics missed was the tragic basis of his philosophy. The idea of perception as a series of 'impressions' came from the work of such contemporary British psychologists as Alexander Bain (1818–1903), author of *The Senses and the Intellect* (1855). Pater's suggestion that these be maximised, so to speak, was not a doctrine of pleasure but a passionate assertion that life is too short to go about drugged by habit:

> Not to discriminate every moment some passionate attitude
> in those about us, and in the very brilliancy of their gifts
> some tragic dividing of forces on their ways, is, on this
> short day of frost and sun, to sleep before evening. With
> this sense of the splendour of our experience and of its
> awful brevity, gathering all we are into one desperate
> effort to see and touch, we shall hardly have time to make
> theories about the things we see and touch. What we have
> to do is to be for ever testing new opinions and courting
> new impressions, never acquiescing in a facile orthodoxy of
> Comte, or of Hegel, or of our own.[53]

This passage brings together many of the themes of this book and in doing so enables us to mark some of the more important changes between 1830 and 1890. There is the sense of change, and the epigraph to the chapter is a quotation from Lucretius: 'All things give way; nothing remains' – a sentiment pervasive in Tennyson and the geologists. But Pater does not struggle against it; for him, and for an increasing number at the century's end, there were no metaphysical absolutes to shore up self or society against the erosions of the relative spirit. This knowledge heightens the aesthetic sense; against the 'awful brevity' of our experience, its 'splendour' is seen more brightly. The developmental theories of Comte or Hegel which had consoled the Victorians for their religious disinheritance are now seen as 'facile' orthodoxies: the only truth we can be sure of, and the only one that matters, concerns 'the things we see and touch'. At the same time science, which in the form of evolution has taken away religious belief, has left in its place a model of mental discipline ('curiously testing new opinions'). However, there is a price to be paid for these developments and liberations, and that price is withdrawal from communal life into the lonely, solitary consciousness. That is what Marius is drawn to when he encounters the Christian community in *Marius the Epicurean* (1885) – not religious belief as such, but the prospect of belonging. More than any other Victorian writer Pater illuminates the threshold between Victorian and Modern. In his philosophy of perception and belief in heightened consciousness as a good in itself he provides an important context for the reading of Henry James, while his religious feeling for the power of beauty and the importance of art in the face of life's transience looks forward to the fiction of Proust and the poetry of Wallace Stevens.

Notes

1. See Dianne S. Macleod, 'Art Collecting and Victorian Middle-Class Taste', *Art History*, 10 (1987), 328–50; also J. Wolff and J. Seed (eds), *The Culture of Capital: Art, Power and the Nineteenth-Century Middle Class* (Manchester, 1988).

2. *Praeterita*, §22; in *Works*, edited by E.T. Cook and A. Wedderburn (39 vols, 1903–12), XXXV, p. 26.

3. *An Autobiography* (1953 edition), p. 109.

4. *Modern Painters* (hereafter *M P*) 3; *Works*, V, 359; from ch. 18 on 'The Moral of Landscape'.

5. *M P 1; Works*, III, pp. 294–5.

6. *M P 1; Works*, III, p. 231.

7. *M P 1; Works*, III, p. 271.

8. *M P 1; Works*, III, p. 308.

9. Wordsworth, 'Tintern Abbey', line 96.

10. *M P 2; Works*, IV, p. 156.

11. *M P 2; Works*, IV, pp. 47, 49, 59.

12. *M P 2; Works*, IV, p. 64.

13. *M P 2; Works*, IV, p. 81.

14. *Victorian Types, Victorian Shadows* (1980), pp. 121–3.

15. *M P 2; Works*, IV, p. 265.

16. *M P 3; Works*, V, p. 18.

17. *Song of Myself*, §51.

18. *M P 5; Works*, VII, p. 262.

19. See *M P 5; Works*, VII, p. 269.

20. Quoted in Bernard Denvir, *The Late Victorians: Art, Design and Society* (1986), p. 6.

21. This is the view argued in Robert F. Jordan's perhaps now rather dated introduction, *Victorian Architecture* (Harmondsworth, 1966), p. 94.

22. *Pre-Raphaelitism and the Pre-Raphaelite Brotherhood* (1905), p. 88.

23. *The Critic as Artist* (1891), Part 2.

24. See *The Pre-Raphaelites*, catalogue of the 1984 Tate Gallery Exhibition, p. 98.

25. *Ibid.*, p. 136.

26. *Ibid.*, pp. 124–5.

27. *Miscellaneous Papers* (1908), p. 237.

28. *The Pre-Raphaelites* (1970), p. 59.

29. For a fuller discussion of the significance of women in the lives and art of the Pre-Raphaelites, see Jan Marsh, *Pre-Raphaelite Sisterhood* (1985) and Gay Daly, *Pre-Raphaelites in Love* (1989).

30. First pointed out by Alastair Grieve in his comments on the painting in the Tate Gallery catalogue, *The Pre-Raphaelites* (1984), p. 209.

31. Quoted by E.D.H. Johnson in *Paintings of the British Social Science: from Hogarth to Sickert* (1986), p. 200. The photographer was Robert Howlett (*q.v.*).

32. Quoted in *The Golden Age of British Photography 1839–1900*, edited by Mark Haworth-Booth (London and Philadelphia, 1984), p. 9.

33. See Sara Stevenson, 'David Octavius Hill and Robert Adamson', in Mike Weaver (ed.), *British Photography in the Nineteenth Century* (Cambridge, 1989), p. 37.

34. See Weaver's essay in *ibid.*, pp. 103–20.

35. Quoted in Amanda Hopkinson, *Julia Margaret Cameron* (1986), p. 22.

36. *The Prelude* (1850), III, line 63.

37. Quoted in Michael W. Brooks, *John Ruskin and Victorian Architecture* (London and New Brunswick, 1987), p. 101. The words come from Patmore's review of *The Stones of Venice* in the *North British Review*, 12 (1854), 89.

38. *Remarks on Secular and Domestic Architecture* (1857), 259–60.

39. Quoted in Roger Dixon and Stefan Muthesius, *Victorian Architecture* (1985), p. 156.

40. For details see John Olly, 'The Reform Club', *Architect's Journal*, 181 (1985), 34–60.

41. Charles L. Eastlake, *A History of the Gothic Revival* (1872; reprinted Leicester, 1970), p. 2.

42. *John Ruskin and Victorian Architecture*, p. 127.

43. *The Stones of Venice*, vol. 2 (1853); *Works*, X, pp. 196–67.

44. Quoted in Peter Davey, *Arts and Crafts Architecture* (1980), p. 95.

45. *My Life*, translated by Andrew Gray, edited by Mary Whittall (Cambridge, 1983), p. 525.

46. Boris Ford (ed.), *The Cambridge Guide to the Arts in Britain* (Cambridge, 1989), p. 281.

47. *The Renaissance*, edited by Adam Phillips (Oxford, 1986), p. 86.

48. Letter 79, July 1877; *Works*, XXIX, p. 160.

49. 'On Whistler and Ruskin', *The Painter's Eye*, edited by John L. Sweeney (1956), pp. 173–4.

50. Two years hard labour: see Richard Ellmann, *Oscar Wilde* (1987), pp. 448–9.

51. Preface to 1873 edition of *Literature and Dogma*; in R.H. Super (ed.), *Collected Prose Works* (Michigan, 1968), VI, p. 150.

52. *Essays on Literature and Art*, edited by Jennifer Uglow (1973), pp. 1–2.

53. 'Conclusion', *The Renaissance*, p. 152.

Postscript

The nineteenth century was the bourgeois century, when the middle classes won their political battle with the aristocracy without having to share much, if any, of their new-found power with the classes below them. To say this is not to endorse the mid-Victorian mood of bourgeois triumphalism, nor is it to ignore what Ruskin called the 'sacrifice of much contributed life'[1] which made it possible for most of the thinkers and artists discussed in this book to write and paint and socialise with their peers as they did – the army of manual workers and domestic servants who swept the daily obstacles from the path of Carlyle's 'brain-workers'. The nineteenth century was bourgeois simply in the sense that the middle classes succeeded in impressing their values – faith in progress, respectability, the importance of work, religious earnestness, belief in moderate political reform – on the culture at large, even on the aspirations of their servants, even on the attitudes of the rebels. It was the bourgeois Dickens who attacked Millais's *Christ in the House of his Parents*. Marx excoriated capitalism for alienating the worker from his labour, but he never escaped from the bourgeois assumption that (non-alienated) labour was the end of man and the goal of history. Even a *fin de siècle* rebel like Oscar Wilde depended utterly on bourgeois assumptions as the springboard for his witty reversals.

Middle-class confidence was justified and sustained by evidence of progress, as they saw it. A male child born in the year of Waterloo (1815) and dying in 1890 would have learned in the nursery that Britain was the leading European power; he would have felt the excitement of the First Reform Bill debates, the anxieties of Chartism and the Hungry Forties, and the reassurance of the 1851 Great Exhibition, when Britain announced its industrial pre-eminence to the rest of the world. Aged 50 at Palmerston's death in 1865, he would have known the confidence of belonging to the most modern and powerful nation on earth, and though that confidence might have faltered a little at the time of the Second Reform Bill, and even more during the economic slump of the 1870s, it would have recovered on the back of the new popular enthusiasm for imperial expansion of the 1880s. As he tottered into his great-grand-children's nursery, this notional middle-class Victorian might have found them reading *King Solomon's Mines* (1885) and the imperial fiction of G.A. Henty (1832–1902), and gone off to his last rest secure in the knowledge that the bounds of Britain would indeed be set, as 'Land of Hope and Glory' (1902) has it, 'wider still and wider'.

That, at least, is one way of looking at the century, and our representative middle-class Victorian now seems guilty of facile optimism. But even at a more intellectually respectable level, science in the form of the evolutionary metaphor provided grounds for believing in a slow and steady development of individuals and communities. The particular attractiveness of the idea of evolution was that it seemed to involve *an incorporation of the past in the present*. We have seen how time-haunted the Victorians were, and how obsessed by history: to steady themselves in a rapidly changing present they reached for the cultural self-understanding represented by historical writing, painting, architecture, and for the private self-understanding of autobiography. Evolution on the dominant neo-Lamarckian model promised a secular redemption of the past. Previous adaptations had not been blind but purposive, and in the developing form of the present the strugglings of the past were embodied and honoured, making up the 'choir invisible' of George Eliot's positivist hymn.

The significance of the 1914–18 war is not that it destroyed the old faith in progress (for in important senses it did not) but that it snapped the evolutionary link between past and present which underlay Victorian confidence. The senseless, mechanical slaughter at Ypres and the Somme and Verdun and Gallipoli threw a bloody light back on the assumptions of the previous century that warfare on this scale could never happen again. As Henry James observed at the time: 'The plunge of civilisation into this abyss of blood and darkness . . . is a thing that so gives away the whole long age during which we have supposed the world to be, with whatsoever abatement, gradually bettering, that to have to take it all now for what the treacherous years were all the while really making for and *meaning* is too tragic for any words.'[2] The Victorians thought they were living one plot of history, a plot of steady improvement; the 1914–18 war revealed that another plot, laid by industrialisation, trade rivalry between nations, and imperial competition, had taken the world's most 'civilised' and advanced societies to Armageddon. Progress in a material sense might still be possible, but the old faith in the historical inevitability of progress died on the Western Front.

The Great War – our sense of its significance lies in our continuing use of the adjective – has sealed off the last century, and it is perhaps the supreme paradox of our contemporary relation to the Victorian age that we do to them and their artefacts what they did to other, past civilisations. The steam railways that Wordsworth once saw as rash invaders of rural peace are now lovingly preserved and run. Industrial archaeology has long been an academic study and is now an increasingly popular leisure activity, with tourists paying to visit the old sites of industrial toil. Victorian architecture and painting have never been more highly valued, nor Victorian furnishings more eagerly collected and carefully restored. Behind it all is nostalgia for the solidity of a vanished world, like the Victorian glass paperweight which means so much to Winston Smith in Orwell's *1984* (1949).

But nostalgia is a distorting emotion, and as Carlyle shrewdly observed there is 'always one most important element . . . surreptitiously (we not noticing it) withdrawn from the Past Time: the haggard element of Fear! Not *there* does Fear dwell, nor Uncertainty, not Anxiety; but it dwells *here*; haunting us, tracking us; running like an accursed ground-discord through all the music-tones of our Existence; – making the Tense a mere Present one!'[3] The period covered by this book had its full share of Fear, Uncertainty, and Anxiety: the social processes, the intellectual and cultural debates – which we see now as settled things – did not look like that to those who experienced them. The solidity of Victorian monuments belies the restlessness of the lives lived in their shadow, and the background to the faith in progress was the fear of decline – a fear sharpened as the century wore on and the darker implications of Victorian thermodynamics became harder to avoid. Both are true, for the defining characteristic of the intellectual and cultural life of Victoria's reign is a shifting debate between certainty and uncertainty in the face of unprecedented change. Confident and anxious by turns, forward-looking and backward-yearning, restless Victorian Britain is not really a convenient bolt-hole for the escapist. Rather it is the place where so many of the characteristic problems of the modern world first make their appearance, in science, religion, politics, industrial development; and if we can no longer accept many of the answers the Victorians found there is a perennial fascination, more perhaps than for any previous period, in studying the questions they asked.

Notes

1. *Sesame and Lilies* (1865), Lecture I, §30n.; in *Works*, edited by E.T. Cook and A. Wedderburn (39 vols, 1903–12), XVIII, p. 108.

2. *The Letters of Henry James*, edited by P. Lubbock (2 vols, 1920), II, p. 398.

3. *The French Revolution*, edited by K.J. Fielding and D. Sorensen (Oxford, 1982), Pt III, bk II, ch. 3, p. 204.

Chronology

Note: Dates refer to the first publication of works, whether in serial or volume form.
        Journals and periodicals (e.g. Fortnightly Review) are listed under OTHER
        WORKS in the year of their first appearance.

Key: D = Drama, O = Opera, P = Painting

DATE	VERSE, DRAMA, FICTION	OTHER 'WORKS'	HISTORICAL/CULTURAL EVENTS
1830	Tennyson *Poems*	Coleridge *On the Constitution of Church and State* Lyell *Principles of Geology*, I (3 vols, 1830–33)	Liverpool and Manchester Railway opened July revolutions in France Accession of William IV
1831	Surtees *Jorrocks' Jaunts and Jollities* (1831–34)	Carlyle *Characteristics* Hegel *Lectures on the Philosophy of History*	Reform Bill crisis BAAS founded Faraday discovers electromagnetic induction Darwin begins voyage of the *Beagle*
1832	Tennyson *Poems*	H. Martineau *Illustrations of Political Economy* (1832–34)	Reform Bill passed Morse invents telegraph
1833	Browning *Pauline*	Carlyle *Sartor Resartus* (–1834) *Tracts for the Times* (1833–37) T. Arnold *Principles of Church Reform*	Factory Act passed Start of Oxford Movement with Keble's Assize Sermon

DATE	VERSE, DRAMA, FICTION	OTHER 'WORKS'	HISTORICAL/CULTURAL EVENTS
1834	Bulwer *Last Days of Pompeii*	Somerville *On the Connexion of the Physical Sciences*	Abolition of slavery in British Empire Poor Law Amendment Act passed
1835	Bulwer *Rienzi*	D. F. Strauss *Das Leben Jesu* Tocqueville *Democracy in America, I (II, 1840)*	Fox Talbot's first photographs Municipal Reform Act (England)
1836	Dickens *Pickwick Papers* (1836–37)	Pugin *Contrasts*	Botanical Society founded
1837	Dickens *Oliver Twist* (1837–38)	Carlyle *The History of the French Revolution*	Accession of Queen Victoria Barry begins work on the Reform Club Government School of Design set up
1838	Dickens *Nicholas Nickleby* (1838–39)	C. Hennell *An Inquiry Concerning the Origin of Christianity* Mantell *The Wonders of Geology* J. S. Mill 'Bentham'	'People's Charter' proclaimed Anti-Corn Law League formed
1839	Thackeray *Catherine* (1839–40)	Carlyle *Chartism* Darwin *Voyage of the 'Beagle'* Faraday *Experimental Researches in Electricity* (1839–55)	Chartist riots Eglinton Tournament Anglo-Chinese Opium War 'Daguerrotype' and Fox Talbot negative process discovered
1840	Dickens *Old Curiosity Shop* (1840–41)	J. S. Mill 'Coleridge' Whewell *Philosophy of the Inductive Sciences*	Marriage of Victoria and Albert Penny post starts

DATE	VERSE, DRAMA, FICTION	OTHER 'WORKS'	HISTORICAL/CULTURAL EVENTS
1841	Browning *Pippa Passes* Dickens *Barnaby Rudge*	Carlyle *On Heroes and Hero-Worship*	Chemical Society founded *Punch* founded
1842	Browning *Dramatic Lyrics* Macaulay *Lays of Ancient Rome* Tennyson *Poems* (2 vols)	Chadwick *Sanitary Condition of the Labouring Population of Great Britain*	Chartist petition rejected; riots Mines Act
1843	Dickens *Christmas Carol* Dickens *Martin Chuzzlewit* (1843–44)	Carlyle *Past and Present* Ruskin *Modern Painters 1* (5 vols, 1843–60)	Ethnological Society founded
1844	Thackeray *Barry Lyndon* Disraeli *Coningsby*	Chambers *Vestiges of the Natural History of Creation* Turner *Rain, Steam, and Speed* (P)	Factory Act limiting working hours
1845	Disraeli *Sybil* Thackeray *Diary of Jeames de la Pluche*	Carlyle *Oliver Cromwell's Letters and Speeches* De Quincey *Suspiria de Profundis* Newman *An Essay on the Development of Christian Doctrine*	Newman converted to Roman Catholicism Start of Irish potato famine
1846	Dickens *Dombey and Son* (1846–48) Lear *Book of Nonsense* Thackeray *Snobs of England* (1846–47)	Grote *History of Greece* (12 vols, 1846–56) Strauss *Life of Jesus* (trans. George Eliot)	Repeal of Corn Laws Railway boom starts

DATE	VERSE, DRAMA, FICTION	OTHER 'WORKS'	HISTORICAL/CULTURAL EVENTS
1847	A. Brontë *Agnes Grey* C. Brontë *Jane Eyre* E. Brontë *Wuthering Heights* Tennyson *Princess* Thackeray *Vanity Fair* (1847–48)	Helmholtz 'On the Conservation of Force [Energy]' Joule 'On the Mechanical Equivalent of Heat'	10 Hours Factory Act Communist League founded Chloroform used as general anaesthetic by J. Y. Simpson
1848	Clough *The Bothie of Toper-na-Fuosich* E. Gaskell *Mary Barton* Thackeray *Pendennis* (1848–50) A. Brontë *Tenant of Wildfell Hall*	*Communist Manifesto* J. S. Mill *Principles of Political Economy*	Revolutions in Europe Public Health Act Pre-Raphaelite Brotherhood formed Collapse of Chartism
1849	M. Arnold *The Strayed Reveller* C. Brontë *Shirley* Dickens *David Copperfield* (1849–50) J. A. Froude *The Nemesis of Faith*	Layard *Nineveh and its Remains* Macaulay *History of England from the Accession of James II* (1849–61) Mayhew *London Labour and the London Poor* (in *Morning Chronicle*) Ruskin *The Seven Lamps of Architecture*	Bedford College for Women founded, London
1850	C. Kingsley *Alton Locke* Tennyson *In Memoriam* Wordsworth *The Prelude*	Carlyle *Latter-Day Pamphlets* *The Germ* (PRB journal) *Household Words* (ed. Dickens) Millais *Christ in the House of His Parents* (P)	Public Libraries Act Natural Sciences Honours School set up at Oxford Roman Catholic Hierarchy restored in England Tennyson becomes Poet Laureate

DATE	VERSE, DRAMA, FICTION	OTHER 'WORKS'	HISTORICAL/CULTURAL EVENTS
1851	Meredith *Poems*	Carlyle *Life of John Sterling* H. Spencer *Social Statics*	Great Exhibition Natural Sciences Tripos set up at Cambridge Owens College Manchester founded
1852	Dickens *Bleak House* (1852–53) Thackeray *History of Henry Esmond*	Newman *Idea of a University* Spencer 'The Development Hypothesis'	Department of Practical Art established
1853	Arnold *Poems* C. Brontë *Villette* Thackeray *The Newcomes* (1853–55)	Froude 'England's Forgotten Worthies' Hunt *The Light of the World* (P) H. Martineau (trans.) *The Positive Philosophy of Auguste Comte* F. D. Maurice *Theological Essays*	Photographic Society set up
1854	Dickens *Hard Times* Gaskell *North and South* (1854–55) Patmore *Angel in the House* (1854–63)	G. Eliot (trans.) *Essence of Christianity* Hunt *The Awakening Conscience* (P) H. Miller *My Schools and Schoolmasters*	Crimean War starts (1854–56) Working Men's College, London, founded
1855	R. Browning *Men and Women* Dickens *Little Dorritt* (1855–57) C. Kingsley *Westward Ho!* Tennyson *Maud* Trollope *The Warden*	F. M. Brown *The Last of England* (P) W. Chappell *The Ballad Literature and Popular Music of the Olden Time*	Woodward and Deane begin Oxford Museum Livingstone discovers Victoria Falls

DATE	VERSE, DRAMA, FICTION	OTHER 'WORKS'	HISTORICAL/CULTURAL EVENTS
1856	Flaubert *Madame Bovary*	Emerson *English Traits* J. A. Froude *History of England*, 1 & 2 (1856–70) Millais *Autumn Leaves* (P)	Bessemer's steel process patented Perkin discovers aniline dye
1857	C. Brontë *The Professor* E. B. Browning *Aurora Leigh* G. Eliot *Scenes of Clerical Life* T. Hughes *Tom Brown's Schooldays* Trollope *Barchester Towers*	M. Arnold 'On the Modern Element in Literature' H. T. Buckle *History of Civilisation in England*, 1 (1857–61) H. Miller *The Testimony of the Rocks* Ruskin *The Political Economy of Art*	Indian Mutiny (1857–59) Neanderthal Man discovered in Germany Manchester Art Treasures Exhibition
1858	Clough *Amours de Voyage* G. MacDonald *Phantastes* Trollope *Dr Thorne*	W. P. Frith *Derby Day* (P)	Hallé Orchestra formed Brunel's *Great Eastern* launched
1859	Collins *Woman in White* (1859–60) Dickens *Tale of Two Cities* G. Eliot *Adam Bede* Fitzgerald *Rubaiyát of Omar Khayyám* Meredith *The Ordeal of Richard Feverel* Tennyson *Idylls of the King* (1859–85)	Beeton *Book of Household Management* (1859–60) Darwin *On the Origin of Species by Means of Natural Selection* J. S. Mill *On Liberty* Smiles *Self-Help* Wagner *Tristan and Isolde* (O) *Macmillan's Magazine* (ed. D. Masson) founded	Foreign Office begun in Italian Renaissance style First oil well drilled in USA

DATE	VERSE, DRAMA, FICTION	OTHER 'WORKS'	HISTORICAL/CULTURAL EVENTS
1860	Dickens *Great Expectations* (1860–61) G. Eliot *The Mill on the Floss* Trollope *Framley Parsonage*	*Cornhill* (ed. Thackeray) founded Dyce *Pegwell Bay* (P) *Essays and Reviews* Ruskin *Unto this Last*	Italian unification Huxley–Wilberforce debate at Oxford BAAS meeting Nile source found
1861	G. Eliot *Silas Marner* Hughes *Tom Brown at Oxford* Palgrave *Golden Treasury* Thackeray *Philip* (1861–62) Trollope *Orley Farm* (1861–62) Mrs H. Wood *East Lynne*	Faraday *Six Lectures on the* *Chemical History of a* *Candle* *Hymns Ancient and* *Modern* J. S. Mill *Considerations on* *Representative* *Government*	American Civil War (1861–65) Death of Prince Albert
1862	M. E. Braddon *Lady Audley's Secret* E. B. Browning *Last Poems* Clough *Collected Poems* Collins *No Name* G. Eliot *Romola* (1862–63) Trollope *The Small House at* *Allington* (1862–64)	Frith *The Railway Station* (P) Colenso *The Pentateuch Examined* Kelvin 'On the Age of the Sun's Heat' J. S. Mill *Utilitarianism* Whistler *Symphony in White No.* *1: The White Girl* (P)	First cricket tour to Australia

DATE	VERSE, DRAMA, FICTION	OTHER 'WORKS'	HISTORICAL/CULTURAL EVENTS
1863	Gaskell *Sylvia's Lovers* Gaskell *Cousin Phyllis* (1863–64) Kingsley *The Water-Babies* Reade *Hard Cash*	Huxley *Man's Place in Nature* Lyell *The Antiquity of Man* Tyndall *Heat as a Mode of Motion*	Anthropological Society formed Football Association founded
1864	Browning *Dramatis Personae* Collins *Armadale* (1864–66) Dickens *Our Mutual Friend* (1864–65) Gaskell *Wives and Daughters* (1864–66) Trollope *Can You Forgive Her?* (1864–65)	Newman *Apologia Pro Vita Sua* Spencer *Principles of Biology*	Pasteur invents 'pasteurisation'
1865	Carroll *Alice's Adventures in Wonderland* Newman *Dream of Gerontius*	Arnold *Essays in Criticism* (First Series) *Fortnightly Review* founded J. Lubbock *Prehistoric Times* J. F. McLennan *Primitive Marriage* Ruskin *Sesame and Lilies*	Lister introduces antiseptic surgery Assassination of President Lincoln
1866	G. Eliot *Felix Holt* Swinburne *Poems and Ballads* Trollope *Last Chronicle of Barset* (1866–67)	*Contemporary Review* founded Ruskin *Crown of Wild Olive*	Gregor Mendel discovers laws of heredity Nobel discovers dynamite

DATE	VERSE, DRAMA, FICTION	OTHER 'WORKS'	HISTORICAL/CULTURAL EVENTS
1867	Arnold *New Poems* Trollope *Phineas Finn* (1867–69)	Arnold *On the Study of Celtic Literature* Bagehot *The English Constitution* Carlyle *Shooting Niagara* Freeman *History of the Norman Conquest* (1867–76) Marx *Das Kapital* 1	Second Reform Act Typewriter invented
1868	Browning *The Ring and the Book* Collins *The Moonstone* Morris *The Earthly Paradise* (1868–70)		Public hangings abolished British Trades Union Congress formed
1869	Arnold *Collected Poems* Blackmore *Lorna Doone*	Arnold *Culture and Anarchy* Galton *Hereditary Genius* *Graphic* magazine founded Mill *On the Subjection of Women* *Nature* founded A. R. Wallace *The Malay Archipelago* Arnold *St Paul and Protestantism*	Suez Canal opened Mendeleev's periodic table of the elements Metaphysical Society formed Girton College, Cambridge, founded

DATE	VERSE, DRAMA, FICTION	OTHER 'WORKS'	HISTORICAL/CULTURAL EVENTS
1870	Dickens *The Mystery of Edwin Drood* D. G. Rossetti *Poems*	Huxley *Lay Sermons* Millais *The Boyhood of Raleigh* (P) Lubbock *The Origin of Civilisation* Newman *A Grammar of Assent* D. G. Rossetti *Beata Beatrix* (P)	Franco-Prussian War (1870–71) Forster's Education Act (England) Devonshire Commission on Scientific Education Death of Dickens
1871	Bulwer *The Coming Race* Carroll *Through the Looking-Glass* G. Eliot *Middlemarch* (1871–72) Hardy *Desperate Remedies* Lear *Nonsense Songs and Verses* MacDonald *At the Back of the North Wind* Swinburne *Songs Before Sunrise* Trollope *The Eustace Diamonds* (1871–73)	Darwin *The Descent of Man* Ruskin *Fors Clavigera* (1871–84) Tylor *Primitive Culture* Verdi *Aïda* (O) Zola *Les Rougon-Macquart* series (1871–93)	Religious tests abolished at Oxford and Cambridge Trade unions legalised Anthropological Institute formed
1872	Browning *Fifine at the Fair* Butler *Erewhon* Hardy *Under the Greenwood Tree* Hardy *A Pair of Blue Eyes* (1872–73)	Darwin *The Expression of the Emotions in Man* Nietzsche *The Birth of Tragedy* W. Reade *The Martyrdom of Man* Whistler *Arrangement in Grey and Black: Portrait of the Painter's Mother* (P)	Edison perfects electric telegraph (Secret) Ballot Act

DATE	VERSE, DRAMA, FICTION	OTHER 'WORKS'	HISTORICAL/CULTURAL EVENTS
1873	Tolstoy *Anna Karenina* (1873–78) Trollope · *Phineas Redux* (1873–74)	Arnold *Literature and Dogma* Clerk Maxwell *Electricity and Magnetism* J. S. Mill *Autobiography* Pater *Studies in the Renaissance* Stephen *Essays in Freethinking and Plainspeaking*	Cavendish Laboratory set up in Cambridge
1874	Hardy *Far from the Madding Crowd* Meredith *Beauchamp's Career* (1874–75) Thomson *The City of Dreadful Night* Trollope *The Way We Live Now* (1874–75)	Brown *St Ives, AD 1630* (P) Fildes *Applicants for Admission to a Casual Ward* (P) Galton *English Men of Science: Their Nature and Nurture* Lewes *Problems of Life and Mind* (1874–79) J. S. Mill *Three Essays on Religion* W. Stubbs *The Constitutional History of England* (1874–78) Tyndall 'Address' to the Belfast BAAS	First Impressionist Exhibition in Paris Moody and Sankey Evangelical revival in Britain (1874–75) Factory Act

DATE	VERSE, DRAMA, FICTION	OTHER 'WORKS'	HISTORICAL/CULTURAL EVENTS
1875	Hardy *The Hand of Ethelberta* (1875–76) Trollope *The Prime Minister* (1875–76)	Arnold *God and the Bible* Bizet *Carmen* (O) Gilbert and Sullivan *Trial by Jury* (O) Symonds *Renaissance in Italy*	Britain buys major holding of Suez Canal shares Theosophical Society founded
1876	G. Eliot *Daniel Deronda* H. James *Roderick Hudson*	*MIND* founded L. Stephen *English Thought in the 18th Century* Wagner *Ring of the Nibelungs* (O) performed entire at Bayreuth	Bell invents telephone Edison invents phonograph Victoria proclaimed Empress of India
1877	James *The American* Mallock *The New Republic* Patmore *The Unknown Eros and Other Poems*	Arnold *Last Essays on Church and Religion* Meredith *The Idea of Comedy* *Nineteenth Century* founded	Bradlaugh–Besant trial Grosvenor Gallery opens Society for the Protection of Ancient Buildings founded
1878	Hardy *The Return of the Native*	Gilbert and Sullivan *H.M.S. Pinafore* (O) W. F. Yeames *And When Did You Last See Your Father?* (P)	Ruskin–Whistler libel trial Salvation Army founded F. M. Brown begins to decorate Manchester Town Hall
1879	Browning *Dramatic Idyls*, First Series Ibsen *A Doll's House* (D) James *Daisy Miller* Meredith *The Egoist* Trollope *The Duke's Children* (1879–80)	Gilbert and Sullivan *Pirates of Penzance* (O)	Electric bulb invented Afghan and Zulu wars

DATE	VERSE, DRAMA, FICTION	OTHER 'WORKS'	HISTORICAL/CULTURAL EVENTS
1880	Browning *Dramatic Idyls*, Second Series Dostoevsky *The Brothers Karamazov* James *The Portrait of a Lady* (1880–81)	Burne-Jones *The Golden Stairs* (P)	Metaphysical Society disbanded
1881	W. Hale White *Autobiography of Mark Rutherford* Stevenson *Treasure Island* (1881–82) Wilde *Poems*	Alma-Tadema *In the Tepidarium* (P) Gilbert and Sullivan *Patience* (O)	First Anglo-Boer War
1882	Hardy *Two on a Tower* Ibsen *An Enemy of the People* (D) Jeffries *Bevis*	J. A. Froude *Carlyle: First Forty Years* Gilbert and Sullivan *Iolanthe* (O)	Married Women's Property Act gives them separate rights Phoenix Park murders Society for Psychical Research founded
1883	G. A. Henty *Under Drake's Flag*	Jeffries *The Story of my Heart* Nietzsche *Thus Spake Zarathustra* J. R. Seeley *The Expansion of England*	Royal College of Music founded
1884	Gissing *The Unclassed*	J. A. Froude *Carlyle's Life in London* *Oxford English Dictionary* ed. Murray (1884–1928) Ruskin *Storm Cloud of the Nineteenth Century* Spencer *The Man versus the State*	Third Reform Act Berlin Conference of European powers on future of Africa Fabian Society formed

DATE	VERSE, DRAMA, FICTION	OTHER 'WORKS'	HISTORICAL/CULTURAL EVENTS
1885	Haggard *King Solomon's Mines*	*Arabian Nights*, trans. Burton (1885–88)	Fall of Khartoum Internal combustion invented by Daimler
	Meredith *Diana of the Crossways*	*Dictionary of National Biography*, 1, ed. Stephen	
	Pater *Marius the Epicurean*	Gilbert and Sullivan *The Mikado* (O)	
	Pinero *The Magistrate* (D)	Ruskin *Praeterita*	
	White *Mark Rutherford's Deliverance*	Whistler *Ten O'Clock Lecture*	
1886	Gissing *Demos*	Nietzsche *Beyond Good and Evil*	Repeal of Contagious Diseases Acts Trafalgar Square riots
	Haggard *She*		
	Hardy *The Mayor of Casterbridge*		
	Hardy *The Woodlanders* (1886–87)		
	James *The Bostonians*		
	James *The Princess Casamassima*		
	Kipling *Departmental Ditties*		
	Stevenson *Dr Jekyll and Mr Hyde*		
1887	Conan Doyle *A Study in Scarlet*	Burne-Jones *The Depths of the Sea* (P)	Queen Victoria's Golden Jubilee Independent Labour Party founded
	Jefferies *Amaryllis at the Fair*	Darwin *Autobiography*	
	Pinero *The Schoolmistress* (D)	Pater *Imaginary Portraits*	
	'Mark Rutherford' *The Revolution in Tanner's Lane*	Verdi *Otello* (O)	

DATE	VERSE, DRAMA, FICTION	OTHER 'WORKS'	HISTORICAL/CULTURAL EVENTS
1888	Kipling *Plain Tales from the Hills* Stevenson *The Master of Ballantrae* (1888–89) Ward *Robert Elsmere*	Arnold *Essays in Criticism* (Second Series) Gilbert and Sullivan *Yeoman of the Guard* (O) Huxley 'The Struggle for Existence' Morris *A Dream of John Ball*	Kodak box camera invented
1889	Gissing *The Nether World* Jerome *Three Men in a Boat* Pinero *The Profligate* (D)	C. Booth *Labour and Life of the People* Gilbert and Sullivan *The Gondoliers* (O) Nietzsche *Twilight of the Idols* Pater *Appreciations*	International Congress of Psychology, Paris Prevention of Cruelty to Children Act
1890	James *The Tragic Muse* Kipling *Soldiers Three* Morris *News from Nowhere* Wilde *The Picture of Dorian Gray*	W. Booth *In Darkest England* Frazer *The Golden Bough* (1890–1915) W. James *Principles of Psychology* Stanley *In Darkest Africa* Whistler *The Gentle Art of Making Enemies*	First underground railway, in London Parnell ruined by O'Shea divorce scandal

General Bibliographies

Chapter 1

The Victorian sense of time has been explored from many directions: the scientific in S. Toulmin and J. Goodfield, *The Discovery of Time* (Chicago, 1965) and S.J. Gould, *Time's Arrow, Time's Cycle* (Cambridge, Mass. and London, 1987); the socio-cultural in S. Kern, *The Culture of Time and Space 1880–1918* (1983); and the literary-historical in J.H. Buckley, *The Triumph of Time: A Study of the Victorian Concepts of Time, History, Progress, and Decadence* (Cambridge, Mass., 1966). P.J. Bowler's *The Invention of Progress: The Victorians and the Past* (Oxford, 1989) is an ambitious attempt to link the historical sciences (geology, archaeology, anthropology) to the Victorian imagination of pre-history and progress.

For autobiography in this period see, as starting-points, J.H. Buckley, *The Turning Key: Autobiography and the Subjective Impulse since 1800* (Cambridge, Mass., 1984), which is a short survey of the field, and the relevant essays in G.P. Landow (ed.), *Approaches to Victorian Autobiography* (Athens, Ohio, 1979).

A. Dwight Culler's *The Victorian Mirror of History* (New Haven and London, 1985) explores different conceptions of history in the period and the ways in which writers used the past to mirror the present. In *The Historical Imagination in Nineteenth-Century Europe* (Baltimore and London, 1973), Hayden White offers an 'analysis of the deep structure of the historical imagination'. More specific studies are J.W. Burrow's analysis of the 'whig' school of historiography, *A Liberal Descent: Victorian Historians and the English Past* (Cambridge, 1981), and Raymond Chapman, *The Sense of the Past in Victorian Literature* (1986), which examines the way different periods from the national past were treated by writers. The same topic is the subject of Roy Strong's extremely interesting and well-illustrated account of Victorian historical painting, *And When Did You Last See Your Father?: The Victorian Painter and British History* (1978).

Richard Jenkyns's *The Victorians and Ancient Greece* (Oxford, 1980) covers the wider cultural manifestations of Victorian Hellenism, Frank M. Turner's *The Greek Heritage in Victorian Britain* (New Haven and London, 1981) its more specifically intellectual formulations. Jenkyns's *Dignity and Decadence: Victorian Art and the Classical Inheritance* (1991) explores the influence of classicism on the art of the period. The intellectual sources and development of Victorian medievalism are the subject of Alice Chandler's *A Dream of Order* (1971), and its influence on conduct is discussed by Mark Girouard in *The Return to Camelot: Chivalry and the English Gentleman* (New Haven and London, 1981). For medievalism in the arts, and Gothic in particular, see Chapter 5. Chapman, *Sense of the Past*, discusses the influence of the English civil war on the Victorian imagination.

A recent survey of the influence of German 'Higher Criticism' on the period is Gerald Parsons, 'Biblical Criticism in Victorian Britain: From Controversy to Acceptance?', in G. Parsons (ed.), *Religion in Victorian Britain*, 4 vols (Manchester, 1988), II, pp. 238–57. G.W. Stocking, *Victorian Anthropology* (New York and London, 1987) is the most recent study of the topic, a rich and ambitious anthropology of the anthropologists. Finally, the influence of the developing science of archaeology on the work of Hardy is explored by Harold Orel in the *Thomas Hardy Annual*, edited by N. Page, IV (1986), pp. 19–44.

Chapter 2

There is a very useful selected and annotated bibliography of 'Recent Studies in Victorian Religion' in *Victorian Studies*, 33 (1989), 149–75, with sections on History by Walter Arnstein, Art and Architecture by Michael Bright, Literature by Linda Peterson, and Music by Nicholas Temperley. Religious art, architecture, and music figure in Chapter 5 of the present study; this bibliography is mainly concerned with the history and literature of Victorian religion.

The standard history of Victorian Christianity is Owen Chadwick's two-volume *The Victorian Church* (1966, 1970), a monumental but highly readable survey of the field, concentrating predominantly on the Church of England. D.W. Bebbington's *Evangelicalism in Modern Britain: A History from the 1730s to the 1980s* (1989) is a recent and challenging survey of its field, while the interaction between the two traditions is the subject of Alan D. Gilbert's *Religion and Society in Industrial England: Church, Chapel and Social Change, 1740–1914* (1976), especially valuable for its tables. There is an excellent introduction to all aspects of Victorian religious belief and practice in the four volumes of *Religion in Victorian Britain* (Manchester, 1988), edited by Gerald Parsons for the Open University. Volume I has essays on all denominations of the period, including Scottish Presbyterianism, Judaism, and Agnosticism; volume II deals with 'Controversies'; volume III reprints extracts from contemporary writings illustrating the variety of Victorian religious debate; and volume IV reprints various recent interpretations of the subject.

All the above recognise the interaction of belief and social experience which this chapter has stressed. Of more purely intellectual history, mention may be made of the three volumes on *Nineteenth Century Religious Thought in The West* (1985), edited by N. Smart, J. Clayton, S. Katz, and P. Sherry, which contain essays by individual scholars on the different religious thinkers and movements of the time; it is comprehensive and helpful, especially on those Continental and European thinkers not covered in the standard surveys. In the latter category Bernard Reardon's *Religious Thought in the Victorian Age: A Survey from Coleridge to Gore* (1971, 1980) is very useful. Basil Willey's *Nineteenth-Century Studies* (1949) and *More Nineteenth-Century Studies: A Group of Honest Doubters* (1956) remain useful for their old-fashioned virtues of clarity and succinct paraphrase.

A lively modern introduction to the Evangelical impact on Victorian life is Ian Bradley's *The Call to Seriousness* (1976). Clyde Binfield, *So Down to Prayers: Studies in English Nonconformity* (1977), provides a number of case studies, including one of Edward Miall, maligned by Arnold in *Culture and Anarchy*. John Briggs and Ian Sellers reprint a selection of contemporary writings in their *Victorian Nonconformity* (1973), and Owen Chadwick does the same for the Oxford Movement in *The Mind of the Oxford Movement* (1960). Longer essays illustrating different aspects of both movements are collected and helpfully annotated in Elisabeth Jay (ed.), *The Evangelical and Oxford Movements* (Cambridge, 1983).

There is a vast literature on the Oxford Movement which cannot be adequately summarised here: Jay provides a useful select bibliography, and there are chapters in all the histories cited above. The best introduction to the movement, and one of the best of all books in the field, is David Newsome's *The Parting of Friends* (1966), which traces the path from Evangelicalism to Catholicism taken by the Wilberforces and Manning. I.T. Ker's *John Henry Newman* (1988) tells the story from Newman's angle. Edward Norman's *The English Catholic Church in the Nineteenth Century* (Oxford, 1984) is a history of the church which held such a fascination for the Tractarians.

The history of Anglo-Jewry is given by David Englander in an essay in Parsons (ed.), *Religion in Victorian Britain*, I, pp. 235–73, and that of

Scottish Presbyterianism by Parsons in the same volume, pp. 117–45. The common ground between the Broad Church party in the Church of England and the Unitarians is explored by D.G. Wigmoore-Beddoes in *Yesterday's Radicals* (Cambridge, 1971). Free thought, secularism, and agnosticism are studied in Susan Budd, *Varieties of Unbelief: Atheists and Agnostics in English Society 1850–1960* (1977), and in two books by Edward Royle, *Victorian Infidels: The Origins of the British Secularist Movement, 1791–1866* (Manchester, 1974), and *Radicals, Secularists, and Republicans: Popular Freethought in Britain, 1866–1915* (Manchester, 1980). I.D. Mackillop, *The British Ethical Societies* (Cambridge, 1986), and T.R. Wright, *The Religion of Humanity* (Cambridge, 1986), throw interesting light on the secular religions of the period, and Victorian agnosticism is reconsidered by Bernard Lightman in *The Origins of Agnosticism: Victorian Unbelief and the Limits of Knowledge* (Baltimore, 1987). There is an essay on British Agnosticism by J.C. Livingston in Smart *et al.* (eds), *Nineteenth Century Religious Thought in the West*, II, pp. 231–70.

The Victorian crisis of faith, and the challenge of modernity, are covered extensively in many of the books mentioned above. Special mention may be made, however, of Owen Chadwick's *The Secularisation of the European Mind in the Nineteenth Century* (Cambridge, 1975), for its authoritative survey of the historical and philosophical influences at work in both phenomena. A. Symondson (ed.), *The Victorian Crisis of Faith* (1970), prints six lectures on or near the topic. Of particular importance in this area is H.R. Murphy's seminal essay on 'The Ethical Revolt against Christian Orthodoxy in Early Victorian England', in *The American Historical Review*, IX (1955), 800–17, which established the importance of the moral objections to Christian doctrine in the mid-nineteenth century. A.W. Brown's *The Metaphysical Society: Victorians Minds in Crisis, 1869–80* (New York, 1947) shows how the crisis affected the intellectual leaders of the time.

The relation between literature and religion is a growing and increasingly sophisticated field, and again it is possible to name only a selection of recent studies. The breezy condescension of titles such as *Search Your Soul, Eustace* (1961), Margaret Maison's survey of the Victorian religious novel, has rightly given way to more sympathetic and detailed treatment of the age's religious culture. Elisabeth Jay's *The Religion of the Heart* (Oxford, 1979) explores Anglican Evangelicalism in the Victorian novel, and Valentine Cunningham's *Everywhere Spoken Against* (Oxford, 1975) does the same for Dissent. The literature of Dissent is also the subject of Donald Davie's Clark Lectures, *A Gathered Church: the Literature of the English Dissenting Interest, 1700–1930* (1976), which, although unsympathetic to the Victorian hymn, has an appreciative chapter on William Hale White ('Mark Rutherford').

Rediscovery of the Tractarian interest in poetry and its place in the Romantic tradition has led to a number of important studies, including Stephen Prickett's *Romanticism and Religion: The Tradition of Coleridge and Wordsworth in the Victorian Church* (Cambridge, 1976), G.B. Tennyson's *Victorian Devotional Poetry: The Tractarian Mode* (Cambridge, Mass., 1981), and John Coulson's, *Religion and Imagination: 'In Aid of a Grammar of Assent'* (Oxford, 1981). Newman figures prominently in each of these studies, as he does in D.J. De Laura's *Hebrew and Hellene in Victorian England: Newman, Arnold and Pater* (Texas, 1969), a book which took Victorian intellectual history into a higher gear.

Finally, in the last decade there has been much interest in biblical typology – the (evangelical) Victorian way of reading the Bible for 'types' prefiguring the life and sufferings of Christ – stimulated by G.P. Landow's *Victorian Types, Victorian Shadows* (1980). Typology and its younger brother 'symbolic realism' have opened up new ways of reading Victorian literature, painting, and architecture, as well as of achieving a genuine integration of these different fields. Two works which show what can be done with the deepened understanding of symbolic modes this old/new approach has brought are Chris Brooks's *Signs for the Times: Symbolic Realism in the Mid-Victorian World* (1984), and Michael Wheeler's ambitious exploration and synthesis of Victorian thinking and imagining about the unknown in *Death and the Future Life in Victorian Literature and Theology* (Cambridge, 1990).

Chapter 3

A recent history of nineteenth-century science is by David Knight, *The Age of Science* (Oxford, 1986), although literary students may find a more useful starting-point in J.A.V. Chapple, *Science and Literature in the Nineteenth Century* (1986), which offers an introduction to the field through commentary on extracts from a variety of sciences. Also of introductory value is Tess Cosslett, *The 'Scientific Movement' and Victorian Literature* (Brighton, 1982) and her *Science and Religion in the Nineteenth Century* (Cambridge, 1984), which prints extracts from the evolutionary controversy with a helpful introduction and notes. There are essays on various aspects of literature and science in J. Paradis and T. Postlewait (eds), *Victorian Science and Victorian Values: Literary Perspectives* (New York, 1981).

For the institutional context of Victorian science see Robert M. Young, 'Natural Theology, Victorian Periodicals and the Fragmentation of a Common Context', in his *Darwin's Metaphor* (Cambridge, 1981) and

Susan Cannon's *Science in Culture* (New York, 1978), which explores various scientific circles and their views in the early Victorian period. The struggle for the development of science as a profession is told by D.S.L. Cardwell in *The Organisation of Science in England* (1957; 1972). The early years of the BAAS are the subject of J. Morrell and A. Thackray, *Gentlemen of Science* (Oxford, 1981). For a detailed study of the development of provincial science in the period see R.H. Kargon, *Science in Victorian Manchester* (Manchester, 1977).

Lynn Barber, *The Heyday of Natural History 1820–1870* (1980) is a lively introduction to the Victorian fascination with the natural world and the intellectual issues it raised; popular writing on the subject is discussed by Lynn Merrill in *The Romance of Victorian Natural History* (Oxford, 1989). Geology and its impact on religious belief before Darwin are explored by C.C. Gillispie in *Genesis and Geology* (New York, 1959), and its implications for the Victorian time-consciousness by S.J. Gould, *Time's Arrow, Time's Cycle* (Cambridge, Mass., 1987). The 1844 edition of Chambers's *Vestiges of the Natural History of Creation* was reprinted by Leicester University Press with an introduction by Sir Gavin de Beer (1969). Milton Millhauser's *Just Before Darwin: Robert Chambers and 'Vestiges'* (Middletown, Conn., 1959) is the standard account but now a little dated: for a more informed contextual reading see J.A. Secord, 'Behind the veil: Robert Chambers and *Vestiges*', in *History, Humanity and Evolution,* edited by J.R. Moore (Cambridge, 1989), pp. 165–94.

For evolution see P.J. Bowler, *Evolution: The History of an Idea* (Berkeley, 1984) and his *The Invention of Progress: The Victorians and the Past* (Oxford, 1989), an ambitious and successful attempt to relate theories of evolution to the other historical sciences and to contemporary ideas of progress.

There is a vast literature on Darwin. Of introductory value are Jonathan Howard's *Darwin* (Oxford, 1982), a short modern study, and John Burrow's lucid introduction to the Penguin *Origin of Species* (1968). Philip Appleman's 'Norton Critical Edition' of Darwin (New York, 1979) is the best point of departure: it reprints selections from *The Origin of Species* and *The Descent of Man,* and a large and representative selection of modern writing on Darwin from various points of view. The nature and consequences of the Darwinian revolution are the subject of D.R. Oldroyd's useful *Darwinian Impacts* (Milton Keynes, 1980). The essays in J. Durant (ed.), *Darwinism and Divinity* (Oxford, 1985), are of particular interest to anyone interested in the contemporary state of that most disputed area of Darwin's achievement.

Of specifically literary studies, there are Lionel Stevenson's *Darwin Among the Poets* (Chicago, 1932) and George Roppen's *Evolution and Poetic Belief* (Oslo, 1956), but recent work has been on Darwin as a narrative artist and on his influence on novelists. The following are valuable: Gillian Beer, *Darwin's Plots: Evolutionary Narrative in Darwin, George Eliot and Nineteenth-Century Fiction* (1983), impressive on Darwin's narrative if less so on the others; George Levine, *Darwin and the Novelists* (Cambridge, Mass., 1988), whose attempt to draw a 'gestalt of the Darwinian imagination' takes in those novelists he could not have influenced in addition to those he did; and Peter Morton's refreshingly independent *The Vital Science: Biology and the Literary Imagination 1860–1900* (1984), which conducts an original argument about the literary use of scientific ideas through an exploration of writers on evolution who are usually neglected. Also of relevance are Patricia Ball, *The Science of Aspects* (1971), on the role of fact and geological study in Ruskin and Hopkins; Allan Hunter, *Joseph Conrad and the Ethics of Darwinism* (1983); and Sally Shuttleworth, *George Eliot and Nineteenth-Century Science: The Make-Believe of a Beginning* (Cambridge, 1984).

The influence of evolution on anthropology and other historical sciences is best approached first through Bowler's *The Invention of Progress* (see above), then J.W. Burrow, *Evolution and Society* (Cambridge, 1966) and George W. Stocking, *Victorian Anthropology* (New York and London, 1987). The development of a post-Darwinian scientific ideology is explored in F.M. Turner, *Between Science and Religion: The Reaction to Scientific Naturalism in Late Victorian England* (New Haven, 1974). For the impact of thermodynamics on Victorian culture see J.D. Burchfield, *Lord Kelvin and the Age of the Earth* (1975), and S.G. Brush, *The Temperature of History* (New York, 1978). The physiology of mind and its cultural implications are discussed in L.S. Jacyna, 'The Physiology of Mind, the Unity of Nature, and the Moral Order in Victorian Thought', *The British Journal for the History of Science*, XIV (1981), pp. 109–32. For the unconscious mind see L.L. Whyte, *The Unconscious Before Freud* (1967) and H.F. Ellenberger, *The Discovery of the Unconscious* (1970). The cult of Mesmerism and its influence on Dickens and his circle is the subject of F. Kaplan's *Dickens and Mesmerism* (Princeton, 1975).

Chapter 4

For the context of intellectual life in the period and the development of a specialised intellectual class see T.W. Heyck, *The Transformation of Intellectual Life in Victorian England* (1982). The sociology of the professional classes who provided so many of the leaders of opinion and so much of the intellectual debate is the subject of Harold Perkin's

The Rise of Professional Society: England since 1880 (1989). For the life of a Victorian man of letters see Noel Annan's *Leslie Stephen: The Godless Victorian* (1984). Stephen is of particular interest to anyone seeking to relate literature to its context: he was the father of Virginia Woolf, the friend and editor of Hardy, a leading agnostic, and the founder of the *Dictionary of National Biography*.

The significance of Scottish influences on the formation of progressive thought in the period was discussed by Walter Bagehot in a famous essay on 'The First Edinburgh Reviewers' (1855) in *Literary Studies* (1878; 2 vols, 1911), and is the subject of Anand Chitnis's *The Scottish Enlightenment and Early Victorian Society* (1986). It has also been an important strand in recent reconsiderations of nineteenth-century political/ intellectual history: see the chapter on 'Dugald Stewart and his Pupils' in *That Noble Science of Politics* by S. Collini, D. Winch, and J. Burrow (Cambridge, 1983). For lively and readable accounts of Malthus and Bentham see G. Himmelfarb's *Victorian Minds* (1968), and for utilitarianism as a movement, W.E.S. Thomas's *The Philosophic Radicals* (Oxford, 1979). There is a very useful account of John Stuart Mill's utilitarianism and its relation to Bentham in Alan Ryan's introduction to his selection, John Stuart Mill and Jeremy Bentham, *Utilitarianism and Other Essays* (Harmondsworth, 1987). This reprints the essays on Bentham and Coleridge as well as *Utilitarianism* and selections from Jeremy Bentham.

Good introductions to the two main political parties can be found in Robert Blake, *The Conservative Party from Peel to Thatcher* (1985) and John Vincent's *The Formation of the Liberal Party 1857–68* (1966), supplemented by Robert Eccleshall's historical anthology, *British Liberalism* (1986), and Michael Bentley's mannered but interesting *The Climax of Liberal Politics: British Liberalism in Theory and Practice 1868–1918* (1987). As the leading ideology of the day Liberalism has attracted less attention from literary scholars than might have been expected, and too much of that has accepted the anti-liberal polemic of the age (Carlyle, Newman, Arnold) rather uncritically. For a study sympathetic to Victorian liberalism and its literary connections see George Watson, *The English Ideology* (1973). The neglected figure of Walter Bagehot is made the link between the political culture and the novels of Anthony Trollope in the chapter on 'Trollope, Bagehot, and the English Constitution' in Asa Briggs's *Victorian People* (Harmondsworth, 1965). See also John Halperin's *Trollope and Politics* (1977) and S.R. Letwin's *The Gentleman in Trollope* (1982), which uses Trollope's fiction to illustrate the ethical character of a social type. The cultural history of gentlemanliness is explored in Robin Gilmour's *The Idea of the Gentleman in the Victorian Novel* (1981). The practical politics of reform are well covered by E.J. Feuchtwanger in his *Democracy and Empire:*

Britain 1865–1914 (1985), and some interesting and unusual voices from the context have been assembled by Barbara Dennis and David Skilton in their *Reform and Intellectual Debate in Victorian England* (1987). See also Patrick Brantlinger, *The Spirit of Reform: British Literature and Politics, 1832–1867* (Cambridge, Mass. and London, 1977).

There is a useful short history of events and issues in C.C. Eldridge, *Victorian Imperialism* (1978). The first two volumes of James (now Jan) Morris's avowedly impressionistic trilogy, *Heaven's Command* (1973) and *Pax Britannica* (1968) are evocative. Edward Said's study of the West's imagination of the East, *Orientalism* (1978), has been immensely influential in modern discussion of imperialism. Martin Green's *Dreams of Adventure, Deeds of Adventure* (1979) is a study of imperialism in English literature. For 'Englishness' see R. Colls and P. Dodd (eds), *Englishness: Politics and Culture 1880–1920* (1986); the part played by the mythologising of English history is well discussed by Sarah Wintle in her Introduction to the Penguin edition of *Puck of Pook's Hill* (Harmondsworth, 1987). Peter Singer's *Marx* (Oxford, 1982) is a good, brief introduction to a vast field. The relationship between socialism and Utopian thought is discussed by James Redmond in his edition of William Morris, *News from Nowhere* (1890; 1970).

Documents from the Victorian women's movement are available in P. Hollis, *Women in Public: the Women's Movement 1850–1900* (1979), and the lives of eight feminists discussed by Margaret Foster in *Significant Sisters: the Grassroots of Active Feminism, 1839–1939* (1984). Two collections of essays edited by Martha Vicinus cover many aspects of women's experience in the period: *Suffer and Be Still: Women in the Victorian Age* (1972) and *A Widening Sphere: Changing Roles of Victorian Women* (1977). Phillip Mallett's 'Women and Marriage in Victorian Society' is a very useful account of contemporary attitudes and legal changes, and can be found in *Marriage and Property*, edited by E.M. Craik (Aberdeen, 1984), pp. 159–89. The literature of feminist interpretations breeds faster than an army of Victorian mothers and it is not possible to list even a representative selection here, but Nina Auerbach's *Woman and the Demon: the Life of a Victorian Myth* (Cambridge, Mass. and London, 1982) shows how literature, art, and contemporary stereotypes are being re-examined today.

Chapter 5

Volume 7 of the Cambridge Guide to the Arts in Britain, *The Later Victorian Age,* edited by Boris Ford (Cambridge, 1989), is a useful survey of the field, with chapters on Architecture, Fine Arts, Design, Music, among others, and a substantial bibliographical Appendix compiled by Norman Vance. The relevant volumes of the Longman 'Art, Design and Society' series provide selections from contemporary writings with Introductions by the editor, Bernard Denvir: see *The Early Nineteenth Century* (1984) and *The Late Victorians* (1986). For the influence of the new middle classes on the formation of Victorian taste and the institutions of cultural dissemination see Janet Wolff and John Seed (eds), *The Culture of Capital: Art, Power and the Nineteenth-Century Middle Class* (Manchester, 1988), and Dianne S. MacLeod, 'Art Collecting and Victorian Middle-Class Taste', *Art History*, 10 (1987), pp. 328–50. The relationship between culture and industry is explored in F.D. Klingender, *Art and the Industrial Revolution* (1947; revised edition 1968) and Herbert L. Sussman, *Victorians and the Machine* (Cambridge, Mass., 1968). William Allingham's *Diary* (1907; Penguin edition 1985) is an entertaining contemporary record by someone who knew most of the leading artists and writers.

There is no satisfactory modern history of Victorian painting. William Gaunt's trilogy – *The Pre-Raphaelite Tragedy* (1942), *The Aesthetic Adventure* (1945), and *Victorian Olympus* (1952), all reprinted in 1975 – are very lively and readable introductions to the field at large, although inevitably superseded in detail. Kenneth Bendiner's *Introduction to Victorian Painting* (London and New Haven, 1985) proceeds from an alternative standpoint, providing detailed and perceptive readings of seven paintings chosen to illustrate the different schools of Victorian painting: it is an excellent starting-point. Victorian narrative art is the subject of E.D.H. Johnson's *Paintings of the British Social Scene* (1986), which takes the story from Hogarth to Sickert, is comprehensively illustrated, and suggests many comparisons with the literature of the period. Another important but today undervalued Victorian genre is the history-painting, which is the subject of Roy Strong's lively and well-illustrated study, *And When Did You Last See Your Father?: The Victorian Painter and British History* (1978).

The literature on Pre-Raphaelitism is predictably huge, but far and away the best modern starting-point is the catalogue of the 1984 Tate Gallery Exhibition, *The Pre-Raphaelites* (1984), introduced by Alan Bowness. This contains reproductions of all the major and some minor paintings and watercolours, the majority in colour, with detailed commentaries by experts in the field. For a vigorous short history of the movement, see Timothy Hilton, *The Pre-Raphaelites* (1970). Two source-books of writing by and about the movement are: Derek Stanford (ed.), *Pre-Raphaelite Writing* (1973), which contains a very full selection of primary material in the form of recollections, reviews, theory, poetry, fiction, and parody; and James Sambrook (ed.),

Pre-Raphaelitism: A Collection of Critical Essays (Chicago, 1974), which reprints writing about the movement from Holman Hunt to John Dixon Hunt: it is a convenient source for finding Ruskin's 1851 defence of Pre-Raphaelitism. Different aspects of the movement are explored in Allen Staley, *The Pre-Raphaelite Landscape* (Oxford, 1973) and Jan Marsh, *Pre-Raphaelite Women* (1987). There has also been interesting recent work on the place of women in the history of the movement: see Jan Marsh, *Pre-Raphaelite Sisterhood* (1985) and Gay Daly, *Pre-Raphaelites in Love* (1989). Pre-Raphaelitism was a highly literary movement and figures prominently in studies attempting to relate literature to painting in the period: see Peter Conrad, *A Victorian Treasure House* (1973) and Chris Brooks, *Signs for the Times* (1984), an ambitious exploration of symbolic realism in Dickens's novels, Pre-Raphaelite painting, and Victorian Gothic architecture.

For contemporary 'realism' in Victorian art see Johnson above and Christopher Wood, *Victorian Panorama: Paintings of Victorian Life* (1976). The other major movement of the period, classicism, was discussed in Chapter 1: see here William Gaunt, *Victorian Olympus* (1952; 1975) and Richard Jenkyns, *Dignity and Decadence: Victorian Art and the Classical Inheritance* (1991).

Victorian photography is surveyed in Mark Haworth-Booth (ed.), *The Golden Age of British Photography 1839–1900* (1984), which covers the technical history of the medium and its various schools and practitioners, for whom there are individual biographical entries, and reproduces some of the period's greatest photographs. The 'Fine Art Tradition' is the subject of the essays in *British Photography in the Nineteenth Century*, edited by Mike Weaver (Cambridge, 1989). The origins of British photography, in the work of Fox Talbot, Adamson, and Hill, are explored by Sara Stevenson and John Ward in *Printed Light* (London and Edinburgh, 1986). For Julia Margaret Cameron see individual entry; for Roger Fenton see Valerie Lloyd's catalogue of the 1988 Hayward Gallery exhibition, *Roger Fenton: Photographer of the 1850s* (1988).

Victorian Architecture by Roger Dixon and Stefan Muthesias (1978; 1985) is the best short introduction to the field; Robert Furneaux Jordan's book of the same title (Harmondsworth, 1966) is written from Modernist premises that no longer seem quite adequate to the period, and is revealing for that reason. The best study of Victorian Gothic is Charles Eastlake's contemporary *History of the Gothic Revival* (1872), reprinted in the Leicester Victorian Library series (Leicester, 1970). Other aspects of Victorian architecture are covered by Mark Girouard in *The Victorian Country House* (London and New Haven, 1979), and Peter Davey in *Arts and Crafts Architecture* (1980). Michael W. Brooks, *John Ruskin and Victorian Architecture* (London and New

Brunswick, 1986) is an important study of a major critic's influence on the architectural thinking and practice of his time. Something of the variety of Victorian architectural styles is captured in Gavin Stamp and Colin Amery, *Victorian Buildings of London 1837–1887* (1980), which covers 101 buildings, each illustrated.

There is a useful survey of Victorian music by Michael Kennedy in Ford (ed.), *The Later Victorian Age* (see above, pp. 270–1). Henry Raynor, *Music in England* (1980) is a good general history. For separate aspects touched on here see F. Howes, *The Folk Music of Britain and Beyond* (1969), Roger Fiske, *Scotland in Music: A European Enthusiasm* (Cambridge, 1983), Nicholas Temperley, *The Music of the English Parish Church* (2 vols, Cambridge, 1979), R. Mander and J. Mitchison, *The British Music Hall* (1965; revised edition 1974). The relationship between literature and music is explored in the special *Victorian Studies* issue on Victorian music, vol. 30 (Autumn 1986): see especially Mary Burgan on 'Heroines at the Piano' (pp. 51–76) and Linda Hughes on Arthur Somervell's song-cycle on Tennyson's *Maud*. See also the discussion of Elgar's music and Newman's poetry in the chapter on *The Dream of Gerontius* in Michael Wheeler's *Death and the After-Life in Victorian Literature* (Cambridge, 1990).

For Victorian sculpture see Benedict Read, *Victorian Sculpture* (New Haven and London, 1982).

There is an anthology of writing by and about the Aesthetic movement edited by Ian Small, *The Aesthetes: A Sourcebook* (1979), which reprints selections from their theoretical and fictional writings, and contemporary reactions. For D.G. Rossetti, Morris, Pater, and Whistler, see individual entries. Graham Hough's *The Last Romantics* (1947; 1961) is a pioneering modern study of the road from Ruskin through Rossetti and Morris to Pater and Yeats; a different but equally important route is charted by David De Laura in *Hebrew and Hellene in Victorian England: Newman, Arnold, and Pater* (Texas, 1969). The road onwards, into Decadence and early Modernism, is explored by the contributors to *Decadence and the 1890s*, edited by Ian Fletcher (1979). See also Gaunt above p. 271, *The Aesthetic Adventure*, R.V. Johnson, *Aestheticism* (1969), and Hilary Fraser, *Beauty and Belief: Aesthetics and Religion in Victorian Literature* (Cambridge, 1986).

Individual Authors

Notes on biography, major works, and suggested further reading

Note: Place of publication is London, unless otherwise stated.

ALMA-TADEMA, Lawrence (1836–1912), born in Dronryp, Holland, was the
son of a notary. He was educated at Antwerp Academy, where he was
influenced by the historical painter Leys and the archaeologist Louis de
Taye. An early career as a national historical painter was transformed
by seeing the Elgin Marbles on a visit to London in 1862 and Roman
remains in Italy. He settled in London in 1870, where he steadily acquired
reputation and wealth by producing paintings of the domestic lives of
Ancient Romans and Greeks. These 'Victorians in Togas' were painted
with great technical brilliance, particularly in the handling of colour and
marble, and in the light of the latest archaeological research, but when
not erotic were sentimental and morally undemanding – like the wealthy
patrons who commissioned them. Alma-Tadema became a Member of the
Royal Academy in 1879 and was knighted in 1899.

> *Sir Lawrence Alma-Tadema,* Sheffield City Art Galleries (1976).

> See: V.G. Swanson, *Sir Lawrence Alma-Tadema: The Victorian Vision of
> the Ancient World* (1977).
> R. Ash, *Sir Lawrence Alma-Tadema* (1989).

ARNOLD, Matthew (1822–88), born in Laleham-on-Thames, was the eldest son
of Thomas Arnold of Rugby School. Educated at Winchester and Rugby,
where the legend of his idleness is belied by a series of prize-essays and
poems in English and Latin, culminating in an open scholarship to Balliol
College, Oxford. There he began his friendship with Arthur Clough,
celebrated in his elegy 'Thyrsis' (1866), and won the Newdigate Prize
with his poem 'Cromwell'. A Second Class in Greats did not prevent
his election to an Oriel Fellowship in 1845, like Newman (*q.v.*) before
him; in 1847, after time spent in France, he became Private Secretary to
Lord Lansdowne, and through Lansdowne's influence, an Inspector of
Schools just before his marriage to Lucy Wightman in 1851. He was to

work in the Schools Inspectorate until his retirement in 1886. Arnold's
literary career falls into three overlapping phases: poetry, literary and social
criticism, and religious debate. From 1849, when *The Strayed Reveller*
appeared, to the publication of *Poems* in 1853, he did the bulk of his
creative work as a poet. The Preface to the 1853 volume is the start of his
literary criticism: the rejection of 'Empedocles on Etna' for its supposed
morbid self-consciousness marks a turn away from romanticism to the
'sound models' of the 'ancients' endorsed in his first lectures as Oxford
Professor of Poetry (1857–67), published as *On Translating Homer* (1861).
His later lectures show more sympathy with the Romantic temperament,
notably *On the Study of Celtic Literature* (1867). Arnold's first collection
of *Essays in Criticism* appeared in 1865, and was devoted to classical and
European subjects, thereby reinforcing the charge of English provincialism
made in the important introductory essay 'The Function of Criticism
at the Present Time'. The concerns of that essay, and its tone of ironic
banter, are developed in *Culture and Anarchy* (1869), his contribution to
the political debates of the 1860s, and in the letters mocking contemporary
attitudes collected as *Friendship's Garland* (1871). Religious concerns
dominate his writings in the 1870s: *St Paul and Protestantism* (1870),
Literature and Dogma (1873), and *God and the Bible* (1875). In his last
decade Arnold went on a lecture tour of the United States (1883–84),
out of which came his *Discourses in America* (1885), and wrote the essays
on English poets (Wordsworth, Byron, Keats, Gray) which make up
the Second Series of *Essays in Criticism* (1888). His introductory essay on
'The Study of Poetry' is a classic expression of his essentially moral and
religious conception of poetry as a 'criticism of life'.

> *Arnold: The Complete Poems,* edited by K. Allott (1965); second
> edition by M. Allott (1979).
> *The Complete Prose Works of Matthew Arnold,* edited by R.H. Super,
> 11 vols (Ann Arbor, Michigan, 1960–77).
> *Matthew Arnold,* edited by M. Allott and R.H. Super (Oxford,
> 1986). (A very useful and well-annotated modern selection from
> Arnold's writings.)

See: K. Allott (ed.), *Matthew Arnold* (1975). (Essays by different scholars
      covering all areas of Arnold's achievement.)
      R. ApRoberts, *Arnold and God* (California, 1983).
      S. Collini, *Arnold* (Oxford, 1988). (Recent, short introduction.)
      R. Giddings (ed.), *Matthew Arnold: Between Two Worlds* (1986).
      (Recent essays.)
      P. Honan, *Matthew Arnold: A Life* (1981). (Modern biography.)
      J.C. Livingston, *Arnold and Christianity* (South Carolina, 1986).

BAGEHOT, Walter (1826–77), born in Langport, Somerset, was the son of
a Unitarian banker and Anglican mother, and educated at local schools
and University College London. There he was an outstanding student,
taking a First in his BA and winning the gold medal for philosophy
when he graduated MA in 1848; he also made a lifelong friendship with
R.H. Hutton (1826–97), the future editor of the *Spectator*. Bagehot studied
for the Bar and was called in 1852, but he decided instead to become
a banker, returning to the family bank at Langport where he began his
career as a journalist. In 1855 he and Hutton founded the *National Review*
with Unitarian backing, and in 1857 he started writing for the *Economist,*

marrying the eldest daughter of the owner the following year, and becoming editor in 1860, a post he held until his death. His classic study *The English Constitution* appeared as a series of articles for the *Fortnightly Review* (1865–67); he also published *Physics and Politics* (1872), an attempt to apply Darwinian ideas to political society, and *Lombard Street* (1873). His *Literary Studies* (3 vols, 1879–95) reveal him as arguably, after Matthew Arnold (*q.v.*), the most lively and readable of Victorian literary critics: the essays on Clough, Dickens, and 'Wordsworth, Tennyson, and Browning; or, Pure, Ornate, and Grotesque Art in English Poetry' are landmarks in Victorian evaluation of contemporary writing.

> *Collected Works,* edited by N. St John-Stevas (15 vols, 1965–86).
> *Literary Studies,* Everyman edition (2 vols, 1911).
> *The English Constitution,* introduction by R.H.S. Crossman (1963).

See: N. St John-Stevas, *Walter Bagehot: A Study of His life and Thought* (1959).
    G. Himmelfarb, *Victorian Minds* (1968).
    C.H. Sisson, *The Case of Walter Bagehot* (1972).
    J. Burrow, S. Collini, and D. Winch, *That Noble Science of Politics* (Cambridge, 1983).

BROWN, Ford Madox (1821–93), born in Calais, studied art in Belgium, Paris, and Rome, where he went with his first wife for her health in 1845–46 and encountered the work of the German Nazarenes. Under their archaising influence he composed his *Wycliffe* (1847–48) and *Chaucer at the Court of King Edward III* (1845–51). Through his lifelong friendship with D.G. Rossetti (*q.v.*) he met Millais (*q.v.*) and Holman Hunt (*q.v.*) and turned to contemporary subjects, experimenting with Pre-Raphaelite techniques of colour and finish. His finest work belongs to his realist phase in the 1850s, and includes *Work* (begun 1852), *The Last of England* (1855), and the charming Hampstead landscape of *An English Autumn Afternoon* (1852–54). He was a founder-member of Morris's decorating firm in 1861, for which he worked until he undertook the murals for Manchester Town Hall (1881–87). Although never so successful as Millais, his paintings of contemporary life are the finest produced by the movement, and his career has an integrity which the more talented Millais lacks.

> Mary Bennett (ed.), *Ford Madox Brown, 1821–93,* catalogue of the 1964 Walker Art Gallery exhibition, Liverpool.
> V. Surtees (ed.), *The Diary of Ford Madox Brown* (New Haven and London, 1981)

See: F.M. Hueffer, *Ford Madox Brown: A Record of his Life and Work* (1896).

BURNE-JONES, Edward Coley (1833–98), born and brought up in Birmingham, met William Morris (*q.v.*) at Oxford, where influence of Ruskin (*q.v.*) and PRB converted them from the church to art. Recruited by D.G. Rossetti (*q.v.*) to paint the Oxford Union murals in 1857, he became a founder-member with them of Morris's decorating firm, for which he provided designs. Visits to Italy in 1859 and (with Ruskin) in 1862 introduced him to the work of Botticelli and others whose influence on his later style was profound. When exhibited at the Grosvenor Gallery (he contributed eight paintings to the opening in 1877) his dreamy maidens, languorous knights, and medieval/mythical subjects won him both popular success and the admiration of the Aesthetic movement: this did not prevent his appearance for Ruskin at the Whistler–Ruskin trial. He was knighted in 1894.

> John Christian (ed.), *Burne-Jones*, Hayward Gallery Exhibition Catalogue (1975).

See: G. Burne-Jones, *Memorials of Edward Burne-Jones* (2 vols, 1904).
F. Spalding, *Magnificent Dreams: Burne-Jones and the Late Victorians* (Oxford, 1978).

CAMERON, Julia Margaret (1815–79), born in Calcutta, was the daughter of an East India Company official and his French-born wife, and educated there and at Versailles with her maternal grandmother. Married the reforming jurist John Hay Cameron in 1838, playing a prominent role as society hostess before returning to England on his retirement in 1848. After several moves and the birth of her younger children, bought a house next to Tennyson's on the Isle of Wight and took up photography on being given a camera by her daughter Julia in 1863. Until 1875, when the Camerons moved to Ceylon to look after the family coffee estates, she threw herself with characteristic energy into the new medium, taking photographs of the children of relatives and friends, of famous Victorians in the Tennyson circle, and of staged enactments of scenes from Tennyson's *Idylls of the King*. She had more success in exhibitions abroad, winning the gold medal at Berlin in 1866, than at home, where her work was considered too unconventional. Generous and commercially inefficient, she never made the money from her brief photographic career that the quality of her work merited.

> D. Cecil (ed.), *A Victorian Album* (1975).
> C. Ford (ed.), *The Cameron Collection* (1975).

See: H. Gernsheim, *Julia Margaret Cameron, her Life and Photographic Work* (1948; revised edition 1975).
A. Hopkinson, *Julia Margaret Cameron* (1986). (Excellent introductory study.)

CARLYLE, Thomas (1795–1881), born in Ecclefechan, Dumfriesshire, was the son of a stonemason, and educated at Annan Academy and Edinburgh University. After spells schoolteaching in Annan and Kirkcaldy, he returned to Edinburgh to study law in 1818, having given up his original aim of going into the ministry. The law too was abandoned and in 1819 he started to study German literature, finding in the writings of the great German Romantics, especially Goethe, both the inspiration for his subsequent literary career and a solution to his religious difficulties. The spiritual crisis of his youth and its resolution is the subject of *Sartor Resartus* (1833–34). In the 1820s he began to acquire a reputation as the translator and interpreter of German literature, with his *Life of Schiller* (1825), translation of *Wilhelm Meister's Apprenticeship* (1824), and four-volume anthology of *German Romances* (1827). In 1826 he married Jane Welsh and in 1828 they moved to the remote farmhouse of Craigenputtock, where in the next six years he published a number of important articles on German and contemporary subjects, including 'Signs of the Times' (1829) and

'Characteristics' (1831) in the influential *Edinburgh Review*, and wrote *Sartor Resartus*. The Carlyles moved to London in 1834 and settled at 5 Cheyne Row, Chelsea. His contemporary reputation was made by the success of *The History of the French Revolution* (1837) and was followed by the first English publication in book form of *Sartor* (1838). Carlyle's influence as a spiritual leader and social prophet was strongest in the crisis-ridden 1840s, when his denunciation of the evils of industrialism and *laissez-faire* in *Chartism* (1839) and *Past and Present* (1843) were highly topical, and his advocacy of strong leadership in his lectures *On Heroes, Hero-Worship, and the Heroic in History* (1841) and implicitly in his edition of *Oliver Cromwell's Letters and Speeches* (1845) made him the first and most widely read of the Victorian 'sages'. His *Latter-Day Pamphlets* (1850) revealed a deepening pessimism about political democracy which, culminating in his apocalyptic response to the 1867 Reform Act, 'Shooting Niagara' (1867), alienated him from advanced opinion, but this period also revealed his skills as a biographer, in the gently affectionate *Life* of his friend John Sterling (1851) and the massive *History of Frederick the Great* (6 vols, 1858–65). He wrote little in his later years, which were saddened by the death in 1866 of Jane Welsh Carlyle, memorialised with other friends of his youth in the posthumously published *Reminiscences* (1881).

> *Works: Centenary Edition,* edited by H.D. Traill (30 vols, New York and London, 1896–99).
> *The Collected Letters of Thomas and Jane Welsh Carlyle,* edited by C.R. Sanders and K.J. Fielding (Durham, N. Carolina and Edinburgh, 1970–)
> *Sartor Resartus,* edited by K. McSweeney and P. Sabor (Oxford, 1987).
> *The French Revolution,* edited by K.J. Fielding and D. Sorensen (Oxford, 1989).

See: J.A. Froude, *Thomas Carlyle: A History of the First Forty Years of his Life, 1795–1835* (2 vols, 1882) and *Thomas Carlyle: A History of his Life in London, 1834–1881)* (2 vols, 1884). (The first and, though flawed, still the best biography; available in an abridged *Life of Carlyle* (1979), edited and annotated by John Clubbe).
F. Kaplan, *Thomas Carlyle: A Biography* (Cambridge, 1983).
A.L. Le Quesne, *Carlyle* (Oxford, 1982). (Good short introduction.)
G.B. Tennyson, *Sartor Called Resartus* (Princeton, 1965). (Excellent modern study of genesis, structure, and style of *Sartor*.)
R. Ashton, *The German Idea: Four English Writers and the Reception of German Thought 1800–1860* (Cambridge, 1980).
J. Clubbe (ed.), *Carlyle and his Contemporaries* (Durham, N. Carolina, 1976).
B.V. Qualls, *The Secular Pilgrims of Victorian Fiction* (Cambridge, 1983). (On Carlyle's influence on the Victorian novelists.)
J.D. Rosenberg, *Carlyle and the Burden of History* (Oxford, 1985). (Excellent study of *The French Revolution*.)

CHAMBERS, Robert (1802–71), born in Peebles, was the son of a cotton manufacturer who was ruined by the coming of the power-loom. The family moved to Edinburgh where he and his brother William set up as booksellers; the business prospered and, encouraged by Sir Walter Scott,

Robert started writing on local and national historical subjects. The brothers' genius was for the popularisation of knowledge in an age of self-improvement, and with the successful launching of *Chambers's Edinburgh Journal* in 1832 the firm of W. & R. Chambers was founded. They published many works of reference, including the famous *Encyclopaedia* (10 vols, 1859–68), but Robert is best remembered for his *Vestiges of the Natural History of Creation* (1844), an ambitious synthesis of contemporary thinking in astronomy, geology, and biology which advanced the then shocking notion of progressive development through species change. At a time when the fixity of species was taken as a guarantee of God's Providence, this argument was so controversial that all eleven editions of *Vestiges* in Chambers's lifetime were published anonymously. It was, nonetheless, a widely read work, and did much to prepare the ground for Darwin's more systematic argument.

> R. Chambers, *Vestiges of the Natural History of Creation* (1844, reprinted Leicester, 1969).

See: M. Millhauser, *Just Before Darwin: Robert Chambers and 'Vestiges'* (Connecticut, 1959).

   J.A. Secord, 'Behind the veil: Robert Chambers and *Vestiges*', in *History, Humanity and Evolution* edited by J.R. Moore (Cambridge, 1989).

DARWIN, Charles (1809–82), born in Shrewsbury, was the son of a doctor and grandson of the evolutionist poet Erasmus Darwin (1731–1802); his grandfather on his mother's side was the founder of the Wedgwood pottery firm. Darwin was educated locally and at Edinburgh University, where his plans to become a doctor did not survive exposure to the realities of illness and pre-anaesthetic surgery. He returned to Cambridge to read for the Church but contact with the Professor of Botany, J.S. Henslow, inspired his interest in biology, and it was through Henslow's influence that he got the post of naturalist to HMS *Beagle*, which in 1831 left England on a scientific survey to the coast of South America. The five years he spent on this trip, circumnavigating the globe, he later described as 'by far the most important event in my life': it not only provided a rigorous training in observation and classification, but also striking evidence, in the Galapagos islands, of species mutation. Publication of the results of his work on coral reefs and volcanic islands made his reputation, and the narrative of his journey, now known as *The Voyage of the 'Beagle'*, was published in 1839 and several times reprinted. But although it had been drafted by 1844, his hypothesis on evolution by natural selection was not published until Darwin was stimulated to do so by knowledge that Alfred Russel Wallace (1823–1913) had come upon it independently. Their joint paper to the Linnaean Society, the publication of the hurriedly written *On the Origin of Species by Means of Natural Selection* in 1859, and T.H. Huxley's dramatic defence in his encounter with Bishop Wilberforce at the 1860 BAAS meeting in Oxford are the stuff of scientific legend, but the popular triumphalist account is unhistorical: natural selection was always under pressure from contemporary physics (see Chapter 3). Cushioned by family wealth and the success of his writings, and exempted from public engagements by an obscure illness whose origins may have been partly psychosomatic, Darwin spent the last forty years of his life in semi-retirement at Deal House in

Kent, where he could devote himself to his family and his work. It is a sign of the humility and attention to detail at the root of his greatness that he could turn from *The Origin of Species* to the fertilisation of orchids for his next book, and that the man who wrote *The Descent of Man* (1871) should end his career with *The Formation of Vegetable Mould through the Action of Worms* (1881).

> C. Darwin and T.H. Huxley, *Autobiographies,* edited by G. de Beer (1974).
> *The Correspondence of Charles Darwin,* edited by F. Burckhardt, S. Smith, and others (6 vols to date, Cambridge, 1985–??).
> *The Origin of Species,* edited by J.W. Burrow (Harmondsworth, Middlesex, 1968).
> *Darwin,* edited by P. Appleman (second edition, New York, 1979). (A useful selection from *The Origin of Species* and *Descent of Man,* with extracts from many twentieth-century commentators.)

See: A. Desmond and J. Moore, *Darwin* (1991). (The fullest and most recent biography.)
J. Howard, *Darwin* (1982). (Short introduction.)
P.J. Bowler, *Evolution: The History of an Idea* (California, 1983; revised edition, 1989).
P. Morton, *The Vital Science: Biology and the Literary Imagination 1860–1900* (1984). (Important study, setting Darwin in context of lesser known evolutionary thinkers and minor writers.)
G. Beer, *Darwin's Plots: Evolutionary Narrative in Darwin, George Eliot and 19th-century Fiction* (1983).
G. Levine, *Darwin and the Novelists* (Cambridge, Mass., 1988).

DYCE, William (1806–64), born in Aberdeen, studied there and at the RA Schools; on visits to Rome he encountered the German Nazarene movement, usually considered an influential precursor of Pre-Raphaelitism. After an early career as portraitist in Aberdeen and Edinburgh, he moved to London in 1837 to take charge of planning the new School of Design, for which his combined scientific and artistic interests qualified him well. Won the competition for the new Houses of Parliament frescoes in 1844, where he painted mainly Arthurian subjects. A devout High Churchman, he celebrated the Madonna and Child in one of his frescoes for Prince Albert at Osborne House (1845) and as the symbol of artistic inspiration in his best-known Pre-Raphaelite painting, *Titian's First Essay in Colour* (1857). Always on the fringes of the movement, he contributed most distinctively to their landscape art, as in *Pegwell Bay* (1859).

> *Centenary Exhibition of the Works of William Dyce, R.A. (1806–64),* Aberdeen Art Gallery (1964).

See: M. Pointon, *William Dyce 1806-64* (Oxford, 1979).
A. Staley, *The Pre-Raphaelite Landscape* (Oxford, 1973).

FROUDE, James Anthony (1818–94), born in Dartington in Devon, was the son of an Anglican clergyman and younger brother of R.H. Froude (1803–36), the leading Tractarian. Froude was educated at Westminster and Oriel College, Oxford, where he came briefly under the influence of Newman (*q.v.*). The process by which he lost his faith is the subject of two autobiographical fictions, *Shadows in the Clouds* (1847) and *The*

Nemesis of Faith (1848). In 1849 he resigned his fellowship at Exeter College and retired to Devon, where he married the sister of Charles Kingsley (1819–75) and embarked on *The History of England from the Fall of Wolsey to the Defeat of the Spanish Armada* (12 vols, 1856–70). Froude wrote extensively for the journals of the day, including *Fraser's*, of which he became editor in 1860, and his essays were collected in four series of *Short Studies on Great Subjects* (1867–83) which, like his *History*, were very popular in their day. He was criticised for a bias towards Henry VIII and the Protestant Reformation, and in this respect his work reveals the influence of Carlyle (*q.v.*), who had replaced Newman as his guiding-star. But hero-worship did not prevent him publishing, as literary executor, the memoirs of Carlyle (1881) and Jane Welsh Carlyle (1883), which were considered shocking in their revelations, nor from writing a controversial *Life* (1882–84) of Carlyle which exposed the tragic unfulfilment of the Carlyles' marriage. In 1892 Froude was appointed Regius Professor of Modern History at Oxford University.

> See: W.H. Dunn, *James Anthony Froude: a Biography* (Oxford, 1961–63).
> B. Willey, *More Nineteenth Century Studies* (1956). (On Froude and religion.)
> A.O.J. Cockshut, *Truth to Life: The Art of Biography in the Nineteenth Century* (1974).
> J.W. Burrow, *A Liberal Descent* (Cambridge, 1981). (On Froude the historian.)

HUNT, William Holman (1827–1900), founder-member of the PRB, was born in London and attended the RA Schools, where he met Millais (*q.v.*). Deeply influenced by Keats and Ruskin's *Modern Painters*, which he read in 1847, he developed symbolic realism as a central Pre-Raphaelite mode. Between 1848, when the PRB was formed after his meeting D.G. Rossetti (*q.v.*), and 1854, when he left for the Holy Land, he painted *The Hireling Shepherd* (1852), *The Awakening Conscience* (1854), and the most famous of all British religious paintings, *The Light of the World* (1854). His two years in the Middle-East produced the painful allegory of *The Scapegoat* (1858) and provided the local semitic detail for *The Finding of the Saviour in the Temple* (1860). Millais and Rossetti soon moved on, but Hunt clung to the original principles of the movement – a fact reflected in his account of it in *Pre-Raphaelitism and the Pre-Raphaelite Brotherhood* (2 vols, 1905).

> M. Bennett (ed.), *William Holman Hunt,* catalogue of the 1969 Walker Art Gallery exhibition, Liverpool.

> See: G.P. Landow, *William Holman Hunt and Typological Symbolism* (New Haven, 1979).
> J. Maas, *Holman Hunt and 'The Light of the World'* (1984).

LEIGHTON, Frederick (1830–96), born in Scarborough, was the son of a wealthy doctor. His mother's ill-health involved family in extensive foreign travel, and gave Leighton the most cosmopolitan of educations: he studied art in Berlin, Florence, Frankfurt before setting up studios in Rome (1852) and Paris (1855). His *Cimabue's Madonna* was a success at the 1855 RA Exhibition and purchased by Queen Victoria. In 1859 he moved to London, acquiring a reputation as a painter of classical and mythological subjects, a sculptor, and an illustrator: he illustrated George Eliot's *Romola* (1862–3) when it was serialised in the *Cornhill*. A loyal servant of the

Academy and Victorian classicism, he became a Member of the Royal Academy in 1868 and its President in 1878, the year of his knighthood. Leighton was the most prominent and publicly distinguished painter of his age, but doubts about the academicism of his art persisted throughout his career: 'so much beauty and so little passion' was Henry James's verdict. It is ironic, then, that he should have achieved the warmth and intensity of colour in *The Garden of the Hesperides* (1892) and *Flaming June* (1895) at the end of his life, when taste had turned against the classicism of his maturity. He became Lord Leighton in 1896, shortly before his death.

See: L. and R. Ormond, *Lord Leighton* (1975).
       C. Newall, *The Art of Lord Leighton* (Oxford and New York, 1990).

LEWES, George Henry (1817–78), born in London, was the illegitimate son of a sometime customs officer and grandson of the comic actor Charles Lee Lewes (1740–1803). After early attempts at medicine and the stage, he became the most versatile of Victorian literary journalists, writing important reviews of the major novelists and introducing German philosophy and modern science to a wider public. He published a 4-volume *Biographical History of Philosophy* (1845–46), an introduction to Comte (1853), *The Life and Works of Goethe* (1855), and two novels, *Ranthorpe* (1847) and *Rose, Blanche and Violet* (1848). In 1850 he became literary editor of the newly-founded *Leader*, with Thornton Hunt as political editor: it was Lewes's acquiescence in Hunt's adultery with his wife which prevented the divorce that would have enabled him to marry George Eliot (1819–80), whom he first met in 1851; from 1854 they lived together. Although his later career was overshadowed by hers, he remained an influential figure in his own right, establishing the progressive character of the *Fortnightly Review* under his founding editorship (1865–66) and writing for it and other periodicals, increasingly on biology and psychology. Lewes never established himself as more than a successful middleman between science and literature, despite the scientific ambitions which inspired the five volumes of his *Problems of Life and Mind* (1874–79), and it is his biography of Goethe that has lasted best.

See: R. Ashton, *G.H. Lewes: A Life* (Oxford, 1991).

MACAULAY, Thomas Babington (1800–59), born in Leicestershire, was brought up in Clapham in a prosperous, abolitionist, Evangelical household, and educated at private schools and at Trinity College, Cambridge, which he entered in 1818. Macaulay inherited the Evangelical energy without the faith, distinguishing himself by twice winning the Chancellor's Medal for poetry and a prize for an essay on William III, later to be the hero of his *History*. Having been elected a Fellow of Trinity in 1824, he pursued a career at the Bar combined with journalism, writing a series of brilliant review-essays for the Whig *Edinburgh Review* which began with a bold reinterpretation of 'Milton' (1825) and included attacks on both Tory and Radical positions. These brought him to the attention of Lord Lansdowne, who gave him the pocket-borough of Calne in 1830: his oratorical triumphs in the Reform Bill debates of 1831–32 made him famous, even if the Act abolished his seat. But Macaulay felt the need of a secure economic platform and broke off his political career to become the legal member on the Governor-General's Supreme Council for India, where he was responsible for drafting legislation at a salary of £10,000 a year.

Between 1834 and 1838, when he returned to England, Macaulay helped to initiate penal and educational reform; he also wrote the bulk of *The Lays of Ancient Rome* (1842) there and his essay on Bacon (1837). He became MP for Edinburgh in 1839 and entered the Cabinet as Secretary-at-War, but continued to write for the *Edinburgh Review* and in 1843 the first collected edition of his *Critical and Historical Essays* was published. The first two volumes of his *History of England from the Accession of James II* appeared in 1848 and was such a success (3,000 copies in the first ten days, 13,000 after four months) that Macaulay decided to devote his energies to completing it – a decision influenced by political defeat at Edinburgh in 1847, personal disappointment in the loss of his sisters' intimate companionship, and failing health after a heart attack in 1852. Volumes 4 and 5 of the *History* were published in 1855, and the following year he resigned from the parliamentary seat he had won back in 1852. He became Baron Macaulay in the year of his death. The fifth volume of the *History* was brought out by his sister in 1861.

> *The Works of Lord Macaulay*, edited by Lady Trevelyan (8 vols, 1866).
> *Letters of Thomas Babington Macaulay*, edited by T. Pinney (6 vols, 1974–81).
> *The History of England*, edited and abridged by H. Trevor-Roper (Harmondsworth, 1979).

See: G.O. Trevelyan, *The Life and Letters of Lord Macaulay* (2 vols, 1876; 1 vol, Oxford, 1978).
    J. Millgate, *Macaulay* (1973). (The best modern introduction.)
    J. Clive, *Thomas Babington Macaulay: The Shaping of the Historian* (1973). (On the biographical roots of Macaulay's historiography.)
    G. Levine, *The Boundaries of Fiction: Carlyle, Macaulay, Newman* (Princeton, 1968).
    W.A. Madden, 'Macaulay's Style', in *The Art of Victorian Prose*, edited by G. Levine and W.A. Madden (New York, 1968), pp. 127–53.
    J.W. Burrow, *A Liberal Descent: Victorian Historians and the English Past* (Cambridge, 1981).

MILL, John Stuart (1806–73), born in London, was the eldest son of James Mill, the utilitarian and historian of British India. Educated at home by his father (*q.v. Autobiography*), in whose steps he followed to a clerkship in the East India Company. A precocious involvement in journalism, debate, and Radical causes (he spent a night in jail for distributing birth-control leaflets when he was seventeen) led to a nervous breakdown at twenty, from which he learned the importance of 'the cultivation of the feelings' as well as the intellect. In 1830 he met and fell in love with Harriet Taylor, then and for the next twenty years a married woman; and in 1835 he founded the *London and Westminster Review*, which he edited until 1840. The death of his father in 1836 freed him to re-examine his philosophical inheritance, which he did in a series of major essays and books: 'Bentham' (1840), *A System of Logic* (1843), *Principles of Political Economy* (1848), and *Utilitarianism* (1863). 'Bentham' apart, his interest for the non-specialist reader today lies in the libertarian writings of his later career, such as *On Liberty* (1859) and *On the Subjection of Women* (1869), as well as in his posthumously published *Autobiography* (1873). His awakening to the wrongs of women he attributed to 'the most important friendship of my life', that with Harriet Taylor, whom he married in 1851 and who died in 1858, the year of Mill's retirement from the East India Company. In the 1860s he turned his attention to political reform, publishing *Considerations on Representative Government* in 1861 and using his three years as Liberal MP for Westminster (1865–68) to speak out for women's votes and proportional representation; his attempt to include them as an amendment to the 1867 Reform Bill was unsuccessful but stands as a high-water mark of principled reformism in the period. The posthumously published *Three Essays on Religion* (1874) and *Chapters on Socialism* (1879) reveal curiosity about, but not commitment to, these phenomena. He died in Avignon, as Harriet had done, in 1873.

> *Collected Works,* edited by J.M. Robson *et al.* (33 vols, Toronto and London, 1963–91).

See: E.J. Alexander, *Arnold and Mill* (1965).
> G. Himmelfarb, *On Liberty and Liberalism: the Case of John Stuart Mill* (New York, 1974). (A provocative approach to a classic text.)
> M. St J. Packe, *The Life of John Stuart Mill* (1954).
> J.M. Robson, *The Improvement of Mankind: the Social and Political Thought of John Stuart Mill* (Toronto and London, 1968).
> A. Ryan, *J.S. Mill* (1975). (Useful survey.)
> William Thomas, *Mill* (Oxford, 1985). (Good short introduction.)

MILLAIS, John Everett (1829–96), the most technically gifted of Victorian painters, came from a wealthy home which encouraged his precocious talent. He was the youngest ever entrant to the RA Schools, and his contributions to the PRB, which was formed in his house in 1848, show the principles and techniques of the movement at their most brilliant, such as *Christ in the House of His Parents* (1850) and *Mariana* (1851). In 1853 he fell in love with Ruskin's wife Effie while on holiday in Scotland, and after their marriage in 1855 turned first to a series of mood paintings set in the country around her Perthshire home, like the haunting *Autumn Leaves* (1856) and funerary *The Vale of Rest* (1859), and then increasingly to a commercial career of painting the famous (Carlyle, Gladstone (twice), Disraeli, Tennyson) and satisfying the contemporary appetite for child-subjects. He painted *The Boyhood of Raleigh* (1870) and *Bubbles* (1886), the apogee of his commercial success and artistic decline. He also illustrated Trollope novels for the *Cornhill* magazine. Millais was knighted in 1885 and elected President of the Royal Academy in 1896.

> M. Bennett (ed.), *Millais,* catalogue of the 1967 Royal Academy and Walker Art Gallery exhibition, Liverpool.

See: J.G. Millais, *Life and Letters of Sir John Everett Millais* (2 vols, 1899).
> M.H. Spielmann, *Millais and His Works* (1898).
> M. Lutyens, *Millais and the Ruskins* (1967).

MORRIS, William (1834–96), born in Walthamstow of wealthy parents, was educated at Marlborough and Exeter College, Oxford, where friendship with Burne-Jones (*q.v.*) encouraged his medievalism: their enthusiasm for Ruskin (*q.v.*) and the Pre-Raphaelites led him to abandon clerical career for art. Recruited by Rossetti (*q.v.*) to paint murals on the new Oxford Union, and founded the firm of Morris, Marshall, Faulkner & Co. to produce well-designed furnishings, including stained glass and the distinctive William

Morris wallpaper. Married Jane Durden, an icon of later Pre-Raphaelitism through Rossetti's obsessive portraits, in 1859, and settled with her in the Red House, an early 'vernacular' building designed for him by Philip Webb. He established his name as a poet with *The Defence of Guenevere* (1858) and *The Earthly Paradise* (1868–70), and in 1878 moved to Kelmscott Manor, the Oxfordshire home associated with the illustrated editions of classic texts produced by the Kelmscott Press. His activities became increasingly political: in 1877 he wrote a manifesto 'To the Working-Men of England' and founded Society for the Protection of Ancient Buildings; in 1883 became a socialist, and in 1884 helped found the Socialist League. Later disenchantment with feuding among socialist leaders did not spoil his idealism, which inspired his Utopian romances *A Dream of John Ball* (1886) and *News from Nowhere* (1890), and his passion for good craftmanship was unabated: he played a leading role in founding the Arts and Crafts Exhibition Society in 1887. The Kelmscott Press was set up in 1890 and produced the *Chaucer* (1896), illustrated by Burne-Jones, which is the embodiment in book-production of Victorian medievalism.

> *Collected Works* (24 vols, 1910–15; reprinted 1966).
> A. Briggs (ed.), *William Morris: Selected Writings and Designs* (Harmondsworth, 1962; reprinted 1984).
> J. Redmond (ed.), *News from Nowhere* (1970).

See: J.W. Mackail, *The Life of William Morris* (2 vols, 1899).
P. Henderson, *William Morris, his Life, Work and Friends* (1967).
P. Faulkner, *Against the Age: an Introduction to William Morris* (1980).
P. Stansky, *Redesigning the World: William Morris, the 1880s and the Arts and Crafts* (Princeton, 1985).

NEWMAN, John Henry (1801–90), born in London, the son of a banker, was educated at a private school in Ealing, where in 1816 he was converted to Evangelical Christianity, and at Trinity College, Oxford. Newman failed to take the first-class degree expected of him but redeemed the failure in 1822 by winning a Fellowship at Oriel College, whose Common Room at that time was a centre of vigorous debate and liberal, Broad Church sympathies. Newman was destined to move away from Evangelicalism and to reject liberalism in politics and religion. The concurrence of the ecclesiastical reform crisis with his discovery of the Early Church – on which he wrote his first book, *The Arians of the Fourth Century* (1833) – convinced him that authority in spiritual matters could only lie with the true heirs of the Apostles and with the forms of worship derived from them, which then raised the question of the authenticity of Anglicanism. From 1833 to 1841 he and the fellow-members of the Oxford Movement published a series of ninety tracts exploring this 'Catholic' heritage of Anglicanism in belief and worship. When members of the group started defecting to Rome contemporary suspicions of 'Romanising' seemed confirmed. Newman lingered longer on his 'Anglican deathbed' than many of those he had inspired, finally converting in 1845 and taking with him a major work of theology which can be read as a justification of his change, *An Essay on the Development of Christian Doctrine* (1845). Rome under the ultra-conservative Pius IX was slow to appreciate his talents: neither the Oratory he founded in Birmingham nor the Catholic University he set up in Dublin received the clerical support they deserved, though out of the latter came his classic series of lectures, *The Idea of a University*

(1859). When rashly accused by Kingsley of condoning untruth, he wrote his *Apologia Pro Vita Sua* (1864) which, by revealing the integrity of his life's journey, won him the respect and affection of many Protestants. A conservative Anglican, he became a reforming Catholic, believing that the Catholic Church had to be 'prepared for converts, as well as converts prepared for the Church'. The new Pope, Leo XIII, had a better sense of Newman's stature, and in 1879 made him a cardinal. Newman was many-sided: a readable novelist, a competent poet, a skilled controversialist and apologist, a great preacher, and a supreme stylist. His cardinal's motto, *cor ad cor loquitur* ('heart speaks to heart'), captures the compelling inwardness felt in all his writing.

> *Apologia Pro Vita Sua*, edited by M.J. Svaglic (Oxford, 1967).
> *The Letters and Diaries of John Henry Newman*, edited by
>   C.S. Dessain, T. Gornall and I.T. Ker (31 vols, 1961–78).
> *An Essay on the Development of Christian Doctrine*, edited by
>   J.M. Cameron (Harmondsworth, Middlesex, 1974).
> *The Idea of a University*, edited by I.T. Ker (Oxford, 1976).

See: W. Ward, *The Life of John Henry Cardinal Newman* (2 vols, 1912).
       I.T. Ker, *John Henry Newman: a Biography* (Oxford, 1988).
       (A modern life, valuable in tracing Newman's intellectual
       development.)
       C.S. Dessain, *John Henry Newman* (1966; 1971). (The best short
       introduction.)
       A.D. Culler, *Imperial Intellect: A Study of Newman's Educational Ideal*
       (New Haven, 1955). (On *The Idea of a University*.)
       D.J. De Laura, *Hebrew and Hellene in Victorian England: Newman,
       Arnold and Pater* (Texas, 1969).
       S. Prickett, *Romanticism and Religion: The Tradition of Coleridge and
       Wordsworth in the Victorian Church* (Cambridge, 1976).
       M. Wheeler, *Death and the Future Life in Victorian Literature and
       Theology* (Cambridge, 1990). (On 'Dream of Gerontius'.)

PATER, Walter Horatio (1839–94), born in London, was the son of a surgeon who died when Pater was three. He was educated at Canterbury and Queen's College, Oxford. Like Newman (*q.v.*) before him, he redeemed a second in finals by winning a fellowship at Brasenose in 1864, and began to acquire a reputation for the subtle, impressionistic appreciations of artists and writers which he contributed to the journals of the time. The first collection of his essays was *Studies in the History of the Renaissance* (1873): it excited the young and shocked the old by its seeming advocacy, in the famous 'Conclusion', of the pursuit of intense sensation as the key to life in a world of relentless flux. Pater himself was an unlikely prophet of the hedonism he was accused of teaching: shy and self-conscious, he lived for most of his life with his two unmarried sisters in Oxford and then in London after he resigned his fellowship in 1883. *Marius the Epicurean* (1885) is his only novel and portrays the growth of a young man in Ancient Rome as he is pulled between the philosophies of paganism and early Christianity; it struck a note with contemporaries similarly divided. In *Plato and Platonism* (1893) he made his contribution to late Victorian Hellenism. But Pater's genius was for a distinctive kind of critical essay, a development from the work of Matthew Arnold (*q.v.*), in which an impressionistic winnowing of aesthetic essences is charged with powerful but undeclared autobiographical urgency. The title of his collection of essays, *Appreciations* (1889), encapsulates his method but does not convey either the sensuous intensity or the subtle command of prose rhythms which make Pater a great stylist. The volume contains his essays on 'Style', 'Wordsworth', 'Aesthetic Poetry', and *Measure for Measure*.

> *Works* (10 vols, 1910; reprinted 1967).
> *The Renaissance*, edited by A. Phillips (Oxford, 1986).

See: T.S. Eliot, 'Arnold and Pater', in *Selected Essays* (1951).
> G. Hough, *The Last Romantics* (1949).
> A. Ward, *Walter Pater: the Idea in Nature* (1966).
> D.J. De Laura, *Hebrew and Hellene in Victorian England: Newman, Arnold and Pater* (Texas, 1969).
> G. Monsman, *Walter Pater's Art of Autobiography* (New Haven, 1980).

PATTISON, Mark (1813–84), was born and grew up in the Yorkshire village of Hauxwell. He was the eldest of twelve children of an austere Anglican parson. At Oxford he came under the influence of Newman (*q.v.*) and the Oxford Movement, but survived Newman's conversion to become a liberal in theology and university politics: the account of the Movement in his *Memoirs* (1885) is penetratingly hostile. As fellow and, from 1861, Rector of Lincoln College, Pattison was a leader of reform at Oxford. He contributed an essay on English religious thought 1688–1750 to *Essays and Reviews* (1860), and projected a history of post-Renaissance learning which was never completed. This failure, his unhappy marriage to a much younger woman, and the fact that he wrote a life of the scholar Isaac Casaubon (1875), have led many to see him as the model for Casaubon in George Eliot's *Middlemarch* (1871–72). But Pattison was no shy pedant; the work he produced shows evidence of high scholarship; and he played an important part in the modernisation of Victorian Oxford.

> Mark Pattison, *Memoirs*, edited by Mrs Pattison (1885; reprinted 1969).

See: J. Sparrow, *Mark Pattison and the Idea of a University* (Cambridge, 1967).

ROSSETTI, Dante Gabriel (1828–82), born and brought up in London, was the son of an Italian political refugee and Professor of Italian. He was a wayward student at art-schools but was inspired by a spell as pupil of F.M. Brown (*q.v.*). Admiration for Holman Hunt (*q.v.*) led to the formation of the PRB in 1848 and to his first painting in the new style, *The Girlhood of Mary Virgin* (1849). The poet of the movement, he published translations of the early Italian poets (1861), produced the short-lived Pre-Raphaelite magazine *The Germ*, and wrote 'The Blessed Damozel' (1847), *Poems* (1870), and 'The House of Life' sonnet-sequence which appeared in *Poems* (1881). His first marriage to Elizabeth Siddal ended in her possibly suicidal death from overdose of laudanum in 1862, and his *Beata Beatrix* (1863) is a monument to her and to his obsession with Dante. Rossetti is the bridge between the first and second phases of Pre-Raphaelitism through his friendship with William Morris (*q.v.*), whose wife Jane became his model: the dream-like qualities of his later paintings emerge from a life of increasing decline and addiction, and yet inspired the Aesthetic movement as his more socially responsible contemporaries did not. Although not a great painter himself, his career exemplifies an important pattern of development in nineteenth-century painting.

> V. Surtees (ed.), *The Paintings and Drawings of Dante Gabriel Rossetti (1828–1882). A Catalogue Raisonné* (2 vols, Oxford, 1971).

See: G.H. Fleming, *Rossetti and the Pre-Raphaelite Brotherhood* (1967).
J. Nicoll, *Dante Gabriel Rossetti* (1975).
A.C. Faxon, *Dante Gabriel Rossetti* (Oxford, 1989).

RUSKIN, John (1819–1900), the only child of an Evangelical mother and wine merchant father, was educated privately before going to Oxford in 1836, accompanied by mother. He won the Newdigate Prize for Poetry in 1839 but his studies were interrupted by ill-health and a consequent foreign tour, 1840–41. He graduated in 1842 and published the first volume of *Modern Painters* in 1843, a passionate defence of Turner, whom he had met in 1840. His first visit to Italy without parents introduced him to Italian Primitive painters and Tintoretto, an enthusiasm reflected in religious orthodoxy of *Modern Painters 2* (1846). In 1848 he married Euphemia Gray and toured Normandy, studying Gothic architecture. The publication of *The Seven Lamps of Architecture* in 1849 was followed by his discovery of Venetian Gothic and its celebration in *The Stones of Venice* (1851, 1853). Meanwhile he had come out as champion of Pre-Raphaelitism with letters to *The Times* and pamphlet in 1851, the year he met Millais (*q.v.*) and Hunt (*q.v.*). A visit to Scotland with Millais in 1853 led to a love affair between the painter and Ruskin's wife and the annulment of Ruskin's marriage on grounds of non-consummation in 1854: it is a sign of Ruskin's largeness of mind that this did not affect his support for the aims of the PRB. *Modern Painters 3* and *4* were published in 1856, volume 5 in 1860. Religious doubts in 1850s culminated in the experience of 'unconversion' in Turin in 1858, the year he met and fell in love with nine-year-old Rose La Touche, with whom he was to conduct a strange and tragic love affair ending in her death, insane, in 1875 and the onset of his own madness in the later 1870s. His career as a social critic began 1860, with articles attacking the doctrines of Political Economy in *Cornhill Magazine* which Thackeray had to limit to four because of readers' reactions; published 1862 as *Unto This Last*. In 1869 he became the first Slade professor of Fine Art at Oxford, and in 1871 began the intermittent series of public letters to 'the workmen and labourers of Great Britain' called *Fors Clavigera*: the fancifulness of his later titles was a symptom of increasing mental instability. His attack on Whistler (*q.v.*) in *Fors* led to his symbolic defeat in the 1878 libel trial, when he was fined a farthing's damages; he resigned his Slade Professorship. Despite passages and articles displaying his old eloquence, the last two decades of his life were a downward passage into silence and insanity, from which only his splendid autobiography, *Praeterita* (1885–89), emerges to compare with his earlier achievements.

> *Complete Works,* edited by E.T. Cook and A. Wedderburn (39 vols, 1903–12).
> J.D. Rosenberg (ed.), *The Genius of John Ruskin* (1979). (Useful selection from all areas of Ruskin's work by leading Ruskin scholar.)
> D. Barrie (ed.), *Modern Painters* (1987). (Excellent scholarly abridgement of Ruskin's work, with notes and illustrations.)

See: J.D. Hunt, *The Wider Sea: A Life of John Ruskin* (New York, 1982).
T. Hilton, *John Ruskin, The Early Years* (1985). (First in projected
two-volume biography, takes story to 1860.)
J.D. Rosenberg, *The Darkening Glass: A Portrait of Ruskin's Genius*
(New York, 1961). (Pioneering modern study.)
G.P. Landow, *Ruskin* (1985). (Short introductory study.)
R. Hewison, *John Ruskin: The Argument of the Eye* (1976).
J.C. Sherburne, *John Ruskin, or the Ambiguities of Abundance: A Study
in Social and Economic Criticism* (Cambridge, Mass., 1972).
M.W. Brooks, *John Ruskin and Victorian Architecture* (London and
New Brunswick, 1986).

SPENCER, Herbert (1820–1903), born in Derby, was the only surviving child
of a Wesleyan-Methodist mother and a deist father. He was educated
locally and then by his uncle, an Anglican parson. In 1837 he became
a railway engineer, involved in the great boom era of Victorian railway
expansion in the 1840s, when he travelled through the Midlands and found
time to develop his interests in science and politics. Early articles for *The
Nonconformist* led to an invitation to edit a radical paper in 1844 and then,
after leaving the railways in 1846, to the sub-editorship of *The Economist*.
In London he joined the circle of intellectuals around the publisher John
Chapman, which included George Eliot and G.H. Lewes (*q.v.*). *Social
Statics*, a critique of utilitarianism and the first stage in his attempt to
create a 'scientific' morality, was published in 1850, to be followed by
articles on evolution (a term he helped to crystallise), 'Progress', and by
Principles of Psychology (1855). A legacy in 1853 enabled him to retire
from *The Economist* and devote the rest of his life to the elaboration of
an evolutionary synthesis of knowledge which he called the 'Synthetic
Philosophy'. This emerged in a series of volumes: *First Principles* (1862),
Principles of Biology (1864, 1867), *Principles of Sociology* (1876–97), *Principles
of Ethics* (1879–93). As a grand system Spencer's life-work has lost its
explanatory power and is today largely unvisited, but his essays early
and late are of considerable interest, and *The Man versus the State* (1884)
is a classic statement of uncompromising individualism and *laissez-faire*
economic theory. Despite the fame and influence which Spencer's writings
brought him abroad, especially in industrialising America, the later years
of his life were clouded by illness and pessimism over the fate of his
philosophical system.

Herbert Spencer, edited by S. Andreski (1971). (A recent selection.)
The Man versus the State, edited by D.G. Macrae (Harmondsworth,
1969).

See: J.W. Burrow, *Evolution and Society* (Cambridge, 1966).
G. Jones, *Social Darwinism and English Thought* (Brighton, 1980).
J.D.Y. Peel, *Herbert Spencer: The Evolution of a Sociologist* (1971).
(Best modern introduction to Spencer's life and background.)
D. Wiltshire, *The Social and Political Thought of Herbert Spencer*
(Oxford, 1978).

WHISTLER, James Abbott McNeill (1834–1903), born in New England, was
the son of a railroad engineer. He had a widely travelled childhood
including five years in St Petersburg, where his father was employed to
build the trans-Russian railway and where he studied at the Academy

of Fine Arts. Failure at West Point in 1854 was followed by a spell in Paris before settling in London in 1859. Whistler brought a cosmopolitan background and an interest in formalism to an English art-world dominated by the moralistic anecdotalism of RA painting. *The White Girl* (1862) was exhibited with the work of the French Impressionists in Paris and his *Nocturne in Black and Gold* (1875), exhibited at the newly opened Grosvenor Gallery in 1877, gave publicity to his art and theories through the Ruskin libel trial. Bankrupted financially, Whistler had to leave the country, but the wit and aesthetic dignity with which he conducted the trial made him a hero with younger artists. His later career coincided with the dispersal of authority from the Royal Academy to the new private galleries, a process his provocative dandyism helped to accelerate. Whistler moved easily and often between London and the continent, especially France, where he was made a Chevalier of the Legion of Honour in 1889. He was also a pioneer of interior design and in 'The Ten O'Clock Lecture' (1885) delivered one of the classic statements of the Aesthetic movement.

> *The Paintings of James McNeill Whistler,* edited by M. MacDonald, H. Miles, R. Spencer, and A.M. Young (London and New Haven, 1980).

See: S. Weintraub, *Whistler: A Biography* (1974).
      J. Walker, *James McNeill Whistler* (New York, 1987).

Index

Wilberforce, Robert, 77
Wilberforce, Bishop Samuel, 112,
  130–1, 136
Wilde, Oscar, 197, 209, 244
  The Critic as Artist, 237, 238
  The Portrait of Dorian Gray, 237
Wilkie, Sir David, 17, 199
Williams, Raymond, 156–7
Williams, Rowland, 97–8
Wills, Mr Justice, 237
Wilson, Henry, 97, 98
Woodward and Deane
  and Oxford Science Museum, 228–9
Woolf, Virginia, 222
Woolner, Thomas, 18, 207, 208

Wordsworth, William, 10, 32, 76, 104,
  126, 132, 157, 199, 200–1, 202, 205,
  222, 236, 246
  The Prelude, 27, 30, 140
Wright, Frank Lloyd, 231
Wynfield, David Wilkie, 51

Xenophon, 156

Yeames, W. F., 19
  *And When Did You Last See Your
  Father?*, 19
'Young England', 48–9

Zola, Emile, 131